Introduction to
Bar and Beverages

Introduction to
Bar and Beverages

Mahendra Singh Negi
Certified Hospitality Educator
Associate Professor
Food & Beverage Services
Amrapali Institute of Hotel Management
Haldwani, Uttarakhand

ISBN: 978-93-89307-79-5

Edition: 2019

Printed at: Rekha Printers

Preface

The present-day modern concept of the hotel is not just a place to provide accommodation, food and beverages but offering to its guest every possible facility, service and convenience. Apart from these services, beverage service is a major component and has remained an important part of hospitality industry. The beverage services are provided by various outlets of food and beverage department in the hotel. This book provides a guide to alcoholic and non-alcoholic beverages, not only for the hospitality management students but also for industry professionals. This book uses simple language to make the student understand the topics. The content, scope and application of this book reflect the best global practices in the field of bar operations from an organization and customer's perspective. This book covers the syllabus of all major universities, technical boards, autonomous bodies and NCHMCT. Photographs, images and tables related to the content ease the understanding of the concerned topic. The book also discusses the new trends in bar and drinks such as mixology, infusion, role of information technology and many more. With the help of SOPs compiled from various five-star hotels, it will help students to understand the right procedures of serving various types of beverages in bar and restaurants. Giving particular emphasis on bar, beverages, cocktails and their services, this book can be utilized by bar, restaurants and hotels who wish to extend the knowledge to their personnel working in food and beverage service department.

This book is also a great help to the students preparing for their placement or interviews, and also suitable for aspiring bartenders.

Divided into two sections — theory aspects and practical aspects — the book elaborates the theoretical knowledge about bar, wines, spirits, cocktails, tobacco and cellar management and in practical aspects the standard operating procedures of beverage services is focused. Practising these SOPs, students can achieve excellence in the bar and restaurant service skills and would be able to understand:

- The role of bartender in the bar
- Duties and responsibilities of bartender
- Bar management skills

- Insight into various alcoholic and non-alcoholic beverages
- Cocktail making methods and recipes
- Right procedure of serving drinks to the guest
- Various trends in bar and restaurant industry

I sincerely hope that its content and design will be found indispensable by the students of Hospitality Management and a useful reference to the industry professionals.

Mahendra Singh Negi

Acknowledgements

From the moment I knew my book was going to be published, I had been anxious about expressing my gratitude to the people for their contribution in creating this book. Without the interest and suggestions offered by a group of individuals this book would have never seen the light of the day. First and foremost, I thank God who gave me the power to believe in my passion and pursue my dreams.

I wish to personally thank Prof. S.K. Singh, COO, Amrapali Institute of Hotel Management and Prof. Prashant Sharma, Dean Academics, Amrapali Institute of Hotel Management for their encouragement, guidance and professionalism. My friend Ms. Archana Sharma (Ex. Duty Manager, Hotel The Grand Star, Gurnsey, United Kingdom), Mukul Tiwari (Corporate Training Manager, The Fern, Ahmedabad) and Kamlesh Bargali (Head Mixologist, J.W. Marrott, Pune) for helping me in designing and compiling the standard operating procedures for drinks services.

I dedicate this book to my darling daughter Riddhima, whose beautiful smile acts as a catalyst to keep me going and inspires me to give my best in whatever I do. My lovely wife Tripti, to whom I am deeply indebted for being my pillar of support and for her unfailing belief in me. My dear students who are one of the major reasons for the conception of this book.

Finally, I would like to acknowledge with gratitude the love and support of my grandparents, parents, parents-in-law and my friends. They all kept me going and this book would not have been possible without their love, blessings and guidance.

Mahendra Singh Negi

Contents

SERVICE OF BEVERAGES

1 The Bar

1.1 INTRODUCTION

After reading this chapter, you will be able to understand:

- Meaning of bar and its history
- Attributes of a bartender
- Rules of a bar
- Colour codes used in bar

Bar is a place or a establishment assigned to serve alcoholic beverages such as wines, spirits, beers, cocktails and other non-alcoholic beverages such as carbonated beverages, mocktails, mineral water and often serve snacks and sometimes full course menu. Through the course of history, alcohol has been bought and sold by people all over the world for profit and enjoyment. Alcohol has always been associated with religion, the bible makes many references to the use of alcohol, the most notable being Christ turning water into wine. It was from this that alcohol became accepted in the western world and drinking became the pass time of most western and far eastern societies. The root of cocktails and mixed drinks lies with the early apothecaries and healers; they would use many different herbs, berries and barks mixed with distilled grain to make potions that could cure all forms of ailments, and as every bartender knows mixed drinks can cause many painful ailments too. The Greek apothecary, Hippocrates is said to have practised the art of blending wine with herbs, roots and berries around the fifth century BC. The origin of the modern cocktail bar lies in the United States, where in the late 1800s the American people started to enjoy the mixed drink. The cocktail gained a great following up until the beginning of prohibition in 1919 but although all consumption was illegal the cocktail thrived in illegal drinking dens called 'speakeasy's'. The cocktail became the favoured way of disguising the illicit alcohol concealed in the glass in case of raids by the police. When prohibition was repealed in 1933, the cocktail emerged as the drink for the newly liberated drinkers.

During prohibition, Europe caught up with the USA in terms of quality and variation in drink making. Many famous bars were opened including Harry's New York Bar in Paris, the home of the Bloody Mary and the White Lady. The hotels in Europe were the bastion of cocktails with the Ritz, Savoy and the George V in Paris retaining their status as the ultimate in cocktail bars. In 1932, a group of British bartenders established the United

Kingdom Bar Tenders Guild, an organization dedicated to the advancement of bartenders and drinks. This became the International Bartenders Association in 1951 and spread throughout the world. In the late 1930s and 1940s, bars began to suffer from the effects of the great depression and World War II, although, many new drinks were created in these years. The 1950s saw interest in the cocktail revived not only in the USA, but also around the world. The interest in alcohol also increased with many books being written about the subject. The 1950s saw the origins of the modern bartender, a service orientated, fine mixer of drinks with the specialist knowledge needed to create the finest drinks. The increased trade in the 1950s also led to the greater availability of new products and the freedom of travel allowed the exchange of information. The 1960s and 1970s saw the increase in the amount of drinks being created and the increase in the numbers of bars especially in the UK and Europe. In the USA and Europe, the cocktail became the destination of the workers after a long day and this led to the 'happy hour'—a period in the early evening when drinks are offered at a reduced price. The boom in the 1980s helped the bar industry spread from the USA into the UK and Europe. Many new American style bars started opening all over the UK, TGI Fridays and Henry J Bean's being examples. These bars offered a new experience for the public, they had great party atmosphere, they offered a huge amount of drinks and were served with '*flair*'. The interest in cocktail bar tending was increased when a certain movie called "Cocktail' was released. The movie caused a great divide in the bartending world, many cocktail bartenders hated the movie, saying it portrayed bartenders as little more than circus performers, while others thought it showed bartending as a enjoyable and worthwhile profession. The late 1980s saw the arrival of the 'designer beer' and at the forefront of this invasion were Mexican beers. Targeted at the young and affluent, these beers soon became very popular and led to a decline in the sales of spirits and wine especially in the 18-25 age group. The Mexican beers were followed by beers from all over the world, countries including Lapland and Zimbabwe all started to import into the UK. Around this time, interest in wines from the New World also started to increase, Australian and Californian wines were becoming particularly popular. The wine lists of bars and restaurants became longer and offered a lot more choice. People who usually only drank wine when eating started to drink wine instead of their usual gin and tonic or beer and began to drink wine at home in larger quantities. The 1990s, so far, has been the best decade for the bartender, not only do they have a better choice of products to sell but they also have a much more enlightened public to sell to. The potential bartender has a number of different styles of bar to choose from, the American style, the Hotel bar, the classic cocktail bar or the European style of café bar. In many cases, the 1990s has seen the rise of the bar and the demise of the pub. The major brewers have closed some of the inner city pubs and converted them into hip and trendy bars, with bottled beers and expensive food. Many of the pubs have been brought off the breweries at a low price and converted at a very low cost by enterprising individuals or companies. These individuals have then become very successful in the process. London has become the bar and restaurant capital of Europe, with places such as Quaglinos, Mezzo, Atlantic and the 5th floor at Harvey Nichol's offering great food and better drinks. With the public wanting a better product and better service, today's bartenders need to be efficient, fast, friendly, sales orientated and great drink makers. For a long time, bartending has never been looked at as a 'proper job' but with the career and earning potential, it is undoubtedly one of the most satisfying professions today. As with the 'celebrity chefs' that have become famous over the last few years, there have been a number of famous bartenders over the last century. These bartenders have become well known for the great drinks they have concocted or by running highly regarded bars around the world. These bartenders include:

- **Jerry Thomas** regarded as the first cocktail bartender, he wrote the world's first cocktail book back in 1862, the 'Bon Vivant's Guide' was the first of many such 'cocktail bibles'.
- **Harry Mac Elhone** was founder of the world famous 'Harry's New York Bar' in Paris. This great bar is responsible for such drinks as the Bloody Mary, the Sidecar, the Blue Lagoon and the White Lady. Harry became notable for serving such people as Scott Fitzgerald and Ernest Hemmingway.
- **Harry Craddock** the late head bartender at the Savoy Grill in London, is renowned for the invention of the 'Blue Blazer'. He is also the author of the 'Savoy Cocktail Book'.

1.1.1 Why People Drink?

- **Thirst:** It may seem obvious, but the most common and important reason people drink is to quench their thirst with something refreshing and tasty.
- **Socializing:** People spend time together and enjoy each other's company over drinks, helping them to relax in a variety of contexts.
- **Pairing:** Alcohol can form part of a guest's culinary experience when certain drinks and their flavours complement the flavours of the food.
- **Flavour:** Every single drink has a flavour which will appeal to certain people. These flavours are varied, with each adding a specific feeling or mood to a drink.

1.1.2 What People Drink?

Factors which determine what people drink generally depends on:

- **Location:** Location is a huge factor in determining what drinks are available. The country you are in and the drinks which are popular in that region also influence what guests want to drink.
- **Weather:** Guests will often order drinks based on what the weather is like, such as a cold drink on a hot day or a warm drink on a cold day. This will determine the preparation of the drinks.

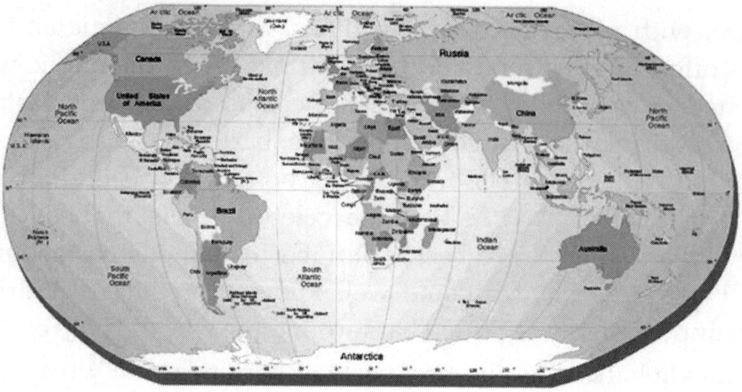

- **Personal preferences:** There are various factors that influence people's preferences. These factors include, but are not limited to, age and gender.

- **Time:** The time of day is another factor that will influence what people will order to drink. Certain drinks suit certain times of day better than others.

1.2 ATTRIBUTES OF A BARTENDER/BARCHEF

The bartender is the central figure in a bar. He is in charge of mixing cocktails, serving drinks, maintaining the supplies and inventory, as well as upholding the law. The bartender is responsible for:

- **Service:** Serving drinks to guests is the most important role of a bartender. When working behind the bar, the bartender needs to be able to prepare whatever is needed but also be an entertainer.
- **Maintaining supplies and the inventory:** The bartender must make sure that there is always enough stock at the bar as well as keep a list of all the supplies that they have at that moment. They also need to decide whether or not more stock needs to be ordered.
- **Mixing cocktails:** There is magic in blending different ingredients to create the most unbelievable flavours. The fashionable name for this elegant mixing of the cocktail is 'mixology'.
- **Upholding the law:** It is the responsibility of every bartender working in a bar to uphold the law such as to ensure all drinkers are of the legal drinking age.

A number of different factors go into making a good bartender.

- **Personality:** Something that cannot be taught, an ideal bartender should have good personal qualities, a great sense of humour and above all, enjoys dealing with people. Personality is very important for every type of employment but maintaining a positive state of mind when working behind a bar is vital. Everyone has a different personality and although you may not be the most energetic and infectious person in the world you may well be a good listener and have a relaxed attitude that is the right thing for your bar. Bartenders must maintain an attractive and well groomed appearance. It is essentially important for bartenders as they represent the hotel's standards of quality in service to guests.
- **Skill:** This is something that can be taught, it takes at least a year working in a good bar to become a good bartender. The main skills are learning to serve and make good quality drinks and to have good customer skills.
- **Awareness and Communication:** First, it is important to be aware of the surroundings while working behind the bar. Make sure you know the bar inside and out, so you always can find anything you need. Always be aware of your customers' needs, making sure they are having a good time. Secondly, a bartender needs to have good communication skills with his fellow staff and with the customers. Good awareness and communication will make everyone's job a lot easier. Interaction between customers and the bartenders is a common element and the extent of which depends on the style and class of the bar/lounge. Warm and courteous attention must be afforded to each guest while maintaining a professional attitude and manner.

- **Cleanliness:** A good bartender will always be clean, neat and tidy. Bars are preparation areas and are regulated under the Health and Safety at Work Act and local environmental health officers. Keeping the bar clean is a fundamental part of bar tending, not just something we do when we are told by a manager. Remember *'if you have time to lean, you have time to clean'*.
- **Politeness:** While dealing with customers and other members of the staff, you must always be as polite as possible. A good bartender always says 'please' and 'thank you' and addresses customers with the appropriate titles.
- **Knowledge:** The best bartenders are the ones who know what products they sell behind the bar and how to sell them. Product knowledge is very important. It is also important for the bartender to take notice of current affairs and to remember the names of their customers and what they drink. Selling points are interesting or quirky information about the product, e.g., Baileys employing 25% of Ireland's cows
- **Professionalism:** A good bartender is always professional, from being accurate when pouring a drink, to dealing with customers and other members of the staff. A good bartender takes pride in everything he does, always keeps the bar clean and tidy and does his job to the best of his ability.
- **Teamwork:** As most bars require more than one bartender to run the bar, if you are a member of a team you must help the team maintain a smooth running bar by working as a team. Many bars have 'bar backs' who support the bartenders by restocking glasses, changing bins, etc. It is important for the bartenders to help the 'bar backs' whenever possible. In most bars and restaurants, you will be dealing with other members of staff such as waiters, chefs and bussers. It is important to remember that you are all part of the same team and help each other whenever possible.
- **Salesmanship:** There are two types of bartender – the salesperson and the order taker. The order taker will just stand behind the bar and serve whatever the customer asks for, e.g., a vodka and tonic using the most convenient and usually the cheapest bottle. The salesperson will always try and sell a better product to the customer, e.g., not vodka and tonic but an Absolut and tonic. A good bartender is always sales orientated and knows all about the products he sells, not just the cocktails but the spirits, wines, beers, soft drinks and liqueurs. Like a lot of jobs, bartending is sales based and therefore the best bartenders are usually the best sales people. At first, selling seems to be a difficult thing to master, but with practice and good knowledge it can become an enjoyable and profitable skill to learn.
- **Confidence:** The most important quality for any bartender, confidence comes from having all of the above qualities. Confidence cannot be taught, it is something that is gained by being 100% certain of your abilities and limitations. A great bartender has the utmost confidence in what he is doing when he is behind the bar and this confidence is communicated to the customers and teammates.

- **Consistency:** A very important factor in working behind a bar, consistency is what makes you, your colleagues and your bar stands out from the crowd. Good consistency means that you and your colleagues produce the same product every time you pour a drink, give the same high level of service. As a bartender, you will be expected to learn how your bar does all of the above and it is in your best interest to follow the guidelines set down by the bar. For instance, if your bar serves gin and tonics in 10oz hi-balls with a squeeze of lime or accepts American Express but not Diners Club as payment, so should you. If the consistency of the bar should slip, the customers will notice and this will adversely affect business.
- **Trust:** Unlike working in an office when you work in a bar, your colleagues rely on you and you on them. If you don't turn up for work one night, you are putting your colleagues under pressure by either forcing a bartender to work a double shift or for the team to work with one less bartender. When you are working a shift, you must trust those around you to help when you are busy or you have a problem with a guest. When you are busy, you should be able to rely on your colleagues to give you a hand, making the drinks or re-stocking your station. This obviously works both ways, you must help others when they need it.

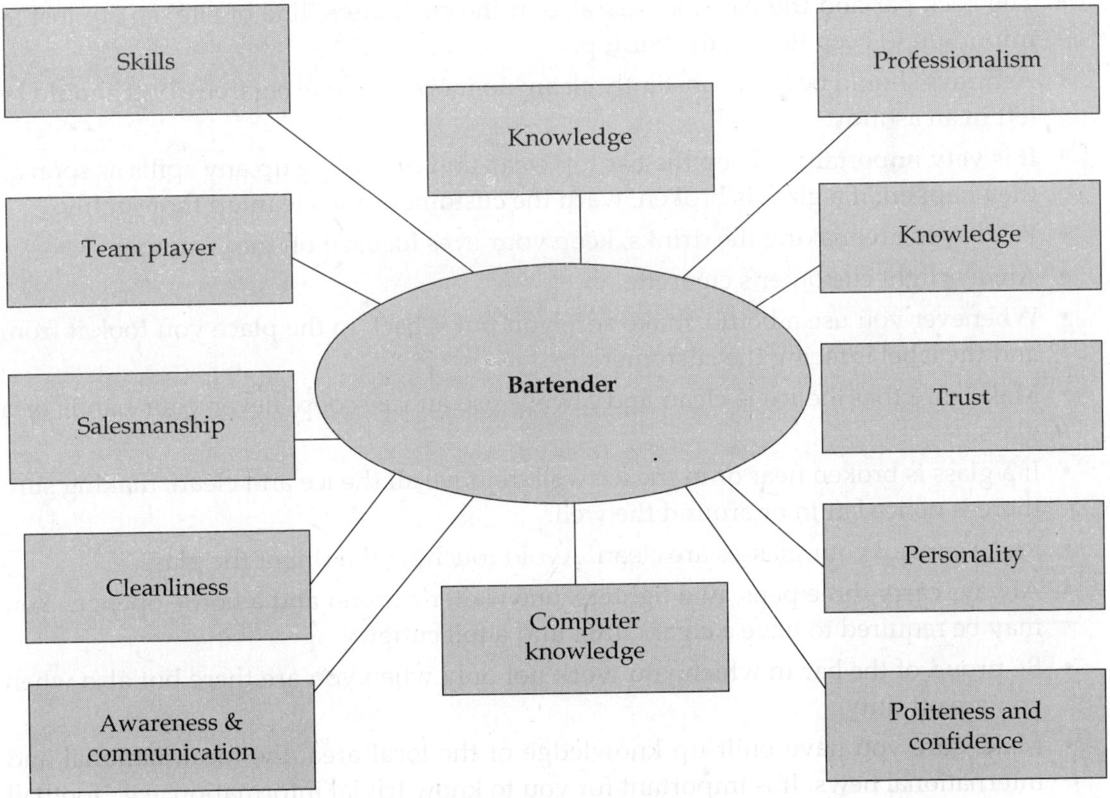

Attributes of a bartender

1.3 RULES IN THE BAR

By following these rules, will you ensure the highest level of service:

- A drink should always be served on a mat or napkin.
- Always place the drink in front of the guest, if possible.
- Flam bottom glass should be held from the bottom whereas stem glass should be held from the stem.
- If napkins become wet or dirty, replace with a fresh ones.
- Try to serve customers in the order they arrive at the bar.
- Always serve sip sticks with rocks glasses and cocktail glasses; always serve soda straws with Hi balls and all blended drinks.
- If rocks, hi balls or collins are served without ice, then no straws are used.
- When a customer orders another drink, always use a fresh glass unless requested otherwise.
- Always use the correct garnish.
- Keep the bar top spotlessly clean of empty glasses, beer bottles, dirty ashtrays, used napkins, etc.
- The back bar and the bar floor are also in the customers 'line of site' so are just as important to keep tidy as the bar top.
- Ashtrays should be kept constantly clean; no more than one cigarette butt should be left in an ashtray.
- It is very important to keep the bar top clean and dry. Wipe up any spills as soon as they happen. If a glass is broken, warn the customers and clean up thoroughly.
- While you are making the drinks, keep your eyes focused on the customers.
- Always light customer's cigarette.
- Whenever you use a bottle, make sure you put it back in the place you took it from and the label is facing the customer.
- Make sure that the ice is clean and always use an ice scoop, never your hands or a glass.
- If a glass is broken near or in the ice well, remove all the ice and clean, making sure there is no ice left in or around the well.
- Make sure all your glasses are clean. Avoid touching the rim of the glass.
- Always carry three pens, two lighters, one waiter's friend and a bottle opener. You may be required to have a cigar cutter and a foil cutter.
- Be proud of the bar in which you work not only when you are there but also when you are off duty.
- Make sure you have built up knowledge of the local area, the local, national and international news. It is important for you to know trivial information, e.g., football results.

Don't's of a bar

- Make unnecessary noise.
- Become over familiar with a customer
- Over fill a glass with a mixer; this will weaken the drink.
- Talk about the customer's last visit, unless they mention it.
- Chew gum, eat food or smoke behind the bar.
- Argue with a customer; if you have a problem with a customer always call the manager to deal with the situation. A good bartender never wins an argument.
- Gossip or tell rude stories, talk about politics or religion.
- Neglect a new customer by standing at the bar talking to a regular customer. Each new customer can be tomorrow's regular. Remember a soda customer today maybe a steak customer tomorrow.
- Interrupt a conversation between customers, be a good listener.

1.4 OPENING DUTIES IN A BAR

- Mis-en-place
  1. Setting a bar.
  2. Stocking up of a bar.
  3. Reading log book.
  4. Slicing fruit garnishes.
  5. Issue requisite items.
  6. Making simple syrup or sugar syrup.
  7. Squeeze lemon or other fruits for juices.
  8. Ready pre-mixes.
  9. Issue alcoholic beverages.
  10. Fill Store-n-Pourers.
  11. Prepare the bar caddy by placing coaster, straws and other required items in it.
  12. Switch on the computers and run software.
  13. Have the floor cleaned by the housekeeping.
  14. Dust chairs and tables and bar counters.
  15. Check for music and lighting.
  16. Switch on ice making machine.
  17. Wiping all glassware and placing them properly in shelves and glass racks.
  18. Place glasses for shilling in glass chillers.
- **Accompaniments:** Issue all accompaniments and store in proper containers.
- **Bottles:** Wipe mineral water bottles, soda bottles, beer cans, beer bottles, tonic water, canned juices and stack them properly in a refrigerator.
- **Refrigerators:** Clean the refrigerators in the under bar as per the standards of hygiene.

Refrigerator: Contents and Cleaning

What goes into a fridge?

Oganising your fridge

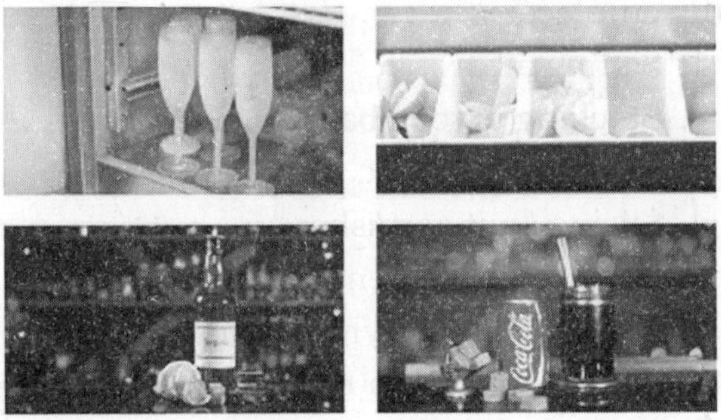

- Know the contents of your fridge.
- Pack your fridge consistently.
- Ensure labels are facing the front.
- All staff must know where everything belongs.

1.5 RUNNING DUTIES IN A BAR

- Refill ice bin, Store-n-Pourer, etc.
- Cutting fresh garnishes
- Stacking glassware
- Putting glasses for chilling in glass chillers
- Emptying trash bin

1.6 CLOSING DUTIES

- Thoroughly clean all used items.
- Place fresh fruits in refrigerators.
- Remove and empty the trash bin.
- Wash and dry all equipment like cocktail shaker, knife, mixing glasses, peg measures and others.
- Clean the bar counter and surface thoroughly.
- Return soiled tablecloth and cocktail napkins to the laundry.
- Store and lock all the alcoholic beverages.
- Leave comments in the logbook.
- Shut down the music, computer and lights.

1.7 STOCK CONTROL

- **Stock control:** It ensures that you always have enough of everything in your store room in case any unexpected sales take place. Stock control means an act of checking the quantities and whereabouts of drinks and ingredients in your bar.
- **Par level of a fridge:** The exact number of a certain drink that you need in your fridge to ensure that you always have enough drinks.
- **Last in, last out:** The 'last in, last out' rule ensures that when packing drinks from your storeroom into the fridge, you always place the coldest drinks at the front and the new stock at the back, allowing them to cool down to the proper temperature. Those placed at the front will be the perfect temperature for guests.

Bar Colour Codes

Items	Colour codes
Margarita Mix	1 Green Stripe; 1 Black Stripe
Lime Mix	1 Green Stripe
Pina Colada Mix	1 Green Stripe
Sweet and Sour Mix	Blank
Bloody Mary Mix	1 Red Stripe
Simple Syrup	1 White Stripe
Grape Fruit Juice	1 Green Stripe; 1 White Stripe
Orange Juice	1 Yellow Stripe
Cranberry Juice	1 Red Stripe; 1 Black Stripe
Pineapple Juice	1 Blue Stripe
Apple Juice	1 Black Stripe

Bar Slang

Items	Codes
86	Not available
68	Available
FHO	Full hands out
FHI	Full hand in
FIFO	First in, first out
FRAPPÉ (OR MIST)	A drink poured over crushed ice
ON THE FLY	Quickly
HANDS	Help
COMING THROUGH	Walking Full Hands
BEHIND YOU	Working Behind
BAR SPOON	A long-handled spoon intended for mixing and laying drinks. Its length ensures it can reach the bottom of a tall tumbler or jug to mix ingredients in the glass.
BITTERS	An herbal alcoholic blend that is used as an additive in cocktails to enhance flavour
CHASER	A chaser is the delicious drink you get to take following the gross one you just took a shot of. You can pretty much use anything to chase anything, let that be a lesson and a warning.
DRY	Refers to the drink or beverage which is less sweet or not sweet.
FREE POUR	Making and mixing drinks without using a measuring device.
DIRTY/BRAVE/ BLACK	Any drink whose name has any of these three words in it, contain Kahlua. Example: Black Russian, Dirty Mother and Brave Bull; all three drinks contain Kahlua, except Dirty Martini.
DOUBLE	A drink with double the amount of liquor.
FROST	To frost a glass, dip it in water, let it drain and stick it in the freezer. This works especially well for beer mugs, because it creates a layer of frost around the glass that will keep the drink cold longer.
NEAT	For a drink made without a mixer or ice, you'd order it "neat". Neat means straight from the bottle, no ice.
PREMIUM	Premium refers to top shelf liquor.
SOUR	'Sour' refers to the sourness of the sour bar mix/lime bar mix/margarita mix which are used in cocktails.
STONE	Any drink that has the word "stone" in it, contains orange juice.
STRAIGHT	This refers to a drink that has been shaken in a shaker and strained into a glass.
SWEET	Refers to drink or beverage which has sweetness in it.
UP	*A drink served up has been chilled by shaking or stirring, and then strained out into a chilled, stemware cocktail glass without ice.*
VIRGIN	This refers to non-alcoholic drinks. You can use this to order common cocktails minus the alcohol, (e.g., Virgin Mojito, Virgin Pina Colada).
(WITH A) SQUEEZE	A lemon "twisted" on top of the drink and dropped into it.
WELL DRINK	An alcoholic beverage served using the low-cost liquors. A well drink is a drink where neither the brand of the liquor or brand of the mix is mentioned (e.g., Vodka Cranberry, Rum & Coke).
PONY	A pony shot is equal to 1 oz.
MUDDLE UP	To crush up ingredients with a tool called a muddler.

Steps to be carried out in a bar

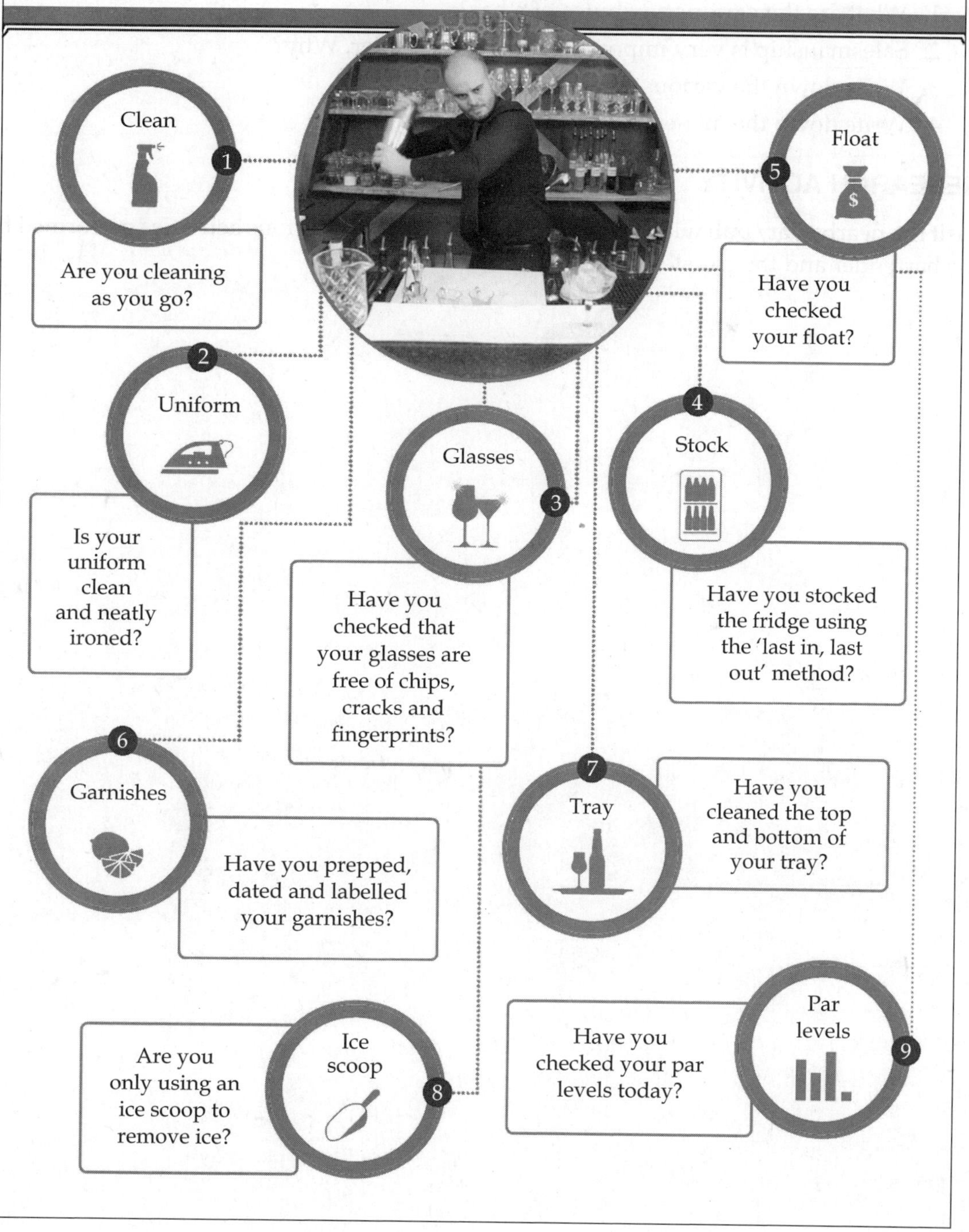

REVISION QUESTIONS

1. What are the various attributes of a bar?
2. Salesmanship is very important for any bartender. Why?
3. Write down the various rules of a bar.
4. Write down the mis-en-place activities in a bar.

RESEARCH ACTIVITY

Visit the nearby bar/pub with a custodian and observe the various activities performed by the bartender and the bar steward.

2

Bar Designing

2.1 INTRODUCTION

> **After reading this chapter, you will be able to understand:**
> - Types of bar
> - Parts of a bar
> - Planning a bar
> - Composition of a bar

Bar is defined as a retail outlet for drinks which are generally consumed standing up or sitting on a bar stool in front of a counter fitted with a wooden bar as a rest and hence the name. The back bar is a set of shelves of glasses and bottles behind the counter. It may be decorated with wood work, etched glass mirror and lights. Alcoholic and non-alcoholic drinks are sold for consumption within the premises. Type of bars range from informal bars to elegant places of entertainment.

2.2 TYPES OF BAR

- **Public house:** These are also referred to as public bars or pubs. These are large in size and offer drinks and light meals at a reasonable rate.
- **Foyer:** Located in the lobby from where the newly arrived guests can have drinks.
- **Saloon/Lounge/Private bar:** These bars offer varying degrees of comfort, elegance and privacy. They are small in size and have restricted entry. These bars are expensive and cater to the elite class.
- **Dispense bar:** This is a bar situated within a food & beverage service area that dispenses only wine and other alcoholic drinks for consumption with meal or are sometimes dispensed from bars situated in the food and beverage service area. The alcoholic drinks are served by a member of restaurant staff known as sommelier or wine waiter.
- **Service bar:** This is a bar where drinks are poured and made ready to serve in some other area like room service, lounge, etc., by the waiter. It does not have a display counter and is usually situated at the back of the house.
- **Cocktail bar:** These modern bars are situated in luxury hotels. They are lavishly equipped and furnished. They introduce new concepts in style and service of exquisite drinks.

Pool side bar

- **Poolside bar:** These are the bars situated near the pool area. Alcoholic and non-alcoholic drinks are provided to the guests frequenting the pool area. The entry to these bars may be restricted for residential guests and members only.

2.3 PARTS OF A BAR

- **The front bar**

1. It is referred as a meeting point for the customers and the bartenders where the customers order for their drinks and are served by the bartenders.

The front bar

2. The bar counter may be round, oval or straight. However, round or oval bar counters look more attractive than a straight bar counter.
3. The counter should be a minimum of 1½ feet wide or 16-18 inches. The height of the counter varies from 4–4½ feet that is approximately 42-48 inches.
4. Bar stools placed in the front of the counter should be 3 feet high with foot rest approximately a foot from the floor. It is always advisable to have a back rest and to fix the bar stool to prevent accidents or guests toppling over.
5. Bar counter should be provided with the speed rail where the pouring brands/ house brands are available.

6. It should be functional and have adequate space for pouring the drinks and serving them.

7. Surface is waterproof and easy to clean (laminated plastic or high quality granite can be used for the same).

8. May have a padded armrest running from one end to other (8 inch space added).

> **Front of House**
> The area in and around the bar where your guests will be. Working in the front of house bar means that you will prepare drinks and garnishes in front of your guests. It also means that you will always be visible to the guests.

9. The waiters pour the drinks along with the mixers, such as soda, water, etc. into the appropriate glass arranged in the glass rail (drip rail) which is recessed for about 3 inches at the bartender's side.

10. Bar die is a vertical structure which supports the front bar. It separates the customer from the bartender's work area.

11. Customer's side may be padded, decorated with carving or left plain.

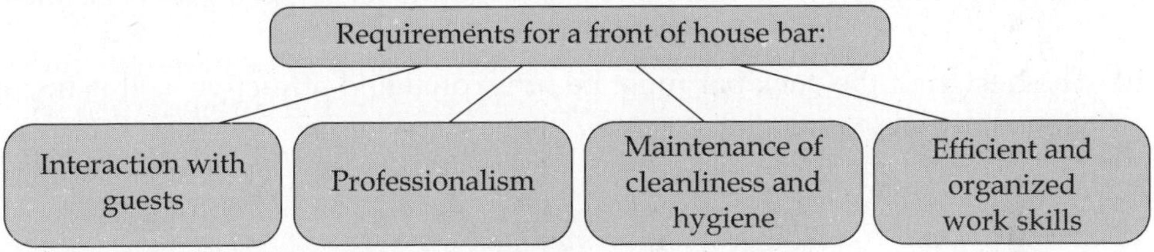

- **The back bar**
  1. Located at the back of the front counter leaving sufficient space for the bartenders to do their work.
  2. It consists of display rack set over the storage cabinets.

The back bar

3. Back bar holds various types of liquor bottles and sparkling assorted glassware in an attractive manner to enhance the appearance of the bar.
4. Back bar may be lined with mirror at the back which reflects the bottle stored in the rack.
5. Many bars include pictures, posters, tainted glass, plants, antiques, etc., to make the back bar more attractive.
6. In back bar, overhead slotted racks are fitted to store the stemware making the bar attractive.
7. Base of the back bar functions as a storage space and the part of it may be a refrigerated cabinet.

Back of House

Unlike the front of house bar, this area is limited to 'staff only' and is where all drinks and garnishes are prepared, as well as stored. This happens out of the guest's sight.

8. The extra stock, such as drinking straws, napkins, cocktail umbrellas, salvers, jugs, condiments, sugars, etc., are stored in a bar caddy.
9. The base of the bar may accommodate special equipment such as bottle cooler, espresso machine, non-alcoholic beverage dispenser, cash register and so on. The base bar is wider than the display rack.
10. The design of the back bar must be functional and attractive as it is in constant view of the customers.

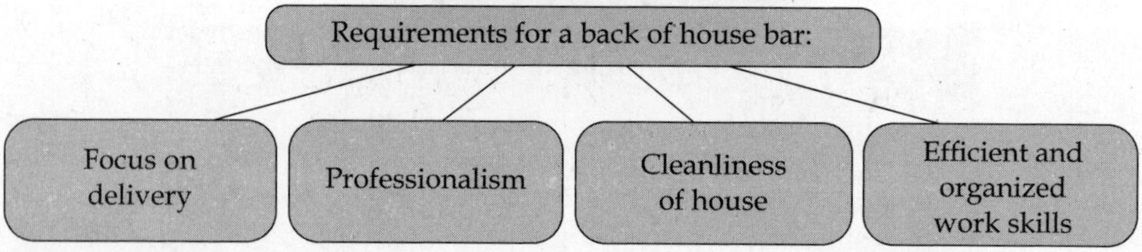

- **The under bar**
  1. It refers to the area under the front bar of the bartender's side.
  2. It is designed keeping in mind the drinks to be made, equipment required and the mixes needed for the drinks.
  3. Work flow must be considered while designing the layout.
  4. It is the centre for the entire bar operations as the bartenders will be facing the guests while preparing their drinks.

5. It may be divided into many workstations according to the volume of the business and the length of the counter.
6. Each station will have its own supply of fast moving liquor, mixes, ice, glasses, blender, sink, garnishes and so on within reach.
7. The liquors in each station are grouped into 'well brands'(house brands) and 'call brands'(requested by the guest).
8. If a blender is required for most of the drinks, then it may be provided to every section: otherwise kept separately at the back bar.
9. Most busy bars have an automatic dispensing system for mixes in each station.
10. If drought beer is served then beer dispensing unit must be provided.
11. Clean glasses should be grouped according to the type and stored in the glass shelves near the station on the back bar or in the overhead racks, and the prepared glasses for the drinks should be kept ready in the glass rail or near the ice box.
12. Storage area should be provided for storing reserve stock of spirits, wines, liqueur, beers and kitchen supplies.
13. Under bar should have provision for waste disposal and hand wash.
14. Some restaurants may not have dispense bar attached to it so the server will have to collect the drinks from the main bar. In that case, one or two sections must be completely devoted to cater to the needs of the restaurant guests otherwise the restaurant staff will be forced to collect the drinks from the stations moving through the customer's station. This will result in chaos.

Under Bar

2.4 PLANNING A BAR

The following factors need to be considered while planning and designing a good bar.

1. Budget
2. Area

3. Clientele
4. Points of service
5. Shape and size of bar counter
6. Guest preferences
7. Seat turnover
8. Average spending power
9. Timings
10. Location and site
11. Décor, ambience, and colours
12. Style of service

- **Location:** The bar should be located from where it is easily visible and accessible to the customers so as to achieve maximum sale. In a hotel, bars are mostly situated near the lobby and are usually visible from it.
- **Space:** There should be sufficient space for the staff to work behind the counter. Ideally, there should be a minimum of 3 feet of space from the back of the counter to the storage shelves at the back.
- **Flooring and plumbing:** The work area should be such which is non-slippery and easy to wipe or mop. The guest area may be wooden or carpeted as these surfaces are able to absorb sound. It is important to have regular supply of hot and cold running water for washing of glassware and other works. A bar should have adequate supply of cold and hot water for sinks and ice machine. Adequate drainage facility is essential for sink, dishwashers, refrigerators, and ice machine. Separate area must be assigned near the bar for washing glasses out of sight of the guests. There will be certain amount of spillage, leftover from used glasses, ice cubes, etc., on the floor. It should be easily cleaned. As the bartenders stand for long hours, the flooring material should be comfortable and safe. The tiles or concrete covered with rubber or plastic mats minimizes slippage and is comfortable for the feet. However, the floor must be cleaned frequently to keep the bar hygienic.
- **Lighting:** Lighting highlights the mood and atmosphere of the bar. Too much lighting is not preferred but should be enough so that the guests can see each other. Indirect lighting is preferred to direct lighting. There should be sufficient lighting at the bar counter for the barman to carry out his work efficiently. A well designed bar will not get the recognition it deserves if the lighting is poor and does not blend with the theme of the décor. The bartenders' efficiency is influenced by the quality of lighting under which they work. Bright lighting is necessary over the under bar and the back bar. It also attracts attention of the guests. Indirect or diffused lighting may be used over the guest area. Bright lighting is better for the guest area as they will be able to appreciate the colour of content in their glasses, behave decently, and will be able to watch their steps under the influence of alcohol.

- **Furniture:** Bar is usually a place where guests meet each other for close interaction and spend plenty of time conversing with each other. Most of the bars serve drinks along with light meals with the guest moving to the restaurant for lunch or dinner. It is therefore advisable that the seating is comfortable. Sofa or soft seating arrangements are preferred with low height for guests to place their drinks and snacks.
- **Electricity:** Modern bars are equipped with a number of electric machines, therefore sufficient power points with proper earthing should be available as most of the equipment run on electricity.
- **POS/register stations:** It is located away from the mix and pickup areas. Each drink served requires entering in integrated computer system installed with various restaurant/bar software such as Micros, POS and so on. Cables connected with the computer system must be avoided running across the work area which may lead to accidents.

A layout/design for a combination of public and service bar as well as the placement of equipment in it.

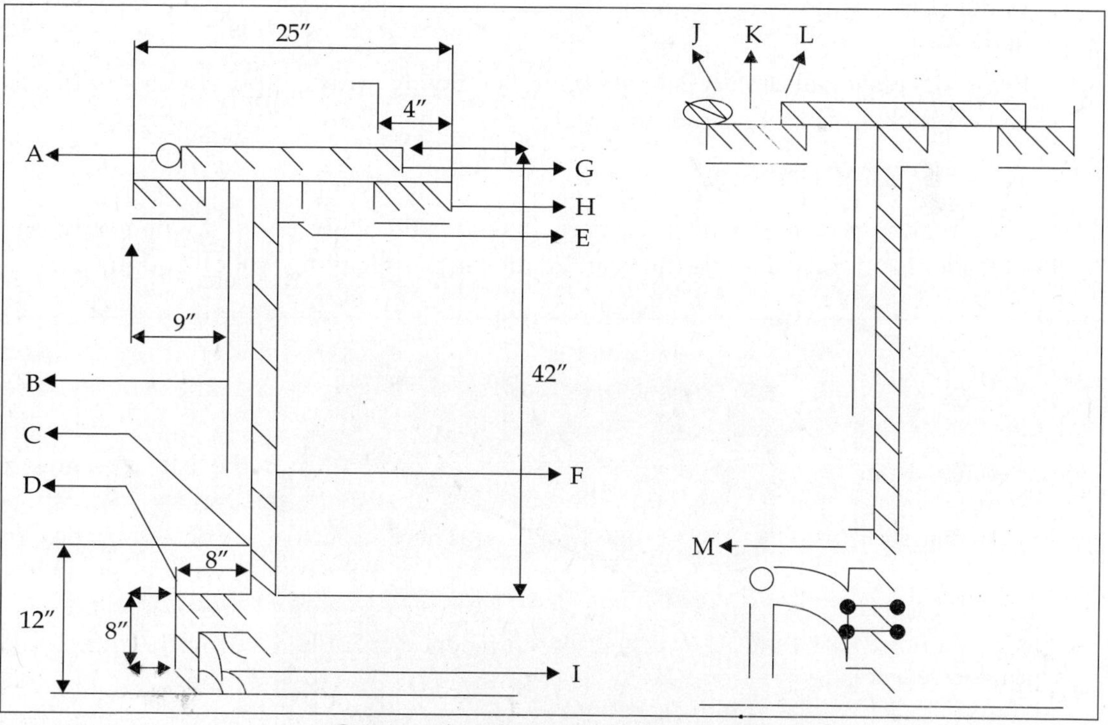

Cross section diagram of a bar counter

2.4.1 Standard Bar Details

A. Arm rest – typical wood shape; many styles are available including finishes.

B. Decorative finish – wood panel, tongue and groove board, carpet, upholstery, ceramic tile, etc.

C. Kick plate – linoleum, formica, etc.

D. Food rest – linoleum, slate, hard wood, etc.

E. Cleat–for securing top to die, varies with manufacturer.

F. Bar die – usually 3/4 inches plywood.

G. Liquor gutter – usually constricted as shown; may be formed in one piece mahogany bar top.

H. Water stop –1/4 inch thick black formica or wood. Cut down for cleaning at ends.

I. Shoe – to prevent moisture from separating laminations of the plywood die, a solid wood base strip or metal channel shoe is desirable.

J. Extended arm rest – wood, formica or upholstery.

K. Extension bar – brass or black iron

L. Water stop – same as 1/4 inch thick black formica or wood. Cut down for cleaning at ends.

M. Brass foot rest – rail usually 2 inches diameter. Swing away support to floor optional. Check thickness of brass rail proposed by supplier. They are rather expensive.

2.4.2 Tips For Bar Planning

- When planning large island type bars, consider the slow periods when only one bartender is on duty. Divide the islands into sections leaving walk through space.

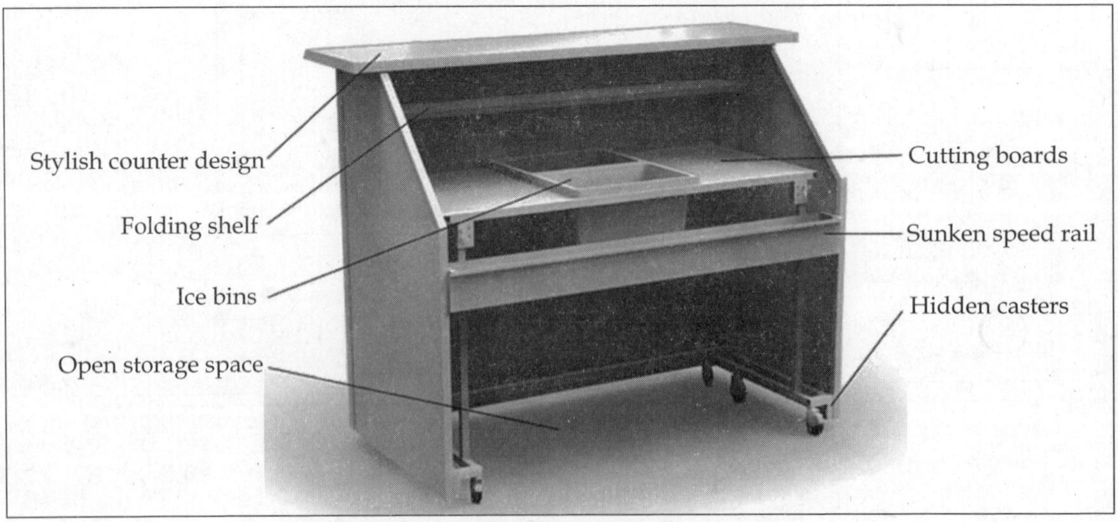

Standard portable bar

- If your preference is for serpentine, round ends or curved bars, weigh carefully the aesthetic value against the much higher construction costs and remember the under bar sinks and coolers. To place a long bottle box, or draft beer unit under a curved bar, not having an exceptionally large radius, could make it impossible for the bartender to reach far enough to be able to serve a customer sitting in front of the under bar unit.
- A fat expenditure on the bar front should be incurred only if it is an absolute necessary and in keeping with the theme. People seldom pay a lot of attention to it.
- Inexpensive paneling or applying carpet to the bar front are usually quite satisfactory.
- Masonry brick fronts provide an attractive rustic appearance.
- Dining and unwinding at a bar can be a pleasant and memorable experience if the ambience is tastefully created. A good design is one that is subtle and unobtrusive while at the same time imbuing a degree of affluence and exclusivity.

2.4.2.1 Keeping Spirits in Shelf

Every bar should have a full range of house spirit in the speed rail and these spirits should be ranged in order from the most frequently ordered spirit closest at hand to the least frequently ordered spirit farthest. These spirits are generally positioned from right to left, as most of the bartenders are right-handed. Example, if Grey Goose Vodka is the most popular spirit in the bar, it should be placed closest to the bartender for easy to reach following with the second popular spirits and so on. In most of the bars, the spirits are kept or stored in shelf in back bar as followed, but it can also be stacked on the shelves as per the hotel policies:

- **Bottom shelf:** Referred as house, rack or basic spirits which are least expensive and lesser quality.
- **Mid shelf:** Referred as Call spirits, slightly more expensive, well-known brands.
- **Top shelf:** Referred as premium, deluxe or exotic spirits; most expensive and highest quality.

Positioning of spirits/ alcoholic beverages also depends on demand, grouping categories and aesthetics as mentioned below:

- **Demand:** The more a spirit/alcoholic beverage is used, the closer it should be.
- **Grouping categories:** Similar products to be placed and positioned together, helping the bartender to find them easily.
- **Aesthetics:** The spirit/alcoholic beverage should look good and appealing when they placed or stacked.

Place the popular spirit/ alcoholic beverage at the service station and slow moving items at back bar. Likewise bottled beer and ready to drink beverages are placed in refrigerators according to their popularity.

2.4.3 Composition of a Bar

- Speed rail (which holds most popular house spirits and liqueurs)
- Glassware
- Cash register
- Ice well
- Sink
- Beer taps
- Soft drink gun/Bar gun
- Juices and mixers
- Cocktail equipment (shakers, spinal mixer, Hawthorn strainer, bar spoon, sifter, blender, knife, cutting board, muddling stick, etc.)
- Cocktail and drink garnishes
- Bottled beers
- Wines
- Spirits and liqueurs
- Straws, coasters and napkins
- Cleaning or wiping cloth
- Bar top
- Fridges

Bar Back Station/Under Bar

- Glass washer
- Ice machine
- Spare equipment and accessories
- Beer cellar (to serve tap beer)

Equipment Placed Together

- Beer taps and beer glasses
- Cocktail equipment, cocktail glasses, cocktail garnishes, ice well, liquor, soft drink gun and sink
- Ice well, sprits, speed well, straws coasters, napkins, soft drink gun and sprit glasses
- Wine and Wine glasses
- Bar top and cleaning cloths

2.4.4 Shapes of the Bar

1. Size of the bar depends upon the volume of the business, variety of drinks on offer and the area available.

2. Shape of the bar depends upon the area available, shape of the area, convenience of operations and the theme of the décor.
3. It may be straight, L-shaped, U-shaped, wave shaped-round, square, etc.
4. All bars have three sections- the front bar, the back bar and the under bar.
5. The location of the back bar is usually behind the front bar, fitted against the wall.
6. In a freestanding square, round, rectangle, and any irregular shapes the back bar will be the focal point located in the centre and the service stations or front bar around the back bar. In this type of layout, the under bar will be exposed to customers. Plumbing work needs extra attention in this kind of layout.

REVISION QUESTIONS

1. What are the various types of bar?
2. Explain in detail about various parts of a bar along with their purpose.
3. What are the various points to be considered while planning a bar?
4. List down the items to be stored in under bar.

RESEARCH ACTIVITIES

- Visit any public bar in nearby location with a custodian and observe the layout of the bar and draw it for better understanding.
- Search two layouts of a bar, observe it and list down the differences.

3

Bar Glassware and Equipment

3.1 INTRODUCTION

After reading this chapter, you will be able to understand:

- Meaning of glassware and its types
- Equipment used in bar
- Rules of a bar
- Don'ts of bar
- Methods of using various bar equipment

Glassware is a term used for all types of glasses used for the purpose of drinking beverages. Glassware can be stem glass and flat bottom glass. Small stem glass is known as *footed glassware* like brandy balloon. Capacity of glassware is measured in fluid ounce and one fluid ounce is 30 mL. Glassware is an essential part of cocktail and should be dust free and neat and clean. Glasses vary in shapes and sizes according to the cocktails.

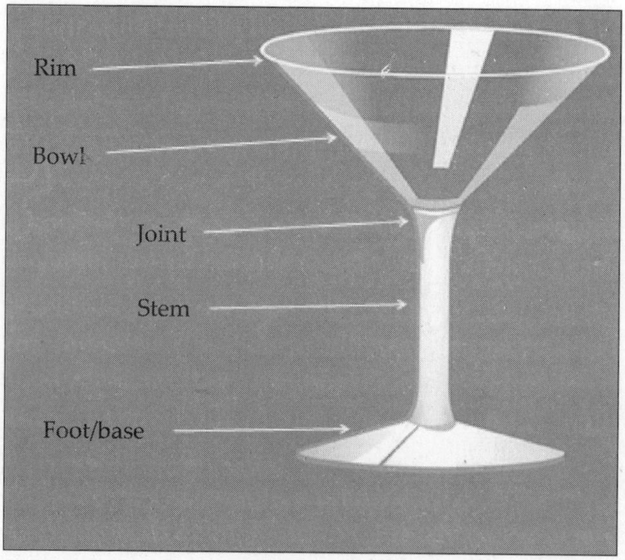

Parts of a glass

Essential bar glassware

	**Brandy snifter/Brandy balloon** **Uses:** To serve aged sprits such as brandy, Cognac, Armagnac, aged rums and specialty aged tequilas. **Capacity:** 8 fl oz.
	**Martini glass** **Uses:** To serve a number of drinks, often cocktails especially Martini **Capacity:** Small Martini glass - 150 mL (5 fl oz.) Large Martini glass - 300 mL. (10 fl oz.)
	**Margarita** **Uses:** To serve Margarita (cocktail) **Capacity:** 425 mL (14 fl oz.)
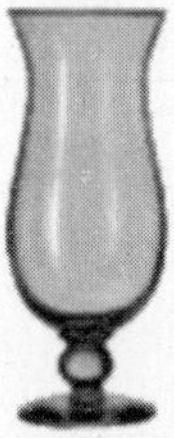	**Hurricane** **Uses:** To serve blended cocktails or cocktails built over ice., e.g., Mai tai **Capacity:** 450 mL (14 fl oz.)
	**Highball glass** **Uses:** To serve long or double spirits as Gin, Vodka, fruit juices, water **Capacity:** 8 fl oz.
	**Irish Coffee Mug** **Uses:** To serve Irish coffee **Capacity:** 300 mL (20 fl oz.)

	**Whisky/Rock glass** **Uses:** Allows the guest to securely hold it and nose the aromas from the whisky. Used to serve whiskies, bourbons and a variety of short drinks. **Capacity:** (9 fl oz.)
	**Sherry glass/Capita** **Uses:** To serve Sherry and fortified wine **Capacity:** 90 mL (3 fl oz.)
	**Shot glass** **Uses:** Designed for a drink to be drunk in a single gulp. Also used as a shooter glass and to drink tequila. Used for straight spirits shots. **Capacity:** 30 mL (1 fl oz.)
	**Red wine glass** **Uses:** To serve Red Wine **Capacity:** 7 fl oz.
	**White wine glass** **Uses:** To serve White Wine **Capacity:** 5.5 fl oz.
	**Pitcher** **Uses:** To serve beer Capacity: 60 fl oz.
	**Pilsner glass** **Uses:** To serve Pilsner beer **Capacity:** 425 mL (14 fl oz.)

	**Champagne flute** **Uses:** To serve Champagne **Capacity:** 6 fl oz.
	**Champagne tulip** **Uses:** To serve Champagne **Capacity:** 6 fl oz.
	**Champagne saucer/Coupe** **Uses:** To serve Champagne **Capacity:** 6 fl oz.
	**Tom Collin** **Uses:** To serve long drinks **Capacity:** 12 fl oz.
	**Slim Gim** **Uses:** To serve long drinks **Capacity:** 12 fl oz.
	**Beer goblet** **Uses:** To serve beer **Capacity:** 10-12 fl oz.
	**Rolly Polly** **Uses:** To erve Bloody Mary (cocktail) **Capacity:** 9 fl oz.

Some other bar glassware

3.2 CARE AND CLEANING OF GLASSWARE

- Glassware is cleaned in the dishwashing machine and goes through the process of washing, rinsing and sterilizing.
- To polish glass, hold glass over boiling hot water until steam condenses on glass. Using a waiter's cloth, the glass is wiped or polished.

- A little lemon juice or white vinegar maybe added in the water to remove any white marks on the glasses due to chlorination.
- Always check for brilliance and any spots against the sunlight.
- All glasses should be held at the base. Those with a stem should be inverted and then held at the stem.
- Check the glasses for chips or cracks. Remove damaged glasses from the stock.
- Always use an ice scoop to fill the glasses with ice. Never use the glass to scoop ice. It can break the ice.
- If you break glass in your ice, throw away all the ice and make sure that there are no pieces of broken glass.
- If a glass is hot, do not put ice in it. The glass can break with the change of temperature.
- If the glass is cold, do not pour anything hot in it.
- Don't carry more glasses than what you can handle on your hands. Use a tray to carry them.
- Glasses must be checked for any lipstick marks.

3.3 STORAGE

- Stored in single rows on paper-lined shelves. Each shelf should be labelled with the names of the items that it holds.
- Should be stored upside down to prevent any dust settling in them.
- Ideally, plastic coated wire racks should be used for stacking, storing and transporting.
- Glasses should never be stacked inside each other. Do not stack the glasses too high.
- Do not stack two different glasses together. They can get stuck together and if you try to separate them, they might break.

1

Be careful when handling, cleaning and serving glassware.

2

Glassware and finger prints should never be seen together.

3

All glassware must always be carried on a tray.

4

When handling stemware, always hold the glass by the stem.

5

6

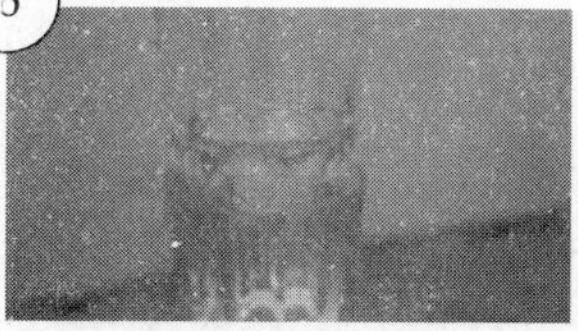

Never stack glasses

Rules of glassware

Except in certain specialty restaurants or first class establishments where either coloured glassware or cut glassware may be used, hotel and bar glassware is usually plain. However, many restaurants and bars use a clear stemmed glass for all wines to cut the cost and quantity. A good wine glass should be clear and plain so that the colour and brilliance of the wine can be clearly seen. It should have a stem for holding the wine glass so that the heat of one's hand does not affect the taste of wine. Wine glasses always have a curving lip to hold the aroma and it should be large enough to hold the wine being tasted. Some of the major brands of glasses used in the hotels and bar are:

> **Did you know ?**
> **Hock** (German white wine) glasses have brown stems same like the colour of the Hock bottle and Moselle glasses (German white wine) have green stems, the same colour as the Moselle bottle.

- Schott Zwiesel (German)
- Imperial Ocean (Thailand)
- Somiya (Local)
- Cisterna (Thailand)

3.4 BAR EQUIPMENT

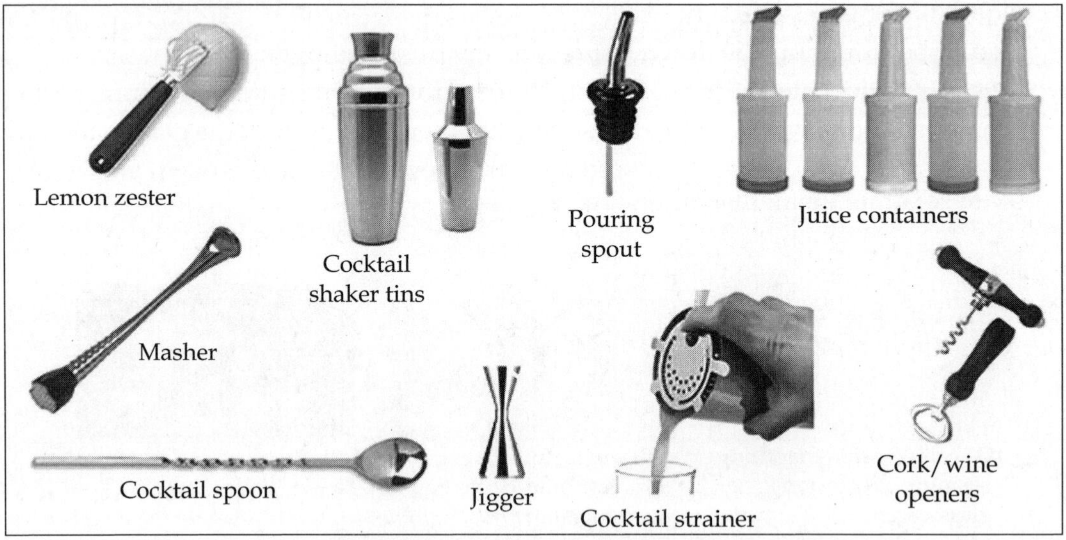

Some essential bar equipment

Table 3.1: Detailed list of bar equipment and their uses

Can opener: For opening cans of fruit and syrup.	
Corkscrew: For opening wine and Champagne bottles.	
Cloths: For wiping surfaces and equipment. These should be damp and not wet.	
Cutting board: For slicing fruit and other garnishes. This should be heavy and laminated.	
Cocktail napkin: To serve with drinks.	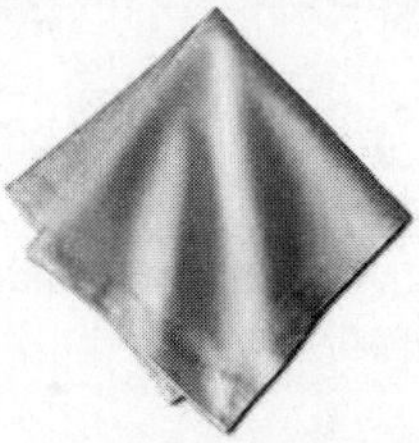
Bottle opener: For opening screw top bottles.	
Bottle sealers: For keeping liquors and other bottle contents fresh.	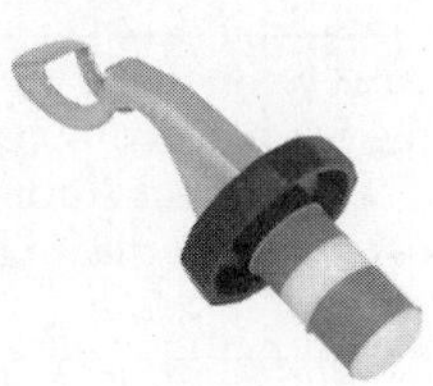

European cocktail shaker: Also known as a cobbler cocktail shaker. It has a cap and built-in strainer which makes it very convenient for use. The cap can often be used as a measure for spirits or other liquids. Most common type of cocktail shaker and is usually made of aluminium. **Note :** Always pour the least expensive ingredient into the cocktail shaker first.	
Boston shaker: The Boston cocktail shaker does the same thing as the cobbler shaker, but looks and works slightly different. It consists of two cone-shaped parts - *metal and a glass* - with the glass part fitting into the shaker. Shaking with this type of shaker is similar to shaking with a cobbler. Instead of using a cap to close the shaker, you tightly fit the two cones onto one another before shaking. One does need to be more careful than with a cobbler shaker. Put the ingredients in the glass cone, put the metal cone over it and give it a slight nudge to seal the two cones.	
Electric blender: Many cocktails require a blender to blend the ingredients smoothly together. Useful for drinks with fruit pieces or ice cream, etc.	
Grater: To grate spices like nutmeg and others.	
Ice bucket: A metal or insulated ice bucket keeps your ice cold and clean.	
Ice scoops and tongs: Use these to add ice to drinks. Never handle ice with your hands, it is not only unhygienic, but the heat from your hand will begin to melt the ice. Don't use glassware as a scoop.	

Ice crusher: Used for crushing the ice.	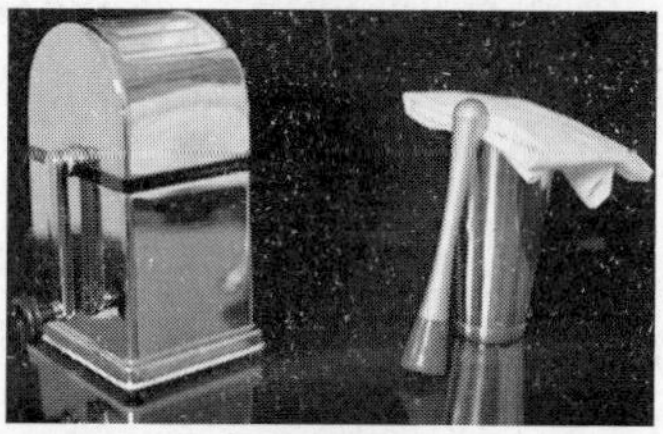
Jigger: Also known as tot or peg measure, is a measurement tool. There are various shapes and sizes, however, the standard single peg measure is either 25 mL or 30 mL.	
Juice squeezer/extractor: Needed for getting the most juice out of your fruits. It helps to soak citrus fruits in hot water before squeezing.	
Bar spoon: A bar spoon with a long handle and a muddler end will allow you to mix and measure ingredients as well as crush garnishes.	
Mixing glass: Useful for long drinks where it is required to mix the ingredients without shaking.	
Sharp knife: For cutting fruit and garnishes.	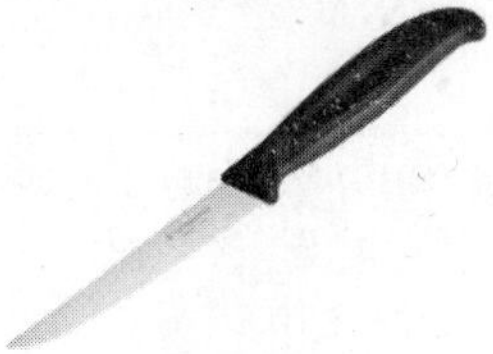
Strainer: Removes the ice and fruit pulp from juices. This may come with a cocktail shaker.	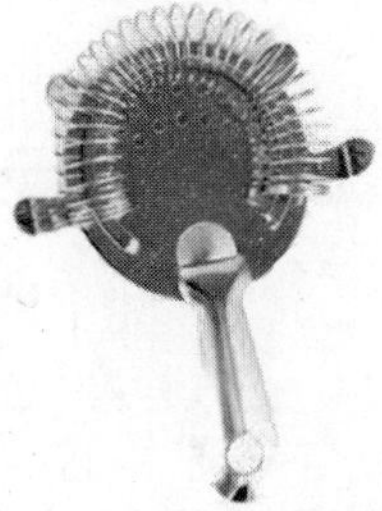

Straws and stirrers: To stir the drink and to drink.	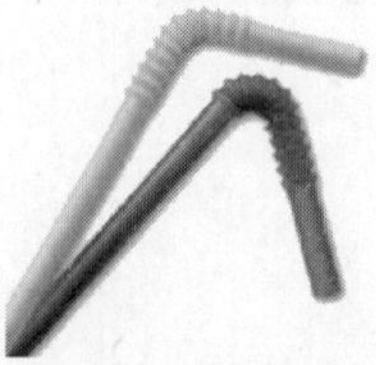
Muddler: To muddle the drink, generally made of wood.	
Garnish tray/condiment tray: To place different garnishes into the tray.	
Salt rimmer: Used to rim the glasses with salt.	
Speed pourer: Helps in pouring drinks.	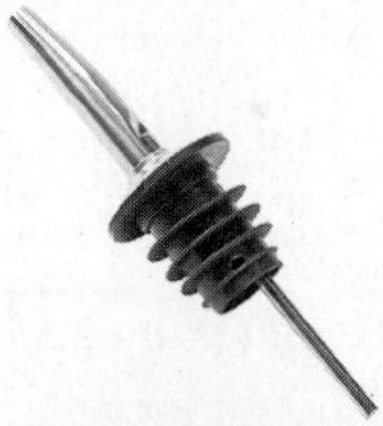
Beverage round/Salver: Used to serve drinks on the table and to carry glasses.	
Coaster: Glasses are placed on the coaster where there is no tablecloth.	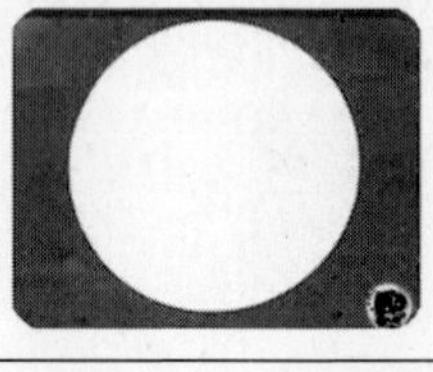

Cocktail umbrella: Used to garnish drinks.	
Ice machine: To make ice cubes.	
Bar gun: A soda gun or bar gun is a device used by bars to serve various types of carbonated and non-carbonated drinks.	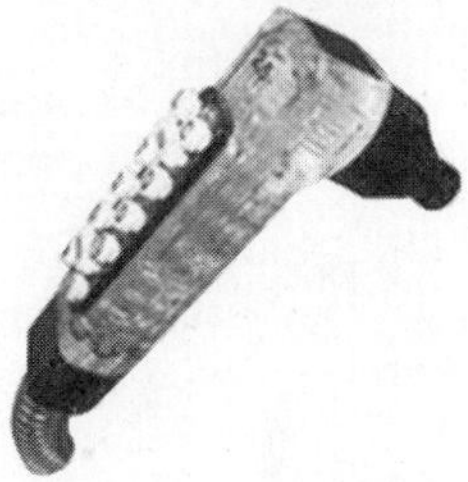
Zester: To remove the zest of citrus fruits.	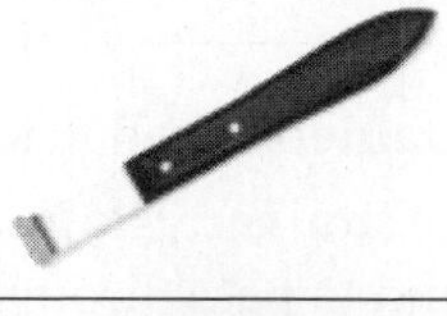
Bar caddy: To put straws, stirrers and paper napkins.	
Bar mats: To provide grip when wet, which prevents tins, bottles and glasses from falling over during service.	

3.4.1 Using Various Bar Equipment

Bar equipment is essential for any bartender for the smooth operation of the bars. These equipment help in mixing and preparing drinks for the guest. It is therefore of utmost importance for any bartender to know the right usage of these equipment.

(i) **Peg measure:** Peg measure, also known as jigger and tot measure, can be used in two ways:

- **The tipping method:** Hold the tot measure between the your thumb and index finger, resting the base on your palm. To avoid the spilling, complete the tipping action quickly and without hesitation.
- **The flicking method:** Hold the tot measure between the thumb and index finger, resting the base on your palm. Raise index finger above the middle finger, and rotate your wrist quickly to tilt the tot measure towards the glass.

Rules of a Tot Measure

1. Always pour into a tot measure over a glass or shaker tin.
2. Always start measuring the cheapest ingredients first to avoid wasting an expensive ingredient should a mistake occur.

(ii) **Strainers:** Used to strain the various cocktails.

- **Fine strainer:** The fine strainer gets its name from the tiny holes in its bowl that allow liquid to pass through.
  1. Place the glass that you'll be straining your liquid into onto your bar mat.
  2. Hold the fine strainer above the glass.
  3. Take the shaking tin in your other hand and carefully pour its contents through the strainer and into the glass.
- **Hawthorne strainer:** The Hawthorne strainer is made up of a disc (the 'rim'), a handle and prongs which are used for stabilising the strainer. There is also a metal spring which rolls inwards to fit inside the glass.
  1. Place the Hawthorne strainer into the mixing tin, with the spring inside the mixing tin.
  2. Place your finger on top of the strainer, making sure it is held firmly in place.

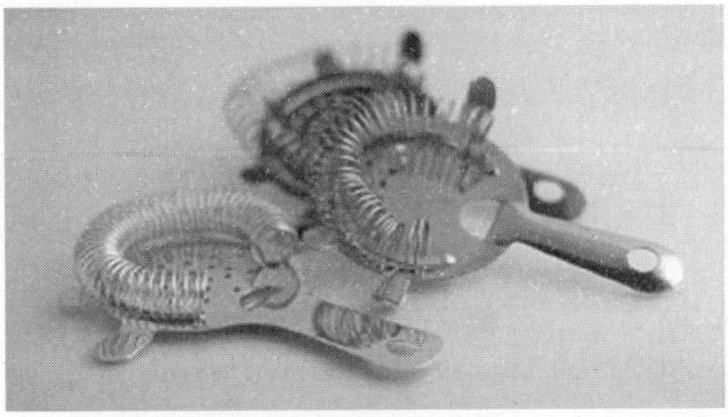

Hawthorne strainer

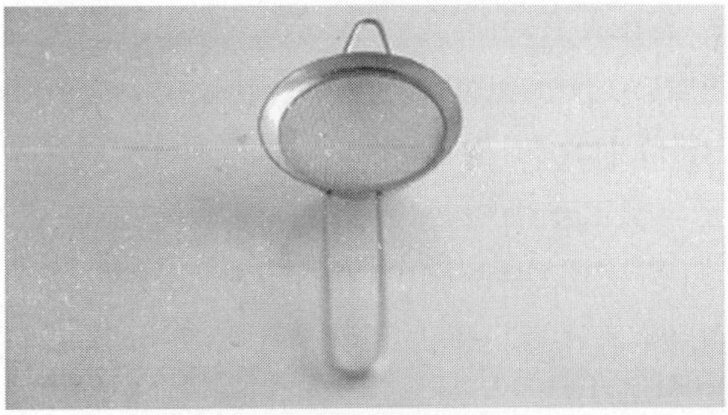

Fine strainer

(iii) Boston shaker: Mixes ingredients effectively and cools down drinks quickly. It also adds performance element to bar service. Once cocktail is mixed, you can use a Hawthorne strainer to strain your cocktail.

Using Boston shaker

- Add all the ingredients to the smaller mixing tin.
- Add ice blocks until it is full.
- Place the large cocktail tin over the smaller mixing tin.
- Tap the tin down, making it fit over tightly.
- Pick up the tins, holding them together firmly.
- Rotate the tins so that the larger tin is facing away from you.
- Shake backward and forward for roughly eight seconds (enough time to cool the drink down).
- With the smaller tin on top and the gap between the tins at twelve o'clock from your body, tap the bottom of the tin.
- If the seal is not released, tap a little harder until it releases.
- Once the tin is released, pull it away. You are now ready to strain the cocktail using the Hawthorne strainer.

(iv) European Shaker

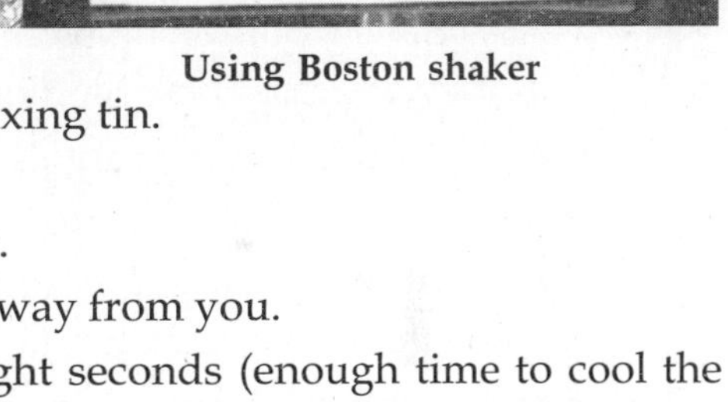

Using European shaker

- Add all the ingredients into the shaker tin, on the bar mat.
- Fill the shaker tin to three quarters with ice.
- Firmly attach the shaker's lid on top of the cocktail tin.
- Place one hand underneath the shaker and one hand on the lid.
- Make sure the underside of the shaker is facing away from you.

- After shaking, remove the shaker's cap.
- Pour the shaken cocktail into the cocktail glass.

Drawbacks of the European shaker

- Fruit pulp is often caught in the built-in strainer. A fine strainer can be used to remove any pulp or fruit bits.
- Ice in the shaker can cause it to contract, which may lead to the lid getting stuck onto the metal tin.
- Shards of ice may break off into the drink. A fine strainer can be used to prevent the drink from being diluted.

(v) Speed pourer: Rubber/plastic attachment that fits into the neck of the bottle to seal in any air or liquid. Long pouring snout allows liquid to flow through when pouring. The air hole allows us to control the pouring of the liquid from the bottle easily. Speed pourer helps in increased accuracy at a fast and even flow.

Use of speed pourer

- Insert the speed pourer into the neck of the bottle.
- Check that the speed pourer is inserted firmly by making sure that there are no gaps between the rubber attachment and the neck of the bottle.

(vi) Bar spoon for layering drinks

- Pour the base layer into the shooter glass using a speed pourer or a tot measure.
- Place the bar spoon at the level where the base layer ends and rest it against the side of the glass.
- Gently trickle the second liquid onto the bar spoon so that it runs off the spoon into the 'wall' of the glass and then gently over the first layer. Because the liquid is added gently, it means that there is no mixture between the two liquids and the layers are easily visible.

(vii) Bar spoon for stirring drinks

- Holding the spoon in your fingers, push and pull the spoon backward and forward from six o'clock to twelve o'clock.
- When you are comfortable with this, change the motion to pushing and pulling from twelve o'clock to three o'clock, to six o'clock to nine o'clock and then all the way around again.
- Once you have got this motion, you will be able to stir smoothly around the glass.

Bar spoon used for layering and stirring drinks

(viii) Blender

- Clean all the fruits and vegetables.
- Remove the blender jug from the base and add the ingredients.
- Place the lid on top of the blender jug and cover the lid with a service cloth.
- Start the blender by giving it a quick 'pulse'. A few short pulses get the blades spinning and give a quick initial blend.
- Turn the blender onto its lowest setting and increase the speed every five to ten seconds until maximum speed, for as long as required.
- Then turn the blender off and remove the lid to check that it is all blended well.
- Turn off the power source and unplug the blender from the wall.
- Remove the blending jug from its base and scoop the contents into your glasses over the bar mat. Avoid making contact with the blades when scooping.

Safety while using blender

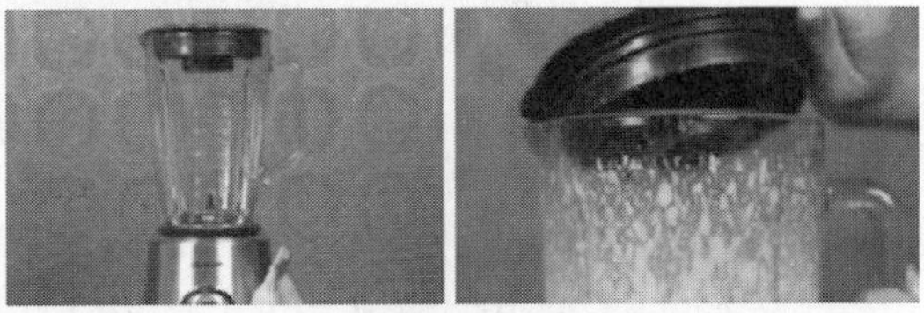

Blending

- Always fill and empty the jug when it is off the base.
- When blending ice ensure that it is only evenly 'crushed ice' as it is less damaging to the blades.
- Avoid using metal objects to stir in the blender as this will also make the blades blunt.

(ix) Grater: Surface of grater has lots of tiny little holes which have sharpened rims. The rims cut off tiny little pieces which are roughly the size of the hole.

Using grater

- Set up your station with a clean chopping board and the washed fruit or vegetables that you intend to use.
- Hold the object that you will be grating or zesting in your strong hand and move your fingers away from the blade to avoid cutting yourself. Use your other hand to stabilise the grater.
- Place the piece of fruit or vegetable firmly against the blade of the grater and move it up and down with consistent movements.
- Be careful while washing it and use hot water for washing the grater.

(x) **Peeler:** A peeler is used to remove the outer skins from fruits and vegetables.

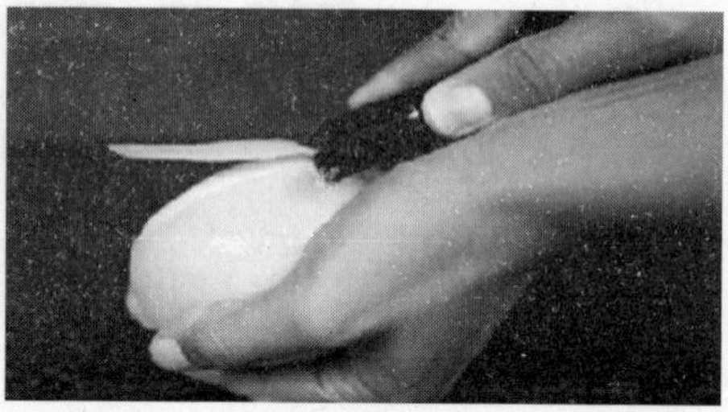

Using peeler

- Grip the item that you will be peeling in your weaker hand, over your clean chopping board or bowl. Always curl your fingers away to keep them safe.
- Place the blade of the peeler firmly into the object you are holding with your strong hand.
- Start at the top of the object, without digging too deeply into it, pull downwards at a consistent speed. Repeat this motion until you have peeled the entire object.

Note: Avoid peeling vegetables over a dustbin as there is always the risk of fruits and vegetables falling into the dustbin.

(xi) **Rinder:** The rinder creates long, thin, 'strings' of skin from either a fruit or a vegetable.

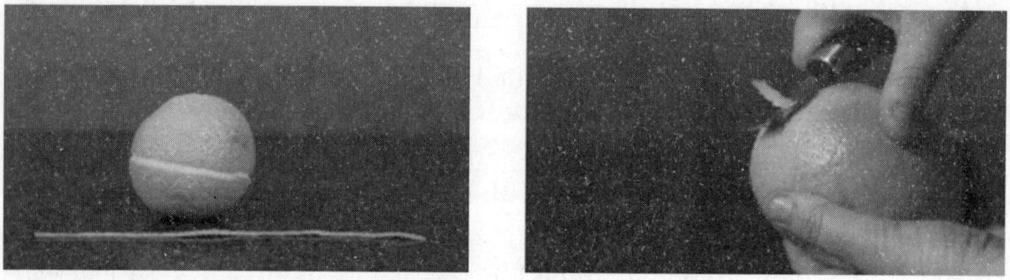

Using rinder

- Always hold the rinder in your stronger hand.
- Insert the sharp end of the rinder into the skin of the fruit at the top.
- Slowly and carefully, turn the fruit in a circular motion, making sure that the blade stays 'under' the skin of the fruit. Make sure that you are making a neat spiral around the fruit.
- Break off the rind when you are finished by twisting the blade upwards and away from the fruit.

Note: This process requires some time and patience, especially when you are dealing with hard or dry skins.

(xii) **Muddler:** A long, blunt tool, made up of a handle and a head. There are various different styles of muddlers, all used for the same purpose.

- Place what you will be muddling into your mixing tin or glass.
- Push the muddling stick down onto the ingredients in the glass until you cannot push any more.
- Twist the muddling stick to help 'grind' the ingredients under it.

- Lift the handle and repeat the process until you have muddled the ingredients enough.
- Never over-muddle ingredients to avoid the release of bitter flavours.
- Always muddle in a hardened glass or cocktail tin.
- Muddle over a chopping board or bar mat.
- Always check that your muddler is longer than the tin or glass that you will be muddling in.

Muddling

(xiii) Knives: Used to make the preparation of garnishes quick and effortless.

- Always curl your fingers inwards and tuck your thumb away underneath your hand to remove any chance of cutting yourself.
- Maintain hygiene and cleanliness by cleaning knives after each use. Wash them by hand in hot, soapy water to prevent them from getting damaged by a dishwashing machine.
- Ensure that you set a place in your bar to store your knives.
- Always use a chopping board when working with knives. Never cut anything with a knife on a bar surface, plate or tray. Chopping boards are specially designed to handle knife-work.

Always remember to set the electrical equipment safely as blenders and juicers have very sharp blades which are extremely dangerous when rotating. Electricity is dangerous if not treated carefully and correctly. Using knives, liquids and glassware can be very dangerous around live wires.

3.5 CONSUMABLES

The bar will stock things which will accompany the drinks that are sent out. These are often not returned as they are not reusable and primarily serve the purpose of decorating or adding flavour to a drink. Examples of consumables are:

- Toothpicks : Used for garnishing and snacks
- Salt and pepper : Used for garnishing and snacks
- Swizzle Sticks : Used for garnishing and stirring
- Dry garnishes and spices : Used for garnishing
- Straws : Used for drinking
- Paper serviette/Tissue paper : Used for guests to wipe clean hands.

REVISION QUESTIONS

1. Differentiate between stem glassware and flat bottom glassware.
2. Name any five stem glassware and any five flat bottom glassware used in bar.

3. Write a note on handling and storage of glassware.
4. List any ten equipment used in a bar.
5. List any five consumables used in a bar.

RESEARCH ACTIVITIES

- Visit any bar or pub nearby your place and list down the various equipment and glassware available along with their purpose.
- Visit any fine dining restaurant or a five-star hotel in a group and find out the brand of glassware they are using.

4

Bar Condiments

4.1 INTRODUCTION

After reading this chapter, you will be able to understand:

- Purpose of condiments
- Types of bar condiments

Condiments are food substances used to heighten the natural flavour of the food, to stimulate the appetite, to aid digestion, or to preserve certain products. The word condiment is derived from the Latin word "Condire", which means to preserve. Many condiments are nowadays available in single-serving packets (sachets), like mustard or ketchup, particularly when supplied with take-away or fast food meals. Condiments are used for making cocktails. Most of the condiments are of vegetable origins, i.e., they are prepared from herbs, spices, aromatic vegetables and others. Condiments vary from one country to another. The types of condiments are listed below in Table 4.1.

Table 4.1: Types of bar condiments

S. No.	Name	Description
1.	HP sauce	• Steak sauce from UK. • Main ingredients in this sauce are malt vinegar, tomato extract, malt vinegar, sugar, raisins, salt, spices, tamarind and onion extract. • This sauce is an excellent accompaniment to all red meats, especially steaks.
2.	Tabasco sauce	• This famous sauce is made with red pepper, salt and vinegar, made in Avery Islands, USA. • This sauce is used to spice up juices, sauces, soups and cocktails. • Comes in different flavours such as green jalapeno peppers, Habanero, Garlic Pepper, Sweet and spicy and many others. • Used in making Bloody Mary.
3.	Powdered sugar and granulated sugar	• Used in bar for making sugar syrup and for making drinks.
4.	Salt	• For making cocktails and to rim a glass.

5.	Ground black pepper	• Used in cocktails.
6.	Cinnamon sticks and nutmeg	• For making cocktails.
7.	Whipped cream	• For making Irish coffee and other drinks.
8.	French mustard	• French mustard is sold in the form of a paste. • The main production is Dijon. • It is prepared with white wine or vinegar. • It is used as a condiment with meat and charcuterie.
9.	English mustard	• English mustard is prepared with milk, mustard powder and cream. • Goes in breakfast • Preferred with poached fish, charcuterie and meat products.
10.	Cayenne pepper	• Cayenne pepper is prepared by coarsely grinding dry pepper, which are long thin variety of red pepper grown in South America and France. • Preferred with pizzas and pastas.
11.	Grated parmesan cheese	• A hard cheese from Italy. • It has a granular texture and yellow colour. • It is offered with pastas and many soups.
12.	Mango chutney	• It is an Indian condiment of worldwide repute. • It is made by cooking mangoes with sugar, spices, and vinegar. • It is a standard accompaniment to Indian food.
13.	Pickles	• An Indian condiment consisting of vegetables or fruits (or both), preserved in spiced vinegar or oil. • A standard accompaniment to Indian food.
14.	Tomato ketchup	• A sweet or sour condiment made from tomato puree, vinegar, sugar and spices. • It is served with fried fish, burgers, omelettes and pizzas.
15.	Vinegar	• Vinegar is an acidic liquid that comes from a variety of sources. ♦ Balsamic - a fruity, mild vinegar ♦ Cider – made from apples ♦ Distilled – made from other vinegars, usually malt ♦ Malt – made from barley ♦ Wine – made from wine that is allowed to age and sour • French vinegar is made by French wine and ageing it in an oak cask.
16.	Soya sauce	• A basic condiment with Chinese and Japanese food. • It is called shoyu in Japan and jiangyong in China. • The sauce is made from soy beans, wheat, water and salt. • Soya sauce comes in light and dark varieties and has the same nutritional value as meat extract. • Soya sauce improves with age.
17.	Worcestershire sauce	• This dark sauce imparts a rich, tangy flavour to the dish. • It consists of barley malt vinegar, spirit vinegar, molasses, sugar, salt, anchovies, tamarind extract, onions, garlic, spices and other flavourings. • Used in Bloody Mary cocktail also.
18.	Maple syrup	• This is classical accompaniment to pancakes and waffles. • This thick syrup is obtained from the fruit of the maple tree. • At times corn syrup, sugar and water is added to enhance the sweetness.
19.	White pepper powder	• This is suited for both, the nutritional and digestive qualities.

20.	Orange marmalade	• This is a bitter preserve placed as part of centre table appointments during breakfast. • It is prepared from oranges, sugar, citric acid and pectin is added as the gelling agent. • It takes approximately 35 g of fruit and 60 g of sugar to produce 100 g of marmalade.
21.	Jams/fruit preserves/jellies	• Sweet condiments usually made from fruit that are used on toast and other bread items. • It is placed as part of centre table appointments during breakfast.
22.	Honey	• It is the sweet product made by bees. • Served in small jars for control purpose. • Served in preserve tray during breakfast.
23.	Barbecue sauce	• It is a spicy tomato based sauce used for chicken and other meats before grilling.
24.	Teriyaki	• It is a mixture of soy sauce in sweet rice wine. It is good in many oriental dishes.
25.	Aioli	• Garlic flavoured mayonnaise.
26.	Capers	• Pickled flower buds lend a piquant sour and salty flavour to salads, dressings, sauces, vegetables and a variety of main dishes.
27.	Béarnaise	• Another French sauce, Béarnaise is a rich accompaniment to grilled meat and fish.
28.	Salsa	• Salsa is a fresh Mexican sauce that is made of fresh chopped tomatoes and other vegetables in an acidic base such as lemon juice or vinegar.
29.	Horseradish	• Horseradish is a uniquely flavoured hot herb that is ground into a paste. • It is good with roast beef and many other meats.

Apart from bar condiments, many establishments put a few small snack items on the bar as accompaniments for the customers to consume while they are drinking. These snack items like salted, spicy or flavoured potato chips are intended to make the customer thirsty and thus buy extra drinks. Other items which are placed in the bar as accompaniments are either complimentary along with the drinks or are sold to the customers:

- Cheese cubes
- Salted biscuits
- Roasted almonds
- Cocktail gherkins
- Dry roasted peanuts
- Plain nuts

Did you know?

Proprietary sauces

These are the industry made sauces purchased from the market and cannot be prepared in the kitchen. These sauces are procured locally or imported, have a unique taste and are multipurpose in use. Every proprietary sauce has a history behind it and a secret recipe or ingredient which is known to its inventor or the family of the inventor or the patenting company only and is sold by the patent company only under its label name following the food laws in bottles.

Example of proprietary sauces are : *H.P sauce, Tobasco, Worcestershire or L.P. (Lea and Perrins), Ketchup and many more.*

- Salted peanuts
- Olives - Black, green or stuffed
- Roasted or fry poppadum
- Potato chips or wafers

REVISION QUESTIONS

1. List down any ten bar condiments used in restaurant and bar.
2. What do you understand by the proprietary sauces? Give four examples of proprietary sauces.

RESEARCH ACTIVITY

- Search and find out the various bar condiments served with food in the bar located at any three five-star deluxe hotels.

5

Non-Alcoholic Beverages

5.1 INTRODUCTION

After reading this chapter, you will be able to understand:

- Non-alcoholic beverages
- Classification of non-alcoholic beverages
- Tea and its types
- Preparation of tea
- Coffee and its types of preparation
- Difference between still water and sparkling water.

The word beverage derives from the Latin word "bever" which means rest from work. After work, one tends to feel thirsty due to fluid loss through perspiration and one is inclined to drink water or other potable beverages. Beverages can be said as potable drinks which have thirst quenching, refreshing, stimulating and nourishing qualities. By refreshing one means the replenishment of fluid loss from the body due to perspiration. Stimulation results in increased heart beats and blood pressure. This is due to the intake of tea and coffee. Nourishment is provided by the nutrients in the beverages such as milk-based drinks. A non-alcoholic beverage is a beverage that contains no alcohol. Such drinks are generally drunk for refreshment, or to quench thirst. Beverages can be classified as non-alcoholic beverages and alcoholic beverages. Non-alcoholic beverages as the name indicates do not contain any molecule of alcohol and they have the thirst quenching, refreshing, stimulating and nourishing qualities.

5.2 TYPES OF NON-ALCOHOLIC BEVERAGES

- **Refreshment:** Non-alcoholic beverages such as plain or carbonated water, lime juice, ginger ale and other bottled beverages, fruit juices and iced tea or coffee are refreshing drinks and are used to relieve thirst.
- **Nourishment:** Pasteurized milk, butter milk, chocolate and cocoa drinks, eggnog made with rum, fruit juices, glucose water, lemonade provide nutrients and help in nourishing the body.
- **Stimulant:** Tea, coffee, cocoa and chocolate beverages help in stimulating the system.

- **Soothing Agent:** Warm milk and hot tea have a soothing effect and are used for this purpose.
- **Appetizers:** Fruit juice and alcoholic drinks in limited quantities increase an individual's appetite and thereby food consumption.

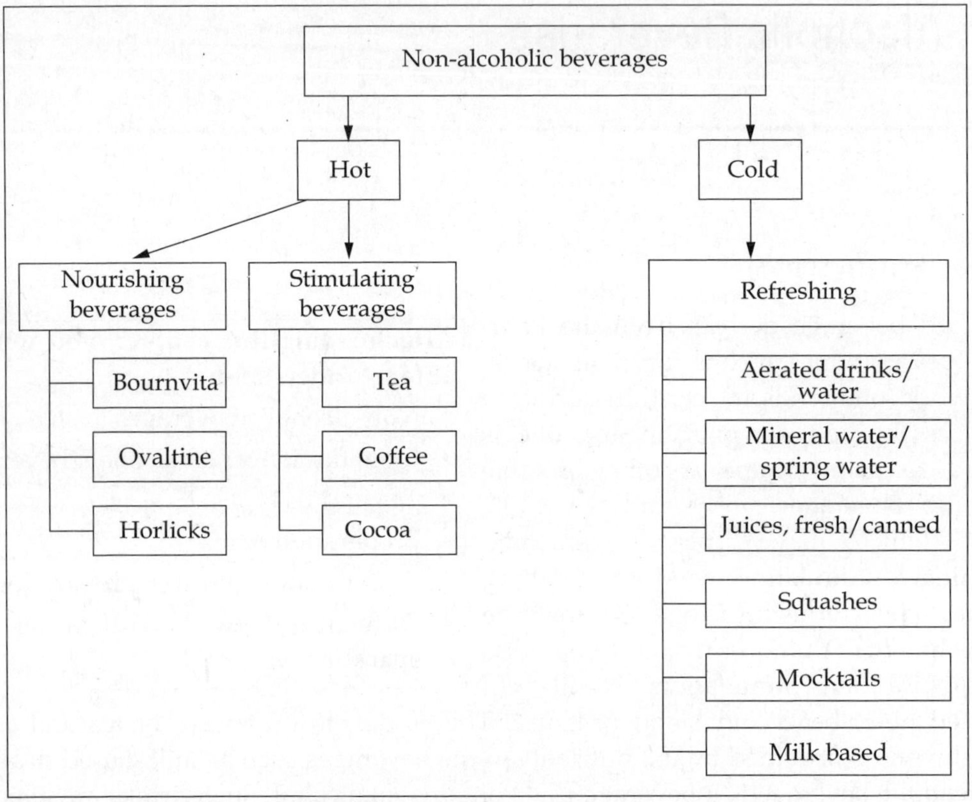

5.3 TEA

> **Note:** Caffeine provides the stimulating effect, tannin the colour, body and taste to the extract and the essential oils contribute the characteristic aroma. It is predominantly grown in India, Ceylon, China and Japan. Chinese tea contains less tannin than the other varieties.

Tea is the most consumed beverage in the world. It is a stimulating non-alcoholic drink. All tea comes from the dried leaves of shrub "*Camellia sinensis*", an evergreen shrub that may grow up to 60 feet in the wild. When cultivated for harvest, the tea bushes are kept to a height of about three feet. There are over 3000 varieties of tea each with their own specific characteristics. Tea leaves have a characteristic oval shape and serrated edge. Younger the leaves, better the quality of the tea. There are main two varieties of tea plants: Indian and Chinese, with numerous local varieties and hybrids. Climate, soil, altitude affect the growth and quality of the plants, and therefore the fragrance, colour and taste of the tea. It contains approximately only half the caffeine of coffee and also aids in muscle relaxation and stimulates the nervous system. It is grown in more than 25 countries with more than 3000 varieties available today. India is the largest producer of tea, followed by Sri Lanka and China. The main flavour components of tea are caffeine, tannin yielding compounds and small amounts of essential oils. The kind of tea obtained is determined by the manufacturing process and treatment.

The top two leaves of the plant are picked by hand. The smaller and younger the leaves, the better the tea. Tea production follows two simple methods. The orthodox hand method and the mechanised CTC method. The CTC method is generally used for mass production as it produces a stronger, darker and more flavoured tea. CTC is harvested by machine. CTC is an acronym for crush, tear and curl. CTC methods cut off a foot or more of the tea plant. The stems are processed along with leaf by the CTC method. Maceration of the leaves takes place by pressing through counter rotating rollers. Tea is mostly named after the region in which they are cultivated. Example: Assam tea is named after the Assam region.

The climate, soil conditions where the tea is grown, and how the tea is processed, determines the flavour characteristics of the tea. Tea is harvested after each flush, the sprouting of the top two leaves and bud. Tea pickers pick two leaves and a bud. The top two leaves and bud are hand plucked and then processed.

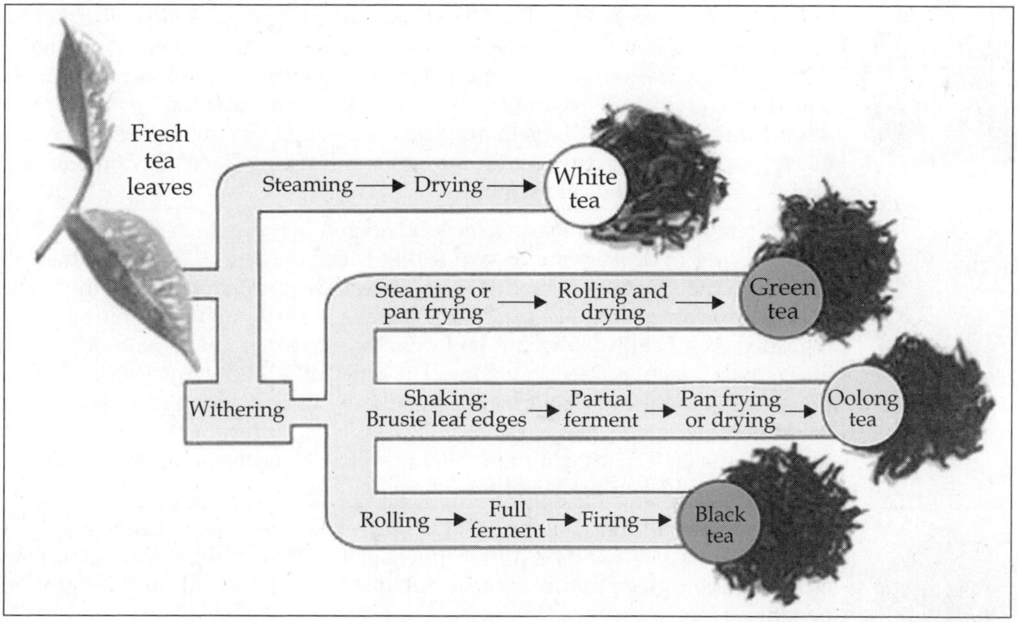

Process of obtaining tea

5.3.1 Tea Manufacturing Process

- **Plucking:** Two leaves and a bud is plucked from every shoot. A bush may be plucked 25-30 times in a year.
- **Drying:** It is removal of excess moisture, using cool air. Leaves are dried out on racks. There is up to 50% loss of moisture, which leads to withering.
- **Rolling:** The withered leaves are machine rolled to break cellular structure and release fermenting enzymes giving the leaves a red hue. Prior to the use of machines in 1887, the leaves were hand rolled in Assam.
- **Fermentation:** This is done at about 82°F for about 3-4 hours. This is essentially done for black tea. It gives the tea strength, taste and coppery hue.
- **Firing:** This is done to check fermentation by passing hot air through leaves at a carefully regulated temperature.
- **Sorting:** The leaves are sorted out as (a) broken or small leaves, and as (b) grades of the leaf.
- **Grading:** The leaves are graded for green tea as per quality and for black tea by size of leaf and leaf particle.
- **Polishing and dying:** This process is practiced only in China. The tea leaves are polished using chalk and dyed using indigo.

5.3.2 Types of Tea

Table 5.1: Four main varieties of tea

	**Black tea:** The leaves are withered, then rolled till they become soft and massy. This is done to break up the fibre and cells of the leaf to liberate the constituents so that their extraction is easy. The leaves are then fermented. During the process of fermentation, some of the acid in the leaves oxidizes and is converted into less soluble forms while more essential oils develop. After fermentation is complete, the leaves are fired in a drying machine. Some of the popular black teas include Assam tea, Darjeeling tea, Ceylon tea, English Breakfast and many more.
	**Green tea:** Green tea is made from unoxidized leaves which are simply heated after picking to destroy the enzymes that cause oxidation. They are then rolled to release their flavour. Green teas are sweet and contain many of the vitamins and antioxidant properties of the fresh green tea leaf, making them highly regarded as a healthy, fragrant and delicious drink. It has a more delicate taste and is pale green/golden in colour. The chief difference between black tea and green tea is the former is fermented while the latter is not. Since the purpose of fermentation is to make tannin less soluble, an infusion of green tea has more tannin in it, astringent and slightly bitter to taste. Green tea is an antioxidant and good for health.
	**Oolong tea (wulong):** Oolong, means Black Dragon, is from China and Taiwan (often called Formosa, its old Portuguese name). It is a semi-fermented tea, a cross between green and black teas, which is widely prized for its digestive benefits.

	**White tea:** White tea is the world's rarest tea as it can only be picked for a few weeks in any one year. Authentic white tea is only grown in the Fujian province in China where the exact method of processing is kept secret. This type of tea is least processed as it is not oxidized or rolled, but simply withered and dried by steaming. The best tea generally produces a pale-coloured infusion. White tea has seen a recent increase in popularity and has well documented antioxidant and detoxifying benefits.

5.3.2.1 Other Varieties of Tea

- **Ceylon (Sri Lanka) tea** is black tea having an aromatic amber liquor and a rich, full astringent flavour. This tea is wonderful with a little cold milk and goes well with a sweet breakfast or afternoon pastry.
- **English breakfast tea** is a blend of fine black teas from India and Sri Lanka. A similar tea was made by a Scottish tea company and marketed as breakfast tea. It became popular in England due to the craze Queen Victoria created for Scottish things. The tea shops in London started marketing the tea as "English Breakfast Tea".
- **Keemun (China)** has a subtle orchid aroma and bright red colour. The flavour is mild with a hint of sweetness, which makes it a good evening tea.
- **Lapsang Souchong (China)** is produced by withering the tea leaves over open fires of pine. It is an assertive dark tea with a smoky fragrance and flavour. It yields a red brown liquor, and is great accompaniment to salty and spicy dishes and with cheese.
- **Assam teas** are black bold teas with a strong malty taste and dark liquor, making them excellent morning teas. Bursting with rich, and round flavour, it is often distinguished had from one garden to another. Assam teas are delicious with a drop of milk. This tea is generally served with milk in the morning.
- **Darjeeling (India) tea** is the rarest and most prestigious black tea. Its excellent quality is the result of climate and elevation. While sometimes difficult to distinguish on garden from another, each harvest period is easily identifiable. Darjeeling teas have a distinctive taste depending on the season. Darjeeling tea is also known as "Champagne of tea" and can be served with milk or without milk along with lemon in the evening.
    - ◊ **First Flush Darjeeling:** Referred to "springtime teas", is harvested from late February to mid-April and yields a light tea with a delicate aroma and flowery taste. This tea is a connoisseur's delight.
    - ◊ **Second Flush Darjeeling:** Referred to as "summer tea", this tea is harvested in May and June before monsoon, and produces a darker, fuller bodied cup.

> **Did you know?**
>
> **Earl Grey** (1764-1845) was the Prime Minister of England under William IV, who is better remembered for the tea named after him. Tea legends say the blend was given to him by a Chinese Mandarin seeking to influence trade relations.

- **Scented tea,** apart from classic teas, there is a large variety of scented teas perfumed with fruits and flowers. Most well known of these is *Earl Grey* that is flavoured with oil of bergamot (*a citrus fruit*). Earl Grey is preferred without milk, and mostly drunk at breakfast time.
- **Matcha tea** is mostly used in the traditional Japanese tea ceremony. For the ceremony, the powdered Match a is measured with a chashku (bamboo spoon) and is placed in a chasen (bamboo whisk) until frothy. The thick frothy tea is consumed straight from the bowl.
- **Tisanes** are fruit flavoured teas and herbal infusions which are often used for medicinal purposes and are gaining popularity with trends towards more healthy eating and drinking. Often these do not contain caffeine as they are natural botanicals which are not related to the actual tea plant.

Herbal Teas	**Fruit Teas**
Chamomile	Cherry
Peppermint	Lemon
Rosemary	Black Currant
Mint	Mango

5.3.3 Grades of Tea Leaves

Leaf grades: This refers to the larger leaves left after the broken grades have been sifted out. In brewing, flavour and colour come out more slowly from leaf grades versus broken grades. Leaf grades are popular in continental Europe and South America.

- **Orange pekoe:** It is simply a size; the term does not indicate flavour or quality. The word "pekoe", which is used in grading black teas, is a corruption of the Chinese word meaning "silver-haired", referring to the silvery down found on especially young tea leaves. "Orange" probably comes from the Dutch royal family.
- **Pekoe:** Shorter leaves than orange pekoe and not as wiry; the liquid generally has more colour.
- **Souchong:** Round leaf, with pale liquid.
- **Broken grades:** Smaller, broken leaves comprise about 80 per cent of the total crop. They make a darker, stronger tea than the leaf grades; only kind used in tea bags.
- **Broken orange pekoe:** Much smaller than the leaf grades; usually contains bud leaf; the mainstay of a blend.
- **Broken pekoe:** Slightly larger than broken orange pekoe, with somewhat less colour; useful as a filler in a blend.
- **Broken pekoe souchong:** A little larger than broken pekoe; also used as a filler.
- **Fannings:** Much smaller than broken pekoe Souchong; main virtues are quick brewing and good colour.

- **Dust:** The smallest grade; useful for a quick-brewing, strong cup of tea; only used in blends of similar-sized leaf, generally for catering purposes.

Brand Names

- **Twining (Kolkata):** Assam, Earl Grey, English Breakfast, Camomile, Darjeeling.
- **Ceylon tea (Watawala Plantations, Sri Lanka):** Low, medium and high grown tea, exotic fruit tea.
- **Tetley:** Standard tea bags used at various hotels.

5.3.4 Preparation of Tea

Tea brewing or preparation is an art that is simple to perform but which also requires some care to do well. While essentially tea is brewed by adding boiling water to the dry leaf, the quantity of leaves, the temperature of the water and timing is of vital concern. The following is a guide for the preparation of tea. The basic rule of thumb to start is 'one teaspoon of loose leaf tea per cup'.

1. Warm your empty tea pot by filling it with hot water. This will prevent the hot water from cooling too quickly when leaves are added.
2. Boil freshly drawn tap water. If the quality of your tap water is poor, try using filtered or bottled spring water. For black tea, use the water when it comes to a boil. Water left boiling too long will deaerate. This will result in a flat tasting tea. For green tea, the water should be heated to a lower temperature (usually approximately 80 degrees Celsius), which may vary from tea to tea.
3. Empty the hot water from your tea pot and add 2.25 g or one rounded teaspoon of tea leaves for each cup of water (or one heaping teaspoon per mug), placing the tea directly into the bottom of the pot or using a basket infuser. Tea ball strainers, while convenient, often yield poorer tasting tea as they are often too small to allow all of the leaves to fully unravel its contents. If you do use a tea ball, be sure to use one that is sufficiently large to pack the tea loosely.
4. Add the freshly boiled water over the leaves in the teapot.
5. Brew tea for the appropriate length of time. Time needed to brew tea varies depending on the leaves being used and the drinker's individual taste. Careful timing is essential for brewing tea. A general rule to follow is the smaller the leaf, the less time required for brewing. Broken grades of tea leaves and most Darjeeling teas usually only need 3-4 minutes to brew. Whole-leaf teas often need 4-5 minutes. All teas, however, will become bitter due to higher tannin extraction if brewed for longer than 5 or 6 minutes. When brewing tea, time with a timer, and not with your eyes. It is a common mistake to brew the tea until it looks a particular colour or shade. The colour of tea is a poor indicator of the tea's taste.

6. If you use a basket infuser or a tea ball, remove these promptly when the brewing time has expired. If you place the tea directly into the pot, pour the tea into the cups through a strainer to catch the leaves. In this instance, if you do not wish to serve your tea immediately, pour your tea through a strainer into another preheated tea pot.
7. Tea, sometimes, is brewed with spices like fresh ginger, dried ginger powder or cardamom to enrich the flavour. Milk and sugar should be added according to individual taste.

Adding of milk first or last does not make any significant difference in the taste of tea - but many people have their choice; some like to add milk first and some afterwards. Sugar must be added last. Tea is also taken hot with sugar and slices of lemon. This is known as **Russian tea.**

5.3.5 Service of Tea

Salvar for tea service

Tea may be consumed with milk or lemon and service would differ as per guest's requirement. Milk if served with tea should be homogenized, i.e., all cream removed and preferably cold. Cold milk brings out the best flavours in tea and lowers the temperature of tea so that it can be drunk. Water used to make tea must be soft and if sugar substitutes are used they should not have any off flavours. Tea may be served from a salver or from a bar tray. The salver is set up with teapot, hot water pot, creamer, tea strainer and drip bowl, sugar basin with sugar sachets and teacup and saucer. Approach from the right and place the teacup in the centre of the cover. Place the sugar basin on the table. Bring salver down to the level of the cup and place the tea strainer on the cup. Pour tea onto the cup. If it is too strong for the guest, add hot water. Ask milk to be served or not and do the needful. The teapot, hot water pot, milk creamer and the tea strainer with drip bowl are left on the table for second helping. *Tea should be served at the temperature of 85°-90° Celcius.*

Lemon tea: Service is the same as for tea service but honey is served instead of milk. A B&B plate with 4 lemon wedges wrapped in a muslin cloth is placed on the table.

Iced tea: Fresh tea infusion is made. Fill a Collins glass with ice and pour over it 15 mL of lime juice. The clear infusion is poured over the ice and served garnished with a sprig of mint. Sugar syrup and lime juice are served separately as well.

Golden Rules for Making Tea

1. Always ensure the water does not have more than 100 ppm of hardness.
2. The temperature of the water is less than boiling point but greater than 80°C.
3. To the pot add 1 level teaspoon per cup or 1-heaped teaspoon per portion.

4. Add hot water and allow the tea to infuse for 3 minutes.
5. Serve with separate pot of hot water and milk.

Storage of Tea

Tea should be kept away from air, moisture and warmth. It should be stored in airtight containers in a cool place, away from strong odours.

5.4 COFFEE

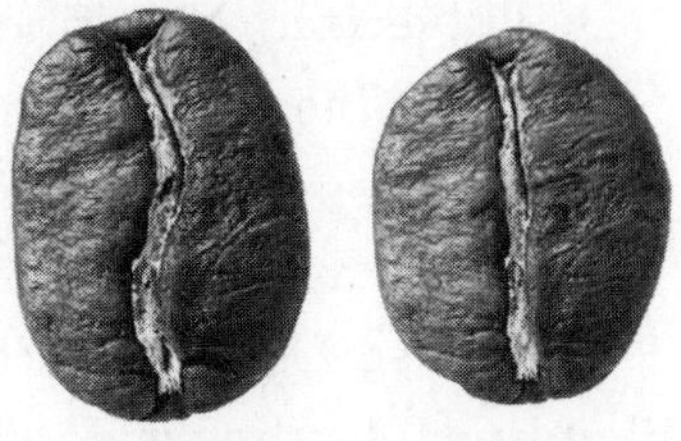

Coffee berries, which contain the coffee bean, are produced by several species of small evergreen bush of the genus *Coffea*. The two most commonly grown species are *Coffea canephora* (also known as *Coffea robusta*) and *Coffea arabica*. These are cultivated in Latin America, Southeast Asia, Africa and certain parts of India. Once ripe, coffee berries are picked, processed to remove the mesocarp, and dried. The seeds are then roasted, undergoing several physical and chemical changes. They are roasted to various degrees, depending on the desired flavour. They are then ground and brewed to produce liquid coffee which is also known as coffee decoction. Coffee can be prepared and presented by a variety of methods to cater the need of local palate. Coffee is always brewed by the user immediately before drinking. In most areas, coffee may be purchased unprocessed, or already roasted, or already roasted and ground. Coffee is often vacuum packed to prevent oxidation and lengthen its shelf-life.

5.4.1 Manufacture of Coffee

Curing: Curing in coffee is done either by wet curing method or hot curing method. Wet curing is the process of soaking the berries in water and washing it well until the parchment and coverings are removed. This is then dried in the sun or in machines before milling. Dry curing is similar to wet curing but there is only one introduction of water after which it is dried. The remaining parchment is removed during milling.

Roasting: This is done at 200–220°C for 5 minutes. To avoid over-cooking, the beans are sprayed with water or cool air. During roasting, the green beans change colour to brown due to caramelisation of the sugars. The oils that ooze out provide the aroma.

Roasting may differ with what the coffee is going to be used for:

- **Light city roast:** Cinnamon colour, light flavours and is very popular in the west.
- **Medium / City roast/American:** Has a flat flavour and is popular in America.
- **Viennese / Full city roast:** Dark brown colour and a hearty flavour.
- **Dark/Spanish/Cuban roast:** Dark brown with a trace of oil on the beans.
- **Continental/French roast:** Burnt amber colour and is very close to Espresso roast.
- **Italian / Espresso roast:** Almost burnt and yields the darkest and the heaviest brew.

Roasting is a specialized job. A heavy roast will lead to burnt coffee and impart bitter taste and coffee roasted for a smaller duration will be weak.

Grinding: The beans are ground to bring out the aroma and flavour from the roasted beans. But grinding also makes the coffee lose its aroma and so it would be best if ground when required. The earliest method of grinding was to use the mortar and pestle and the grinding electric mill. The modern machines can be programmed to grind a specific quantity of beans to ensure a fresh grind at all times.

The types of grinds are:

- **Pulverized:** Very fine grind, used for Turkish coffee.
- **Very fine:** Used for filter coffee.
- **Fine Espresso:** Used in espresso machine and applied for the Espresso roast.
- **Medium:** Used for percolators, vacuum machines, coffee jugs, etc.
- **Coarse:** Used for jug coffee.

Blending: Blending is done to produce uniform taste and flavour, to enhance the taste of coffee and to reduce costs. Blending may be done at the bean phase or after the beans have been ground. Arabica and Robusta blends well as the 'body' of Arabica helps mask the harshness and inferiority of Robusta. Some examples of blends are Mocha Java, Neapolitan and Roma.

> **Did you know?**
>
> **Decaffeinated coffee**
>
> In 1900, in Germany, a large consignment of coffee fell into the sea. To retrieve the coffee, Dr. Ludwig Rosarius tried many methods and discovered that he had deprived the coffee of its caffeine. To remove the caffeine, the beans are immersed in a solvent and agitated. The caffeine gets dissolved in the solvent. The beans are then dried and coffee manufactured. The solvent used is methylene chloride. In the modern Swiss water process, the beans are washed with hot water to remove the oils and caffeine. This is a much longer process than the former one. Some brands of decaffeinated coffee are Nestle Gold, Café Hag and Sanka.

5.4.1.1 *Instant Coffee*

Satori Kato, a Japanese scientist attempted to make instant tea but in vain. Though instant tea failed, the idea was adopted and instant coffee was discovered. The two methods of manufacturing instant coffee are:

- **Spray drying:** The percolated extract of coffee is passed through fine atomizers and the resulting spray is subjected to a blast of heated air, which evaporates the coffee percolation, and coffee powder is obtained. To make it flavourful, oils may be introduced along with the percolation into the atomizer.
- **Freeze drying:** First, the coffee is allowed to sit so the water evaporates naturally, leaving a concentrated coffee solution. This concentrate is then frozen to around –40°C. The remaining water freezes into ice crystals. Sublimation (a natural process similar to evaporation) is used to remove the ice, leaving dry grains of coffee.

5.4.1.2 Coffee Brews

General methods of preparation of coffee are given below. This is followed by specific methods of brewing coffee.

(i) **Brewing:** Coffee can be brewed in several different ways, but these methods fall into two main groups depending on how the water is introduced to the coffee grounds.

- If the method allows the water to pass only once through the grounds, the resulting brew will contain mainly the more soluble components (including caffeine).
- If the water is repeatedly cycled through the beans (as with the common percolator), the brew will also contain more of the relatively less soluble, and bitter compounds found in the bean, to avoid this coarse ground beans of coffee are used.

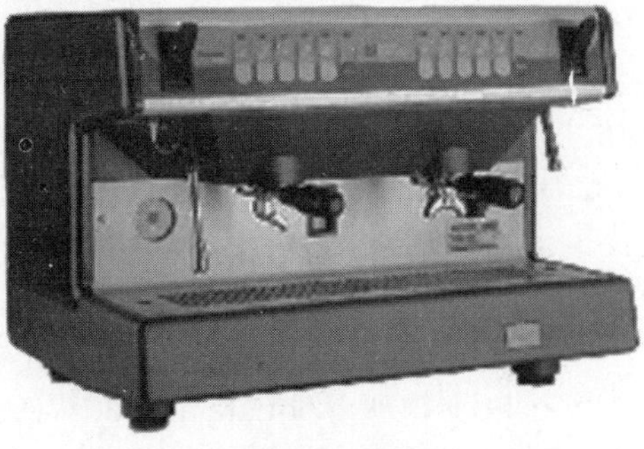

Coffee machine

(ii) **Boiling:** Despite the name, care should be taken not to actually boil coffee for more than an instant because the decoction becomes bitter. The simplest method is to put the ground coffee in a cup, pour in hot water and let it cool while the grounds sink to the bottom. This is a traditional method also for making a cup of coffee (known as "mud coffee"). "Cowboy coffee" is made by simply heating coarse grounds with water in a pot, letting the grounds settle and pouring off the liquid to drink, sometimes filtering it to remove fine grounds. The above methods are sometimes used with hot milk instead of water. Water temperature is crucial to the proper extraction of flavour from the ground coffee. The recommended brewing temperature of coffee is 93°C (199.4°F). If cooler, some of the solubles that make up the flavour will not be extracted. If the water is too hot, some undesirable, bitter components will be extracted, adversely affecting the taste. If coffee is heated to boiling point only very briefly, the taste will be little affected; the longer it is kept at a high temperature the worse the taste becomes. Coffee is brewed by the following ways.

Coffee plunger

Cona coffee machine

- **Jug coffee:** Coffee is allowed to infuse with water in a jug and served with cream.
- **Plunger or cafetiere:** This is a glass jug with a filter attached to the plunger. The coffee is added and allowed to infuse with water for a few minutes and then the plunger is depressed.

- **Cona coffee machine**: It consists of two bowls, one above the other. Water is boiled in the lower bowl and the vapour travels to the upper bowl where coffee is placed over a filter. When the pot is removed from the fire, the vacuum created, pulls the vapour down through the filter.
- **Machinetta**: This consists of two jugs one on top of the other. In between the two jugs is a basket of coffee. The water is allowed to boil in the top jug and then it is upturned to allow the water to infuse. It is also known as the Nepolitan flip.
- **Filter coffee**: Works on the same principle as the machinetta. The proportion of coffee to water used in this case is 1:10.
- **Espresso:** Literally means a 'strong and frothy' coffee. The basic principle used in the espresso machine is steam pressure giving strong concentrated coffee. The blend used is 30% Robusta and 70% Arabica which is fine ground. The grind if right would give coffee with proper trickle and golden froth. Too coarse a grind will give watery coffee. An ideal grind would be removed as firm cakes after the coffee is made. The normal proportion is 7-10 gm of coffee per portion.
- **Percolator**: This consists of a cabinet where coffee is allowed to infuse with hot water. The electric models of the same have a pump, which introduces spurts of hot water into the coffee.
- **Turkish coffee:** This coffee is made in an apparatus called Ibrik, which is the original apparatus that was used in Arabia to brew coffee. The green bean is pulverized with cardamom, cloves and cinnamon. The grind is brewed and allowed to boil three times resulting in a raft. This coffee is very bitter and is served along with the raft and lots of sugar.

5.4.2 Dos and Don'ts for Coffee Making

- Never reuse coffee grinds.
- Never boil coffee. Boiled coffee is spoilt coffee.
- The water temperature should be always at least 2°C less than boiling temperature.
- The optimum serving temperature is 85°C.

5.4.3 Reasons for Bad Coffee

(i) Weak coffee

- May be due to the water not having reached boiling point
- The coffee used being insufficient
- The infusion time being short
- The coffee used being stale
- Usage of incorrect grind

(ii) Flat coffee: The reasons for weak coffee are also a part.

- The coffee is stored in the urn for too long
- The equipment is dirty
- Water used is not fresh
- Reheated coffee

(iii) Bitter coffee

May occur due to excess of coffee used:

- Too long an infusion time
- Incorrect roasting of coffee beans
- Presence of sediments in the serving compartment
- The temperature of infusion being too high
- Coffee left in the urn for too long

5.4.4 Storage of Coffee

- Coffee should be stored in airtight containers to avoid evaporation of oils.
- The material used to contain coffee should be inert in nature.
- It should be stored away from moisture, and strong smells.
- Stored in a well ventilated room.
- It is best if coffee is stored in the form of beans and ground when necessary.
- Coffee powder should not be stored for more than one week's supply.

5.4.5 Types of Coffee Preparation

- **Espresso or Caffè Espresso:** Espresso is a concentrated coffee beverage brewed by forcing very hot, but not boiling water under high pressure through coffee that has been ground to a consistency between extremely fine and powder. The defining characteristics of espresso include a thicker consistency than drip coffee, a higher amount of dissolved solids than drip coffee per relative volume, and a serving size that is usually measured in shots, which are between 25 and 30 mL. Properly brewed espresso has three major parts: the *heart, body, and the most distinguishing factor, the presence of crema,* reddish-brown foam that floats on the surface of the espresso. It is served in demitasse cup with demitasse spoon along with Demerara sugar.

Other types of Espresso

- **Ristretto:** It is a double strength espresso.
- **Doppio:** A double espresso.
- **Lungo:** Half strength of Espresso, served in a teacup.
- **Chocolaccino:** Cappuccino without cinnamon but topped with abundant chocolate shavings.

- **Espresso Macchiato:** A shot of espresso stained with a dollop of frothed milk. Also called 'Cortado' in Spain and Portugal, means quick and smooth sip of heaven. Macchiato is also known as Piccolo Latte.
- **Instant Coffee:** A thick coffee decoction is prepared first and then it is either spray-dried to a fine powder or freeze-dried to granules. When added to hot water, it dissolves completely leaving no residue.

Espresso in demitasse cup with demitasse spoon

- **Caffè Americano/Long black:** Single or double-shot of espresso combined with hot water resulting in rich and nutty flavour of espresso but with a lot less intensity.
- **Latte:** Single or double-shot of espresso combined with steamed milk and a little foam. A latte is usually a little milder than its cousin cappuccino. Serve in latte cup.
- **Flat white:** A flat white is a coffee primarily found in Australia and New Zealand. It is made the same way as a cappuccino except it does not have any foam or chocolate on top. It is made with 1 shot of espresso into a cup and steamed milk is added into the cup but with no micro-foam.

> **Did you know?**
>
> **Affogato**
>
> Affogatos aren't a coffee at all really, as they're a shot of espresso poured over a desert (usually ice cream).

- **Café viennois:** Brewed coffee with a little whipped cream.
- **Mochaccino:** Single or double-shot of espresso, part hot chocolate and part frothed milk.
- **Cappuccino:** Single or double-shot of espresso, part steamed milk, part frothed milk and cinnamon or cocoa to top it off – slightly stronger than a latte.

Cafe Amaretto

Irish coffee

- **Café au lait:** Half brewed coffee and half warm milk. Typically served in a bowl, à la Française.

- **Espresso Romano:** A shot of espresso with a little curl of lemon peel in Rome.
- **Iced coffee:** Fresh brewed coffee, cooled and served over ice.

5.4.5.1 Liqueur Coffee

Liqueur coffees are prepared by using alcoholic beverages. These coffees are made by using a shot of liqueur or liquor and coffee along with sugar and cream.

Table 5.2: Types of liqueur coffee

Name of Coffee	Alcoholic Beverages Used
Highland Coffee	Scotch Whisky
Irish Coffee	Irish Whisky
Brandy Coffee	Brandy
Cafe Mendoza	Brandy and Kahlua
Keoke Coffee	Brandy and Kahlua
English Coffee	Gin
French Coffee	Grand Marnier
Russian Coffee	Vodka
Jamaican Coffee	Tia Maria and Rum
Baileys/Sultan Special	Baileys Irish Cream
Calypso Coffee	Tia Maria or Kahlúa and Rum
Seville Coffee	Cointreau
Corfu Coffee	Koum Quat Liquor
Cafè Corretto (From Italy)	Grappa, Brandy or Sambuca
Shin Shin Coffee	Rum
Monk's Coffee	Bénédictine

Rules to Observe While Making Coffee

- Use freshly roasted and ground coffee.
- Buy the correct grind for the right type of machine.
- Clean the equipment.
- Use a set measure.
- Add boiling water to the coffee.
- Infusion time is according to the type of coffee being used and the method of making.
- Control the temperature. Do not boil it.
- Strain and serve.
- Add/milk/cream separately.
- Serving temperature : Coffee 72°C, Milk 67°C.

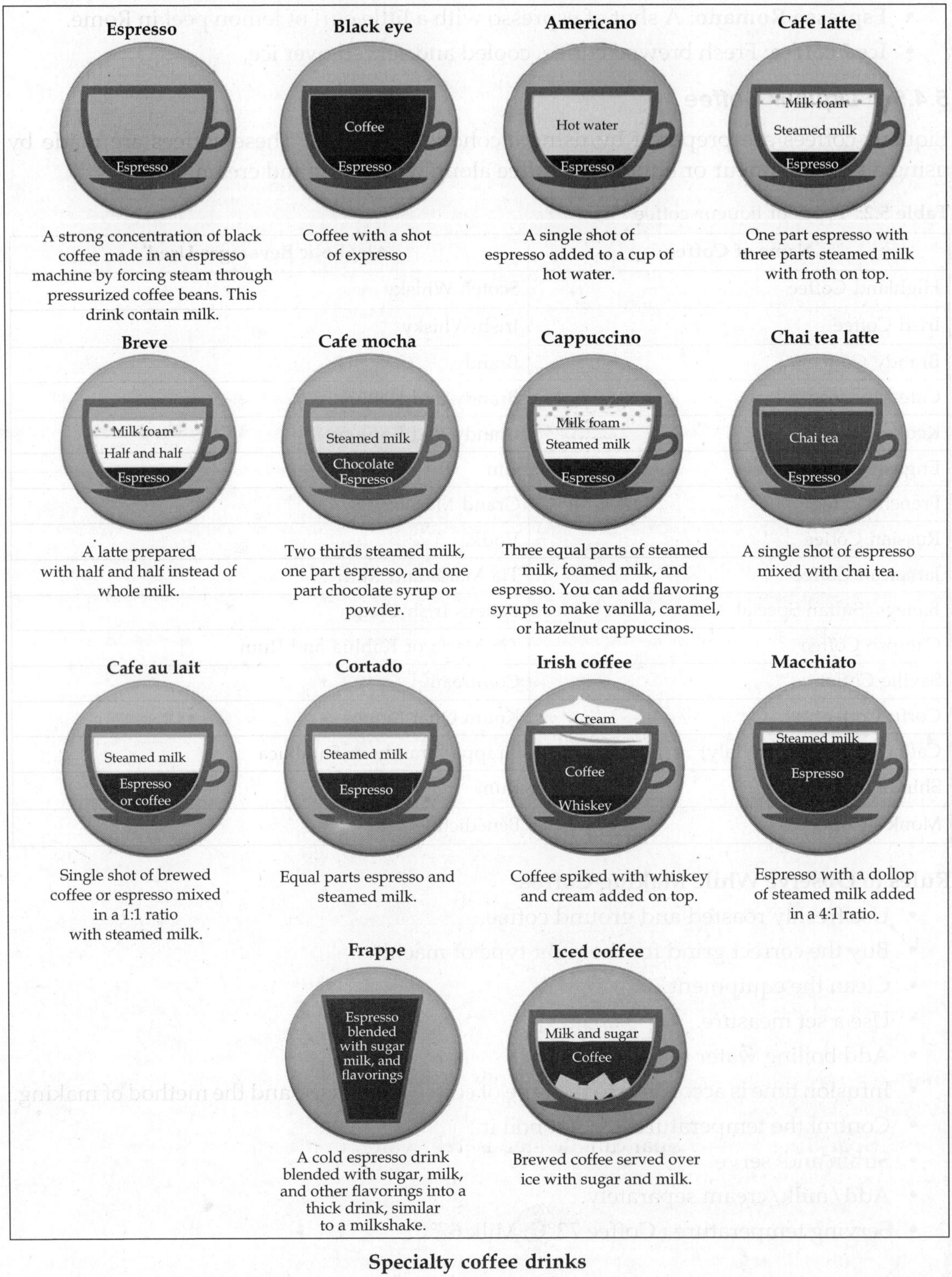

Specialty coffee drinks

5.5 COCOA

Cocoa, besides being a stimulant, is also a food. It is prepared from the seeds (beans) of a tree called *Theobromo cacao*, grown in South and Central America, The West and East Indies and along the Gold Coast and adjacent areas in Africa. Common commercial varieties are criolo (fine quality) and trinitario (medium quality). The pods are gathered in heaps and cut open with sharp rounded knives. The cocoa beans which are covered with a moist, glistening sweet white pulp (mucilage) are scooped out. Oxidation begins almost at once causing the beans to become brown. Therefore, as soon as possible, they must be placed on fermenting heaps and are spread in the sun to remove the moisture so that spoilage does not set in. However, fermentation is necessary to get the finest possible flavour. This is accompanied by a rise in temperature and the transformation of natural sugars to acetic and other acids. After several days, this operation is complete and the beans are allowed to dry. They are then ready to be packed and shipped. Cocoa contains bromine and caffeine as well as starch fat, nitrogenous compounds and salts. So, apart from being a stimulating drink, it is also a food. Cocoa can be prepared in milk only, or in milk and water, mixed to suit the taste of the individual. The powder is mixed with sugar to avoid lumping. A little cold milk is added and a thick even paste is made. The preparation is then allowed to boil for a few minutes which improves the flavour.

5.6 CARBONATED BEVERAGES

Carbonated beverages are also known as soft drinks or mixers. They are popular items of bar stock as they are either sold on their own or as mixers with spirits, e.g.,

- **Soda water:** Colourless and tasteless
- **Tonic water:** Colourless and quinine flavoured
- **Dry ginger:** Golden straw coloured with a ginger flavour
- **Aerated drinks:** Coca Cola, Pepsi, Thumps Up, Limca
- **Lemonade:** Lemon flavoured, sweet aerated water.

> **Did you know?**
> Sparkling waters are often consumed on their own and can be served either plain or with a twist of lemon or lime as garnish. They may also be used as the base for various cocktails and are sometimes recommended as a home remedy for an upset stomach.

5.7 BOTTLED WATER

It is of two types: **Mineral water** (which has a mineral content, which is strictly controlled) and **spring water** (which has fewer regulations apart from those concerning hygiene). Waters can be classified as:

- **Sparkling water:** Sparkling water is the water that contains carbon dioxide or hydrogen sulphide gas, whether naturally occurring or introduced on purpose to create an effervescent drink. It goes by many names like fizzy water, seltzer and sometimes soda water.

- **Still water:** Still water is plain water. This can be tap water, spring water or plain bottled water.

Table 5.3: Types of bottled water

Name	Type	Country
Appolinaris	Naturally sparkling	Germany
Contrex	Still	France
Perrier	Naturally sparkling (or in fruit flavours)	France
Royal Farris	Naturally sparkling	Norway
San Pellegrino	Carbonated	Italy
Spa	Still, naturally sparkling (or in fruit flavours)	Belgium
Spa Monopole	Still or sparkling	Belgium
Vichy Celestine	Naturally sparkling	France
Vittel	Naturally sparkling	France
Volvic	Still	France
Ashboure	Still or sparkling	England
Evian	Still	France
Highland Spring	Still or carbonated	Scotland

Examples of Mineral Water		Examples of Spring Water	
Vittel	France	Ashbourne	England
Contrex	France	Buxton	England
Perrier	France	Badoit	France
Spa	Belgium	Evian	France
San Pellegrino	Italy	High Land Spring	Scotland

5.8 SQUASHES

A squash is a sweetened fruit pulp. Squashes may be served on their own, mixed with spirits or cocktails, or used as the base for such drinks as fruit cups. They are indispensible in the bar and an adequate stock should always be held. Examples,

- Orange
- Lemon
- Grapefruit
- Lime juice

5.9 SYRUPS

The main use of these concentrated, sweet, fruit flavourings is used as a base for cocktails, fruit cups or mixed with soda water as a long drink.

Items	Flavour
Grenadine	Pomegranate
Cassis	Blackcurrant
Citronelle	Lemon
Orgeat	Almond
Cerise	Cherry
Fromboise	Raspberry
Gomme	White sugar syrup

5.10 JUICES

Fresh fruit juices are prepared just before the order and a little extra is prepared for contingencies. Juices should not be stored for more than an hour. They have a low shelf-life due to absence of preservatives. Fresh juices are generally served in hi ball glasses. Fruit juices are also available in tetra packs or cans. The brand names are:

- Morton (Indian)
- Tropicana (Indian)
- Ocean Spray (USA)

5.11 HOT NON-ALCOHOLIC BEVERAGES

Item	Description
Hot chocolate	Drinking chocolate mixed with milk. May also be served with whipped cream.
Bournvita	A milk drink flavoured with proprietary brand Bournvita, characterized by a caramelized chocolate flavour.
Horlicks	A nutritional health drink mixed with either milk or water. Available in different flavours like chocolate, cardamom, etc.

REVISION QUESTIONS

1. Draw a classification chart of non-alcoholic beverages.
2. Write down the golden rules of making tea.
3. What is the serving temperature of tea?
4. List down various coffee preparations.
5. Differentiate between mineral water and spring water along with examples.

RESEARCH ACTIVITIES

- Visit a nearby departmental store and collect various types of tea like Green tea, Earl Grey, Darjeeling tea and Assam tea. Prepare, drink and differentiate their taste and aroma.
- Visit a nearby cafe and try cappuccino, cafe latte and espresso and differentiate their taste.

6

Alcoholic Beverages

6.1 INTRODUCTION

After reading this chapter, you will be able to understand:

- Meaning of alcoholic beverage
- Classification of alcoholic beverage
- Meaning of distillation
- Pot still and Patent still
- Scales for measuring alcoholic strength
- Proof and its uses

Beverage means any potable liquid. It is a term derived from the Latin word *bever* that means *to rest*. Beverages can be alcoholic and non-alcoholic. Non-alcoholic beverages can be classified as refreshing (juices, soft drinks), stimulating (tea, coffee) and nourishing (milk base drinks, horlicks). Whereas alcoholic beverages are those beverages which contain alcohol. The word alcohol derives from the Arabic word *al-kohl*. Kohl is a black very fine staining powder which was used for cosmetic purpose by the Arab ladies for staining their eyelids. Afterwards the name was applied to highly refined chemical powders and essences and then to spirits produced by distillation. Alcohol in a better way can be regarded as a colourless, flammable, volatile and intoxicating liquid containing sugar, the strength of which can be further increased by distillation process. Beverages that contain 0.5% of alcohol by volume to 75% of alcohol by volume are considered to be alcoholic beverages. The beverages with higher than 75% of alcohol by volume are known as "medicines", such as anaesthesia. The only consumable alcohol is *ethyl alcohol/ethanol,* rest all other alcohols like *methyl alcohol/ methanol* are poisonous. Alcoholic beverages can be made by fermentation, distillation and brewed and fermented methods. Fermentation is the process whereby unique cellular organisms called yeast break down the simple sugars in a substance, converting them into ethyl alcohol and carbon dioxide.

Did you know?

ABV: Alcohol by volume; a measure of how much alcohol is in an alcoholic beverage

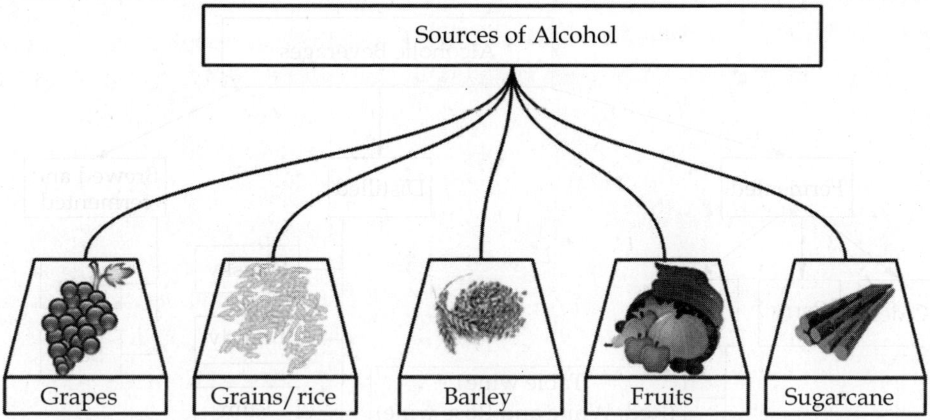

6.2 CLASSIFICATION OF ALCOHOLIC BEVERAGES

All alcoholic beverages have been classified into three categories as below:

(a) **Fermented beverages:** All alcoholic beverages begin with the fermentation of a liquid food containing sugar. Fermentation is the action of yeast upon sugar in solution, which breaks down the sugar into carbon dioxide and alcohol. The carbon dioxide escapes into the air, and the alcohol, remains behind, which thus becomes a fermented beverage. Cider, perry and all types of wines like table wine, sparkling wines, fortified wines, aromatized wines come under the category of fermented beverages. Wines can be made from fermented grape juice and fruits.

(b) **Distillation/ distilled spirits:** Spirit is a potable alcoholic beverage obtained from the distillation of an alcohol containing liquid. The process of separation is called distillation. The liquid is heated in an enclosed container called a still. Brandy, whisky, rum, gin, vodka, tequila are examples of distilled spirits.

(c) **Brewed and fermented:** Certain fermented alcoholic beverages like beer, sake, etc., are brewed before they are fermented, i.e., the mixture of grist (mashed cereals) and hot water is brewed to extract flavour, taste and aroma before fermentaction.

6.3 DISTILLATION

Distillation comes from the Latin word 'distillare' which means to 'drip down' or 'trickle'. It was first discovered in ancient times, being used for things such as cosmetics, perfumes, essential oils and potable seawater. Distillation is actually a simple process wherein the more volatile elements, such as alcohol are separated from the less volatile elements, such as water, by applying heat to alcohol containing liquid (which is called the wash) because alcohol evaporates at 78.37°C and water at 100°C then capturing the resultant alcohol vapours, cooling them back into liquid and thus separating them from water.

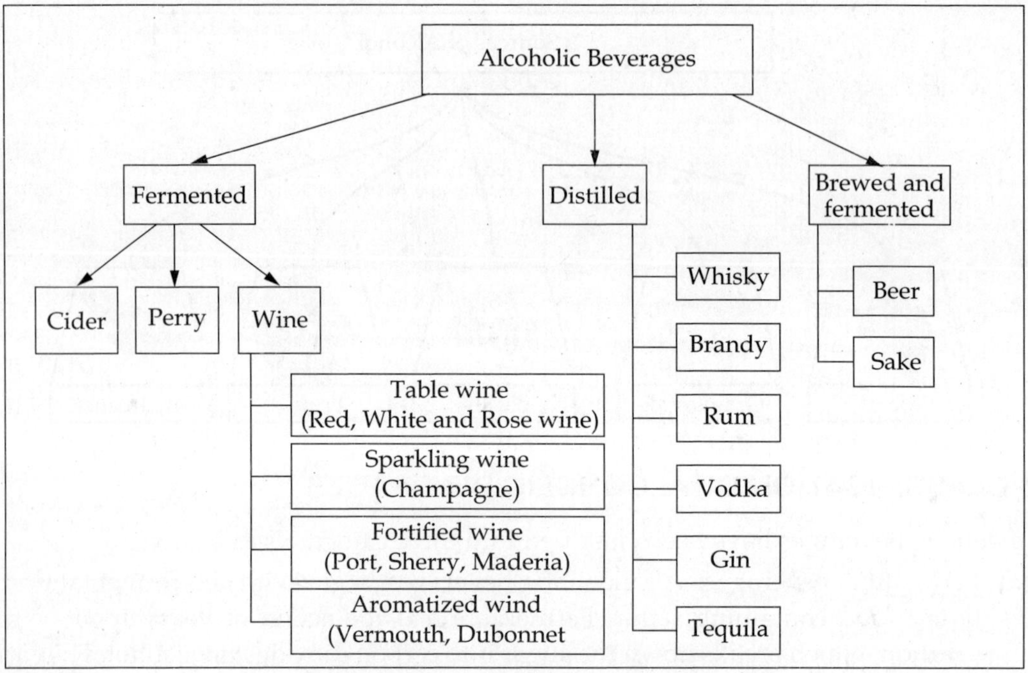

Classification of alcoholic beverages

Distillation may also be known as a process whereby two liquids are separated based on differences in their volatilities. It is a process where liquid is boiled to such an extent that it leaves vapour behind and then condenses back to liquid form. The liquid obtained is colourless. Equipment used to distill the spirit is called *Still* or *Alembic*, it has three main parts:

1. Original container
2. Condenser
3. Receiver

6.3.1 Types of Distillation

I. Pot Still

1. A pot still is a type of still used in distilling spirits such as whisky or brandy. Heat is applied directly to the pot in which the wash (in the case of whisky) or wine (in the case of brandy) is contained.
2. This is the oldest and simplest form of still, it is made of copper, as that is the only metal that does not interfere with the taste of the spirits. Distillation in a pot still produces spirits with strong flavours, such as Cognac and malt whiskies.

3. The pot consists of a copper kettle with a neck, because of its shape called a 'swan's neck', which is connected to a condenser surrounded by cold water.
4. The fermented liquid: alcoholic wash, is placed in the kettle and heated, and as the liquid boils, the vapour rises through the still head, over the neck, and around the coil, where the vapour is cooled, and condensed back into liquid form.
5. Using this method, most spirits have to be distilled twice to produce sufficient alcohol strength.
6. Distillation by a pot still often required two distillations in separate stills. This is called batch distillation, as opposed to continuous distillation.

The first distillation produces a product with a strength of about 25-35% alcohol by volume, which is then distilled a second time to produce the colourless spirit, collected at about 70% alcohol by volume. The liquid that comes out of the still, known as the distillate, is divided into three parts:

- **Heads or foreshots:** They are made up of volatile compounds that are toxic and unpleasant to taste. They are not discarded, but collected and redistilled in a later batch.

Congeners

These are biologically active chemicals which exert an effect on the body or brain and are often contained in alcoholic beverages, in addition to alcohol. Congeners are produced during the process of fermentation or ageing, when organic chemicals (chemicals from plants) in the beverage break down. These may also be added during the production process to impart special character to the beverage like taste, smell and appearance of the beverage. Darker liquors, brandy, tequila, whisky contains more congeners as compared to white spirits like vodka and white rum. Following are some types of congeners available in the alcoholic beverage:

- **Fusel oil:** It is a congener produced in the process of alcoholic spirit distillation. In high concentrations, it causes an off flavour. In low concentrations, fusel oil adds to the flavours and aromas of alcoholic beverages.
- **Furfural:** This congener inhibits yeast metabolism. It may be added to alcoholic beverages during the fermentation stage.
- **Tannins:** This is found in wine. Tannins contain powerful antioxidants such as polyphenols.
- **Acetaldehyde:** Acetaldehyde is a toxic congener produced by the breakdown of ethanol.

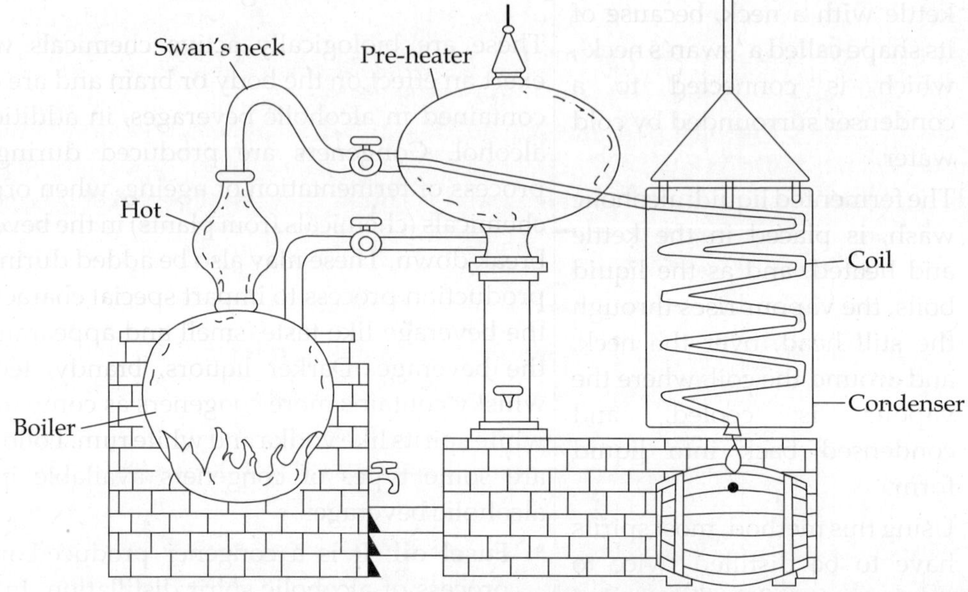

Pot still

Pot still type of distillation

- **Hearts or spirit:** This is the major part of the post distillation division, and produces potable or drinkable spirit. The heart from the second distillation is the fraction that has matured, and at this stage the spirit is water white in colour with an alcohol content around 70%, with the remainder being water.
- **Tails or Feints:** This last part, like the heads is not drinkable, and again is reserved for a later batch for redistillation. The residue left in the still after all usable spirit has been removed is known as 'spent lees' and is runoff to waste. The pot still is energy inefficient, but the resulting spirit will retain some of the character of the original alcohol wash. All spirits distilled in this way must be matured in casks before being ready to drink, and time scales vary with the product.

Disadvantages of pot still

1. Needs cleaning after every boiling.
2. Requires constant attention to maintain the temperature of 78 to 100°C.
3. Spirits may carry impurities.
4. Impurities take time to mature, therefore distillers are bound to mature spirit made pot still for minimum of 2 years.
5. Distillation needs to be carried out twice.

II. Patent Still/Continuous Still/Coffey Still/Column Still

Patent still is a variety of still that consists of two columns. The first, called the rectifier and the second column called the analyzer. Steam is fed into the base of the analyser and hot wash into the top. As the two meet on the surface of the perforated plates, the wash boils and a mixture of alcohol vapours and uncondensed steam rises to the top of the column. The spent wash runs down and is led off from the base. The hot vapours enter the rectifier at the base and as they rise through the chambers, they partially condense on the sections of a long coil through which wash is flowing. The spirit vapour condenses at the top of the rectifier and is run-off through a water-cooled condenser to the spirit safe and on to the spirit receiver. Once the spirit begins to be collected, it runs continuously until the end of distillation. Because of the rectifying element present in this process, the distillate is generally lighter in aroma than most Malt whiskies. It consequently has a milder character and requires less time to mature.

- The patent still is also known as the continuous or coffey still, the latter being the name of an 18th century custom officer Aeneas Coffey, credited with its inventor.
- The patent still is a great deal larger and far more complex than the original pot still, and consists of two main parallel columns known as the analyzer and the rectifier.
- Patent still is, unlike the pot still, a continuous operation. With the alcohol wash being pumped into one side, and the spirit collected from the other.
- The patent still condenses spirit vapours at a higher strength than its smaller counterpart, normally around 94-96% volume. This higher alcohol strength means greater purity, and consequently less flavour and character than those spirits produced in the pot still.

- The patent still is used for grain whisky, some rum, vodka, and the base spirit for gin, but unlike pot still spirits, not all patent still spirits require a period of maturation.

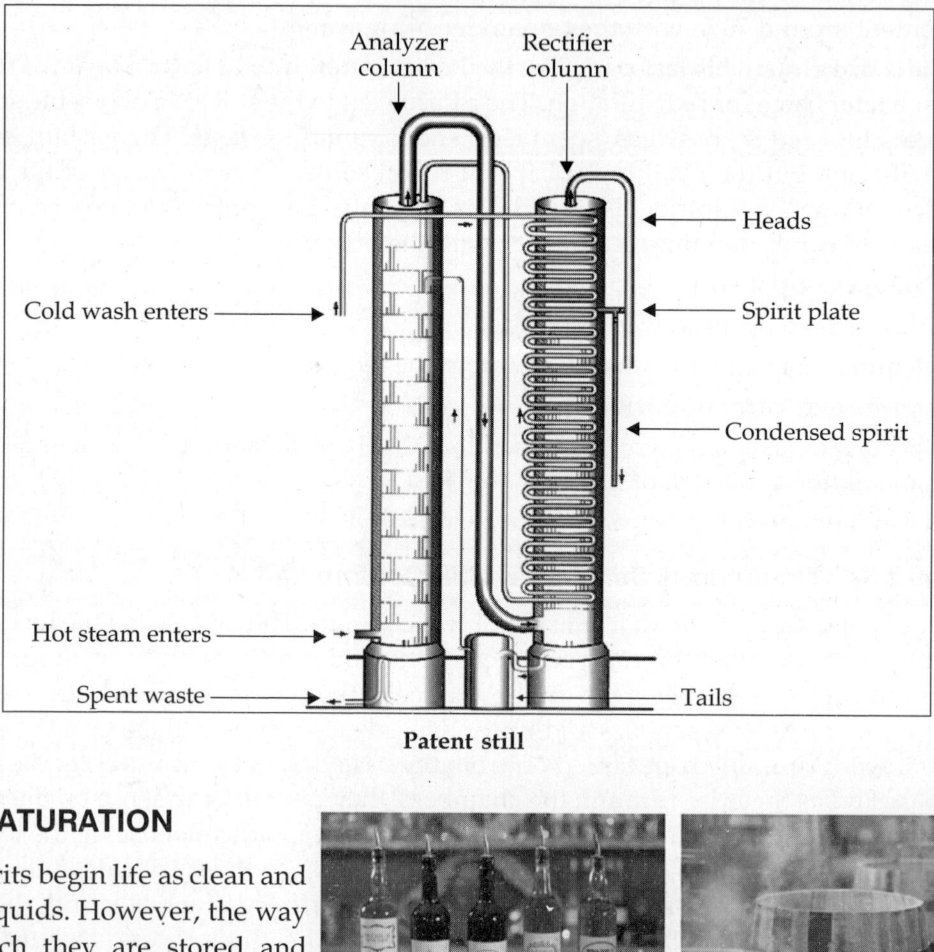

Patent still

6.4 MATURATION

All spirits begin life as clean and clear liquids. However, the way in which they are stored and aged/matured, develops various new colours and flavours. After distillation, all spirits are clear regardless of what their base liquids looked like. These spirits get their colour when they are stored in oak barrels, from the charred wood inside the cask. Apart from the colours which develop, spirits also develop many different flavours from the barrel, depending on the type of barrel and for how long they are matured. Many spirits have a minimum period of maturity such as whisky, which must mature over at least three years. The longer the maturation, the softer and gentle flavours a spirit has.

6.5 MEASURING ALCOHOLIC STRENGTH

Alcohol proof is a measure of how much alcohol (ethanol) is contained in an alcoholic beverage. Earlier the strength of a spirit was tested or proofed, by mixing equal amount of the spirit and gunpowder together, then the mixture was ignited. If the gunpowder didn't ignite, it meant the alcohol was too weak and if it burned rapidly, the alcohol was too strong. If alcohol burned with a steady blue flame, the alcohol was of an appropriate strength. Three types of system/scales for measuring alcoholic proof are:

- Sikes system/The British system
- Gay Lussac system
- American system

Strength of different beverages

Low alcohol beer	0.9% ABV
Light beer	3% ABV
Beer	5% ABV
Table wine	9-14% ABV
Fortified wine	17-22% ABV
Spirits	40% ABV
Over proof rum	58% ABV

Note: ABV stands for Alcohol by Volume

Sikes system/ The British system

Bartholomew Sykes introduced a famous hydrometer in 1816. He determined that the steady blue flame is produced when the percentage of alcohol by volume in the spirit was 57.1% which is regarded as 100° proof. To convert the British proof into % by alcohol by volume, simply multiply the proof by four and divide by seven. Example: if according to British system spirit containing 70°, will be containing the percentage of alcohol by volume as:

$$\frac{70 \times 4}{7} = 40\%$$

Used mainly in Canada and Great Britain. Now a new system called OIML (Organisation Internationale de Metrologie Legale) , which is similar to Gay Lussac system is used.

Gay Lussac or The G.L. system

Much easier to understand and adopted throughout Europe. Gives the exact amount of alcohol by volume. This system uses a scale of 0-100 which means a spirit containing 60 contains 60% alcohol.

In this system, degree is equal to percentage.

American system

Here the proof of the spirit is precisely twice the alcohol content in the bottle by volume. Therefore, a spirit marked at 90° proof would contain 45% alcohol by volume. Remember that in America, alcoholic beverages are measured differently. Spirits are measured by proof, beer by weight, and wine by volume

Table 6.1: Types of spirts

Type of spirit	Country of origin	Alcoholic percentage by volume	Flavour description
Scotch Whisky	Scotland	40-43	Pungent, dry, smokey
Irish Whisky	Ireland	37.5-40	Smooth, mellow, light
Canadian Whisky	Canada	37.5-40	Smooth, sweetish
Tennessee	U.S.A.	37.5-43	Complex, full bodied mellow
Bourbon	U.S.A.	37.5-50.5	Rich, sweetish, caramel overtones
Vodka	Russia/Polland	37.5-40	Odourless, weak, flavourless
Gin	England/Netherlands	37.5-40	Juniper and citrus infused bouquet
White Rum	West Indies	37.5-57.5	Light, dry and slightly sweet
Dark Rum	West Indies	37.5-57.5	Rich, sweet and caramelised
Cognac	France	37.5-40	Sweet bouquet complex
Tequilla (white)	Mexico	37.5-40	Subtle, gentle bouquet
Mezcal	Mexico	37.5-50	Bitter, raw, strong

REVISION QUESTIONS

1. What do you mean by alcoholic beverages?
2. Differentiate between pot still method and patent still method.
3. What is the alcoholic percentage of table wine, fortified wines and beer?
4. Draw a classification chart of alcoholic beverages.
5. What is the other name of patent still?
6. What do you mean by proof?

RESEARCH ACTIVITY

If a peg of 60 mL whisky is 70° Proof, then what would be the amount of water and alcohol in the peg using :

(a) Sikes system

(b) G.L. system

(c) American system?

7

Beer

7.1 INTRODUCTION

The word beer derives from the word *baere*, an Anglo Saxon word which means barley. It is one of the world's most ancient and satisfying drinks which has played an important role in many of the major cultures of the past. Brewing is the process by which beer is made. Many believe that the Middle East and Egypt were the birthplace of beer and developed brewing to a fine art, however at the same time the Africans were making their own intoxicating drink by brewing method using millet and Chinese were brewing beer using more advanced technique using millet and rice as a prime ingredient. In Latin America, the Aztecs in Mexico boasted their own beer gods, and Brazilian Indians produced dark, smoky tasting brews from manioc roots and grain roasted over hardwood fires. Some even argue that in very early times, the crop was cultivated not for food but to brew beer. By 6000 B.C. brewing was well established in Babylon. The Egyptians, Greeks and Romans all produced beer of acceptable quality. The Normans are credited with bringing their brewing skills to England. One belief that many of these very early brewers shared was that the beer they brewed was a gift from the Gods. Beer in this modern world is one of the widely consumed beverages.

After reading this chapter, you will be able to understand:

- Meaning of beer
- Ingredients for making beer
- Manufacturing process of beer
- Different styles of beer
- Beer glassware
- Various brands of beer

7.2 INGREDIENTS FOR BEER MAKING

Ingredients used in beer making which provide distinct flavour to the beer are described below:

(a) Grain: The best cereal to produce beer is barley as it contains the natural sugars required for fermentation. Barley in its malted form gives a unrivalled taste to beer. Barley is very rich in starch, around 60%-65% and also in the enzyme called diastase.

It converts the starch into sugar which is important for fermentation. Other grains such as wheat, rice and maize are also used for brewing beer but mostly in conjunction with barley to add some balance.

Barely

(b) **Sugar:** Graded or refined sugars are added for fermentation and to add sweetness. It acts as a catalyst for the fermentation process. Heated sugar or caramel is sometimes used instead of coloured malts to darken beers.

(c) **Yeast:** It is a single cell living microorganism, essential to induce fermentation. It occurs everywhere but only a few types are suitable for fermentation in beer. During fermenting process, the yeast converts the sugar into alcohol and releases carbon dioxide. Any one of the two types of brewer's yeast – *Saccharomyces cerevisiae* and *Saccharomyces carlsbergensis/ Saccharomyces uvarum* are used in beer production. *Saccharomyces carlsbergensies* is used in making bottom fermented beer like lager, while *Saccharomyces cerevisiae* is used in making top fermented beer such as ales and stouts.

Yeast

(d) **Finings:** These are brightening agents added to clarify the beer. Beer gets hazy and cloudy due to yeast and proteins, therefore to clarify the beer fining agents are added. Finings clear and brighten the beer. These fining agents attract all the sediments to the bottom of the cask, making beer clear and bright. Example: natural agents such as Isinglass (obtained from air bladders of various fish, especially sturgeon), Irish moss (it is not actually a moss, but a seaweed) or synthetic fining agents.

(e) **Hops (female cone-shaped flower):** These plants are tall climbing plants, members of the hemp family distantly related to both cannabis and the nettle. Botanical name of hops is *Humulus lupulus*. A single hop plant carries male or female flowers, however female flower is used for brewing. The female cone is made up of a number of petal-like structures called bracts. As the cone ripens, the bases of these bracts bear glands filled with a yellow resinous oily substance known as *lipulin*. It is this *lipulin* that contains alpha acids, which give a characteristic bitterness and distinct flavour to beer. Hops can be used in various forms while

Hops

brewing beer such as in the form of entire cone, slightly crushed, powdered form or hop extract. Hops are added in beer:

- as a preservative and aiding longevity to beer;
- to prevent the beer from going sour;
- to add a characteristic bitter flavour and aroma; and
- to aid in digestion.

Fuggles, Saaz, Crystal, Goldings, Bramling Cross, Spalter, Admiral, Chinook, Orion are some types of hops used by brewers to produce beer.

(f) Water: Beer is mainly made up of water. The composition of water can influence the brewing process and ultimately result in a softer, harder or sweeter beer. Water contains six main minerals: bicarbonate, sodium, chloride, calcium, magnesium and sulphate. The proportions of these minerals in the water greatly affect the flavour and sometimes colour of the finished product. Brewers have even given water their own name - liquor. Hard water is ideal for lager and soft water more suitable for heavier beers. Approximately six litres of water is required to produce one litre of beer.

(g) Adjuncts: Some brewers add substances to the mash other than malt called *adjuncts*. These adjuncts are added to the grist when the malt is cracked in the mill. Adjuncts can be used to provide a cheaper substitute for part of the malt or when there is a short supply of malt. Sometimes, however the extra ingredients can simply be added to enhance the flavour of beer, to reduce costs or to improve colour. Some of the common adjuncts are:

- **Sugar:** It is the common adjunct as it ferments easily and quickly to produce more alcohol and makes beer lighter.
- **Caramel:** It is used instead of dark malt to give colour to beer.
- **Flaked maize:** It is used to make dry, light coloured beer.
- **Rice:** Used as an alternative to the malt.
- **Roasted barley:** Unmalted roasted malts are sometimes used to darken or blacken the beer along with a harsh and dry flavour.

Other ingredients are also added while brewing beer like honey, chilly, ginger, herbs and fruit peels as flavour enhancers.

7.3 BEER MANUFACTURING PROCESS

Beer manufacturing also known as brewing process has several steps as described below:

1. **Malting:** Barley when steeped or soaked in water is known as Malt. To produce good malt, the barley must be of good quality and low in nitrogen as nitrogen may affect the fermentation. Malting has three distinct steps:

- Steeping: After screening the barley to remove any extraneous matter, it is put in a large tank and steeped in water to a moisture content of about 45%. This is simply an accelerated version of the absorption of water which would normally occur over several weeks in the soil. The grain absorbs the water and oxygen which leads to germination.
- Germination: This is the commencement of growth when the food reserves in the grain, namely, starch and protein are broken down into sugars and amino acids. The moist grain is spread onto a malting floor which is air conditioned to assist germination. Each grain sprouts tiny rootlets and at the same time, the enzymes begin to convert the starch into sugars.
- Kilning: After about five days when germination has reached the desired stage, further development is stopped by kilning. The grain is gently dried by hot air and moisture is removed. Depending on the intensity and duration of kilning, different coloured malts are produced such as pale malt, lager malt, crystal malt and chocolate or black malt.

2. **Milling:** Malted barley is lightly crushed by passing it through a mill producing a fine black powder called grist. At this stage other cereals can be introduced, such as wheat, unmalted barley, rice and flaked maize to give more subtle characteristics of flavour and colour to the finished brew.
3. **Mashing:** The grist is transferred to a very large vessel known as *mash tun* where it is mashed with hot water keeping the temperature at 65° centigrade, allowing the enzymes formed during malting to convert the starch into fermentable sugars that will determine the alcohol content of the beer. The resulting sweet brown liquid is known as *wort* (pronounced as wert). Some brewers also use the decoction method in which the brewer has not one but two or three mash tuns. Here the mash is heated at 50° centigrade but instead of everything being heated in a single mash tun, a third of the mash is transferred to another mash tun, where it is brought to boil. The boiling mash is then added back to the remaining mash and in this way the higher temperature of around 65° centigrade, is reached. This process is repeated to achieve a temperature of 75° centigrade.

Mash tun

4. **Lautering:** In this process, the mash is transferred to a straining (or lautering) vessel which is usually cylindrical with a slotted false bottom two to five centimetres above the true bottom. The liquid extract (wort) drains through the false bottom and is run-off to the brew kettle. Water is "sparged" (or sprayed) though the grains to wash out as much of the extract as possible. The "spent grains" are removed and sold as cattle feed.

5. **Boiling or brewing:** The wort is now taken to a copper vessel, a sort of massive kettle usually made of stainless steel, where hops and sugar are added and boiled for an hour and half. Boiling enables the wort to be brought to the desired density and to kill the enzymes and bacteria that are still present, thereby sterilizing the brew. Hops are added at various phases of boiling process. Hops that are added for their aromatic qualities will often be added only a few minutes before the end of the boiling process, so that not too much aroma is lost. Hops used for bitterness are added at the start of the boiling process.

Brewing kettle

6. **Whirlpooling:** As a result of addition of the hops and the precipitation of proteins during the brewing/boiling process, the wort is filtered using a whirlpool separator. With this device the brewer circulates the wort at high speed in the vessel, causing the loose particles to pile up in the centre. At the same time, the clear liquid is drained away on the outside of the vessel. The remaining hops are sold as fertiliser.
7. **Cooling:** After the boiling process, hops is removed and the wort is pumped through to a paraflow (heat exchanger) where it is cooled to a temperature of 15° centigrade and is now ready for fermentation.
8. **Fermentation:** During fermentation process the yeast is added which absorbs the nutrients and feeds on the sugar, converting them into alcohol and release carbon dioxide. Two types of fermentation; top fermentation and bottom fermentation are done depending on the style of beers. For top fermentation, the yeast *Saccharomyces cerevisiae* is added and the fermentation takes place either open or closed. The yeast floats on the wort and converts the sugars into alcohol and carbon dioxide. The temperature during this process varies between 15 to 25 degrees centigrade and the time required ranges from 3 to 7 days. Whereas in bottom fermentation, the yeast *Saccharomyces carlsbergensis/Saccharomyces uvarum* is added and the yeast eventually sinks to the bottom. One of the main advantages of bottom fermentation is that it is less prone to infection and the process is more predictable. The fermentation proceeds very slowly for two weeks and requires a temperature between 5 to 10 degrees centigrade. After the fermentation process, the beer is known as *green beer.*
9. **Maturing and conditioning:** After fermentation, the liquid known as *green beer* is run into conditioning tanks where it is left for maturing. The length, nature and location differs from beer to beer. For top fermented beers, this settling period is short and for bottom fermented beers it can last for many weeks. Conditioning builds up the carbon dioxide in the beer and it is this gas that will give the beer its head in the glass when poured. Addition of yeast and some fresh wort for the

fermentation of the more stubborn sugars is also done known as *krausening*. Some traditional beers are racked directly into wooden or metal casks ready to go to the consumers without filtration or any other processing. These beers are known as bottle conditioned beers. Finings are also added to the cask to clear the beer in addition to yeast with some sugar to encourage further or secondary fermentation, which is known as *priming*. Dry hops may also be added to impart extra aroma. Cask conditioned beer or bottle conditioned beer continue to mature until they develop complex fruity flavours.

10. **Filtration:** After conditioning and maturing, beer develops cloudiness due to dead yeast protein cells. This unwanted sediment is known as lees and is removed by filtration process. A sterile filtering system or fine sheets filters are used to filter the unwanted substances in beers.
11. **Pasteurization:** Pasteurization named after Louis Pasteur, who discovered the process involves briefly heating the beer so as to stop the microbiological activities in the beer. Pasteurization is used to prolong the beer's storage life. Beers that are bottle conditioned are not pasteurized. Pasteurization may be performed before bottling by heating the beer to 60 to 80 degrees centigrade and at the same time passing through the tube known as flash pasteurization. Another method is to send the beer through a heated tunnel known as tunnel pasteurization after it has been bottled.

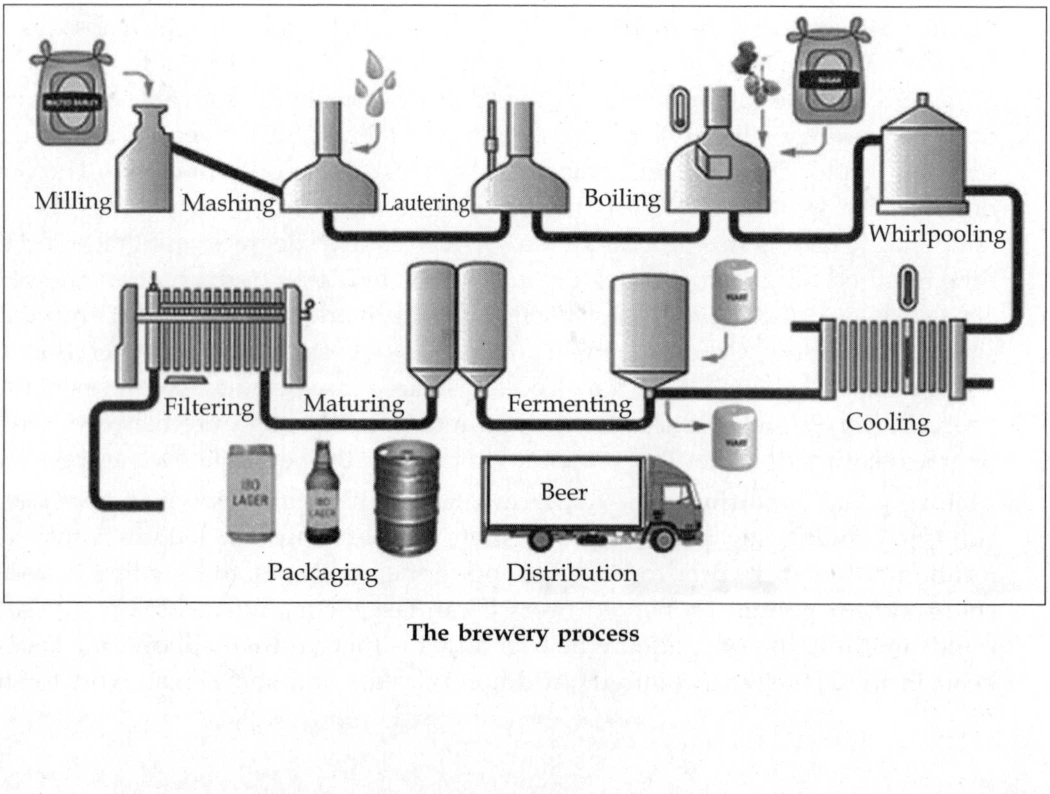

The brewery process

7.4 TYPES OF BEER

A broad classification of beer types can be made based on the type of fermentation. Generally beer can be classified on the basis of types of fermentation:

- bottom fermentation,
- top fermentation; and
- spontaneous fermentation.

Table 7.1: Comparison between bottom fermented beer and top fermeneted beer

Criteria	Bottom fermented beer	Top fermented beer
Type of yeast	*Saccharomyces carlsbergensis/ Saccharomyces uvarum*	*Saccharomyces cerevisiae*
Fermentation	Yeast sinks to the bottom of the wort	Yeast floats on the wort
Temperature	Primary fermentation takes place at cool temperature from 5°C to 10°C.	Primary fermentation takes place at warm temperature -15°C to 25°C
Holding	Lasts two weeks	Lasts for three to seven days
Secondary fermentation	In the form of Krausening	In the form of priming
Service	4-6°C	8-20°C
Composition	These beers are thick and dark.	These beers are thinner and clearer.
Infections	Susceptible to infections.	Less susceptible to infections.

7.4.1 Top Fermented Beer

- **Ale:** is a generic term for the top fermented beers brewed in the British style. The colour is usually amber, though not necessarily so, while the flavour is generally bitter to sweet but may also be sourish. Most ales are full bodied and fruity.
- **Porter:** This ale gets its name from its popularity among porters in London and Dublin. It is brewed from charred malt and is highly aromatic and flavoursome.
- **Stout:** Made from scorched, very dark malt and generously flavoured with hops. Stout has a smoothy, malty flavor and creamy consistency.
- **Trappist:** There are only six brands in the world that are allowed to call their beer Trappist. They all make top fermented beers that are close to the Belgian Ales and Barley wines.
- **Alt:** Beer from Germany is a top fermenting beer and undergoes a cold maturation from three to eight weeks. The colour is usually fairly dark, bronze coloured, though lighter version can also occur.
- **Amber:** Is a fairly modern name for an ale refering principally to the colour. Both Belgian special beers and American ales bear this designation.
- **Barley wine:** Kind of an ale having heavy, fruity taste, consists of higher alcohol content nearly about 10% closer to wine than beer that is why it is known as barley wine rather than beer. It has a bronze to mahogany colour.

- **Kolsch:** It is a top fermented beer from a German city, Cologne. Kolsch means Cologne. It is a straw beer, light and soft, but with substantial carbon dioxide content. It may also be brewed with a small amount of wheat malt.

7.4.2 Bottom Fermented Beer

- **Lager:** This beer gets its name from the German word *lagern* which means to store and was originally made in central Europe. It is a bottom fermented beer. It is stored at low temperatures for up to six months after fermentation in order to condition and mature before it is sold either in bottle or on a draught. The long storage period also helps the beer to withstand variations of temperature without cloudiness.
- **Bock:** Comes from the German village of Einbeck is bottom fermented beer having a somewhat higher alcohol content and characterised by the malty sweetness.
- **Pilsner:** Originally a beer from the Czech town of Plzen, it is always a straw, bottom fermented beer with a moderate hop bitterness and light maltiness. The alcohol percentage is 4.5 and 5.55 by volume. Pilsner is nowadays a thin neutral beer.
- **Malt liquor:** It is a strong lager often made with huge amount of sugar to produce a thin brew.

7.4.3 Spontaneous Fermentation

- **Lambic beer:** It is a special style among beers from Belgium. It is a spontaneous fermentation using wild airborne yeast beer. Brewed with 30% wheat, it is a sourish beer that undergoes a long maturation process in oak. It contains little alcohol and its plain version has few adherents. It is usually sweetened, blended or prepared with fruit.
- **Geuze:** When a mature lambic and a young lambis are blended and bottled together, the mixture evolves further to form a sweet sourish beer that is livelier than Lambic itself known as Geuze.
- **Faro:** It is simply a lambic to which sugar has been added so as to sweeten the sourish beer. Mixtures of Lambic with sweet top fermenting beers also occur as Faro.

7.4.4 Others

- **Draught beer:** Draught beer system uses a plastic chamber in the bottom of the can. The can is filled with beer containing dissolved gas and it is then sealed. When it is eventually opened the pressure pushes the beer down, then up through a small hole in the chamber which releases a very fine stream of bubbles. As we finish pouring, a pub style, smooth creamy head is formed.

Draught beer

- **Ice beer:** New concept in beer where the beer is made by cooling beer to below freezing point and then removing the ice crystals formed. Ice beer has a higher alcoholic content. Many ice beers were originally developed in Canada.
- **Root beer:** Root beer is not actually a beer but a soft drink originally flavoured with sassafras root bark and is boiled but not fermented. It is very famous in America.
- **Weisse or weizen:** This wheat beer style has come from Bavaria. The white or wheat beers of Bavaria are made with 50 to 60% malted wheat. These pale, often cloudy brews became a popular summer refresher in Germany.
- **Non-alcoholic beer:** For making non-alcoholic beverages, many brewers used vacuum distillation. In this the brew can be boiled at a lower temperature, about 140 degrees, lessening the cooked taste. The brew lacks character, therefore 10% real beer is added to the final product for taste. Alcohol remains below 5%, lower than orange juice. Compared with other methods for the production of non-alcohol beer, this novel approach produces a favourable alternative to regular beers with similar flavour characteristics and satisfactory stability. Non-alcoholic beer brands like Moussy, Kingsbury, Kaliber and Barbican among others are made by vacuum distillation.

Importance of the 'head'

It is important that beers are served with a head that is a maximum of two finger-widths high. This preserves the coolness and aromas of the beer. A larger head indicates that the beer has been poured too quickly, whereas a lack of a head indicates that it was poured either too slowly or into a dirty glass.

7.5 BEER GLASSWARE

Beers are served mostly in the following glassware:

- Pilsner glass – To serve Pilsner beer
- Beer goblet – To serve lager beer
- Beer mug/ Dimple glass
- Pitcher
- Weizen beer glass- To serve wheat beer

			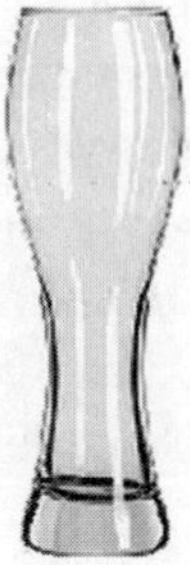	
Beer goblet	**Pilsner**	**Pitcher**	**Weizen**	**Beer mug**

Beer measures

- Pint: 330 mL
- Bottle: 650 mL

Beer strengths

The average strength of beer is 4% alcohol by volume, however beer ranging from 4%- 11% alcohol by volume is also available along with low alcohol and alcohol-free beer.

- Super strength : 8-11% alcohol by volume
- Premium strength : 4-6% alcohol by volume
- Standard strength : 3-4% alcohol by volume
- Low alcohol : 0.5-1.2% alcohol by volume
- Alcohol free : not more than 0.05% alcohol by volume

Table 7.2: International beer brands

Beer Name	Country
Foster, Godfather	Australia
Corona	Mexico
Tiger	Singapore
Carlsberg, Tuborg	Denmark
Castle lager	South Africa
Stroh, Budweiser, Miller	U.S.A.
Heineken, Amstel Light	Netherlands
Kalyani Black Label, Kingfisher	India
Brahma	Brazil
Murphys, Guiness	Ireland
Stella Artois, Hoegarden	Belgium
Asahi	Japan

Did you know?

Microbrewery

A microbrewery is one where beer is brewed fresh. These breweries are independently owned and produce a small amount of beer as compared to traditional/large-scale corporate breweries. The brew master here can use a variety of ingredients to turn out a diverse selection of craft beers. Apart from lager, various flavours such as Wheat beer and The English Brown Ale are offered. Such breweries are generally characterized by their emphasis on quality, flavour and brewing technique.

7.6 TERMS RELATED TO BEER

- **Abbey:** Commercial Belgian beers licensed by abbeys. Not to be confused with Trappist ales.
- **Adjuncts:** Materials, like rice, corn and brewing sugar, used in place of traditional grains for cheapness or lightness of flavour.
- **Ale:** The oldest beer style in the world. Produced by warm or top fermentation.
- **Alt:** Dark brown top-fermenting beer from Düsseldorf.
- **Alpha acid:** The main component of the bittering agent in the hop flower.
- **Attenuation:** The extent to which brewing sugars turn to alcohol and carbon dioxide.
- **Beer:** Generic term for an alcoholic drink made from grain. Includes both ale and lager.
- **Bitter:** British term for the pale, amber or copper coloured beers developed from the pale ales in the 19th century.
- **Bock or Bok:** Strong beer style of the Netherlands and Germany.
- **Bottle-conditioned:** Beer that undergoes a secondary fermentation in the bottle.
- **Brew kettle:** Vessel used to boil the sugary wort with hops.
- **Cask-conditioned:** Beer that undergoes a secondary fermentation in the cask. Known as "real ale", closely identified with British beers.

- **Decoction mashing:** A system mainly used in lager brewing in which portions of the wort are removed from the vessel, heated to a higher temperature and then returned. Improves enzymic activity and the conversion of starch to sugar in poorly modified malts.
- **Dry-hopping:** The addition of a small amount of hops to a cask of beer to improve aroma and bitterness.
- **Dunkel:** A dark lager beer in Germany, a Bavarian speciality that predates the first pale lagers.
- **Entire:** The earliest form of porter, short for "entire butt".
- **Ester:** Flavour compounds produced by the action of yeast turning sugars into alcohol and carbon dioxide. Esters may be fruity or spicy.
- **Fining:** Substance that clarifies beer, usually made from the swim bladder of sturgeon fish; also known as Isinglass.
- **Framboise or Frambozen:** Raspberry-flavoured lambic beer.
- **Grist:** The coarse powder derived from malt that has been milled or "cracked" in the brewery prior to mashing.
- **Gueuze:** A blend of Belgian lambic beers.
- **Helles or Hell:** A pale Bavarian lager beer.
- **Hop (Latin: Humulus lupulus):** Herb used when brewing to add aroma and bitterness.
- **IBU:** International Bitterness Units. An internationally-agreed scale for measuring the bitterness of beer. A "lite" American lager may have around 10 IBU's, an English mild ale around 20 units, an India Pale Ale 40 or higher, an Irish stout 55 to 60 and barley wine 65.
- **Infusion:** Method of mashing used mainly in ale-brewing where the grains are left to soak with pure water while starches convert to sugar, usually carried out at a constant temperature.
- **Kölsch:** Top-fermenting golden beer from Cologne.
- **Kräusen:** The addition of partially-fermented wort during lagering to encourage a strong secondary fermentation.
- **Kriek:** Cherry-flavoured lambic beer.
- **Lager:** In German, it means "to store". It is a type of beer which is stored at a low temperature for ageing after it has been brewed.
- **Lambic:** Belgian beer made by spontaneous fermentation.
- **Lauter tun:** Vessel used to clarify the wort after the mashing stage.
- **Malt:** Barley or other cereals that have been partially germinated to allow starches to be converted into fermentable sugars.
- **Mash:** First stage of the brewing process, when the malt is mixed with pure hot water to extract the sugars.

- **Märzen:** Traditional Bavarian lager brewed in March and stored until autumn for the Munich Oktoberfest.
- **Mild:** Dark brown (occasionally pale) English and Welsh beer, lightly hopped. The oldest style of beer that once derived its colour from malt cured over wood fires. One of the components of the first porters.
- **Milk stout:** Stout made with the addition of lactose, which is unfermentable, producing a beer low in alcohol with a creamy, slightly sweet character.
- **Pilsner or Pilsener or Pils:** International brand name for a light-coloured lager.
- **Porter:** Dark brown or black beer that originated in London.
- **Priming:** Addition of sugar to encourage secondary fermentation in beer.
- **Reinheitsgebot:** Bavarian beer law of 1516 (the "Purity Pledge") that lays down that only malted grain, hops, yeast and water can be used in brewing. It now covers the whole of Germany.
- **Shilling:** Ancient method of invoicing beer in Scotland on strength. Beers are called 60, 70 or 80 shilling.
- **Sparging:** From the French esparger, to sprinkle; sprinkling or spraying the spent grains in the mash tun or lauter tun to flush out any remaining malt sugars.
- **Square:** A traditional, open fermenting vessel.
- **Steam beer:** American beer style saved by the Anchor - Brewery in San Francisco.
- **Stout:** Once an English generic term for the strongest ("stoutest") beer in a brewery. Now considered a quintessentially Irish style.
- **Trappist:** Ales brewed by monks of the Trappist order in Belgium and the Netherlands.
- **Union:** Method of fermentation developed in Burton-tn-Trent using large oak casks.
- **Ur or Urtyp:** German for 'original'.
- **Weizen or Weisse:** German for wheat or white beer.
- **Wort:** Liquid resulting from the mashing process, rich in malt and sugars.

REVISION QUESTIONS

1. List down various ingredients along with their purpose in making beer.
2. Differentiate between top fermented beer and bottom fermented beer.
3. Name any ten international beer brands along with their countries of origin.
4. List down various top fermented beers and bottom fermented beers.

RESEARCH ACTIVITIES

- Visit a nearby public bar or wine shop and list down the various imported brands of beer available.
- Search and list down the top ten strongest beers of the world.
- Search and list down ten beer brands which are not made from barley.

8

Whisky

8.1 INTRODUCTION

Whisky is defined as an alcoholic beverage distilled from cereal grains and matured in wood casks. The word whisky is derived from ***'acqua vitae'*** - the Latin equivalent of the Gaelic ***'usige beathe'***, or 'water of life'. It is said that the spirit was first produced in Ireland. Irish monks brought the craft of distillation with them when they settled in Scotland. Thereafter, the Scots set about making whisky the most internationally enjoyed spirit, helped of course with input from Irish, American and Canadian producers, the invention of coffey still revolutionized the whisky industry. As a result lighter whisky was produced with the grains like maize, barley and rye. Previously only high flavoured pot still were available. Whisky usually comes with a strength of 40-55% alcohol by volume. Along with Scotland other countries like America, Ireland, Canada also produced world renowned whiskies. Japan is also coming up with some excellent whiskies in this modern era.

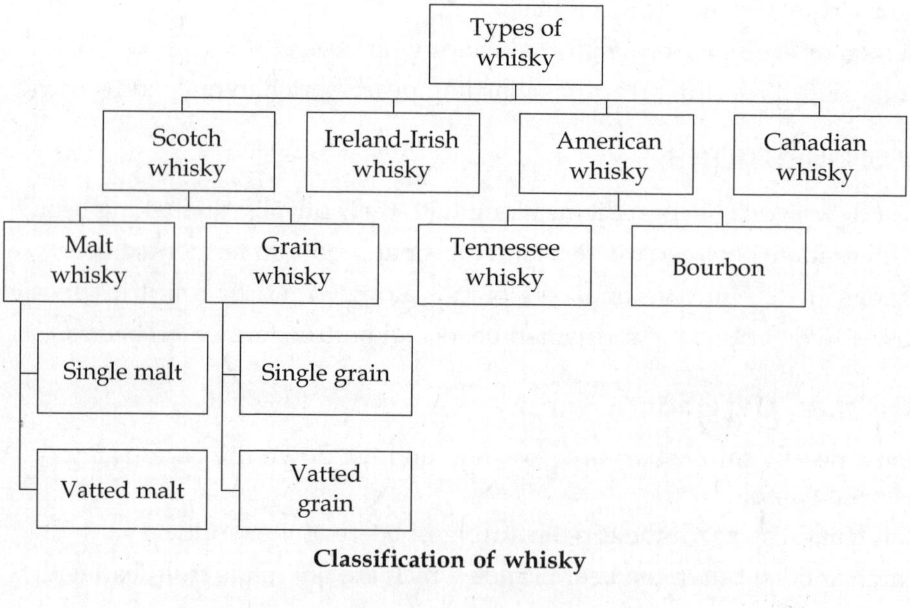

Classification of whisky

8.2 WHISKIES FROM SCOTLAND

This is a whisky made in Scotland which dominates the whisky world. Its flavour and quality are governed by the type of cereal used, the malting process, the peat used, the water, the distilling equipment, and the skills of the distiller and the blender. In Scotland, whisky is spelled as whisky and in general, whisky from Scotland is referred as Scotch. Whiskies from Scotland can be blended, grain and malt whisky. Scotch whisky is mostly retailed at the standard dark spirit strength of 40% alcohol by volume or perhaps slightly above. A small proportion of the best grades are bottled from the barrel undiluted. These are known as 'cask strength' whiskies.

8.2.1 Types of Scotch Whisky

(a) **Grain whisky:** These whiskies are made by grains such as maize, wheat, millet and some barley plus a little malted barley. Maize is usually the main ingredient and when ground, it is cooked under steam pressure to convert the starch of the grain into fermentable sugar. These whiskies are produced by Coffey still and are light bodied by nature. It is usually a quicker process and cheaper than malt whiskies.

(b) **Blended whisky:** For making blended whiskies 50% blend of malt and 50% grain whiskies are used; using more amount of malt can be referred as deluxe whiskies. These whiskies spend longer time in cask and are expensive and smoother in taste. More than 90% of whiskies produced in Scotland are blended whiskies. The object of the blending is to iron out the rough edges of individual whiskies and produce something that will appeal to a broader taste. Blended whiskies also state the number of years in their label indicating the time taken by the whiskies to mature in cask.

Table 8.1: Blended whiskies from Scotland

Ballantine	The Antiquary
Bells	Chivas Regal
Black and White	Haig's Dimple
Cutty Sark	Johnnie Walker Balck label
Henkey Bannister	Old Parr
Teachers	Usher's Deluxe
Vat 69	Red Hackle

(c) **Malt whisky:** All Scotch Malt whiskies must be produced only with malted barley. You will find malt whisky sold as either Single Malts or Vatted Malts.

- **Single malt:** It is produced by a single distillery from a single year; it must be made from 100% barley malt and distilled in pot stills only—the majority are twice distilled. The alcohol levels cannot exceed 165 proof.

- **Vatted/blended malt:** These whiskies are made from 100% barley malt and are blended from at least two different distilleries. The alcohol levels also cannot exceed 165 proof. Blended Malt whiskies were previously called Vatted Malts.

Single malt whisky

The defining feature of single malt whisky is the fact that it is made in a single distillery, using a pot still and a malted rain such as barley.

Blended whisky

These whiskies are made by blending a variety of malt and grain whiskies from different distilleries into a single blend.

8.2.2 Whisky Regions of Scotland

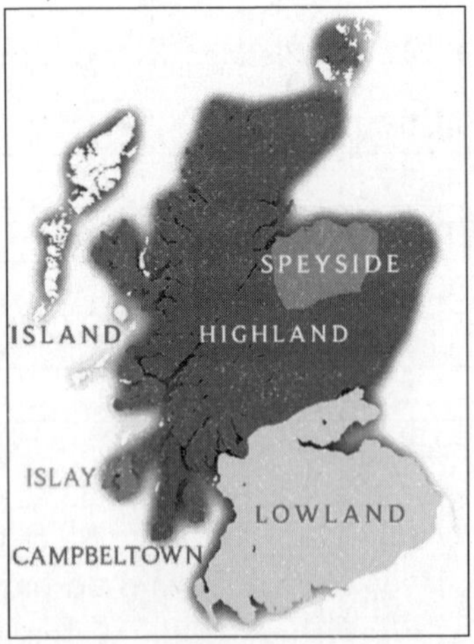

1. **Lowland**
   - Whiskies are smooth and slightly fiery.
   - Light, salty and neat.
   - Most of the lowland whisky is served as an aperitif.
   - Brands: *Auchentoshan, Bladnoch, Glenkinchie, Ladyburn, Littlemill, Highland, Rosebank.*
2. **Highland**
   - Largest whisky producing region.
   - Highland whiskies are powerful, rich in flavour and quite smoky.
   - Many of the famous distilleries are located around the river Spey.
   - Brands - *Maccalan, Knockando, Singleton, Glenmorengie Oban, North Port, Glenlivet, Glenmorangie, Glenfarclas, Glenfiddich, Glengrant, Glenord* (Glen means valley)

3. **Islands**
   - There are many fine malts made in the islands which consist of Islay, Jura, Mull, Orkney and Skye.
   - Brands: *Arran, Blackwood, Jura, Talisker, Tobermory, Highland Park, Scapa, Laphroiag, Isle of Jura.*
4. **Spey Side**
   - Received its name from the river Spey.
   - Good choice of rich flavour, complexity and relatively mild character.
   - Brands: *Glen Morey, Glen Spey.*
5. **Campbeltown**
   - Once known as the whisky capital of Scotland.
   - Whiskies are heavy and smoky.
   - Brands: *Glengyle, Glenscotia, Springbank, Longrow.*

Table 8.2: Single-malt whiskies and whiskies from glen family

Single malt whiskies	Whiskies from glen family
Springbank	Glengyle
Longrow	Glenscotia
Knockando	Glen Morey
Macallan	Glen Spey
Singleton	Glenfiddich
Tormore	Glenlivet
Rosebank	Glenmorengie
Talisker	Glenkinchie
Highland Park	Glengrant
Laphroaig	Glenfarclas
Langavulin	Glenord

8.2.3 Whisky Manufacture

The whisky making process has changed a little over years. All whiskies are made of grain (barley, maize, corn, rye), water and yeast. Most of the distillers use barley as a grain, specially Scotch whiskies. Distillers also require lots of pure, cold water in order to make whisky. Most of them use spring water but loch sources and even town supplies are also used. Yeast is also used in whisky making for fermentation. Following process is carried out in distilleries (where whisky is being made) for whisky manufacturing.

1. **Malting:** Barley when steeped or soaked in water is known as Malt. To produce good malt, the barley must be of good quality and low in nitrogen as nitrogen may affect the fermentation. Malting has three distinct steps.

- **Steeping:** After screening the barley to remove any extraneous matter, it is put into a large tank and steeped in water to a moisture content of about 45%. This is simply an accelerated version of the absorption of water which would normally occur over several weeks in the soil. The grain absorbs the water and oxygen which leads to germination.
- **Germination:** This is the commencement of growth when the food reserves in the grain, namely starch and protein are broken down into sugars and amino acids. The moist grain is spread onto a malting floor which is air conditioned to assist germination. Each grain sprouts tiny rootlets and at the same time, the enzymes begin to convert the starch into sugars.
- **Kilning:** After about five days when germination has reached the desired stage, further development is stopped by kilning. The grain is gently dried by hot air and moisture is removed. This will help in stopping germination but will not impart any flavour. The second method of kilning is to dry the barley over a peat fire imparting a smoky flavour. Peat is a fuel made from decomposed vegetation.

Barley **Steeped barley** **Germinated barley**

Physical changes during malting process

2. **Milling:** Malted barley is taken to the distillery where the malts are ground by passing them through a mill producing a fine black powder called grist.
3. **Mashing:** The grist is transferred to a very large vessel known as *mash tun* where it is mashed with hot water keeping the temperature at 65° centigrade, allowing the enzymes formed during malting to convert the starch into fermentable sugars. The resulting sweet brown liquid is known as *wort* (pronounce as wert). The final water is then retained as the first water of the next batch.

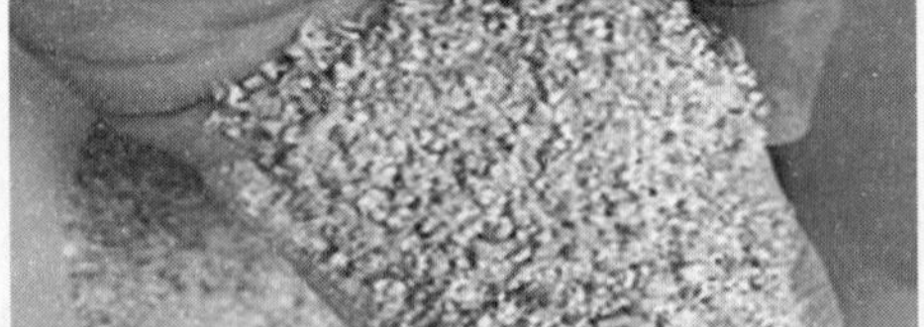

Fine black powder obtained by milling

4. **Fermentation:** During fermentation process, yeast is added which converts the sugars into alcohol which can be done in open-ended vessel or close-ended vessel. In Scotland malt distillers prefer close-ended vessel whereas grain distillers used both open-ended and closed vessels, though the latter are widely favoured in the United States. The speed and vigour of fermentation can be controlled by having a cooling system. This may be in the vessel itself or in the hall where the fermentation vessel stands, known as *tun-room.* Wooden fermentation vessels are still widely used sometimes co-existing with stainless steel in the same *tun-room.* Short fermentation (nearly 48 hours) produces malty character whiskies whereas long fermentation (nearly 55 hours) produces lighter, complex and fruity flavoured whiskies.
5. **Distillation:** The wash has an alcoholic strength of 8% alcohol by volume (abv). This is then distilled twice in pot stills. The first distillation in a wash still will produce a spirit of 23% abv 'low wines' which is then redistilled. This time the distillate is divided into three: *foreshots, heart* and *feints.* Only the heart is retained for maturation. The foreshots and feints are recycled with the next batch of low wines.
6. **Maturation:** It is the mellowing of whisky by being stored in oak barrels/casks. Scotch whisky must be matured for three years and the American classics are usually aged for not less than four years. The optimum period varies according to the whisky. Maturation helps in oxidation of some components of the whisky which is one of the phenomena that takes place during ageing, and extraction of flavours from the wood is another. Vanilla (in Bourbon whiskies) and tannins may come from the oaks. Maturation of single malt whiskies takes place in Ex Bourbon, Ex Sherry and Refill casks. It takes time for whisky to mature.

Whisky maturing in a cask

Bottling

7. **Bottling:** Before bottling, chill filtration is done which stops a whisky from becoming cloudy and sometimes spirit caramel is also added to standardize colour.

8.2.4 Factors Affecting Scotch Whisky

1. Maximum flavour and aroma of the spirits retains in Scotch whisky due to pot still.
2. Spring water contains the essential minerals giving a distinctive character to the whisky.
3. Scotch whisky uses peat fire to impart smoky flavour.
4. Whisky maturing in cask helps in giving a distinctive flavour to the Scotch whisky.

8.3 TYPES OF WHISKY

8.3.1 Irish Whisky

Irish whisky spelt as 'whisky' is from Ireland made from malted and unmalted barley and very small quantities of other grains. It is *triple distilled* and as a result it has less congenerics–flavouring elements–which make it light and easy on the palate. No peat is used in the kilns, so that there is none of the smoky pungency that is present in some degree in most Scotch whiskies. As per Irish law, it must be matured for at least five years in oak casks which gives it a distinctive and smooth finish. Most Irish whiskies are blend of the coffey and pot still products. Important features of Irish whisky are listed as below:

- Generally made from mash of mixed malted and unmalted grain.
- Produced by using both 'pot still' & 'patent still'.
- Produced by using 'unpeated malt' except Connemara Peated Irish Malt.
- Triple distilled except Connemara Peated Irish Malt.
- Matured for at least 'Five Years' before blending.

Brand Names - *Tullamore Dew, Bushmills, Jameson, Paddy's, Middleton Rare, Power's Gold label.*

Note: Congeners are impurities which give whisky a flavour and aroma, however their presence are to be judged as excess congeners will result in the spirit being undrinkable. These are generally chemical compounds which are produced while making whisky during fermentation and maturation in casks. They include methanol, furfural, fusel oil, tannin, acetaldehyde. Congeners are present in darker spirits such as brandy and whisky (except tequila) and in wine which also causes hangover and has greater intoxication.

8.3.2 Canadian Whisky

Canadian whisky is made from mixture of grains like rye, malted barley, corn and wheat. Canadian whiskies are produced by coffey still and aged in charred oak casks for three years. It is somewhere between scotch and Bourbon to taste, being light in body and flavour and slightly sweet. A curiosity of Canadian whisky is that the regulations permit the additions of a tiny quantity of other drink products, such as sherry or wine made from grapes or other fruits. While this may account for no more than a hundredth part of the finished product imparting fruitiness in the whiskies.

Brand Names- *Canadian Club, Crown Royal, Black Velvet, Royal Reserve.*

8.3.3 American Whisky

In America, whisky is spelled with an 'e' as it is in Ireland. It was Britishers and Irish settlers who brought their own whisky with them from the old countries and helped in the development of American whisky. The first American whiskys were made with malted barley and rye. Soon a group of distillers started producing pure corn whiskies in Bourbon County, Kentucky.

Following are some types of American whiskies

1. **Bourbon whiskies:** These are classic American whiskies made from maize, rye and malted barley. Bourbon takes its name from Bourbon County, Kentucky thus also known as Kentucky whiskies. It must contain at least 51% corn plus rye, wheat or malted barley. It is distilled in continuous still (coffey still) and is matured in charred oak casks for a minimum of four years. Kentucky Bourbon must be distilled and matured in Kentucky for a minimum of these years.

   Brand Names – *Jim Beam, Wild Turkey, Early Times, Old Grand Dad, Maker's Mark, Four Roses.*

2. **Rye whisky:** The whisky is distilled mainly from a mash containing a minimum of 51% rye, is distilled in a continuous still and aged for a minimum of two years (but usually four years) in new, charred oak barrels. No colouring and flavouring is allowed.
3. **Corn whisky:** This American whisky is made from 80% corn mash as compared to 51% for Bourbon.
4. **Sour mash:** This is made by using some of the spent mash from one fermentation to start the next fermentation. This will continue the

Tennessee

- Gentleman jack
- Jack daniels
- Georage a dickel
- Ezra brooks

flavour and style. Makers mark is an example of sour mash whisky. The term sour mash means that some of the fermented mash from a previous run of a still is used to help the fermentation process in a new batch of mash. Upto 25% of the volume of the new mash should be the mash obtained from previous batch.

5. **Tennessee whisky:** This is a sour mash whisky which is charcoal filtered before being matured in barrels.

   Most American whiskies are matured in charred oak barrels which gives a distinctive flavour to the whiskies.

8.4 JAPANESE WHISKY

Scotch inspired Japanese whisky. Scottish academic institutions trained the first whisky makers of Japan. Scotch whisky and Japanese whisky are closely related but each with a slightly different character. Most obvious distinction between Scotch whiskies and Japanese whiskies is the extent of their peatiness. The classic Scotch whiskies have a definite peatiness though its extent varies from one to another. In Japan too, peatiness is usually present but in a very subtle manifestation. Water in Japan is also crystal clean like Scottish Highland flowing over granite and peat too, giving a hint of peat in the whisky. Japanese whisky has a light nose. The Japanese whisky is made from millet, corn and rice. Both pot still and continuous still (coffey) methods of distillation are used. Sometimes genuine scotch whisky is added while blending. The peat is imported from Scotland to give the distinguishing flavour.

Brand names- *Hibiki, Yamazaki, Hakushu, Komagatake,Yoichi, Nikka.*

Understanding a whisky label

A whisky label will display the brand name, where it was made, how much alcohol it contains and how long it has taken to mature in the barrel.

Table 8.3: Comparison between Irish, Scotch, Bourbon, and Canadian whiskies

Criteria	Irish	Scotch	Bourbon	Canadian (Rye)
Principle flavouring	Unmalted barley	Malted barley	Corn	Rye
Number of distillations	3	2	2	1, 2 or 3

Blend of	Pot still, grain whisky and pot malt whisky	Pot malt whisky and grain whisky	Mixed cereal/grain whiskys	Mixed cereal/grain whiskys
Stills used	Pot still and column still	Pot still and column still	Column still only	Column still only
Maturation	3 years minimum	3 years minimum	2 years minimum	3 years minimum
Oak barrels	Used charred bourbon, sherry & port	Used charred bourbon, sherry & port	Used new charred	Used charred bourbon
Colour	Medium	Varies on blend/malt	Darker	Lighter
Smell	Perfumery	Smokey	Sharp	Delicate
Taste	Roundness	Sweet/dry	Sharp/woody bitter	Grainy

8.5 INDIAN MADE FOREIGN LIQUOR (IMFL)

Did you know?
Paul John and Amrut are India's single malt whiskies.

Indian Made Foreign Liquor, often abbreviated as IMFL, is a term used to denote western-style hard liquors such as whisky, rum, vodka, etc., which are manufactured in India. It is used to differentiate them from indigenous recipes such as fenny and arrack, which are collectively called country liquor. A common characteristic of many IMFLs, distinct from spirits elsewhere in the world, is that irrespective of the final product the starting ingredient is a neutral spirit distilled from molasses, a byproduct of the sugar industry. For example, whereas a whisky in most countries would be distilled from grain, Indian whisky is made by adding whisky-like flavouring and colouring to neutral spirit obtained from molasses. The same applies to other IMFL spirits, like rum or vodka.

8.6 SERVICE OF WHISKY

1. **Scotch whisky and irish whisky:** Served straight or with a splash of spring water or ice in old fashioned glass.
2. **Malt whisky:** Served straight with a few drops of spring water.
3. **Canadian whisky:** Served straight or on the rocks or with a splash of soda/water.

REVISION QUESTIONS

1. Differentiate between single malt whisky and Irish whisky.
2. Differentiate between Canadian whisky and Bourbon whisky.
3. Name any five brands of single malt whisky.
4. What do you mean by IMFL? List any five brands of IMFL.

RESEARCH ACTIVITY

Visit a public bar nearby and list down the available brands of the following:

- Single malt whisky
- Indian whisky brands
- IMFL
- Scotch whisky

9

Rum and Tequila

9.1 INTRODUCTION TO RUM

After reading this chapter, you will be able to understand:

- Meaning of rum and tequila
- Their manufacturing process
- Types of rum
- Classification of tequila
- Difference between Tequila and Mezcal
- Brand names of various rum and tequila

Rum is a distilled beverage made from sugarcane byproducts such as molasses and sugarcane juice by fermentation and distillation. The distillate, a clear liquid, is then usually aged in oak and other casks. Rum can be referred to in Spanish by descriptors such as *ron viejo* ("old rum") and *ron añejo* ("aged rum"). World's best rum comes from the Caribbean countries and Latin America. Nations like Barbados, Bermuda, Guyana, Cuba, Jamaica, Honduras, Puerto Rico, Costa Rica, Haiti and Martinique produce world's best rums. However, India and Philippines is also famous for producing quality rums.. Some major rum brands include *Bacardi, Barbancourt, Brugal, Captain Morgan, Appleton Estate, Havana Club, Stroh, Matusalem, Mount Gay, Bundaberg, Myers, Malibu Rum, Gosling's, Cruzan, Pusser's, Flor de Caña, Don Q, and Ron Zacapa Centenario.* "Overproof" rums, such as Wray and Nephew, contain a higher alcohol content. Rum is produced in a variety of styles. Light rums are commonly used in mixed drinks, while golden and dark rums are appropriate for use in cooking as well as cocktails. Premium brands of rum are also available that are made to be consumed neat or on the rocks. Rum plays a part in the culture of most islands of the West Indies, and has famous associations with the British Royal Navy and piracy. Rum had a host of other names like "Kill-devil", "Barbados Water" and "Nelson's Blood".

9.1.1 Rum Manufacturing Process

Rum is an alcoholic beverage distilled with sugar. The sugar maybe either pure cane sugar, syrup or molasses. Rum is one of those few spirits, which retains a lot of character of its base ingredient. Therefore, Rum varies with: variety of sugarcane, mineral content of the soil, sugar level and climate.

- **Extraction of juice:** Freshly cut sugarcane is stripped of its leaves and crushed between rollers to extract juice. Spent sugarcane called bagasse is again crushed several times to extract all juice.
- **Formation of sugar:** The liquid sugar extract is heated almost to a boiling point and is then immediately cooled. This leads to crystallisation of the sugar and formation of sugar crystals in a syrupy liquid.
- **Separation of sugar crystals:** The syrup is placed in a centrifuge where it is spun until sugar crystals are separated. These are removed to make commercial sugar, leaving a very dark, treacly mother liquid – the molasses or black strap.
- **Fermentation:** At this point molasses is transferred to clean, well-aired tanks for 3-4 months. Rested molasses gives rum a better fragrance and it helps in even fermentation. To the molasses yeast, and potentially water, are added to start fermentation. While some rum producers allow wild yeast to perform the fermentation, most use specific strains of yeast to help provide a consistent taste and predictable fermentation time. Dunder, the yeast-rich foam from previous fermentations, is the traditional yeast source in Jamaica. Distillers that make lighter rums, such as Bacardi, prefer to use faster working yeasts. Use of slower working yeasts causes more esters to accumulate during fermentation, allowing for fuller-tasting rum.
- **Distillation:** There is no standard method used for distillation. Some producers work in batches using pot stills, however most rum production is done using column still distillation. Pot still output contains more congeners than the output from column stills and thus produces fuller-tasting rum. Light rums are distilled in patent still, therefore, they have less congeners. Dark rums are distilled in pot still, thus they are high in congeners.
- **Ageing and blending:** Many countries require rum be aged for at least one year. This ageing is commonly performed in used bourbon casks, but may also be performed in stainless steel tanks or other types of wooden casks. Due to the tropical climate common to most rum-producing areas, rum matures at a much faster rate than Scotch or Cognac. After ageing, rum is normally blended to ensure a consistent flavour. The new spirit takes the colour from the oak wood and a small part of the flavour while mellowing and loses its harsh taste. As part of this blending process, light rums may be filtered to remove any colour gained during ageing. For darker rums, caramel may be added to adjust the colour of the final product.

9.1.2 Classification of Rum

- **Light rum**
  - ◊ Light rums are also referred to as Silver or White Rum.
  - ◊ Light rums are often filtered after aging to remove any colour.
  - ◊ These are light flavoured hence, more suitable for cocktails.
  - ◊ **Brands:** *Bacardi Superior, Mount Gay, Ronrico, Havana Club Anejo Blanco, Appleton White Rum.*
- **Gold rum**
  - ◊ Gold rums are also called Amber rum.
  - ◊ These are medium bodied rums, which are generally aged.
  - ◊ This gains its colour from aging in wooden casks.
  - ◊ **Brands:** *Mount Gay, Havana Club, Appleton, Captain Morgan Spiced Gold, Bacardi Gold.*

- **Dark rum**
  - ◊ It is generally aged longer in heavily charred barrels.
  - ◊ It has much stronger flavour.
  - ◊ Often caramel is added for darker colour.
  - ◊ **Brands:** *Captain Morgan, Lamb's Navy Rum, El. Dorado, Old Monk, Wood's Old Navy Rum, Myers.*
- **Flavoured/spiced rum**
  - ◊ These rums are infused with flavours of fruits and spices such as mango, cinnamon, orange, citrus and coconut, etc.
  - ◊ **Brands:** *Lemon Hart, Shell Back, Sailor Jerry, Malibu.*

- **Overproof rum**
  - ◊ These rums have much higher alcohol than the standard 40%, around 75% of alcohol by volume. Most of these rums bear greater than 75%, in fact, and preparations of 151 to 160 proof occur commonly.
  - ◊ **Brands:** *Captain Morgan 100 Proof, Bacardi 151°, Holey Dollar, Bounty.*

9.1.3 Rums Around the World

Within the Caribbean, each island or production area has a unique style. These styles can be grouped by the language that is traditionally spoken.

- **Spanish speaking** islands traditionally produce light rums with a fairly clean taste. Rums from Cuba, Puerto Rico and Dominican Republic are typical of this style.
- **English speaking** islands are known for darker rums with a fuller taste that retains a greater amount of the underlying molasses flavour. Rums from Jamaica, Bermuda, and the Demerera region are typical of this style.

- **French speaking** islands are best known for their agricultural rums (*rhum agricole*). These rums, produced exclusively from sugarcane juice, retain a greater amount of the original flavour of the sugarcane. Rums from Martinique and Guadeloupe are typical of this style.
- **Premium rum:** As with other sipping spirits, such as Cognac and Scotch, a market exists for premium and super-premium spirits. These are generally boutique brands which sell very aged and carefully produced rums. They have more character and flavour than their "mixing" counterparts, and are generally consumed without the addition of other ingredients.

Light rums
- Bacardi
- Ron Rico
- Dry Cane
- Rhum St. James
- Mount Gay
- El Dorado
- Malibu
- Carriba
- El Dorado

Dark rums
- Captain Morgan
- Lambs Navy
- Appleton
- Myers
- Woods
- Hansen
- Coruba
- Barbancourt
- Old Monk

Some light and dark rum brands

9.1.4 Brands

9.1.4.1 Caribbean Rums

- **Barbados:** Cockspur Rum, Malibu Rum, Mount Gay
- **Bermuda:** Gosling's Rum
- **Cayman Islands:** Tortuga Rum Company Ltd. (Tortuga)
- **Cuba:** Havana Club
- **Dominica:** Soca Rum
- **Dominican Republic**: Brugal, Bermudez, Barcelo (The Three B's), Matusalem
- **Grenada:** Westerhall Plantation
- **Haiti:** Rhum Barbancourt
- **Jamaica:** Appleton Estate, Myers's, Captain Morgan, Charley's
- **Martinique:** Clement, DePaz, St. James
- **Puerto Rico:** Bacardi, Castillo, Don Q, Palo Viejo
- **British Virgin Islands:** Pusser's Ltd. (Pusser's)

9.1.4.2 Central/South American Rums

- **Costa Rica:** Ron Centenario
- **Colombia :** Ron Santa Fe, Ron Caldas
- **Guatemala:** Ron Zacapa Centenario, Ron Zacapa Centenario XO, Ron Botran.
- **Guyana (Demerera):** El Dorado, Lemon Hart
- **Nicaragua:** Compañía Licorera de Nicaragua, S.A. (Flor de Caña and Ron Plata)
- **Panama:** Carta Vieja, Varela Hermanos (Ron Abuelo, Ron Cortez)
- **Venezuela:** Cacique, Ocumare, Pampero, Ron Santa Teresa 1796.
- **Mexico:** Porfidio

Rum can be used

- In cocktails.
- As an excellent cold weather drink.
- As a base in the manufacture of a number of liqueurs.
- As a flavouring agent in cakes and pastries.
- In some ice creams often with raisins.
- In cooking and in flambe.

9.1.4.3 Rums From Other Areas

- **Austria:** Stroh, often considered a rum but, due to the addition of aroma, is not.
- **Australia:** Bundaberg, Beenleigh
- **Canada:** Lamb's
- **India:** Old Monk
- **Mauritius:** Green Island
- **Philippines:** Tondeña, Tanduay
- **Spain:** Arehucas, Barceló
- **Sweden:** Träkumla

9.2 TEQUILA

Tequila is not produced from the typical grains or fruits that most alcoholic beverages are made from. It is made from the distillation of an alcoholic wash obtained from the roasted centre (*piña*) of the blue agave plant and is obtained from the delimited Tequila region at the Jalisco district in Mexico.

Agave plant

Pina

9.2.1 Tequila Manufacturing Process

Harvesting of agave

- **Harvesting:** Tequila is made from the root or piña of the blue agave plant, which looks like a large pineapple or pinecone. The blue agave plant is allowed to grow for 6 to 8 years. The shoot is cut off causing the *piña,* the base (root), to swell and fill with juice. A mature *piña* usually weighs 80 to more than 300 pounds. The plant is then harvested by hand and the spikes are cut off leaving the carbohydrate-rich *piña* or root which is sent off to the ovens.

Brick oven

- **Cooking and crushing:** Traditionally the pinas are cooked in horno (brick ovens) and nowadays in autoclaves (big pressure cookers). Oven cooking traditionally takes 50-72 hours and autoclave cooking takes 6 hours. This turns the complex carbohydrates into fermentable sugars and softens the *piña* so they can easily release their juice. After the cooking, the *piñas* are rested for a few days, and then placed in a ring of stone or concrete of about 12 ft diameter, where a large stone wheel attached to a post in the middle is rolled around, crushing the *piñas.* Modern makers usually cook the piñas in huge stainless steel ovens and then crush them with mechanical crushers. The juice is referred to as *aguamiel.*

Mosto (juice) treated with yeast

- **Fermentation:** The must (*mosto*) is fermented in wooden or stainless steel tanks for 4 to 30 days, depending on the kind of yeast used. Some manufacturers use cane or corn sugar to speed up fermentation to be able to use immature and fewer plants. This type of tequila called *mixto* can be sold in bulk for shipping out of the country, and can be bottled anywhere, but will not be labelled 100% agave. The fermentation process is generally between 7-12 days unless accelerators are used, which reduces it to just 2-3 days. Longer fermentation results in a more full bodied tequila. After fermentation is finished, the mosto may be left for another 12 hours to condition and settle before distillation.

- **Distillation:** The mosto is then put into traditional copper pot stills or in stainless steel column stills. It is then heated to around 200°F with steam injection. The vapour then rises up through a pipe where it is cooled and run-off to a holding tank. The product is called *ordinaro.* The *ordinaro* is then used in the second distillation and the product of this process is tequila. Tequilas are distilled twice.
- **Colouring and ageing:** All tequila is clear right after distillation. The colour comes later, from aging in wooden barrels or from additives like caramel (in mixto only) or wood essence. Depending on the intended tequila to be made, the aging process varies greatly. It is aged between two months to seven years depending on the type of tequila to be made.
- **Blending and bottling:** The final product is usually blended with other barrels of similar age to create consistency of taste and aroma. Representatives of the Tequila Regulatory Council oversee the production to ensure the distillers meet the standards and quality controls in place under Mexican legislation. The resulting mix is then bottled or tanked for shipments. All 100% agave tequilas must be bottled in Mexico and marked, "Hecho en Mexico" meaning Made in Mexico. Only mixto tequila is allowed to be sold in bulk and bottled outside the country. Before bottling, most tequila is filtered through activated carbon or cellulose filters and most distillers add demineralized water to bring the alcoholic strength down to 80 (40% Alc./Vol.).

There are two types of tequila:

- **100% Blue Agave Tequila:** Made with 100% Blue Agave juice.
- **Mixto:** At least 51% Agave juice and at most 40% other sugars added.

9.2.2 Classification of Tequila

- **Blanco** *or* **Plata** (white or silver): It is 'un-aged' and is under 60 days old, and may be bottled fresh from distillation.

Mezcal

Mezcal is also made from the pulque of agave plants other than the blue agave variety. Bottles of Mezcal contain the worm whereas Tequila will never have a worm. There is a worm called *gusano,* properly a butterfly caterpillar (*Hipopta agavis*) in some types of Mezcal. Sometimes, there is also a bag of 'worm salt' - dried gusano, salt and chilli powder tied to the mezcal bottle.

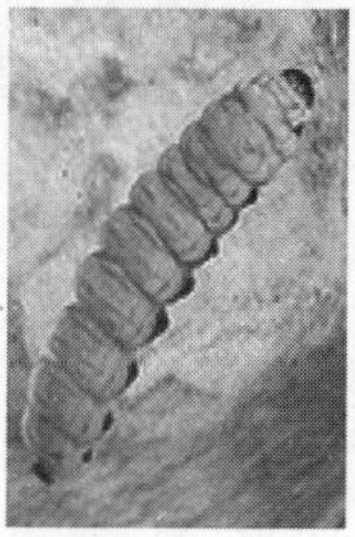

There are two types of gusano in mezcal: the red (*gusano rojo* - considered superior because it lives in the root and heart of the maguey) and the less prized white or gold (*gusano de oro*), which lives on the leaves. The red gusano turns pale in the mezcal, the gold turns ash-grey.

- **Joven Abocado** or ***Oro*** (gold): Basically, the same as *Blanco*, but with colouring and flavouring ingredients added to make it look aged (generally with caramel or oak essence, up to 1% total weight).
- **Reposado** (rested): This is aged from two months up to a year in oak casks or barrels.
- **Añejo** (aged or vintage): They are aged for a minimum of one year. They may be aged as long as eight to ten years.

The most important identifier on the label is "100% agave" or "100% agave azul" - *cien por ciento de agave azul*. This means that the tequila has been made only from the blue agave plant, and was approved by a government inspector to ensure purity. If it doesn't say this, it legally can be mixed up to 49 per cent with other ingredients.

Tequila Myth

There is no worm in Mexican-bottled tequila. Though some American-bottled brand(s) put one in their bottle as a marketing ploy but not as a Mexican tradition. Worm will be in the bottle of Mezcal only.

Service of Tequilla

The traditional "caballito" (2 oz.) is the glass to enjoy Blanco and Reposado. Anejo is preferably served in a snifter so that its aroma is fully appreciated. The tequila shot with salt on one hand and a bite of lime is Hollywood stuff which is also known *as Lick, Sip and Suck method*. First lick the salt then immediately sip the tequilla by shot glass and then suck the bite of lime. Tequilla is usually served at room temperature.

Tequila as a shooter

Glassware:
shot glass

Temperature:
well chilled

Guest preferences:
Served with salt and a slice of lemon, or with cinnamon and a slice of orange

Tequila as an ingredient

Glassware:
As an ingredient in a cocktail or long drink; it will be served in a coupe or highball glass.

Golden rule:
Only use blanco or gold tequila when making cocktails as aged tequilas are often more expensive

Tequila as an aged spirit

Glassware:
Brandy balloon

Temperature:
Room temperature, never refrigerated

Guest preferences:
Serve with an accompanying ice bucket, along with a small jug of water.

9.2.3 Brands

- Sauza
- Two Fingers
- Camino Real
- Jose Cuervo
- Don Julio
- Centinela
- Corralejo

REVISION QUESTIONS

1. What are the various kinds of rum?
2. Differentiate between dark rum and white rum.
3. Write down the tequila manufacturing process.
4. Name any five brands of tequila and mezcal.
5. Differentiate between tequilla and mezcal.

RESEARCH ACTIVITIES

- Search five international brands of white rum.
- Read the label of a tequila bottle and list down the information from the label.
- Collect the empty bottles of white rum, spiced rum, mezcal and tequila.

10

Brandy

10.1 INTRODUCTION

The word brandy derives from the Dutch word "*brandewijn*" meaning burnt wine. Brandy, in its broadest definition, is a spirit made from fruit juice or fruit pulp and skin. Brandy usually contains 40–60% ethyl alcohol by volume. In addition to wine, this spirit can also be made from grape pomace or fermented fruit juice. Unless specified otherwise, brandy is made from grape wine. It is normally consumed as an after-dinner drink. Brandy, like rum and tequila, is an agricultural spirit. Unlike grain spirits such as whisky, vodka, and gin, which are made throughout the year from grain that can be harvested and stored, brandy depends on the seasons, the ripening of the base fruit, and the production of the wine from which it is made. More specifically, it is broken down into following group:

After reading this chapter, you will be able to understand:

- Meaning of brandy
- Difference between Cognac and Armagnac
- Reading Cognac and Armagnac labels
- Grapes used in making cognac
- Other brandies
- Brand names of Cognac and Armagnac

Fau de vie

It is a French term for a colourless brandy, particularly from the Alsace region of France and from California and is distilled from fermented fruit juice. The term is informally used for like beverages from non-French speaking countries. It is distilled from young fruit and rarely aged in wooden casks, thus preserving the freshness and aroma of the fruit. Typical spirit in this category is *kirschwasser*, a cherry-based beverage or *framboise*, which is made from raspberries. When the *eau de vie* is made from the pomace, the result is called Pomace brandy or in France *Marc* (*wine*), sometimes *eau de vie de marc*.

(a) **Grape brandy** is distilled from fermented grape juice or crushed but not pressed grape pulp and skin. This spirit is aged in wooden casks (usually oak) which gives it colour, mellows the palate, and adds additional aromas and flavours.

(b) **Pomace brandy/Marc brandy** is produced from fermented grape pulp, seeds, and stems that remain after the grapes are pressed for their juice for wine. They often tend to be rather raw, although they can offer a fresh, fruity aroma of the type of grape used, a characteristic that is lost in regular oak-aged brandy. Examples include the Italian grappa and the French marc.

(c) **Fruit brandy:** Fruit brandies are distilled from fruits other than grapes. Apple, plum, peach, cherry, raspberry, blackberry, and apricot are the most commonly used fruits. Fruit brandy is usually clear, 80 to 90 proof, and usually drunk chilled or over ice. Fruit brandy should not be confused with fruit-flavoured brandy, which is grape brandy that has been flavoured with the extract of another fruit. Fruit brandies, except those made from berries, are generally distilled from fruit wines. Berries tend to lack enough sugar to make a wine with sufficient alcohol for proper distillation, and thus are soaked (macerated) in high-proof spirit to extract their flavour and aroma. Calvados, the Apple Brandy from the Normandy region of northwestern France, is probably the best known type of fruit brandy. Apple is pressed into cider, fermented with yeast and double distilled. **Kirschwasser** is a fruit brandy made from cherries. **Slivovitz** is a fruit brandy made from plums.

10.2 MAJOR TYPES OF BRANDIES

10.2.1 Cognac and Armagnac

Cognac is one of the world's greatest drinks and may be defined as a distilled and blended Appellation d'Origine Contrôlée brandy made in the delimited region of Cognac in France situated at northwest of Bordeaux region. The region of Cognac is characterized by chalky soil, wet winters, and sunny summers. The Charente soil in the Cognac region is ideally suited to three kinds of grapes: *Ugni Blanc* (locally also known as Saint Emilion), *Folle Blanc* and *Colombard* by which Cognac is made. The Cognac producing region is divided into six areas or districts.

Did you know?

For a brandy to be called Cognac, it must be made from specified grape varieties grown in the AOC (a majority of Ugni Blanc, with small portions of Colombard and Folle Blanche allowed), double-distilled in copper pot stills and aged at least two years in Limousin or Tronçais oak barrels. Cognac must be at least 40 per cent alcohol.

- **Grande Champagne:** The heart of the Cognac district is located around the town of Segonzac, enclosing 13,766 hectares of clay and compact chalk soil; its grapes are considered best of all and it produces very fine Cognac. It is known as the Premier *Cru du* Cognac.
- **Petite Champagne:** Enclosing 16,171 hectares of clay and a more compact chalky layer of soil surrounds Grande Champagne. The next-best grapes comes from this area.

Fine Champagne: An appellation, but not a geographic area, this means that 50 per cent or more of the product's grapes came from Grande Champagne and the balance came from Petite Champagne.

- **Borderies:** Located around the town of Burie, enclosing 4160 hectares of soil on the plateau above Charente river, they produce Cognac with rich, flowery aromas.
- **Fins Bois:** Encloses 37,000 hectares of soil. It has rich, full, strong aromas with a touch of the maritime climate.
- **Bon Bois:** Encloses 16,000 hectares of less chalky but earthier soil.
- **Bois Ordinaires et Bois Communes (Bois a Terroir):** Encloses 30,000 hectares of soil.

10.2.1.1 Manufacturing Process

Cognac is consumed in the Brandy Balloon glass, also known as Brandy Snifter or Brandy inhaler. This glass has a short steam and a large bowl. The large bowl and narrow top is designed to trap the aroma from bandy. Cup the glass with palm; this will generate heat from the palm and will gently warm the glass. This releases brandy's aroma. A gently warmed Brandy is preferred by many. That is why Brandy is either served warm or at room temperature. Besides warming the brandy through palm, enthusiasts may also use an alcohol burner.

- **Vinification:** Grapes used in making Cognac are:
  - ◊ Ugni Blanc/Saint Emilion
  - ◊ Colombard
  - ◊ Folle Blanc

  The grape harvest usually begins in this region around the 3rd or 4th week in September. The majority of grapes are harvested mechanically, then pressed and fermented to make white wine. However, the process follows three important exceptions: sulphur dioxide addition and chaptalization are forbidden, as is use of a continuous press. The grapes may only be pressed in traditional horizontal plate presses or in pneumatic presses.
- **Distillation:** Distillation starts in November of the year following the year of harvest, as soon as the fermentation is over. The closing date for the process is March 31st. The distillation process is carried out in two chauffes in a particular type of still called **alambic charentais** comprising a characteristically shaped boiler, heated with a naked flame, and topped with an onion-shaped cowl. There is a swan-neck tube, which leads off from this, becoming a condensing coil, and passes through a cooling tank known as 'the pipe'.

  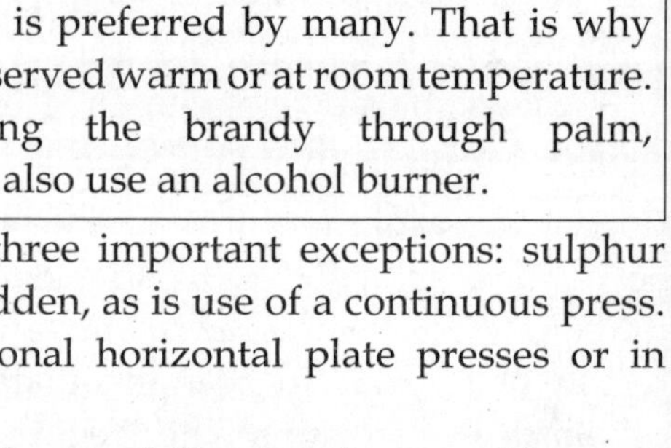

  The charentais still for making cognac

  The *Charentais Still* often has an energy saving **wine reheater**. This optional device, in which heat is provided by the alcohol vapours passing through it, preheats the wine, which is to be distilled in the next cycle.

  The unfiltered wine is put into the boiler and brought to a boil. Alcoholic vapours are given off and collect in the cowl, entering the swan-neck then passing into the coil. On contact with the coolant, they condense, draining away as the liquid known as ***brouillé***. This slightly cloudy liquid, with an alcohol content of 27 to 30% vol., is returned to the boiler for redistillation, called ***la bonne chauffe.***

Subsequently, the feints are separated, to obtain the *heads*, the *heart,* and the *tails*. The ***tails*** are separated when the alcoholmeter registers 60% vol. The heads and tails are redistilled with the next batch of wine or '*brouillé*'.

- **Ageing and maturing:** Cognac is aged in Limousin or Tronçais oak casks (barrels) that hold between 270 and 450 litres. Its aging period is between 2 to 50+ years. Once transferred out of the oak wood casks into bottles, Cognac stops aging. However, during this process about three per cent of Cognac evaporates; this loss is referred to as the angel's share. The quantity and age of the product must be verified by Bureau National Interprofessionnel du Cognac, the Cognac industry's governing body.
- **Blending:** It is guided by the nose of the cellar master, by the legal requirements, and by the market demands. All Cognac sold must be at least 40% volume. Since the eau-de-vie, at the end of distillation, has high alcohol content, the producer must blend its product. Generally distilled water is used as the prime reduction component, as well as a different eau-de-vie. The colour could be adjusted with the use of sugar, caramel and oak chips.

10.2.1.2 Reading a Cognac Label

It is important to note that regulations for Cognac label depend on the export market for which the Cognac is intended. In France for example, a Cognac labelled with 3 stars must be at least one and half years old , while in United States, 3 stars must be at least two years old. Whereas in Britain 3 stars means a Cognac, that is atleast three years old, the star system however, has largely given way to the letter system but nowadays many production houses do not use the 3-star system. Instead, a universal system of letters indicating is used:

- **V.S. (Three Stars):** The average aging period of the cognac is 5-9 years.
- **V.S.O.P.- Very Superior Old Pale - The Reserve:** The average age of Cognac used in the blend is from 12 to 20 years.
- **X.O., Napoleon, V.V.S.O.P. (Very Very Superior Old Pale), Vielle Reserve, Grand Reserve, Royal and Vieux:** The Cognac is even older and therefore contains a very high percentage of Cognac that has been aged for 20, 30, 40 years or more.

Brandy symbols explained

V	Very
S	Special
O	Old
P	Pale
X	Extra
F	Fine
B	Brandy

Very special = 3 years

Very special old pale

Cognac is also labelled by its geographic location such as:

- A Grande Champagne or Fine Grande Champagne cognac is assembled with 100% Grande Champagne spirits.
- A Petite Champagne or Fine Petite Champagne cognac is assembled with 100% Petite Champagne spirits.
- A Fine Champagne Cognac is the result of the grapes from Grande and Petite Champagne wines with a minimum of 50% from Grande Champagne.
- A Borderies or Fine Borderies cognac has 100% of spirits from the Borderies area.
- A Fins Bois or Fine Fins Bois cognac has 100% of spirits from the Fins Bois area.
- A Bons Bois or Fine Bons Bois cognac has 100% of spirits from the Bons Bois area.

10.2.1.3 Cognac Producers/Brands

- Braastad
- Hennessey
- Courvoisier
- Martell
- Rémy Martin
- Hine
- Larsen
- Camus
- Meukow

10.2.2 Armagnac

Armagnac may be defined as a distilled, blended Appellation d'Origine Contrôlée brandy from the Armagnac region of Gascony in southwest France. It lies between the Adour and Garonne rivers in the foothills of the Pyrenees. The summers here are warm and sunny whereas icy winds sweep down from the Pyrenees in winter. Armagnac is made of the same grapes as Cognac and undergoing the same aging in oak barrels, but without double distillation. Armagnac production is overseen by a Bureau National Interprofessionel de l'Armagnac (BNIA). Armagnac is the only true rival to Cognac for recognition as the finest producer of brandy in the world. Along with Cognac and Jerez in Spain, it is one of only three officially demarcated brandy regions in Europe. Its quantity of production is significantly lower than that of the Cognac region; for every six bottles of Armagnac sold around the world there are one hundred bottles of cognac sold. Armagnac has been making brandy for around 200 years longer than Cognac. Armagnac has clayey and sandy soil. Grapes used are same as for Cognac. The Armagnac has three producing areas.

- **Bas-armagnac or black armagnac:** The famous area of production. Sandy and silty soil of this area produces prune flavour and gives an aroma to the brandies made here.
- **Tenarèze:** Around the small town of Condom, it represents about 40% of the vineyards planted for distillation. The soil in this region is chalky and clayey. The brandies produced here have a prune flavour and a hint of violets which reach maturity after a long period of ageing.
- **Haut-armagnac:** Also known as White Armagnac because of the abundance of limestone and its chalky soil. This region produces excellent brandies and table wines.

10.2.2.1 Manufacturing Process

Armagnac is made by distilling white wine mainly from the grapes used for making Cognac *Ugni Blanc, Folle Blanc and Colombard*. The wine is high in acid and low in alcohol and is distilled with *lees*.

(a) **Vinification:** The white wine for distillation is traditionally vinified, with three important exceptions: sulphur dioxide addition and chaptalization are forbidden, as is use of a continuous press. The grapes may only be pressed in traditional horizontal plate presses or in pneumatic presses. Only wines vinified traditionally and containing fine lees can be used to produce Armagnac.

(b) **Distillation:** It starts in November of the year following the year of harvest, as soon as fermentation is over. The closing date for the process is March 31st.

Distillation is carried out:

- either on the estate, often using the travelling distillers which tour the country; or
- by a professional distiller or in a co-operative cellar.

A small quantity is distilled in a double-distillation still, such as in Cognac. But most of the production or the essence of Armagnac (approximately 95%) is distilled in the small continuous still known as **alambic Armagnacais** or the Armagnac still. This type of still has some features of the pot still used in Cognac making. Its distinguishing feature is a short rectifying column above the *chaudiere*.

(c) **Ageing and maturing:** After distillation, the Armagnac is aged much in the same way as Armagnac. The resulting Armagnac which is colourless, is put into 400 litre barrels for ageing. Ageing is done in dark oak casks from the forest of Monlezun. The wood is dark, sappy, contains high tannin but is not very porous, thus less evaporation takes place which is 2-3% per year. On ageing it draws colour from the cask. End product is nutty brown with flecks of gold deepening to black. Armagnac is at its best or prime between 5 and 10 years. After 10 years, it starts deteriorating and becomes like any other Brandy. The barrels are stored in temperature and humidity controlled cellars. Three important phenomena happen during the ageing process:

- The extraction of tannic compounds from the oak barrel.
- The partial evaporation of the spirit and the reduction of alcoholic strength (approximately 0.5% vol. alc. per year).
- The evolution of Armagnacs due to a micro-exchange with oxygen through the oak barrel, which will highlight delicate vanilla, plum, prune, nut, spices, candied fruits aromas.

The spirit remains in new oak barrels for as long as the optimal substances can be extracted from the wood (it is at this stage that Armagnac gains its colour). It is then transferred to older barrels and continues to develop, the alcohol decreasing progressively by evaporation. The spirit takes on fine amber, then mahogany colour.

(d) Blending: When the cellar master considers the ageing satisfactory, he starts blending different Armagnac to make a harmonious finished product. It must reach a minimum of 40% of alcohol.

10.2.2.2 Reading Armagnac Label

The word Armagnac on the bottle of a brandy means that it was made within the delimited Armagnac area and the name of the producing areas (Bas-Armagnac, Tenareze or Haut-Armagnac) means that the brandy is made entirely within that area.

The blending listed below refers to the time the youngest Armagnac used in the blending remained in oak barrels:

- Three stars, Crown, letters and so on or the words Monopole or Selection de Luxe means that the Armagnac is at least 1year old in France and at least 3 years old in United States and in Great Britain.
- V.O., V.S.O.P., and Reserve: Means that Armagnac is at least 4 years old.
- Extra, Napoleon, X.O., and Vielle Reserve: Means that Armagnac is at least 4 years old.

Recent Nomenclature: In 1999, there was a unanimous decision to make labels simpler and clearer:

Armagnac	Less than 6 years in oak barrels
Vielle armagnac	Blending aged more than 6 years in oak barrels
Vintage	Unchanged, with no blending
Blanche d'Armagnac	The distilled spirit, with no ageing

10.2.2.3 Armagnac Producers/Brands

- Delord
- Jean Sempe
- Janneau
- Chabot
- Alain Dauriac
- Sempe
- De Montal
- Darozze

Cognac

Country: France
Areas: Bon Bols, Bols ordinaires, Grande champagne, Borderies and fins bois.
Grapes: White grape varietals, Ugni Blanc.
Flavour: Big, bold and spicy.

Armagnac

Country: France
Areas: Armagnac, Gascony
Grapes: Baco 22A, Colombard, Folle-Blanche and Ugni Blanc.
Flavour: Dry, medicinal and floral.

10.3 OTHER TYPES OF BRANDIES

10.3.1 Spanish Brandies

Brandy de Jerez is made by the Sherry houses centred around the city of Jerez de la Frontera in the southwest corner of Spain. Virtually, all Brandy de Jerez; however, is made from wines produced elsewhere in Spain – primarily from the Airen grape in LaMancha and Extremadura – as the local Sherry grapes are too valuable to divert into Brandy production. Nowadays most of the distilling is likewise done elsewhere in Spain using column stills. It is then shipped to Jerez for aging in used Sherry casks in a solera system similar to that used for Sherry wine. A solera is a series of large casks (called butts), each holding a slightly older spirit than the previous one beside it. When brandy is drawn off (racked) from the last butt (no more than a third of the volume is removed) it is replenished with brandy drawn from the next butt in line all the way down the solera line to the first butt, where newly distilled brandy is added. This system of racking the brandy through a series of casks blends together a variety of vintages (some soleras have over 30 stages) and results in a speeding up of the maturation process. Basic Brandy de Jerez Solera must age for a minimum of six months, Reserva for one year and Gran Reserva for a minimum of three years. In practice, the best Reservas and Gran Reservas are frequently aged for 12 to 15 years. The lush, slightly sweet and fruity notes to be found in Brandy de Jerez come not only from ageing in Sherry casks, but also from the judicious use of fruit-based flavour concentrates and oak essence (boise). Penedès Brandy comes from the Penedès region of Catalonia in the northeast corner of Spain near Barcelona. Modelled after the Cognacs of France and made from a mix of regional grapes and ...lly grown Ugni Blanc of Cognac, it is distilled in pot stills. One of the two local producers (Torres) ages in soleras consisting of butts made from French Limousin oak, whereas the other (Mascaro) ages in the standard non-solera manner, but also in Limousin oak. The resulting Brandy is heartier than Cognac, but leaner and drier than Brandy de Jerez.

10.3.2 Italian Brandies

Italy has a long history of brandy production dating back to at least the 16th century, but unlike Spain or France there are no specific brandy producing regions. Italian brandies are made from regional wine grapes, and most are produced in column stills, although there are now a number of small artisanal producers using pot stills. They are aged in oak for a minimum of one to two years, with six to eight years being the industry average. Italian brandies tend to be on the light and delicate side with a touch of residual sweetness.

10.3.3 Pomace Brandies

Italy produces a substantial amount of Grappa, both of the raw, firewater variety and the more elegant, artisanal efforts that are made from one designated grape type and frequently packaged in hand-blown bottles. Both types of Grappa can be unaged or aged for a few years in old casks that will tame the hard edge of the spirit without imparting much flavour or colour. Marc from France is produced in all of the nation's wine-producing regions, but is mostly consumed locally. Marc de gewürztraminer from Alsace is particularly noteworthy because it retains some of the distinctive perfumed nose and spicy character of the grape. California pomace brandies from the United States are broadly in the Italian style and are usually called Grappas, even when they are made from non-Italian grape varieties. This is also true of the pomace Brandies from Canada.

10.3.4 German Brandies

German monks were distilling Brandy by the 14th century and the German distillers had organized their own guild as early as 1588. Yet almost from the start, German brandy called *weinbrand* has been made from imported wine rather than the more valuable local varieties. Most German brandies are produced in pot stills and must be aged for a minimum of six months in oak. Brandies that have been aged in oak for at least one year are called uralt (meaning older). The best German brandies are smooth, somewhat lighter than Cognac, and finished with a touch of sweetness.

10.3.5 United States Brandies

Brandy production in California dates back to the Spanish missions in the late 18th and early 19th centuries. In the years following the Civil War, brandy became a major industry, with a substantial export trade to Europe by the end of the century. For a time Leland Stanford, founder of Stanford University, was the world's largest brandy producer. Phylloxera and National Prohibition almost shut down the industry in the 1920s. Repeal started things up again, but as with the bourbon industry, the advent of World War II resulted in the brandy producers further marking time. Soon after the end of the war, the industry commissioned the Department of Viticulture and Oenology at the University of California at Davis to develop a prototype "California-style" brandy. It had a clean palate, was lighter in style than most European brandies, and had a flavour profile that made it a good mixer. Starting in the late 1940s, the California brandy producers began to change over to this new style. Contemporary California brandies are made primarily in column stills from table grape varieties such as the Thompson Seedless and Flame Tokay, although a handful of small new-generation Cognac inspired pot distillers, such as Jepson and RMS, are using the classic Ugni Blanc, Colombard, and Folle Blanche grapes. California brandies are aged for two to 12 years in used American oak (both Brandy and Bourbon casks) to limit woodiness in the palate, although the pot distillers also use French oak. Several California distillers, most notably Korbel, utilize the Spanish solera method of maturing their Brandy. California Brandies do not use quality designations such as V.S.O.P. or stars. The more expensive brands usually contain a percentage of older vintages and pot-distilled brandies in the blend.

10.3.6 Latin American Brandies

In Mexico a surprising amount of wine is made, but it is little known outside the country because most of it is used for brandy production. Mexican brandies are made from a mix of grapes, including Thompson Seedless, Palomino, and Ugni Blanc. Both column and pot stills are used in production whereas the solera system is generally used for ageing. Brandy now outsells tequila and rum in Mexico. South American brandies are generally confined to their domestic markets. The best known type is Pisco, a clear, raw brandy from Peru and Chile that is made from Muscat grapes and double-distilled in pot stills. The resulting brandy has a perfumed fragrance and serves as the base for a variety of mixed drinks, including the famous Pisco Sour.

10.4 OTHER BRANDIES FROM AROUND THE WORLD

Greece produces pot-distilled brandies, many of which, such as the well known Metaxa, are flavoured with Muscat wine, anise, or other spices. Winemaking in Israel is a well established tradition dating back thousands of years. But brandy production dates back only to the 1880s when the French Jewish philanthropist Baron Edmond de Rothschild established what has become the modern Israeli wine industry along French lines. Israeli brandy is made in the manner of Cognac from Colombard grapes, with distillation in both pot and column stills and maturation in French Limousin oak casks. In the Caucasus region, along the eastern shore of the Black Sea, the ancient nations of Georgia and Armenia draw on monastic traditions to produce rich, intensely flavoured pot still brandies both from local grapes and from such imported varieties as Muscadine (from France), Sercial and Verdelho (most famously from Madeira). South Africa has been producing brandies since the arrival of the first Dutch settlers in the 17th century, but these early spirits from the Cape Colony earned a reputation for being harsh firewater (witblits, white lightning, was a typical nickname). The introduction of modern production techniques and government regulations in the early 20th century gradually led to an improvement in the quality of local brandies. Modern South African brandies are made from Ugni Blanc, Colombard, Chenin Blanc, and Palomino grapes, produced in both pot and column stills, and aged for a minimum of three years in oak.

10.5 FRUIT BRANDIES

Normandy is one of the few regions in France that does not have a substantial grape wine industry. Instead it is an apple country, with a substantial tradition of producing hard and sweet cider that, in turn, can be distilled into an apple brandy known as Calvados. The local cider apples, which tend to be small and tart, are closer in type to crab apples than to modern table apples. This spirit has its own appellations, with the best brands coming from Appellation Controlee Pays d'Auge near the Atlantic seaport of Deauville, and the rest in 10 adjacent regions that are designated Appellation Reglementee. Most Pays d'Auge and some of the better Appellation Reglementee are produced in pot stills. All varieties of Calvados are aged in oak casks for a minimum of two years. Cognac-style quality and age terms such as V.S.O.P. and Hors d'Age are frequently used on labels, but have no legal meaning. In the United States, Applejack, as apple brandy is called locally, is thought by many to be the first spirit produced in the British colonies. This colonial tradition has continued on the East Coast with the Laird's Distillery in New Jersey (established in 1780 and the oldest distillery in America). Apple brandies that are more like *eau-de-vie* are produced in California and Oregon. The fruit-growing regions of the upper Rhine River are the prime *eau-de-vie* production areas of Europe. The Black Forest region of Bavaria in Germany, and Alsace in France, are known for their Cherry Brandies (Kir in France, Kirschwasser in Germany), raspberry brandies (Framboise and Himbeergeist), and pear brandies (Poire). Similar *eaux-de-vies* are now produced in the United States in California and Oregon. Some plum brandy is also made in these regions (Mirabelle from France is an example), but the best known type of plum brandy is Slivovitz, which is made from the small blue Sljiva plum throughout Eastern Europe and the Balkans.

10.5.1 Calvados

Calvados is an apple brandy from the French région of lower Normandy. Like most French wines, Calvados is governed by appellation contrôlée regulations. The Appellation Calvados contrôlée area includes all of the Calvados, Manche, and Orne départements and parts of Eure, Mayenne, Sarthe, and Eure-et-Loir. The more restrictive Appellation Calvados Pays d'Auge contrôlée area is limited to the east end of the département of Calvados and a few adjoining districts. Calvados should be aged in oak for several years before bottling. The phrases *vieilli en chêne* and *vieilli en fûts de chêne* are indicators of this.

The longer it is aged, the smoother the drink becomes (up to a point; eventually the quality of the drink will fall off). A half-bottle of twenty-year-old Calvados can easily cost the same price as a normal-sized bottle of ten-year-old Calvados. Calvados is the basis of the tradition of le trou Normand, or "the Norman hole". This is a small drink of Calvados taken between courses in a very long meal, supposed to reawaken the appetite.

10.5.2 Cut Brandy

Cut Brandy is liquor made of brandy and hard grain liquor. Sugar is used to soften taste.

Grades Cut brandies are graded by the relative amount of brandy it contains. Grades are represented by stars.

- **0 Star:** almost no brandy at all, only some bringing colour to the grains liquor.
- **1 Star:** one-third (1/3) of brandy.
- **3 Star:** three-fourths (3/4) of brandy.

Did you know?

Neutral Brandy is a brandy produced at more than 170° proof.

10.5.3 Lees Brandy

This brandy distilled from the lees of standard grape, citrus, or other fruit wine, and shall be designated as Lees Brandy qualified by the name of the fruit from which such lees are derived.

10.5.4 Pisco

It is grape brandy manufactured in Peru or Chile in accordance with the laws and regulations of the country of manufacture, governing the manufacture of Pisco for consumption in the country of manufacture.

REVISION QUESTIONS

1. What do you mean by cut brandy?
2. What does V.S.O.P, V.S. and X.O. indicate in a label of cognac?
3. Differentiate between Cognac and Armagnac.
4. What is Grande Champagne and Fine Champagne?
5. What do you mean by eau-de-vie?
6. List down various brand names of Cognac and Armagnac.
7. Name the grape varieties used in making Cognac.

RESEARCH ACTIVITIES

- Collect the label of any two brands of Cognac and list down the information mentioned in the label.
- Collect and paste the pictures of various grapes used in making Cognac and Armagnac in your notebook. Also give the description of the grapes used.

11

Gin and Vodka

11.1 INTRODUCTION TO GIN

After reading this chapter, you will be able to understand:

- Meaning of gin and vodka
- Gin and vodka manufacturing process
- Types of gin
- Common mixers of gin
- Flavoured vodkas
- Brands of gin and vodka

Gin is a spirit made from the distillation of white grain spirit and juniper berries (best juniper in the world comes from the hills of Tuscany) which provide its distinctive flavour. Gin originally called *Genever* (French word for Juniper berries) originated in Holland by a Dutch Doctor, Franciscus Sylvius. The juniper berries, which have medicinal value, were infused in the neutral spirit and the resultant product was *Genever*. The taste of ordinary gin is very dry, and as such it is frequently mixed with other beverages. Gin is also regarded as national drink of England. The Dutch gin reached England in the 16th century. English soldiers preferred fighting after drinking this. They got courage and so they called it 'Dutch Courage', and they took gin back to England. It arrived into England through Plymouth, Portsmouth and Bristol. By 17th century, Gin was produced in England and it overtook the sales of brandy and rum. In the beginning it was sweet (sugar was added), there was no malt wine, only neutral spirit, sugar and botanicals. Gin became very popular in England after the government allowed unlicensed gin production and at the same time imposed a heavy duty on all imported spirits. This created a market for poor quality grains that were unfit for brewing beer, and thousands of gin shops sprang up all over England. By 1740 the production of gin had increased to six times that of beer, and because of its cheapness it became extremely popular with the poor. Of the 15,000 drinking establishments in London, over half were gin shops.

Juniper berries

11.1.1 Manufacturing Process

> **Did you know?**
> The key feature of all gins is their defining flavour. During distillation these powerful flavours are infused into the spirit. Gin's flavours can be infused by passing alcoholic vapours through a 'gin basket' with botanicals in the head of the potstill. Popular flavours include citrus, juniper and spices.

- **Mashing:** Gin can be made from a variety of ingredients. Nowadays, it is made mostly from grains like maize and rye. Other grains and molasses are also used for making it. The grain is pressure-cooked and ground. This mash is cooled and mixed with water. Malts or special enzymes are added to convert the starch into sugar.
- **Fermentation**: Yeast is added, and the wort ferments, much as in whisky making.
- **Distillation:** The wash goes into a continuous still, where it is distilled to a very high proof to extract all flavouring elements. To produce a neutral spirit, the fermented wash is distilled in patent still. Dutch gins are distilled in pot still to retain more body and flavour.
- **Filtration:** Continuous stills have two columns; one for distillation and one for rectification. Stills for neutral spirits have at least one additional column, where the distilled alcohol is further purified. High quality gins are also filtered through tanks containing charcoal.
- **Infusion:** The next stage is the infusion of the botanicals into the neutral spirit. The most common flavourings called botanicals apart from juniper berries, coriander seeds, orris root, angelica, orange peel, cassia bark and calamus roots are some examples of flavouring agents.
- **Ageing:** Gin doesn't require ageing; it can be drunk the day it is made. Some companies age their gin in wood, giving it a pale-gold colour. This type of spirit is known as *golden gin.*
- **Bottling:** Demineralized water may be added to the finished gin to reduce the alcoholic strength. It may also be filtered to remove any visible trace of botanicals.

11.1.2 Types of Gin

- **London dry gin:** It is an unsweetened gin. Having high proof, produced in a patent still and redistilled after the botanicals are added to the base spirit. It is smooth, crystal clear and is very dry. All American and English gins are made in London dry style.
- **Dutch gin:** Also known as *Hollands, Genever or Schiedam*. Dutch *genever* falls into two categories *jonge* (young) and *oude* (old). The difference between the two is manufacturing technique, not age. Former is made by a newer process that produces a lighter spirit whereas latter is made using an older process that produces a heavier spirit with a distinct and intense flavour. Dutch gin is double distilled in pot still, and retains some of the basic flavour of the grains used.

- **Plymouth gin:** It is a pungent, aromatic gin from Plymouth, England. It is famous for its softness and smoothness which comes from using water to dilute the spirit to bottling strength.
- **Old tom:** Pungent and heavily sweetened (2-6% sugar syrup). Used in Tom Collins Cocktail and it is very rarely made nowadays.
- **Sloe gin:** Flavoured with Sloe berries and not with Juniper berries .Traditional way of making it is to infuse gin with the berries. (It is also important to know that Sloe gin is a liqueur).
- **Flavoured gins:** In addition to standard Juniper oil flavouring these gins are flavoured with lemon peel, orange peel, mint and others.

11.1.3 Brand Names

London dry gin

- Bombay Sapphire
- Beefeater
- Tanqueray
- House of Lords
- Gordons Dry Gin
- Gilbeys
- Grenall's
- Silver Wolf
- Seagram

Dutch gin

- Bols
- Damrak

Bombay sapphire: Distilled with the following ten botanicals.

- **Juniper berries:** Give dry, fragrant, herbal aroma.
- **Lemon peel:** Help in lifting the other botanical notes and give citrus flavour.
- **Grains of paradise:** A relative of the ginger plant, these seeds offer a spectrum of exotic flavours from a strong peppery bite to light lavender notes as well as along finish.
- **Cubeb berries:** Provide a dry, hot flavour which lingers on the tongue.
- **Coriander:** Coriander seeds are the key flavour contributor.
- **Orris root:** Provide full floral flavours while distillation.
- **Almonds:** Bitter almonds bring out and tie together all of the flavours of botanicals, delivering the silky smoth feel.
- **Cassia bark:** Gives light warmth and sweetness to gin.
- **Liquorice:** Provides the deep, warm and sweet flavour to gin.
- **Angelica:** Brings a distinct earthy tone to Bombay Sapphire whilst also holding the other nine botanicals in perfect balance.

Botanical names of plants used for making gin

11.1.4 Premium/Famous Brands

- Aristocrat gin
- Beefeater
- Bols
- Bombay Sapphire
- Boodles
- Booth's
- Broker's Premium London Dry Gin
- Burnett's Gin
- Calvert Gin
- Cork Dry Gin Geek Gin
- Gilbey's Gin
- Gordon's
- Seagram's Gin
- Silver Wolf Gin

Serving gin

Gin can be taken:

- Neat/straight
- On the rocks
- Along with mixers (tonic, soda, lemonade, ginger ale, juices, squashes, syrups)
- In cocktails
- It can be used as marinating agent.
- It can be used to flambé.

- Taaka - a London Dry Gin with a secret formula
- Tanqueray

11.1.5 Common Mixers for Gin

- Vermouth - in a Martini
- Tonic water - in Gin and tonic
- Soda water - in Gin Rickey
- Orange juice
- Orange soda
- Lemon juice
- Lime juice
- Grapefruit juice
- Ginger Ale or Ginger Beer
- Cranberry juice
- Milk for 'Gin Milk Punch'
- Kool-Aid
- Fresca

11.1.6 Cocktails With Gin

- Martini
- Tin Roof
- Tom Collins
- Maiden's Prayer
- Salty Dog
- Singapore Sling
- Gimlet
- Gin and Tonic
- Pink Lady
- Pimm's Number 1

11.2 VODKA

Vodka known as Wódka in Poland and Voda in Russia means *'water'*. Vodka however, means *'little water'*, which signifies the love of the Russians towards it. Vodka may be defined as a neutral spirit distilled from any fermented material and treated in a way so as to be without any distinctive colour, aroma, or taste. Vodka, a clear, colourless, tasteless and a neutral spirit originated in a laboratory at St. Petersburg in 1810. Vodka is generally made from agricultural products such as rice, wheat, corn, rye, molasses and sometimes with potato. The main feature of any vodka is the purity after distillation. To reach this purity, vodka must be distilled multiple times as well as filtered to remove any impurities. Vodka exported from Russia, Poland, England, Finland, Sweden and United States are made up of grains.

Factors that differentiate Vodkas

- The grains used or the percentage of grains in the mixture (which directly affect the flavour).
- The equipment used.
- The size of the patent still.
- The quality of distilled water used.

11.2.1 Manufacturing Process

> **Did you know?**
>
> **Neutral spirits** are distilled spirits produced from any material at or above 190° proof, and, if bottled, bottled at not less than 80° proof.

- **Mashing and fermentation:** Vodka can be manufactured from anything that contains starch and sugar including potatoes, molasses, corn. However, the tasteless, neutral style typified by world popular Smirnoff is principally made with corn. Most vodka is made from cereals. Traditionally, rye was most used, and is still the main ingredient of most Polish vodkas. Wheat is the main cereal used in other countries. Other cereals such as oats and barley are also used. It is also believed that vodka is made only from potatoes; potatoes are used, but it is difficult to do so as they have complex starches, which do not get easily converted into fermentable sugar. Potatoes are still sometimes used in Poland and Russia. Other materials such as molasses are also used. Wort is made from the milled, malted grain or potatoes and heated to convert the starch into fermentable sugars. This is then fermented to produce a *wash*.
- **Distillation and rectification:** The wash is then distilled to produce a high-proof spirit (about 95% v/v alcohol). Distillation is generally done in a patent still. However, some full-bodied types of vodka are distilled in a pot still. High purity and alcohol content is obtained by multiple distillations; many types of vodka are triple distilled, some even more.
- **Filtration and purification:** The distillate is then filtered, usually through charcoal and sometimes through river sand. Other coagulants are added to bind impurities so that they can be filtered out more readily.
- **Dilution and bottling:** The spirit after purification is diluted, usually to about 80 proofs (40% alcohol) for bottling. To keep tl[illegible]ality of the product, distilled water can be used, but it is cheaper to deionize and t[illegible] water. This is also considered

to produce better-flavoured vodka. No aging is required, so the vodka can be bottled the same day it is made, however, few varieties are aged in wooden barrels.

- **Addition of flavourings:** Most vodka are sold as plain vodka, some however, are flavoured. There are much traditional Polish and Russian flavoured vodkas, and in recent years, many Western producers have released many flavoured vodkas, typically flavoured with citrus, pepper or fruits.

11.2.2 Service

Vodka is traditionally drunk neat and freezing chilled in a special glass known as Toto glass (30 mL) The style is '*bottoms up and throw the glass back*' in its Eastern European and Scandinavian homeland, its growth in popularity elsewhere owes much to its usefulness in cocktails and other mixed drinks, such as the Bloody Mary or Bloody Caesar, the Screwdriver, the White Russian, Geezer Sauce, the Gimlet, and the Vodka Martini (also known as a Vodkatini), a dry martini made with vodka instead of gin. Whereas Vodka in the West is generally drunk mixed. In Eastern Europe and Scandinavia, however, it is traditionally drunk straight and freezing chilled in a special glass known as Toto glass (30 mL). In Poland, Vodka is sipped neat in a long glass with a bulb at the base and is had chilled.

The elite indulge in this practice and generally have it with sharp tasting appetizers like caviar and smoked salmon. Vodka can be drunk with meals or as an accompaniment to snacks and goes well with strong or greasy food that would overpower a lot of wines.

11.2.3 Brands of Vodka

- **Absolut:** Swedish vodka is made in the Åhus distillery in southern Sweden. Absolut Vodka comes in following flavours.
  - ◊ **Apeach:** Peach flavour launched in 2005.
  - ◊ **Citron:** Lemon flavour launched in 1988. Displays curious sweet/tart interplay of lively citrus. Develops an interesting salty tang in the finish.
  - ◊ **Kurrant:** Blackcurrant flavour launched in 1992.
  - ◊ **Mandarin:** Orange and mandarin flavour mix launched in 1999.
  - ◊ **Pears:** Pear flavour launched in January 2007.
  - ◊ **Pepper:** The first flavoured Absolut Vodka launched in 1986, chilli pepper flavo

- ◊ **Raspberri:** Raspberry flavour launched in 2004.
- ◊ **Ruby red**: Grapefruit flavour launched in June 2006.
- ◊ **Vanilia:** Vanilla flavour launched in 2003 in 750 mL bottle.

- **Danzka:** Danish vodka packaged in an aluminium bottle.
- **Finlandia:** The classic export vodka of Finland.
- **Iceberg:** Canadian vodka made from Ontario sweet corn, and iceberg water.
- **Belvédère:** Polish vodka made by Polmos Zyrardów in Zyrardów.
- **Chopin:** A potato vodka from Poland, with a lingering aftertaste.
- **Polish Pure Spirit:** A very high proof vodka (being sold at 160 proof).
- **Wyborowa:** This 100% rye vodka is the biggest selling Polish vodka.
- **Smirnoff:** The most popular vodka in the world.

Did you know?

Black Vodka - Blavod

Black Vodka is a type of vodka made by using black catechu as a colouring agent. Catechu is an extract from the Acacia shrub, which is distilled by boiling the wood in water and evaporating the resultant brew. Blavod from U.K. is a famous and premium black vodka brand popular during Halloween.

- **Stolichnaya:** The most popular Russian export vodka.
- **Grey Goose Vodka:** The most famous produce of France
- **Vor :** Russia
- **Wodka Gorbatschow** : Germany
- **Evolution Vodka** : Poland

Flavoured Vodkas ***(Many Polish and Russian Vodkas are flavoured by the addition of herbs and grasses)***

- **Limmonaya:** Stolichnaya flavoured with lemon.
- **Okhotnichya:** Popular vodka flavoured with various herbs and heather honey, also known as 'Hunter's Vodka'.
- **Pertsovka:** Russian pepper vodka. Made with black and red pepper pods and cubeb berries, it is a traditional Russian antidote to the cold.
- **Wisniówka cherry vodka:** A deep cherry-red, dessert vodka from Poland.
- **Zubrówka:** The famous bison grass flavoured vodka from Poland (a blade of the grass is included in the bottle). The vodka is slightly yellow and aromatic.
- **Starka:** This in Russian means 'old'. After production it is matured in wine soaked oak casks for 10 years, which imparts to it an amber colour with a wine flavour. It is also known as the 'Brandy Lover's Vodka'.
- **Yubileyneya osobaya:** Very popular vodka flavoured with brandy, honey, etc. It is also known as 'Jubilee Vodka'.

Some flavoured vodkas

REVISION QUESTIONS

1. What is the purpose of Juniper berries in the manufacturing of gin?
2. Differentiate between neutral vodka and flavoured vodka.
3. List and five brands of dry gin and flavoured vodka.

RESEARCH ACTIVITIES

- Search the Internet and find out the ingredients used in making the Bombay Sapphire Gin along with their purpose and paste their pictures in your note book.
- Visit any two liquor shops nearby and find out the available brands of flavoured vodka along with their flavours.

12

Liqueurs

12.1 INTRODUCTION

After reading this chapter, you will be able to understand:

- Meaning of liqueurs
- Differentiate between liqueur and cordial
- Types of liqueur
- Manufacturing of liqueur
- Differentiate between proprietary liqueur and generic liqueur

Liqueur should not be confused with the term liquor which means a wide range of alcoholic spirits. Liqueur is a flavoured and sweetened alcoholic beverage made by the method of infusion, distillation or sometimes flavourings are just soaked or macerated in an alcohol base. Various botanicals such as berries, fruits, herbs, nuts, honey and sometimes cream are used to flavour the liqueurs. In short, liqueurs are flavoured sweetened spirits which are characterized by their flavourings and not base spirit. It is very important to distinguish between the spirits and liqueurs to understand what contributes a liqueur. For example, Kirsch is a spirit but Cherry brandy is a liqueur. The distinction lies in the fact that spirit is not sweetened but liqueurs is. Liqueurs contain at least 2.5% sugar by volume which differentiates them from flavoured spirits. Liqueurs containing from 2.5 to 10% sugar fall under dry range whereas most of the liqueurs contain up to 35 or 45% sweeteners. Liqueurs are not allowed to age for a long time, however they may have resting periods so that liqueurs may obtain the flavour. Liqueurs with large amount of sugar are called crème liqueurs as word crème indicates a liqueur with base flavour and ingredient the same as its name like crème de cassis. The French often call liqueurs digestives because they are usually served after a meal as an aid to digestion. Historically, liqueurs were thought of as after-dinner drinks and nightcaps, but as cocktail culture is shifting and growing, they're showing up more and more in mixed drinks.

- Liqueurs with *large amount of sugar are called creme liqueurs*, due to the creamy consistency.
- Cremes indicates a liqueur with base flavour and ingredient the same as its name. Example: *Créme de casis* is based on black currants.
- Liqueurs with cream are called cream liqueurs. They combine alcohol and diary cream. Example: Bailey's Irish Cream.

12.2 HISTORY OF LIQUEURS

> **Did you know?**
> **Digestifs**
>
> As aperitif is a before meal drink so as digestifs is a *after meal drink.* It can be sweet, dry or bitter flavour and served at the end of the meal as they aids in disestion. Digestifs are generally taken straight Following can be served as digestifs :
>
> - Grappa
> - Brandy and Cognac
> - Cordials and liqueurs
> - Bitter digestifs like Amari
> - Ouzo
> - Schnapps

Charles Schumann (1995) in his famous book *American Bar: Artistry of Mixing Drinks,* defines liqueurs as, "Sweetened liqueurs that are flavoured and scented by the addition of spices, herbs, flowers and so on". Nowadays, liqueurs are also flavoured with ingredients like fruits, roots, plants, barks, and sometimes cream. The word liqueur derives from the Latin word *liquifacere* which means 'to dissolve' or 'melt' referring to the dissolving of flavourings. Liqueurs should contain at least 2.5% sugar by volume but most liqueurs contain 35-45% sugar. In some parts of the world, liqueurs and cordials are considered same, however there is a difference between the two as cordials are generally prepared with fruit pulp or juices. Egyptians were the first to start the production of liqueurs. The first documented liqueur used caraway seeds, to produce the world famous Kummel, which was distilled first in 1575 by Lucas Bols of Amsterdam, Holland. Some liqueurs are centuries old, many have monastic connections and in medieval times it was a common practice for monks tending those suffering from colds and fever to make their medicine from a base spirit and an infusion of herbs and spirits. Benedictine liqueur was developed by monks for curing and treating malaria. By the fifteenth century, liqueur making had progressed into the public domain and specialist liqueur elaborations were in production through Italy and France. Major liqueur producing countries are Italy, France, Holland, Hungary, Germany, Japan, England, Russia, Ireland, United States and Denmark. Liqueurs also have a lower alcohol content than spirits ranging from 15% - 30% by volume but some liqueurs do have higher alcohol content as much as 55% by volume. At one time, certain liqueurs were considered for their medicinal purposes and most of their ingredients were chosen for their healing properties. In modern world, liqueurs are drunk as a necessity rather than a medicine and used as a prime ingredient while making cocktails or can be used as digestives.

12.3 COMPONENTS OF LIQUEUR

To be labelled as a liqueur it should include three components: First one is the base which is spirit and sometimes wines, secondly it must be flavoured, and third it must be sweetened. As mentioned, mostly liqueurs have three elements which can be divided as:

- The spirit (or occasionally wine) base
- The flavouring agent
- The sweetener

1. **The base:** Most liqueurs have a neutral or grain spirit base, but some use brandy (even Cognac), whisky or rum as a base spirit. It provides an essential element in their character. Example: Grand Marnier has a base of cognac and Irish Mist is based on Irish whisky.
2. **Flavouring agents:** Liqueurs have complex mixtures of flavours although sometimes one flavour predominates. Some of the common flavours are described below.

   Herbs and spices: It may include *barks, flowers, roots and seeds.* They specially dominate the flavourings.

   Fruits and their peels and stones: Many liqueurs include small quantities of fruits or fruit peels in their complex mixtures. Some of the finest are: flavoured dried lime, lemon and orange peels.

   Nuts: Walnut, almonds and many more.
3. **Sweetener:** Sweetening agents or sweeteners were originally referred to as 'lacing' agents which described the process of threading or weaving the sweetener into liqueur. This was always done after blending. Sugar syrup is used, but sometimes honey is used as a sweetener. Example: *Drambuie and Irish Mist* use honey to provide sweetness. Sometimes eggs and cream are also used as other ingredients.

12.4 TYPES OF PRODUCTION

Liqueurs can be produced by various methods such as infusion, percolation, distillation or by maceration where flavouring agents are soaked in the base spirits. All the methods are described below.

1. **Infusion:** In the infusion method chopped fruits, herbs and spices are simply added to cold water and kept for up to one year. When the water absorbs the colour and flavour, it is then filtered and kept for further use.
2. **Maceration:** In this method, the flavouring agents are immersed in the alcohol till the time spirit absorbs the flavours and characteristics. This may take as long as a year and is used for those flavouring agents which may lose their flavours upon heating. Resulting product is known as *tincture* and is used during liqueur production.
3. **Percolation:** This method is somewhat like *brewing coffee.* The spirit is pumped up over the flavourings and allowed to percolate through it carrying down, i.e., extracting, the aroma and flavours. The pumping and percolation is repeated continuously for weeks or months. The percolate is then sweetened with sugar syrup and filtered.
4. **Distilled with water:** This method is used for delicate fruits, flowers and herbs. They are soaked in water and distilled slowly in a pot still. The colourless water is then sent for blending.
5. **Distilled with alcohol:** The flavouring agents are soaked for several hours and then distilled slowly in a pot still to achieve a colourless flavoured spirit.

6. **Percolation and blending:** After collecting 'coloured or flavoured' and 'water' they are blended together with sugar syrups, honey, vegetable dyes and alcohol to achieve the desirable character.

12.5 TYPES OF LIQUEUR

Liqueurs can be generally classified as fruit flavour, botanical mixture flavour and cream base. Fruit flavour liqueur as the name suggests are flavoured with various types of fruits such as apricot, cheery, orange, raspberry and strawberry to name a few. Botanical mixture flavour liqueurs can be flavoured with herbs, spices, seeds, nuts or flower or sometimes mixture of these can be also used to flavour a liqueur on the other hand, cream base liqueurs are flavoured with dairy cream. For example, Bailey's Irish Cream.

12.5.1 Proprietary Liqueurs

Proprietary liqueurs are expensive. Imported liqueurs have distinctive recipe, brand name and bottle shape.

Table 12.1: Some widely used proprietary liqueurs

Name	Origin	Name	Origin
Cointreau	France	Drambuie	Scotland
Benedictine	France	Galliano	Italy
Bailey's Irish Cream	Ireland	Grand Marnier	France
Kahlua	Mexico	Tia Maria	Jamaica
Malibu	West Indies	Miodri	Japan
Pernod	France	Pimm's No. 1	England
Mandarine Napolean	France	Frangelico	Italy

12.5.2 Generic Liqueurs

Generic liqueurs are cheaper liqueurs without a protected name, recipe or bottle shape. They are cheaper than proprietary liqueurs. For example, while preparing Margarita an expensive liqueur, Cointreau is used as a substitute to a generic liqueur, Triple sec as both have a orange flavour but latter is much cheaper.

Table 12.2: Some widely used generic liqueurs

Name	Flavour	Name	Flavour
Crème de cacao	Chocolate	Creme de menthe	Peppermint
Blue Curacao	Orange	Triple Sec	Orange
Cherry Brandy	Cherry	Banana liqueur	Banana
Mango liqueur	Mango	Creme de cassis	Black currant
Sambuca	Licorice	Amaretto	Almond
Sloe gin	Sloe berrries	Melon liqueur	Melon

Table 12.3: Substitutes for proprietary and generic liqueurs

Proprietary	Generic
Cointreau	Triple Sec
Midori	Melon Liqueur
Malibu	Coconut Liqueur
Kahlua	Crème de cafe
Lena	Banana Liqueur
Tia Maria	Crème de Cacao

Table 12.4: World famous liqueurs

S. No.	Name	Flavouring	Base	Colour	Alc%	Origin
1.	Amaretto	Almond, Apricot	Brandy	Russet	28	Italy
2.	Aurum	Orange	Brandy	Golden	40	Italy
3.	Bailey's Irish Cream	Cream	Irish Whisky	Beige	17	Ireland
4.	Benedictine	Herbs	Brandy	Dark amber	40	France
5.	Chartreuse	Herbs	Brandy	Green, Yellow	55, 40	France
6.	Cointreau	Orange	Brandy	Clear	40	France
7.	Crème de banane	Bananas	Brandy	Yellow	30	France
8.	Crème de Cacao	Cocoa, Vanilla	Brandy	Dark Brown, Clear	27	France
9.	Crème De Cassis	Black currant	Brandy	Red-brown	30	France
10.	Crème de Menthe	Mint	Brandy	Green, Clear	30	France
11.	Curacao	Orange	Rum	Clear, Red, Yellow, Green, Blue	25-35	Dutch
12.	Drambuie	Honey, Herbs	Scotch	Amber	35	Scotland
13.	Fraise de bois	Strawberry	Brandy	Red	30	France
14.	Frangelico	Light hazelnut	Alcohol	Clear Pale Gold	20	Italy
15.	Framboise	Raspberry	Brandy	Red	30	France
16.	Galliano	Vanilla, Liquorice, Anise	Neutral Spirit	Yellow	35	Italy
17.	Glayva	Heather honey, Oranges	Scotch	Amber	35	Scotland
18.	Goldwasser	Aniseed, caraway, gold	Neutral spirit	Clear with gold specks	40	Poland

19.	Grand Mariner	Orange	Cognac	Amber	40	France
20.	Irish Mist	Honey, Herbs	Irish Whisky	Amber	35	Ireland
21.	Kahlua	Coffee	Neutral Spirit	Dark brown	26.5	Mexico
22.	Kummel	Caraway seeds	Neutral spirit	Clear	39	Germany
23.	Malibu	Coconut	White rum	Clear	24	West Indies
24.	Mandarine Napoléon	Tangerine	Cognac	Amber	38	France
25.	Maraschino	Cherry	Neutral Spirit	Clear	30	Italy
26.	Midori	Melon	Neutral Spirit	Green	23	Japan
27.	Parfait Amour	Fruits, spices, violets	Brandy	Purple	30	Holland
28.	Peach Schnapps	Peaches	Spirit	Clear	23	Scandanavian
29.	Pimm's	Fruit extracts	Gin	Deep red	25	England
30.	Sambuca	Anise	Neutral Spirit	Clear	40	Italy
31.	Southern Comfort	Peaches	Bourbon	Amber	40	U.S.A.
32.	Tia Maria	Coffee	Jamaican rum	Dark Brown	26.5	Jamaica
33.	Van der Hum	Orange, nutmeg	Brandy	Amber	25	South Africa
34.	Wisniowka	Cherry	Vodka	Dark red	40	Poland

12.6 SERVICE OF LIQUEUR

Almost each liqueur are served in its own way. The various ways by which liqueurs can be served in day-to-day life are described below.

- In many restaurants, liqueurs are served from liqueur trolley after sweet course. The trolley displaying assorted liqueurs like Grand Marnier, Chartreuse and others along with glassware is carried to the guest and served from the trolley to the guest.
- Ideally, liqueur should be served in small brandy balloon. Liqueurs can also be served in a liqueur glass known as

cordial/pony glass. This classic stemmed liqueur glass is designed to hold about 1 oz. (30 mL) of liqueur, but nowadays many people refrain from using this glass as it is very difficult to drink from and also looks odd in the hands of most grown-up people.

> **Did you know?**
> In bottle of the Liqueur Benedictine a word **DOM** is mentioned which stands for - ***Deo Optimo* Maximo** meaning, *Praise be to God, Most good, Most great.*

- When consumed with water without ice they can be served neat, on the rocks, or with crushed ice (in a Champagne saucer or cocktail glass) as *Frappe;* as the ice melts it slightly dilutes the drink, reducing its intense flavours and making it a more little approachable.
- Liqueurs can also be served as shooters in a shot glass, as a cocktail ingredient, sipped straight from a stemmed glass after drink, added to coffee, mixed with cream, topped over ice cream or in a champagne flute.
- Liqueurs are also used as flavouring agents in cakes and as a prime ingredient in cocktails.

Always keep liqueur bottles in a dark cool cupboard. Most should last three years if unopened. Once opened oxidation speeds up and spoils the drink, therefore it is suggested to consume the bottle within six months except cream liqueurs as they can be used within eight months if refrigerated after opening.

12.7 FAMOUS LIQUEUR DRINKS

- **Specialty coffee:** Liqueurs have always been a popular choice to prepare specialty coffees like Irish Coffee (made with Irish cream) and Caffe Corretto (made with Sambuca).
- **Side car:** A famous classic cocktail made with brandy and orange liqueur.
- **White Russian:** This cocktail evolved from the Black Russian (a mix of vodka and coffee liqueur) with the addition of cream.
- **Harvey wallbanger:** A classical cocktail made with orange liqueur and herbaceous-vanilla Galliano mixed with vodka.
- **Pousse café:** Liqueurs are also great for layered drinks, known as pousse cafés, because they vary in density. When building a layered cocktail, always pour the heaviest ingredient first, which contains the most sugar and least alcohol. The last ingredient should be the lightest.

REVISION QUESTIONS

1. Name any three liqueurs having the following flavours:
   (a) Coffee
   (b) Herb
   (c) Orange

(d) Anise
(e) Cream
(f) Chocolate

2. List down any three methods of serving liqueur.
3. Differentiate between proprietary liqueur and generic liqueur with examples.
4. Draw a classification chart of liqueurs.
5. Write down the various liqueur compositions and also explain various liqueur making methods.

RESEARCH ACTIVITIES

- List down the various liqueurs along with their flavours, base spirit and country of origin.
- Paste the pictures of any 10 liqueurs in your scrap book. Also paste five creme liqueurs and cream liqueurs.

13

Other Famous Spirits

13.1 INTRODUCTION TO SAKE

After reading this chapter, you will be able to understand:

- Types of spirits

Sake is a naturally fermented alcoholic beverage from Japan that is made from fermented rice. Sake is sometimes called "rice wine" but the brewing process is more akin to beer, converting starch to sugar for the fermentation process. In ancient times the production and serving of sake was entrusted upon experienced brewers called ***'toji',*** who had to be virgins. Sake means "the essence of the spirit of rice".

13.1.1 Sake Production

- **Rice polishing:** Depending upon the type of final product desired, rice is polished by removing approximately 30 to 50 per cent of its original surface.
- **Steaming:** The polished rice is rinsed, soaked and steamed in a *koshiki* (steaming tub). About a quarter of the resulting steamed rice is cooled to about 30ºC (86ºF) and set aside for making **koji** (molded rice). The remainder is cooled to 5ºC (41ºF) and used for the actual sake fermentation process.
- **Making "Koji":** As the basic ingredient required to convert rice starch into glucose, koji is made by sprinkling fungi spores (***Aspergillus oryzae***) over steamed rice in a special room (koji room) where high temperature and humidity level complete the process in about 48 hours.
- **Making "Moto":** Koji and yeast are placed into a tank of water and mixed. Steamed rice is then added to make what is known as **moto** (seed mash). During this stage, the yeast multiplies and fermentation begins.
- **Fermentation-"Moroni"**, a mixture of solids and liquid, is created from the fermentation process. The liquid must be separated from the solids by filtration. The remaining solids are called "sake cake" and the remaining liquid is called "sake".

- **Pasteurization:** Before pasteurization the sake is racked, filtered and matured in casks for 90 to 100 days. Sake is generally pasteurized at approximately 65ºC (149ºF) to terminate enzyme activity.
- **Bottling:** After maturing in the ageing tanks, sake is ready to be bottled and shipped to consumers. If kept cool and out of direct sunlight, sake retains its original delicate flavour for approximately two years in an unopened bottle.

13.1.2 Types of Sake

The type and origin of the rice used in sake production determines what the final product will taste like, for e.g., sake from Hiroshima – full bodied and robust, Akita – heady in its bouquet with higher alcoholic content, Kyoto – lighter and driest of all the sakes.

But different sakes could be classified under four major styles:

- **Mirin** – mi = taste, rin = sweet. Mostly used for cooking.
- **Toso** – It is aged in Yoshino wooden casks which gives it a dark colour, is full bodied and has a spicy sweet taste.
- **Nigori** – semi-refined sake.
- **Seishu** – also known as ama – kara – ping (ama = sweet, kara = lightly, ping = delightful effect).

13.1.3 Serving and Storing Sake

The Japanese traditionally serve sake warm between 100°F to 110°F. To serve, warm the sake by placing the bottle into a pot of boiling water to release the bouquet, then decant the sake into small ceramic serving bottles called **'tokkuri'**. It is then poured into porcelain cups or bowls called **'sakazuki'** and **'ochoko'**, which hold a little more than an ounce. These cups are always filled to the brim. Sake can also be served chilled or on the rocks with a twist of lime. Sake should be stored in a cool dark place prior to opening. Unlike wines, it does not improve in the bottle with age and should be kept refrigerated after opening.

Brands: *Gekkeikan, Genji, Ozeki, Hakutsuru, Fuki, Shogun.*

Did you know?

A tokkuri is a sake flask, and it usually comes as part of a sake set with drinking cups. Sake cups come in different varieties – the basic three types are- *sakazuki* (flat saucer-like cup), *ochoko* (small cylindrical cup), and *masu* (wooden box cup). Often, sake set comes with a tokkuri and a set of ochoko shown below.

13.2 SCHNAPPS

Schnapps is a type of distilled beverage and is of two types. The first one is the traditional German kind. In Germany itself, as well as in Austria and the German-speaking part of Switzerland, the spelling Schnapps is virtually unknown and Schnapps, as a purely colloquial term, can refer to any kind of unsweetened distilled beverage. Outside of German-speaking countries, German Schnapps refers to usually clear alcoholic beverages distilled from fermented cereals, roots or fruits, including cherries, apples, pears, peaches, plums and apricots. Often, the base material for making schnapps is the pulp that is a byproduct in juice production. True Schnapps has no sugar or flavouring added. Traditional German Schnapps is similar in flavour and consistency to vodka, with light fruit flavours, depending on the base material. The alcohol content is usually around 40% by volume or 80 proof. The second type of Schnapps is of American origin. These distilled beverages are liqueurs, such as peach schnapps and butterscotch schnapps. They can be the result of differing processes that do not involve direct fermentation. Some of these use a primary alcohol, such as schnapps, vodka or rum, to extract flavours out of fruit. Often, additional ingredients are added, most commonly sugar. The alcohol level of these schnapps may be only half that of the German kind, usually around 20% by volume or 40 proof.

13.3 SLIVOVITZ / SLJIVOVICA / RAKIJA / PRAKIJA / SLIVOVKA

Slivovitz is a distilled beverage made from black plums called Madjarka, which imparts a rich heady scent to the spirit. It is frequently called plum brandy. Slivovitz is primarily produced in Slavic regions of eastern and central Europe notably Bulgaria, Hungary, Germany, Austria and Italy. To make Slivovitz, black plums are crushed along with their stones and fermented very slowly over a period of three months. A double distillation is carried out, and then the new spirit is aged in wooden casks made of Slavonian Oak. Slivovitz is usually bottled at about five years and at 35-40% A.B.V. and it comes in a variety of beautifully shaped bottles like round, flask shaped, tall, thin and so on. This superb brandy lends itself well after a fine meal and good conversation. Slivovitz is commonly drunk at normal tempeature, as a digestif.

13.4 PASTIS

Pastis is an anise-flavoured liqueur and apéritif from France, typically containing 40-45% alcohol by volume, although there exist alcohol-free varieties. When absinthe was banned in France in 1915, the major absinthe producers (then Pernod and Ricard, who have since merged as Pernod Ricard) reformulated their drink without the banned wormwood component, a heavier focus on the aniseed flavour using more star anise, sugar and a lower alcohol content creating pastis, which remains popular in France today. Pastis has changed considerably since its first creation based on market preference. Pastis is normally diluted with water before drinking (generally 5 volumes of water for 1volume of pastis). The resulting decrease in alcohol percentage causes some of the constituents to become insoluble, which changes the liqueur's appearance from dark transparent yellow to milky soft yellow. The drink is consumed cold, with ice, and is considered a refreshment for hot days. Ice cubes can be added after the water to avoid crystallization of the ethanol in the pastis. However, many pastis drinkers refuse to add ice, preferring to drink the beverage with cool spring water. Although it is consumed throughout France, especially in the summer, pastis is generally associated with southeastern France, especially with the city of Marseille.

13.5 OUZO

Ouzo is an anise spirit, produced exclusively in Greece. It is produced by blending alcohols flavoured by means of distillation or maceration using aniseed and possibly fennel seeds and other aromatic seeds, plants and fruits. Ouzo is a colourless spirit which contains a minimum alcoholic strength of 37.5% ABV with a sugar content of 50 grams per litre or less. The label on the bottle of ouzo may bear the word aperitif but not the words like 'from distillation', 'double distilled', or 'redistilled'. Only if the alcohol content of the ouzo is exclusive, the product of distillation is permitted to declare '100% distilled'. Nowadays most of the ouzo are labelled as 100% distilled. When water or ice is added to ouzo, which is clear in colour, it turns cloudy white and reveals an entirely different character. This is because anethole, the essential oil of anise, is soluble in alcohol but not in water. Diluting the spirit, the alcoholic strength decreases and the essential oils become insoluble which causes the spirit to separate creating an emulsion. The addition of water not only changes the colour, but also the aroma, setting it free to flood the senses. This process is called louching, and is also found while preparing absinthe.

13.6 GRAPPA / MARC

Grappa is a fragrant grape-based pomace brandy of between 40% and 60% alcohol by volume of Italian origin. Literally a word for "grape stalk", grappa is made by distilling pomace, grape residue (primarily the skins, but also stems and seeds) leftover from winemaking after pressing. It was originally made to prevent wastage by using leftovers at the end of the wine season. It quickly became commercialized, mass produced, and sold worldwide. The flavour of grappa, like that of wine, depends on the type and quality of the grape used as well the specifics of the distillation process. In Italy, grappa is primarily served as a "digestivo" or after dinner drink as strong tannins present in grappa make it unsuitable for mixing. Its

purpose is to aid in the digestion of the heavy Italian meals. Grappa may also be added to espresso coffee to create a *caffè corretto*. Another variation of this is the "*amazza caffè*" , the espresso is drunk first, followed by a few ounces of grappa served in its own glass. Among the most well-known producers of grappa are *Nonino, Sibona, Nardini* and *Jacopo Poli*. While these grappas are produced in significant quantities and exported, there are many thousands of smaller local and regional grappas, all with distinct character. Most grappa is clear, indicating that it is an un-aged distillate, though some may retain very faint pigments from their original fruit pomace. Lately, aged grappas have become more common, and these take on a yellow, or red-brown hue from the barrels in which they are served.

13.7 RAKI

Raki is a Turkish anise spirit derived from an Arabic word *araql* meaning 'of liquor'. Different regions of Turkey distil the spirit from various fruits including raisins, figs and plums. The pomace (the pulp of pips, skins and stalks) of grapes may also be used. Some producers also use *suma* (concentrated grape distillate) rather than fruit for making raki. Aniseed is also used in raki production process, sometimes at the beginning with the other botanicals (herbs, roots, plants, spices, bark, peels) or at the end. Raki contains 40-60% alcohol by volume and turns cloudy when mixed with water. Raki is drunk traditionally ice cold mixed in equal amounts with water to accompany light foods such as salads and fish.

13.8 ARAK

Also known as Arrack or Arraki. It refers to the strong spirits distilled mainly in Middle East and Asia from fermented fruits, grains, sugarcane, or the sap of coconuts or palm trees. The word itself originated from the Arabic word 'araq', which means "juice" and is applied to a variety of strong spirits made variously from rice, palm, sap, raisins, coconut, molasses, sugarcane and other fruits. Arrack is mainly produced in Sri Lanka and Indonesia. In India, it is distilled from palm trees. It is generally distilled between 37-50% alcohol by volume 70° to 100 ° proof. Arrack is traditionally taken straight or with water. Owing to its rough potency, arrak is not generally served chilled and it is safer to sip it rather than gulp it down in one go. Contemporarily it is also often taken with ginger ale or soda, or as a component of various cocktails. The quality and character of arrack depends upon its ingredients and country of origin.

13.9 EAU DE VIE

Eau De Vie, the French phrase for the Latin *aqua vitae* (water of life) refers to all spirits distilled from fermented fruits, starting with wine based Cognac and Armagnac. Apart from their base ingredients, the main attributes that distinguishes eau de vie from Cognac and Armagnac is that they are colourless because they have not been aged in wood. It is distilled from young fruit and rarely aged in wooden casks, thus preserving the freshness and aroma of the fruit. *The term Eau de vie is reserved for other fruit brandies*. The flavourings includes strawberries, raspberries, pears, plum and many other types of berries. Eau de vie are served chilled and neat. They also blend well with soda but any other mixers or flavourings are avoided as they can dominate the fruit aromas of eau de vie.

13.10 KIRSCH/KIRSCHWASSER/SCHWARZWALDER

Kirsch is a colourless pure distillate, a true brandy or *eau de vie* made from cherries. Kirsch is also known as true cherry spirit but it is included separately as it is seen as distinctive product from the other fruit brandies. Kirsch should not be confused with cherry brandy. For making kirsch, cherries are pressed along with their stones for the initial fermentation. The stones impart a characteristic, slightly bitter note to the spirit. It is aged for a short period of time in large earthenware vats so that it remains colourless. Kirsch is served lightly chilled in small glasses making a refreshing after-dinner alcoholic drink.

13.11 AQUAVIT/AKVAVIT

Aquavit, also known as akevitt, is a Scandinavian distilled beverage of typically about 40% alcohol by volume. Like vodka, it is distilled from potato or grain. It is flavoured with herbs such as caraway seeds, anise, dill, fennel, coriander, and grains of paradise, among others. The recipe differs between the different brands, but typically caraway is the dominating flavour. Aquavit usually has a yellowish hue, but is available in many colours, from clear to light brown depending on how long it has been aged in oak casks. Normally, darker colour suggests higher age or the use of young casks, but this may also come from the use of artificial colour or caramel. Clear akvavits called Taffel akvavits are typically matured in old casks which do not colour the finished product.

13.12 SAMBUCA

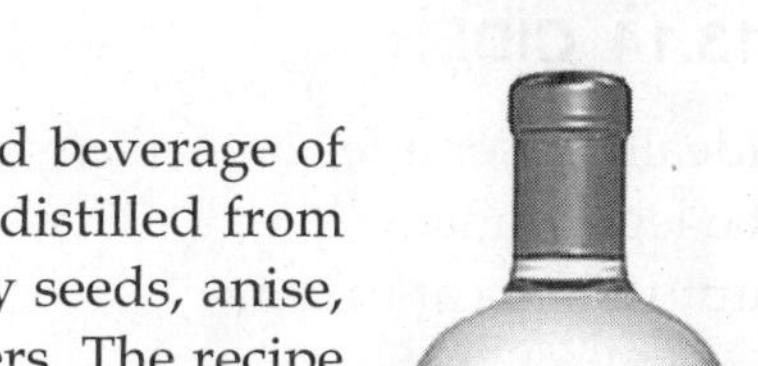

Liquorice

Sambuca is an anise and elderberry flavoured liqueur made in Italy. Using elderberries distinguishes sambuca from other anise based spirits like pastis and ouzo. Sambuca is made by macerating anise, elderberries, liquorice and other herbs and spices in alcoholic spirit. Sambuca is generally clear known as 'white sambuca' but it also comes in deep blue colour known as 'black sambuca' which is little sweeter. French anise liqueur is known as anisette. Sambuca is drunk as an aperitif mixed with water.

Black and white sambuca

Elderberries

13.13 CYNAR

Globe artichoke

Cynar is an Italian liqueur owned by Campari and is being made by using globe artichokes as the primary ingredient. Cynar is characterized by its bitterness and is drunk with ice, soda or lemonade or is used as an ingredient in a cocktail.

13.14 CIDER

Ideally, cider is fermented apple juice but it can also be legally made from a mixture of apple juice and upto 25% pear juice.

> Cider strength may vary between **1.14% and 8.5%.** Beyond this strength, the product becomes ***apple wine.***

- It came to prominence in England after the Norman quest.
- Cider is made in many countries such as France, Spain, Germany, Italy, Switzerland, Canada, New Zealand where it is known as hard cider.

13.14.1 Making of Cider

To make a cider, balance of flavours and characteristics is required.

- Dessert apples give sweetness, cooking apples acid, and cider apples through their tannin content, give bitterness and preserving qualities.
- In England cider apples are cultivated principally in the southwest in Hereford, Devon, Dorset, Sommerset and Worcester.
- Some cider companies also use concentrated apple juice from France and Germany.
- Apples in prime condition are machine gathered in September through October.
- Then they are cleaned and taken to a mill where they are reduced to a pulp known as *pomace*.
- The pulp is wrapped in coarse cloth to form a cheese which is pressed and the resulting juice fermented.

- Fermentation lasts for about one month and the new cider is then put through a centrifuge.
- This device spins and helps to get rid of suspended solid particles which otherwise would cause cloudiness.
- Before reaching its point of sale, the cider may also be fined and filtered to make it brilliant in appearance

13.14.2 Styles of Cider

(a) **Draught cider:** This may be dry and still or slightly sweet and sparkling. The sweetness is added in the form of sugar or concentrated apple juice. The sparkle is induced by adding yeast and sugar to the cask. Draught cider is generally filtered and it will have a hazy appearance as a result. When completely dry, it is often called scrumpy or farmhouse cider.

(b) **Keg cider:** These are pasteurized filtered ciders, bright in appearance. They are usually sweetened and carbonated.

(c) **Bottle cider:** These ciders are pasteurized and filtered and brilliant in appearance. Many are sparkling may be due to carbon dioxide being injected or through an addition of yeast and sugar. This may be added to the cider in a closed tank or in bottle where it goes through a classic second fermentation. This produces what used to be known as **Champagne cider**, the term can no longer be used but an equivalent standard is marketed as ***pomagne.*** Many bottled ciders are sold as **Special** or **Vintage.** These are high quality ciders, the product of one year.

13.15 PERRY

- Perry is the fermented juice of pears.
- It is made in a similar way to cider and the producers are even allowed to use up to 25% apple juice in the blend.
- The most popular styles of perry are carbonated, either through the injection of carbon dioxide or by the inducement of a second fermentation which takes place in a sealed tank.

13.16 ABSINTHE

It is a distilled, highly alcoholic, anise-flavoured spirit derived from herbs including the flowers and leaves of the medicinal plant *Artemisia absinthium,* also called grand *wormwood.* Although it is sometimes incorrectly called a liqueur, absinthe is not bottled with added sugar and is therefore classified as a liquor or spirit.

13.16.1 Absinthe Production

Anise is one of the three main herbs used in the production of absinthe Grande Wormwood. The main herbs used are grande wormwood, florence fennel and green anise, often called the 'holy trinity'. Many other herbs may be used as well, such as hyssop, melissa, star anise and petite wormwood (*Artemisia pontica* or Roman wormwood). Various recipes also include angelica root, sweet flag, dittany leaves, coriander, veronica, juniper, nutmeg, and various mountain herbs. The simple maceration of wormwood in alcohol without distillation produces an extremely bitter drink, due to the presence of the water-soluble absinthe, one of the most bitter substances known. Authentic recipes call for distillation after a primary maceration and before the secondary or 'colouring' maceration. The distillation of wormwood, anise and Florence fennel first produces a colourless distillate that leaves the alembic at around 82% alcohol. It can be left clear, called a Blanche or la Bleue (used for bootleg Swiss absinthe), or the well-known green colour of the beverage can be imparted either artificially or with chlorophyll by steeping petite wormwood, hyssop, and melissa in the liquid. After this process, the resulting product is reduced with water to the desired percentage of alcohol. Over time and exposure to light, the chlorophyll breaks down, changing the colour from emerald green to yellow green to brown. Pre-ban and vintage absinthes are often of a distinct amber colour as a result of this process. Non-traditional varieties are made by cold-mixing herbs, essences or oils in alcohol, with the distillation process omitted. Often called 'oil mixes', these types of absinthe are not necessarily bad, though they are generally considered to be of lower quality than properly distilled absinthe and often carry a distinct bitter aftertaste. Alcohol makes up the majority of the drink and its concentration is extremely high, between 45% and 89.9%, though there is no historical evidence that any commercial vintage absinthe was higher than 74%. Given the high strength and low alcohol solubility of many of the herbal components, absinthe is usually not imbibed 'straight' but consumed after a fairly elaborate preparation ritual. Historically, there were five grades of absinthe – ***ordinaire, demi-fine, fine, supérieure and Suisse*** (which does not denote origin) in order of increasing alcoholic strength and production quality.

13.17 MEAD

Mead or honey wine is an alcoholic beverage produced by the fermentation of water and honey. For producing mead pure, clean water, premium honey and yeast are required. The water is required to reduce the BRIX or sugar content of the honey to a range at which the yeast can effectively ferment it. Mead's alcohol content can vary between mild and strong, and it can range between still and sparkling. Similar to grape wine, mead can be dry, semi-sweet, or sweet. Mead had been accidentally discovered when old tree stumps serving as homes for honeybees were flooded during the rains and the fermentation process took place naturally. Mead can be served cold, at room temperature or warm. These variations change the flavour, mouth feel, and personality of the mead.

REVISION QUESTIONS

1. Give short notes on the following:
   (a) Sake
   (b) Cider
   (c) Grappa
   (d) Slivovitz
   (e) Arak
   (f) Ouzo
   (g) Pastis
   (h) Aquavit
   (i) Kirsch
   (j) Mead
2. Absinthe is not considered a liqueur. Why?
3. Write down the serving procedure of sake.

RESEARCH ACTIVITY

- Search the Internet and find out more about the other spirits mentioned in the chapter.

14

Wine

14.1 INTRODUCTION

After reading this chapter, you will be able to understand:

- Meaning of wine
- Classification of wine
- Grape varieties used in winemaking
- Winemaking process
- Types of wine openers
- Wine cork
- Common flavours of wine
- Decanting a wine
- Serving temperature of wine
- Storage of wine

The term wine indicates an alcoholic beverage made by the fermentation process from the juice of freshly gathered grapes. However, wine may also be made from a variety of fruits which contain water and sugar as nowadays many producers are making wines from fruits like litchi, guava, mango, berries and many more which is better known as fruit wine. When another fruit is used to produce the wine, the name of the fruit used is included on the label, for example, strawberry wine. The practise of drinking wine for pleasure is centuries old-dating at least as far back as Ancient Egypt. Wine is mentioned in documents three thousand years sold as well as in the Bible and in the literature of the Greeks and Roman. Ever since the time man started enjoying his food, he has known the art of making wine to go with it. Art of winemaking was developed by the ancient Greeks and Romans; they were the ones responsible for spreading it to Italy, Spain, Portugal, France, Germany and Central Europe. There are varied types of wine to discover, but new styles are emerging all the time. This is not only due to improvements in technology, but a result of new grape varieties and the emergence of new winemaking regions with their own unique soils and climate. Wine is about far more than production and consumption.

14.2 FACTORS AFFECTING THE QUALITY OF WINE

14.2.1 The Terroir

There are many factors that determine the quality of wine. The same grape grown in same area can make two totally different wines, yet different grapes grown apart can produce wines that are very similar. A term commonly used to describe these factors is '*terroir*'. The term *terroir* means all the natural and climatic elements linked to a particular vineyard. The *terroir* is the primary influence on the character of the wine, though the grape variety and the methods used by the wine producer remain important factors. *Terroir* does not simply refer to the soil and what lies beneath the vines (granite, limestone, etc.) but also includes other local factors such as the slope (hillsides or plain), altitude, exposure, environment and climate. The *terroir* is the combination of all these factors and it gives each wine producing site its unique identity. Among many factors responsible for quality of wine, some of the very important ones are:

- Soil: the best terroirs are those of poor soil on well drained hillsides where excess water is avoided, and the vines enjoy good exposure to sunlight in order for their fruit to ripen effectively. The best wines are often grown in limestone, gravelly, sandy or stony soil and on a hillside rather than on a plain.
- Climate: for a good harvest climate needs a good balance of moisture and heat.
- Grape variety: size, skin and the sugar content
- Method of cultivation: viticulture
- Fermentation process
- Vinification: the process of making wine
- Ageing and maturing process
- Bottling and storage
- Other factors which are loosely termed the 'luck of the year'.

14.2.2 The Grape

Many varieties of grapes are used to produce wine. They are all based on the grafting of the scions of European varieties of the species *Vitis vinifera* on to American rootstocks *Vitis rupestris, Vitis riparia* and *Vitis berlandieri*. Grafting began in the 19th century because the louse Phylloxera attacked the European rootstocks. As the American rootstocks are resistant to *Phylloxera,* European growers found the solution by grafting *Vitis vinifera* onto the roots of wild American vines. Since then, vine stocks have been composed of a graft (the part of the plant that grows above the ground) attached to a rootstock. The former is always a *Vitis vinifera,* while the rootstock is nearly always from another species. It is also important to know that table grapes consumed at home differ from wine grapes.

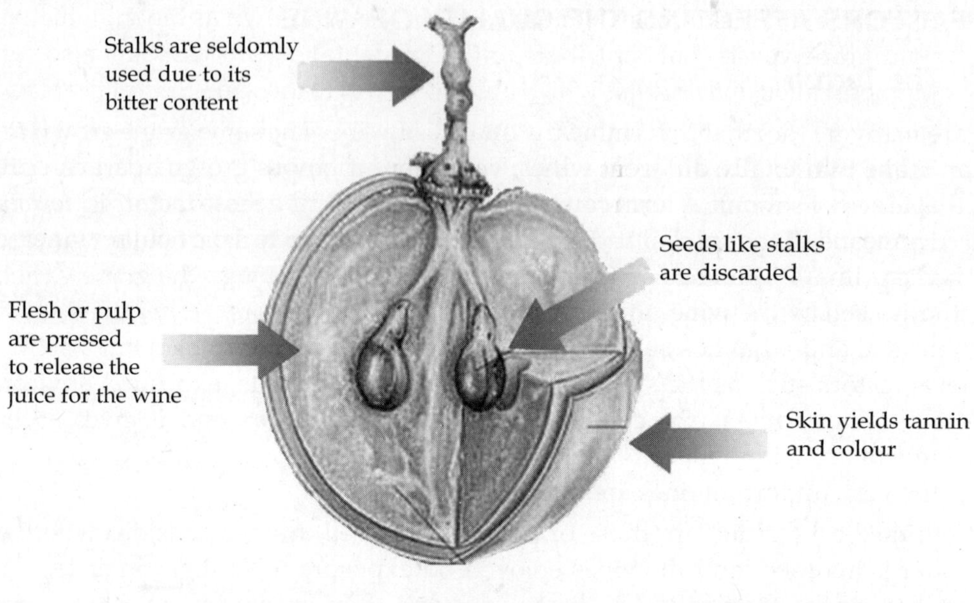

Anatomy of wine grape

Table 14.1: Composition of grape

Wine grape	Table grape
Brix level is 24-26	Brix level is 17-19
Grapes are lean and thin	Grapes are fat and sassy
Grapes are smaller, riddled with seeds	Grapes are larger, seedless with thicker pulp and thinner skins
Note: Brix is the scale to measure percentage of sugar in a liquid.	

The character of a wine – its aroma, taste and structure – is shaped by the grapes from which it is made. The grape variety (or varietals) used are usually given on the label of the bottle of New World Wine but not always on Old World Wines. The grape is made up of stalk, skin, pips and pulp. Smaller the fruit, the more concentrated the flavour, therefore all classic grape varieties have small berries. Grapes are classified as red grape and white grape. The purpose of the following parts of grape is as follows:

Enemies of grape

1. **Phylloxera:** Lives in the root.
2. **Mildew or oidium:** Mildew, odium are diseases that can ruin the vine. It is a fungus, which attacks the root of the plant. The remedial measure is *Bordeaux mixture.*
3. **Mould:** Grey rot.
4. **Grubb of the Cochylis:** Eats the flowers.
5. **Red Spider:** Sucks the sap.
6. **Bad climate:** Frost, hail, rain and storms.

1. **Skin:** The outer skin has a whitish or cloudy coat known as bloom which contains wild grape yeasts that contribute to the fermentation process. Skin also contains a pigment called *anthocyanins* which imparts colour to the wine. Skin of the black grapes provides the colour and tannin in red wine. Skin also adds character to the wine.
2. **Stem/Stalk:** The stalks are usually removed before the grapes are crushed or pressed. Previoulsy the stalks were left on the grapes for red wines, and this increased the tannin content of the wine. The characteristics of the wine will vary according to the variety of grape used and the vinification process.
3. **Pips:** These are not crushed in the vinification as they contain tannic acid, oils and water which can spoil the wine.
4. **Pulp:** The pulp produces the grape juice known as *must* in France and *mosto* in Italy and Spain. The juice provides the water content and the fruit flavours which come from the sugars and acids. Sugar content dictates the alcoholic level and acidity or sweetness in the wine. The pulp supplies the sugar required for the fermentation process.

14.2.2.1 Grape Varieties

Grapes are classified as red grape and white grape. Most of the white wines are produced from *"white grapes"* that can range in colour from green to amber-yellow. On the other hand, red and rose wines are made from *"black grapes"*. White wines can also be made from black grapes after removing the skin. However, red wines cannot be made from white grapes.

Major red grape varieties

Some white grape varieties

Table 14.2: Principal varieties of white and red grapes

White grape	Red grape
Chardonnay (shar-du-NAY): Famous grapes from Alsace region in France produces greatest dry wines in the world.	**Cabernet Sauvignon (cab-er-NAY soh-vee-NYOHn):** Dark red in colour, it has aroma of blackcurrant when young. Wine made from this variety becomes brick red with cedar wood aromas as it develops. High on tannin and often blended with many varieties.
Colombars: Produces thin, acidic wine. Ideal for distillation of Cognac and Armagnac.	**Merlot (mehr-LO):** Produce supple and fruity wines with aromas of blackcurrant and plums.
Chenin blanc: Has good acidity level, thin skin and high sugar content. Good for making sparkling wine.	**Grenache:** Sweet grapes. Makes strong wines with character and not much colour.
Folle blanche: Traditionally used for making Armagnac.	**Gamay:** Wines made are light, rich in primary aromas and have the flavour of ripe red fruit. Has little tannin and is often acidic.
Sauvignon Blanc (SOH-veenyohn-BLAHn): Produces dry and aromatic white wines.	**Cabernet Franc (cab-er-NAY FRAHNK):** Produces wines with fresh fruity aromas with a flavour of ripe red or black fruits.
Gewurztraminer: Makes aromatic and spicy wines; it is a grape from Alsace.	**Petit Verdot (peh-TEET-vehr- DOE):** Produces rich and tannic wines that improve with age.
Muller thurgau: From Germany, makes aromatic wines, low in acidity.	**Pinot Noir (PEA-no Nwahr):** Fairly delicate grape, also used to make Champagne. Makes scented, flavourful and full bodied wines.

Pinot blanc: White variant of Pinot Noir, low in substance and aroma.	**Pinot Meunier:** Produces supple fruity red wines, also used in making Champagne.
Riesling *(REES-ling)*: A classic German variety produces wines with a good balance of acidity and sweetness.	**Zinfandel (ZIN-fan-dell):** An American multipurpose grape variety, rich in sugar and fruity aromas.
Aligoté: Thin skinned grapes, make wines of moderate alcoholic content which are dry and crisp.	**Syrah (sih-RAH):** In Australia known as Shiraz make peppery, structured wines with violent aromas.
Trebbiano: Major grape variety of Italy produces fresh light white wines, often blended with one or more other varieties.	**Nebbiolo:** Also known as Spanna from Italy, produces world famous Barolo and Barbaresco wines.
Se´million: Produces good white wines, sometimes blended with Chardonnay and Sauvignon Blanc.	**Sangiovese:** From Italy; used as a blend in producing Chianti wines.

- **Sparkling wine:** These wines get sparkle or effervescence from carbon dioxide. Cava from Spain, Prosecco and Asti Spumante from Italy are the names of a few sparkling wines. The term Champagne is reserved for the sparkling wines made in Champagne region of France whereas other countries produce similar wines known as sparkling wines.
- **Fortified wines:** A fortified wine is a wine strengthened with the addition of grape spirit brandy. The spirit also preserves the wine for longer periods after the bottle is opened. Fortified wines include sherry, port, madeira, marsala and malaga.
- **Aromatized wines:** These wines are fortified and flavoured with botanicals such as herbs, fruit peels, fruit extracts, quinine. Examples: Vermouth (wormwood), Dubonnet (herbs and quinine), Lillet (herbs, fruit peel and fortified with brandy).

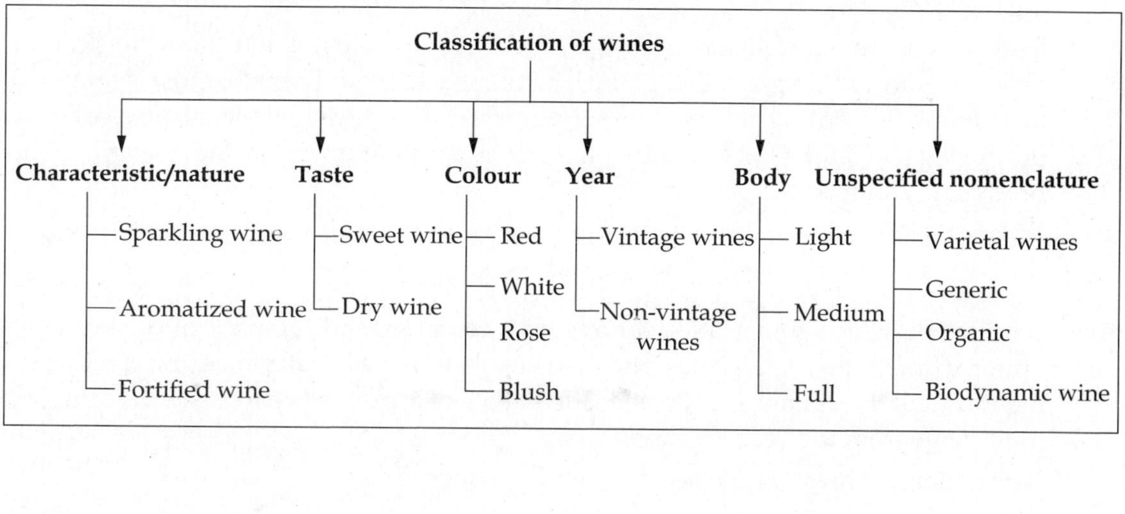

14.3 CLASSIFICATION OF WINES

14.3.1 Characteristics of Wine

14.3.1.1 Nature

Generally, wines are as follows:

- **Natural or still wine:** These are further classified into
  - ◊ **Red:** Being fermented with the grape skins from which the wine gets its colour.
  - ◊ **White:** Usually produced from white grapes and the grape juice is fermented away from the skins.
  - ◊ **Rosé :** The colour is controlled by regulating the duration the grape juice is kept in contact with the skin.

14.3.1.2 Taste

- **Sweet wine:** Has a high sugar content. The sugar may remain in the wine after the fermentation has finished.
- **Dry wine:** These wines are low in sugar. This is usually arrived at by allowing the fermentation to use up the grape sugar (any added sugar) in the fermentation.

14.3.1.3 Colour

- **White wine:** Usually produced from white grapes and the grape juice is fermented away from the skins. White wines can also be made from red grapes after removing the grape skin.
- **Red wines:** Fermented with the grape skins from which the wine gets its colour.
- **Blush wines:** An American invention, blush wine is a pale pink-blue wine made from red grapes. The skins are only in contact with the must for an hour or two during fermentation.
- **Rose wines:** They are made from the black grapes. Must is left with the skin for about one day or till the desired pinkish colour is achieved. Then the must is removed to continue fermenting at a low temperature elsewhere. Rose wines can also be made by mixing red and white wine to the desired colour in many new world wine producing countries.

14.3.1.4 Year

- **Vintage wines:** The term vintage in wine refers to *harvest*. It means the year of the production, which sometimes features on a collar around the neck of the bottle, is optional for both AOC wines and Vin de pays wines, but almost all producers mention it. If the vintage is specified, atleast 85% of the wine, whatever is the category must come from the year indicated.
- **Non-vintage wines:** These are the blended wines.

14.3.1.5 Body

- **Light bodied wines:** Light bodied wine is usually below 13% alcohol by volume.
- **Medium bodied wines:** These are wines which are round, fairly fat with good body, texture, and flavoursome.
- **Full bodied wines:** Wines which are high in alcoholic content that is 13% abv (alcohol by volume) upwards as classed as full bodied wines.

14.3.1.6 Unspecified Nomenclature

- **Varietal wines:** They carry a variety label, that is the label tells you the variety of the grapes from which the wines are made. Common white varietal wines include chardonnay, riesling, sauvignon blanc, and gewurztraminer whereas cabernat sauvignon, pinot noir and shiraz are red varietal wines. Often two or more varieties are blended, for instance traminer-riesling or cabernet shiraz.
- **Generic wines:** These wines are named after the long established European area. Many north American and Australian wines are labelled as Claret, Burgundy, Chablis Sauternes, Graves, Hock and even Champagne. A generic wine should possess the distinctive colour, flavour and aroma of its own.
- **Organic wines:** These are produced by organic farming method. Organic farming refuse to use any conventional chemicals, relying instead on natural treatments or the prevention of diseases through better maintenance of the vineyard. Organic farming concentrates on farming techniques, forbidding any synthetic chemicals, fungicides, pesticides or fertilizers. Organic viticulture is not looking to feed the plant directly, but to ensure soil fertility by maintaining biological activity within it.

Different types of wine

- **Biodynamic wine:** Regarded as a branch of organic farming, biodynamic goes much further than simply excluding the use of artificial chemicals. It uses basic products such as cowdung. Instead of bringing in outside fertilizers and pesticides, biodynamic farmers build soil fertility and manage pests by encouraging biodiversity among crops, livestock and wildlife and by using specially prepared farm-generated outputs like composted animal manures, plants and minerals. These farmers also aim to conserve their farm's resources, especially water and soil. Once the vineyard is certified as biodynamic, its grapes are considered biodynamic, but the finished product—the wine itself—cannot be labelled as biodynamic unless it goes through secondary verification programme for processed agricultural products.

14.4 WINEMAKING PROCESS OR VINIFICATION

Refractrometer

Wine is made through the natural process of fermentation. In this process, sugar is converted into alcohol and carbon dioxide by yeast that is present on the skin of the grape called ***bloom***. Under normal conditions the yeast will go on working until all sugars in the grape is converted into alcohol, or until the alcoholic percentage is about 14-16% of the volume. Left to nature, almost all the wines would be dry. But it is possible to stop fermentation before all the sugar is used up, either by adding alcohol to raise the level up to 15%, or by adding sulphur both of these kill the yeast, so another alternative is to filter the wine. These methods are applied to manufacture ***sweet wines***. There are five basic components or steps to making wine:

1. **Harvesting:** Knowing when to pick the grape is very important and critical for the winemaker. The vintage is made by the weather. Therefore, the decision when to pick depends on the weather, white wines generally need high acidity therefore should be picked early vis a vis black grapes which are generally picked later when they have achieved a balance in colour and sugar content. Before the harvest, wine-makers spend a lot of time in the vineyard sampling the grapes, checking sugar content with **refractometer.** Harvesting can be done manually as well as mechanically. Manual harvest ensures quality of grapes however, is a time consuming and labour-intensive process. On the other hand, mechanical harvest is a fairly quick and inexpensive process however, desired quality of grapes might not be achieved.

Picking of grapes by hand

Picking of grapes by machine

2. **Crushing or destemming:** Crushing is done to break the berries without crushing the seeds. Destemming separates the berries from the stem. After this, the grapes are immediately transferred to the wine press by pumping.

Crushing of grapes

Stem separated by destemmer

3. **Pressing:** During pressing, all the juice is extracted from the grapes. It results in a clear juice without crushing the seeds. If they were crushed, the wine might taste grassy. This process must be done immediately to avoid oxidation. Resulting grape juice is known as 'must'. The *French Vaslin Press, Wilmes or Pneumatic Press* or *Continuous hydraulic* and *Archimedes presses* are used for pressing the wines. Following is to be kept in mind while pressing is carried out:

Pressing of grapes in a pressing machine

- In white wines the grapes are pressed immediately after harvest, and only the juice is used for fermentation. Sufficient yeasts are run off with the juice for fermentation to take place.
- In red wine, the fermentation takes place with the skins still present in the must; this practice is known as *cuvasion*. Skins are removed when sufficient colour and tannins have been extracted.

- In rose wines, skin is kept in contact with juice for a very short time and skin is immediately removed as soon as the desired pinkish colour is achieved.

  Note: Unfermented must contains perhaps 24% sugar content together with malic acid, tartaric acid, cream of tartar, protein, tannin, colouring matter and glycerol. The alcohol formed in the production of wine is ethyl alcohol or ethanol. The alcohol percentage will depend on the sugar content of the must and variety of yeast whereas maceration means contact between the juice known as must and the solids including the skin or film.

  - **For red wines:** The distinctive feature of making red wine is its maceration. The must containing juicy mass of crushed grapes is transferred into fermentation vats that can be thermo-regulated stainless steel tanks or wooden vats. The duration of fermentation, involving maceration and fermentation can range from a few days to three weeks, depending on the style of wine. During this stage the colouring matter, tannins and aromatic compounds contained in the solid parts of the grape (skin and pulp) are dissolved in the juice giving the wines its colour and character.
  - **For white wines and rose wines (clarifying the must and addition of sulphur):** The must after the pressing is cloudy, it contains solids or sedimentary material that can make wine taste bad so it should be removed. To do this the juice may be moved to the centrifugal extractor, which is quick and efficient. The other method is stabilization by cold (at almost 32°F or 0°C) is better as the juice is prevented from getting fermentated while the sediment naturally falls to the bottom of the tank. During this stage, the sulphur dioxide is added to the must to prevent oxidatation and to neutalize the development of any microorganism. Excessive uses of sulphur dioxide can mask all the wine's flavours. Another useful preservative is potassium sorbate.

4. **Fermentation:** Fermentation is the process where yeast consumes the sugar available in grape juice and produces alcohol and carbon dioxide. Yeast is a unicellular microorganism which reacts on sugar favourable temperatures and produces alcohol and carbon dioxide. Apart from yeast naturally present in outer skin of grapes also known as *bloom*, cultured yeast is also used in winemaking. Cultured yeast refers to the yeast made in a laboratory. Yeast named *Saccharomyces ellisoideus* and *Saccharomyces apiculatus* are generally used for winemaking. During fermentation process, heat is also generated so the temperature has to be carefully controlled. Cultured yeasts are also added for fermentation. Fermentation is different for red and white wines. Red wines are fermented with their skins and seeds as these not only pass colour but also tannin and additional

Fermentation process

ingredients that provide flavour whereas in white wines the grapes are first pressed to extract the juice which is then fermented on its own in vats or barrels.

- **Fermentation for white wines:** White wines are fermented slowly for one to four weeks. Fermentation can be stimulated by an injection of cultured yeast or by adding fermenting juice from another vat. The temperature required for yeast in white winemaking process is 15°C and 20°C to impart delicacy and fragrance. The temperature determines the extent of fermentation and hence the style of wine desired. The lower the temperature, the more time the wines will take to ferment resulting in higher quality wines. The higher the temperature the quicker the fermentation but also often lower quality wines. Fermentation vats can be made of stainless steel tanks or wooden vats. Also note that while making white wines, winemakers prevent the malolactic fermentation.
- **Fermentation for red wines:** The duration of fermentation involving maceration and fermentation can range from a few days to three weeks depending on the style of wine which takes place in a wooden vat or thermo-regulated stainless steel container. Red wines are fermented more quickly and at a higher temperature between 25°C and 30°C which helps to extract colour and body for the wine.

Maturing wines in barrel

When the winemaker considers the optimal maceration time complete whether alcoholic fermentation is complete or not the wine is *run off.* A valve is opened at the bottom of the tank to flush out the liquid permanently separating it from solids. The juice that is run off is of the finest and high quality and is known as *free run wine* or *vin de goutte.* Afterwards, the grape skins and lees (solid still containing liquid) are pressed to extract any remaining juice known as *press wine* or *vin de presse*. These are matured separately, classically in oak casks where they undergo a malolactic fermentation. During malolactic fermentation (MLF) in red wine, the malic acid is converted into lactic acid providing a texture and buttery flavour to the wines and does not affect the alcohol content of wine. A bacteria named *Oenoccocus oeni* is responsible for malolactic fermentation and not the yeast.

5. **Maturation:** When the must has been transformed into wine by fermentation, maturation begins and comes to an end at the point of bottling. Maturation refines and develops the qualities of wine. Maturation is done to clarify the wines and to allow the wines to develop and acquire flavours. Maturation can take place in large scale in tanks but majority of the winemakers use oak barrels for ageing. After the wine has been made it still has made many tiny particles of grape material, yeast and bacteria suspended in the liquid known as lees. These lees can result in second fermentation on contact with residual sugars which are generally removed. For

clarifying the wine racking, fining and filtering are the most common methods used. Some white wines are matured *sur lie* – on the lees which means they are not racked or filtered before bottling. This gives a greater depth of flavour to the white wines and an enhanced freshness and liveliness.

Winemakers typically check the maturing red wine barrels at regular intervals, and top them up as some of the wine evaporates during the maturation process.

- **Racking:** It is the most common method complemented by filtration before filtering. Racking means separating the wines from the lees by carefully pouring it from one container to another. Racking eliminates the lees that had settled naturally at the bottom of the tank or barrel and optionally oxygenates and softens the wine. It also releases residual carbon dioxide produced during fermentation. When the wine must be stored in tanks or barrels for a long time, racking is done two to four times per year. But this frequency may greatly increase when the maturation period is short or after fining.

Plate filters for wine

- **Fining:** This method is often used before bottling, whether or not racking has already taken place. The fining agent when comes in contact with wine forms sediment by binding with any miscroscopic impurities and settles down and is later on removed by racking. The best agent for red wines is beaten egg white (six eggs per barrel) while for white wines casein is the best. After fining, red tannin wines lose some of the roughness caused by tannins and gain softness and finesse.

Bottling of wine

- **Filtering:** This sometimes complements the racking carried out during maturation, but more often takes place before bottling. The plate or membrane filters used here have smaller or larger pores. When they are tiny pores, the wine not only has the lees removed, but is also sterilized because bacteria too are unable to pass through the very tiny holes.

Bordeaux **Burgundy** **Flute**

6. **Bottling:** Wines are also sometimes blended before bottling which helps in harmonious combination of wines sourced to offer different characteristics. Dark colour bottles are used so that sunlight does not affect the wine. Wine producers also use bottles of various shapes and sizes to identify different types of wines. The three most common shapes of wine bottles are Bordeaux, Burgundy and Flute.

Did you know?

The most common preservative used in winemaking is sulphur dioxide. Another useful preservative is potassium sorbate.

14.4.1 Aspects of Winemaking

14.4.1.1 *Sparkling Wine*

Sparkling wines are those wines which contain carbon dioxide. There are four methods to add sparkle to the wine:

Champagne method

- Charmat method (Methode cuve close)
- Transfer method (Methode transvasement)
- Carbonation method (Methode gazifie)

14.4.1.2 *Alcohol Free Wines*

These wines contain a maximum of 0.05 alcohol by volume. De-alcoholised wines conatins a maximum of 0.5% alcohol by volume. Low alcohol wines contain a maximum of 1.2% alcohol by volume. Reduced alcohol wines contain a maximum of 5.5% alcohol by volume. These wines are made by normal method and later on the alcohol is removed by distillation process or reverse osmosis method.

14.4.1.3 *Aerating the Wines*

Red wines along with some white wines need aeration when starting to mature This is provided either by racking, by slow diffusion of oxygen through the seams of the barrel, but the amount of oxygen should remain minimal. Except in rare cases such as wines fortified with alcohol , the producer always avoids direct and prolonged contact between wine and air. Oxygen promotes the growth of bacteria such as acetobeter, which can turn

Did you know?

Buttery Taste in Wine - Malolactic fermentation

While sipping a wine, have you ever wondered why some wines have a creamy or buttery taste giving a rich texture to the wine? This is due to the process of malolactic fermentation in a winemaking process that gives still wines both red and white wines a richer and creamier texture. It is also very surprising to know that malolactic fermentation is not technically a fermentation at all because it does not use yeast at all, instead a bacteria provides a wine with buttery and creamy aroma by releasing an impact compound called diacetyl. Malolactic fermentation, also called malo or MLF, is a process of the conversion of malic acid in the wine to lactic acid (the same acid found in milk) naturally or added bacteria where tart is softer and creamier. Malic acid in wine is converted to lactic acid thus reducing and softening the acidity of the wine.

A special kind of bacteria called *Oenoccocus oeni* (along with a few other *Lactobacillus* strains) eat the malic acid in wine and poop out lactic acid. Malic acid has a sharper acidity like unripe apples, whereas the acidity of lactic acid is softer (more like milk). During the process of malolactic fermentation aromas of primary (fruit) get reduced as a result wine gets a creamy, almost oil-like texture on the middle of your tongue, that adds a marvellous, velvety texture to the wine.

Genearally, all red wines and some white wines such as Chardonnay undergo malolactic fermentation. One way to recognize MLF in a wine is to note if it has a creamy, oily mid-palate texture. Another easy way to identify the malo is to see if the wine was aged in oak, since MLF typically occurs while wines age in oak barrels.

the alcohol into vinegar. It also alters the colour and taste of wine to avoid this sulphur is added.

14.4.1.4 Role of Barrel Ageing

Oak barrel

Maturation in oak barrel is common for wines that need to be aged for a long period. The word barrel is a generic term for all wooden containers used to house wine. Oak of the Limousin forest of France is considered best for ageing of wines however oak supplies also come from Poland, Slovenia and Russia. Oak is porous, light and easy to handle. New wooden barrel provides the wine with the most aroma and flavour. When used for the first time, tannins and other substances are transferred to the wine and tartar crystals, even a portion of wine are deposited in the wood. The thicker the tartaric layer, the less effect the wood will have. Although some barrels are made of chestnut, oak is universally appreciated for its physical properties and its flavour contributions. Oak provides various flavours to the wines, the most significant being vanilla. In addition to the notes of vanilla various aromas such as pepper, coconut, smoke is also imparted by the oak in the wine. The oak also provides the wine with tannin apart from those transmitted by the skin and stalk of the grapes. It is also possible to obtain the oak-like flavours with oak chips placed into stainless steel tanks. Most of the new world wine areas like Chile and New Zealand are using this technique.

14.4.1.5 Points to be Considered While Making Wine

- During fermentation process, sulphur dioxide is added to the must to kill any harmful wild yeast and any bacterial contamination.
- Unfermented must contains approx. 24% grape sugar together with various acids, cream of tartar,

Did you know?

How does wine get so many flavour?

Grapes are an incredibly impressionable and delicate fruit. Each decision the winemaker makes throughout the process, from how and where the grapes are grown, to what occurs to them after they are juiced, impact how the wine tastes and smells at the end. Good farming equals great wine, and it is at this stage where the grapes also first come in contact with elements that can impact the wine's ultimate characteristics. Many insects are important to the health of grapes, but bees play an important role. As the grapes grow in a vineyard surrounded by plants such as wild herbs, flowers and grasses, the bees fly around the vineyard distributing pollen, and as the grapes ripen they absorb the subtle flavour characteristics from these plants.

Elements such as the air also have an impact on the flavour of the grapes as they grow. In many regions of the world, such as Spain and Greece, much of the white wine is grown on cliffs that overlook the sea. As the waves crash into the rocks and spray salt water into the air, the saline air is absorbed by the grapes as they ripen, adding a delicious mineralogy to the grapes that can taste and smell like a fresh sea breeze.

Ageing wine in oak barrels also imparts a distinctive flavour and characteristics to the wine.

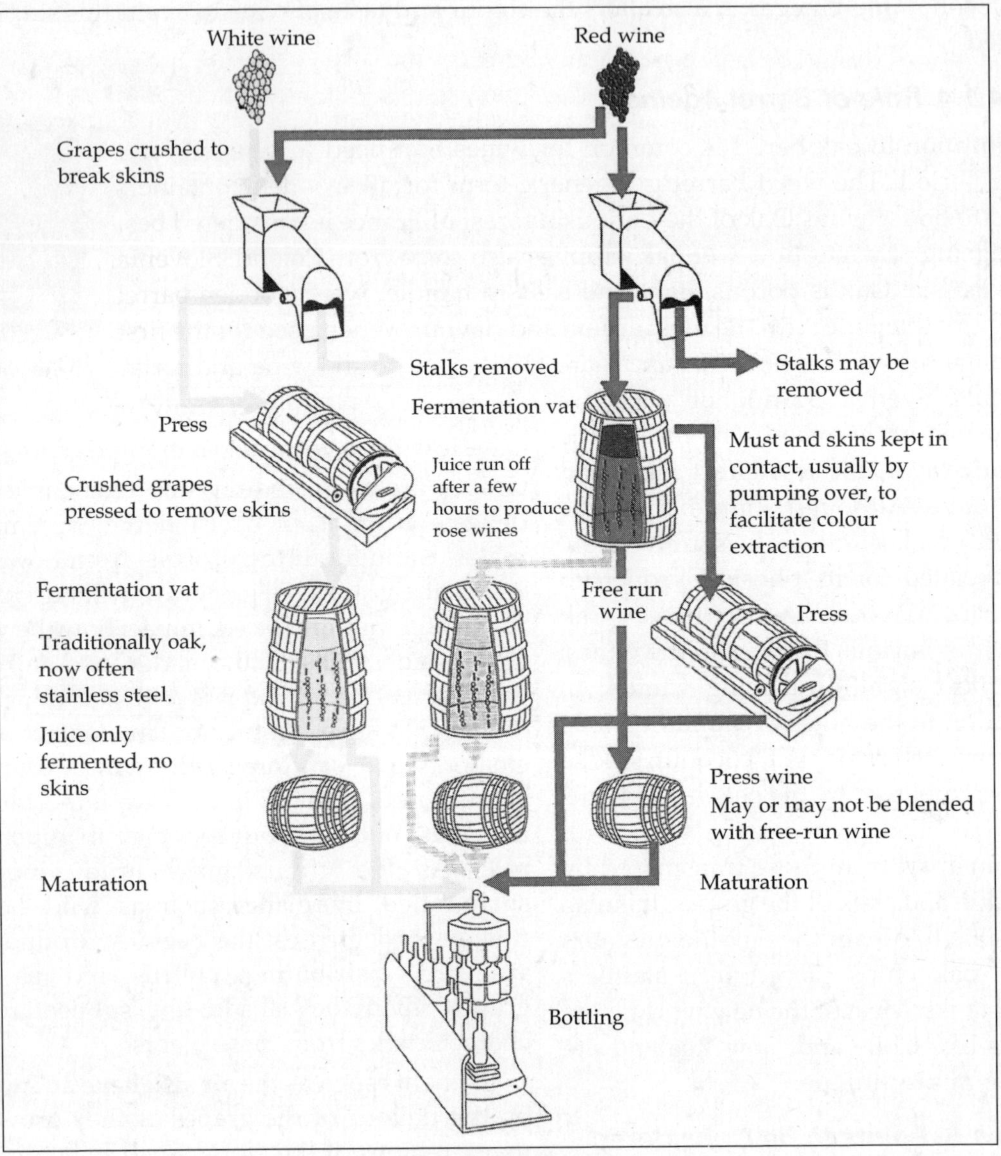

Winemaking process

protein, tannin and minerals. If the must does not contain enough natural sugars to produce the required amount of alcohol, then a small amount of sugar is added known as *chaptalization*. It is subject to local regulations.

- Every gram of sugar in the must is converted to about half a gram of ethyl alcohol.
- Red wine requires a lot of attention.
- Fermentation stops when all the sugar is converted to alcohol or when all the yeast is killed.

14.4.1.6 Storage of Wines

Storing wine horizontally

The wines should be kept horizontally lying for the cork to remain moist and to make sure that wine should not be exposed to light as light damages wines, especially white wines and sparkling wines. An ideal place to store wine is a *cellar*. It is situated underground to avoid any vibrations. The cellar should have good ventilation but no drafts, it should be dark, clean, without odours, quiet, damp, a gravel floor with stone or a brick wall. The temperature of cellar should be cool and constant between 8°C to 18°C and humidity should be 75-80% as too much humidity can cause wine labels to peel off and lack of humidity will result in the dryness of cork. Wine in the glass is poured as:

- Red : $\frac{1}{3}$
- White : $\frac{1}{2}$
- Sparkling Wine : $\frac{3}{4}$

14.5 COMMON FLAVOURS FOUND IN WINE

In general dry white wines should have a pleasantly citrus nose (lemon, grape fruit), and a grassy or green fruit aroma. Fuller white wines might have a vanilla or butter aroma. The lighter reds typically have aromas of red fruits and the heavier reds, black fruits. Aged red will have aromas of earth, smoke, oak and even spice smells. Young wines have lively aromas, aged wines have more ripe and complex aroma. A good red wine balances the key elements of acidity, alcohol, fruit and tannin. Cheaper wines lack the complexity of more expensive red wines whereas a good white wine balances the fruit/sugar, acidity and alcohol. Common aromas found in wines are:

- Fruit
- Smoke
- Spice
- Herbs
- Vanilla
- Flowers
- Wood
- Vegetables

14.6 SERVICE TEMPERATURE OF TABLE WINES

Temperature has a big impact on the taste of wine. Each style of wine has an optimum serving temperature at which it releases its aromas and flavours. Following is the serving temperatures of various wines.

Types of wine	Serving temperatures
Light, crisp white wines	4-6°C (39-43°F)
Juicy aromatic white wines	6-8°C (43-46°F)
Full opulent white wines	10-12°C (50-54°F)
Rose	4-6°C (39-43°F)
Fruity lively red wines	12-14°C (54-57°F)
Ripe smooth red wines	16-18°C (61-64°F)
Rich dense red wines	18-20°C (64-68°F)
Sparkling	6-8°C (43-46°F)
Sweet and fortified	6-8°C (43-46°F)
Note: Always remember that over-chilling the white wines not only numbs the taste buds but also can change the taste characteristics.	

14.7 WINE FAULTS

Poor storage conditions or vinification process resulting in unpleasant characteristics and bad odours in a wine are known as wine faults or wine defects.

- **Oxidation:** It results in deterioration of the bouquet, caused by the prolonged contact with air and insufficient dosage of sulphur dioxide during ageing.
- **Reduction:** During production of wine and ageing when wine does not get enough exposure to oxygen, the reduced wine starts giving a foul smell of sulphur or rotten eggs.
- **Smell of sulphur:** It is caused by the excessive usage of sulphur during winemaking. This lingers mostly in white wines which are very sensitive to oxidation and protected by more sulphur oxide.
- **Mercaption:** It is also a sulphur related fault in which fermentation yeast reacts with sulphur in the lees. It produces an unpleasant smell of rotten eggs, onion or burnt rubber.
- **Acetification:** Also known as acteic spoilage is caused by a bacterium (acetobacter) and produces an acetic wine which gives a taste of vinegar.
- **Crystals of Tartarate:** Generally appears at the bottom of white wine spoiling its appearance, however perfect to drink after decanting the wine.
- **Cork Wines:** These are wines affected by a diseased cork caused through bacterial action or excessive bottle age. The wine will have rancid, fungal smell and taste. The term should not be confused with cork residue - little harmless bits of cork which may splinter into the wine on opening a bottle.

14.8 DECANTING OF WINE

Decanting is a delicate operation, requiring a degree of dexterity to achieve three objectives:

- to separate any sediment from the wine,
- to aerate the wine, and
- to modify the temperature of wine.

Decanting of wine

Corky wines are decanted to remove the withered particles of corks from the wine. However, wines can also be decanted to remove the sediment which has formed in the wine and to allow the wine to breathe. Utmost care is to be taken of the corky wines or wines which have sediment so that sediment does not get mixed up in wine, causing it to become cloudy. If this happens, then the wines should not be decanted but rather left opened to allow the sediment to settle. For decanting a wine, a clean decanter along with decanting funnel or muslin cloth and a candle is required. The decanting funnel, if used, is placed on the decanter and a piece of muslin cloth is placed in the funnel if required. Light the candle beside the decanter. Now hold the bottle firmly with one hand and pour the wine steadily into the top of the funnel or decanter with the shoulder of the bottle held over the candle flame. If the bottle is held too close to the flame, soot may form at the bottom of the bottle, which will prevent the person decanting from seeing the sediment moving up the bottle to the neck. Continue pouring until the sediments reach shoulder of the bottle. At this point, pouring must stop before any of the sediment passes into the decanter.

14.9 TERMS RELATED TO WINE

(a) **Acidity:** It refers to the crispness or refreshing taste at the end of the wine. It is found more commonly in white wines than red wines.

(b) **Aroma:** Refers to the overall smell of the wine. It specifically has to do with the smell of the particular grape varietal. This term is generally used more often in younger wines.

(c) **Astringency:** Mostly found in red wines due to the tannin present in red wines absorbed from the seeds, stem and skin.

(d) **Appellation:** A legally defined and protected geographical indication used to identify where the grapes for a wine were grown.

(e) **Balance:** It tells you that whether the wine is smooth and harmonious. Differing flavours should balance each other, for example, acid should balance against sweetness.

(f) **Body:** Refers to the weight of a wine in your mouth, how thick or thin does the wine feel. Grape variety, alcohol content and age of the wines affect the body of the wine.

(g) **Bright:** It means how the wine tastes in your mouth. The higher the acidity or fresh wines, the brighter the wine is. Bright sometimes refer to the clarity of a wine if you are technically analyzing a wine's colour.

(h) **Bouquet:** Refers to the smell of a wine based on its ageing process. A mature wine will have a complex bouquet as compared to the recently fermented wine.

(i) **Creamy:** Term used for describing white wines and sparkling wines fermented or aged in oak.

(j) **Decanting:** It is a process that allows a wine to breathe by adding oxygen. Sometimes higher quality styled red wines with thicker grape skins (like Cabernet) are decanted to soften the tannins in a younger version of the grape. Decanting can also be used for releasing and separating sediment from an older red wines. This process is done by using decanter.

(k) **Earthy:** Used to describe wines that do not have "fruit-forward" flavours. Flavours such as soil, wet grass or dirt are associated with earthy wines and these flavours are typically found in red wines.

(l) **Finish:** Referred as the aftertaste a wine leaves in your mouth. The better quality wines tend to have a longer finish, that is rich, complex and flavourful.

(m) **Flabby:** Refers to wine that is lacking acidity.

(n) **Flamboyant:** Abundance of wine.

(o) **Fruit-forward:** Used for those wines that leave a more fruit driven taste on your palate and have a fruit forward sense of aroma.

(p) **Opulent:** Describes style of wine that is rich, smooth and bold.

(q) **Oxidized:** Oxidation for wine is the most common wine faults, which leads the wine to a loss of colour, flavour and aroma. Sometimes referred to as leaving the wine flat.

(r) **Palate:** It describes the flavours and complexities of a wine on your tongue and within your month.

(s) **Tannin:** Tannins are biomolecules found in leaf, bud, seed, root, and stem tissues. These add structure to the wine's taste. Tannin is primarily found in red wine as the juice spends more time in contact with all of these elements during the fermentation process. However, some tannins are desirable. To be noted that this is one of the major reasons to decant wine to soften young tannins in winemaking the wine more silky and smooth in texture. An aggressive amount of tannin can be referred to as "chewy".

(t) **Lees:** It is unwanted dead protein yeast cells that generally sink to the bottom of a wine. Lees are stirred up once a day to make a wine have a thicker, more oily, and creamy texture.

(u) **Legs:** When a wine is swirled , it leaves behind drops that slide down the side of a wine glass. These droplets are referred as legs, tears or curtains. The higher the alcohol content in a wine, the thicker the droplets form on the side of your glass.

(v) **Nose:** The smell of the wine in the glass.

(w) **Structure:** The more structure a wine has the more layers of flavour you will taste. It is a way to describe the relationships between the acid, tannins and alcohol in a wine. Better structure and a stronger relationship (equally) between these elements sometimes mean a wine will age better

(x) **Varietal:** Refers to the different varieties of the grapes.

(y) **Vintage:** This refers to the year in which the grapes were harvested, that made the wine.

14.10 PRONUNCIATION OF WINE TERMS

For any food and beverage personnel/bartender/wine waiter, it is important to know and learn the right pronunciation of relevant wine terminologies. Below is the list of some wine terminologies along with their right pronunciation which hospitality professionals come across during their day-to-day working.

Name	Pronunciation and Description
Agrafe	(Ah-grahf) - Metal cap for secondary fermentation in Champagne
Alsace	(Ahl-zahss) -Vineyard region in northeastern France
Anjou	(Ahn-zhoo)-Vineyard area in the Loire Valley in France
Assemblage	(Ah-sem-blaushj) -Blending a still wine before secondary fermentation
Asti Spumante	(Ah-stee Spoo-mahn-tee)- A sparkling white wine from Piedmont, Italy
Auslese	(Owss-leh-zeh)-Selected picking of fully-ripened grapes
Ausone	Château Ausone is a very famous vineyard located in Bordeaux and famous for producing quality wines.
Avignon	(Ah-veen-yong)-Major city of the Cotes du Rhone region of France
Bacchus	(Ba-kus)-The Roman God of Wine
Bandol	(Bahn-dohl)-A red Premier Cru in Savigny
Barbaresco	(Bar-ba-ress-ko)-A red Premier Cru in Savigny
Barbera	(Bar-beh-ra)-A red grape
Bardolino	(Bar-doh-lee-no)-A Veronese red wine
Barolo	(Ba-roll-oh)-A fine red wine from Piedmont
Barrique	(Ba-reek)-Bordeaux wine barrel containing 54 gl
Beaujolais	(Bo-zho-lay)-Red wine region of Southern Burgundy
Beaune	(Bone)-The capital of Burgundy
Beerenauslese	(Beh-ren-owss-leh-zeh)-Individually selected overripe grapes
Bellet	(Bell-lay)-Small appellation in Cote de Provence
Bianco Toscano	(B'yahn-ko Tohs-ka-no)
Blanc	(Blohng)-White

Blanc fume	(Blohng Fu-may)-Sauvignon Blanc as known in the Loire
Bordeaux	(Bor-doh)-Major city in the department of Gironde
Brut	(Broot)-The driest Champagne (lowest in sugar)
Cabernet Franc	(Ka-behr-nay Frahng)-A red wine grape of Bordeaux
Chablis	(Sha-blee)-White wine region, north of the Cote d'Or
Champagne	(Shawm-pine)-Vineyard region, northeast of Paris
Chateau	(sha-toh)-A specified viticultural holding; a winery or wine produce
Chianti	(K'yahn-tee)-The famous red wine from Tuscany
Cotes de Provence	(Koht duh Pro-vawnss)-The wine region of Provence
Degorgement	(Day-gorj-mahn)-Removing frozen sediment from Champagne
Dom Perignon	(Dohm Pay-reen-yohng)-The Benedictine monk famous in Champagne
Eiswein	(ICE-vine)-Perfectly ripened, partially frozen grapes, with concentrated sugars
Frascati	(Fra-ska-tee)-A strong red wine from Latium (Italy)
Fuisse	(Fwee-say)-White wine village in the Cote Maconnais
Gamay	(Ga-may)-A red wine grape used mainly in Beaujolais
Gewurztraminer	(Guh-VERTS-tra-mee-ner)-A superior quality and spicy wine grape
Hermitage	(Air-mee-tahzh)-Red wine area in the Cotes du Rhone
Lafite-Rothschild	(La-feet Rohts-sheeld)-A classified first growth in Medoc (Pauillac)
Latour	(La-toor)-A classified first growth in Medoc (Pauillac)
Loire	(L'war)-Vineyard in a valley area along the Loire River
Lombardy	(Lom-bar-dee)-One of Italy's largest regions, Lombardy lies in the north of the country, sharing a border with Switzerland
Malbec	(Mahl-bek)-A red wine grape of Bordeaux
Marc	(Mark)-Press loading in Champagne totaling four tons
Marsala	(Mar-sa-la)-A sweet fortified wine from Sicily
Medoc	(May-dohk)-The major red wine district of Bordeaux
Merlot	(Mair-lo)-A red wine grape, originally used as a blending wine in Bordeaux winemaking, now a widely produced standalone varietal as well.
Mit Pradikat	(Mitt Pray-dee-kaht)-Superior grade of Qualitatswein (with distinction)
Muscadet	(Muss-ka-day)-Vineyard region of the Loire Valley
Nahe	(Na-heh)-A vineyard area of the Rhine
Nebbiolo	(Nebb-yo-lo-)A red wine grape of Italy
Petrus	(Pay-truss)-A Great First Growth in Pomerol

Phylloxera	(Fy-lox-eh-ra)-Native American plant (root) lice
Piedmont	(Peed-mont)-A Department in northeast Italy
Pomerol	(Po-may-rol)-A red wine district of Bordeaux
Pommard	(Po-mar)-The best known commune in the Cote de Beaune
Pouilly-Fuisse	(Poo-yee Fwee-say) Famous white wine from the Cote Maconnais
Pouilly-Fume	(Poo-yee Foo-may)-The important wine from the Loire Valley
Pouilly-Loche	(Poo-yee Lohsh)-White wine commune in the Cote Maconnais
Pouilly-sur-Loire	(Poo-yee sur L'war)-White wine vineyard town in the Loire Valley
Premiere taille	(Pruh-m'yair tie)-The second pressing in Champagne
Pupitres	(pu-peetr)-Slanting cellar racks (riddling) used in Champagne
Qualitatswein	(Kua-lee-taits-vine)-Quality German table wine
Rebeche	(ruh-besh)-The fourth pressing in Champagne
Remuage	(ruh-m'wahzh)-Riddling process Champagne in secondary fermentation
Rheingau	(Rine-gow)-A vineyard area of the Rhine
Rheinpfalz/Palatinate	(Rine-pfahlz)-A vineyard area of the Rhine
Riesling	(Rees-ling)-The noble grape in Alsace and Germany
Rose d'Anjou	(Ro-zay dahn-zhoo)-A vin rose from Anjou (Loire)
Saar	(Zar)-A vineyard area of the Upper Moselle
Sauvignon Blanc	(So-vee-yohng Blahng)-Major white wine grape of Grave
Sec	(Sek)-Very Sweet
Semillon	(Say-meel-yohng)-Major grape of the Sauternes
Sicily	(Sis-sil-ly) Island Department at southern tip of Italy
Spatlese	(Shpayt-leh-seh)-Late-picked fully-ripened grape
St. Emilion	(Seng-tay-meel-yohng)-Red wine district of Bordeaux
Sylvaner	(Sil-va-ner)-White wine grape used in Alsace and Germany
Syrah	(See-ra)-Red wine grape of the Cotes du Rhone
Tafelwein	(Tah-fel-vine)-Ordinary German table wine
Tavel	(Ta-vel)-Vin Rose commune in the Cotes du Rhone
Traminer	(Tra-min-ner)-White wine grape used mainly in Alsace
Tuscany	(Tuss-ca-nee)-A Department in central Italy
Verdicchio	(Vair-deek-yo)-A pale white wine from Marche
Vin Santo	(Veen Sahn-toh)-A white dessert wine from Tuscany
Vouvray	(Voov-ray)-Important white wine in the Coteaux de Touraine
Zeltinger	(Tsel-ting-er) A large vineyard town on the Moselle

14.11 WINE OPENER

Various wine openers are used to open the wine but the most popular wine opener is waiter's friend.

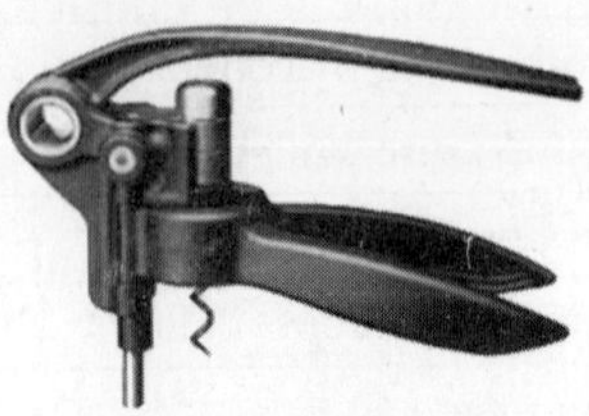

Lever style Corkscrew/the rabbit

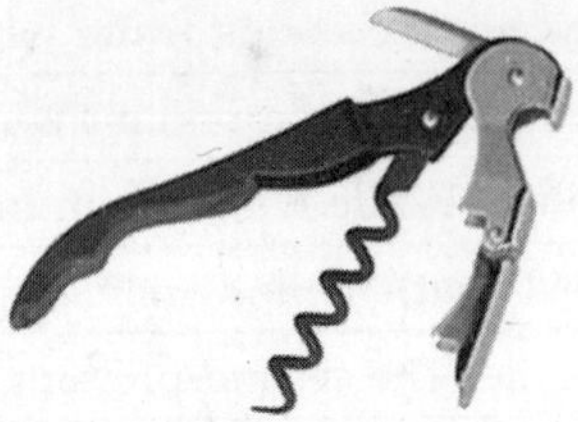

Waiter's friend

Winged corkscrew

Twisting pull cork

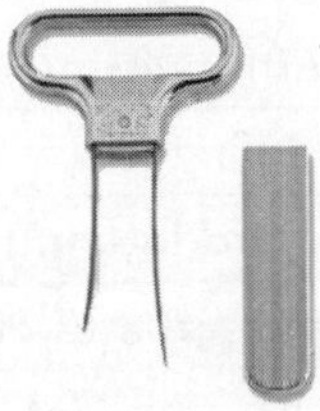

Two pronged wine Opener/Ah so wine opener

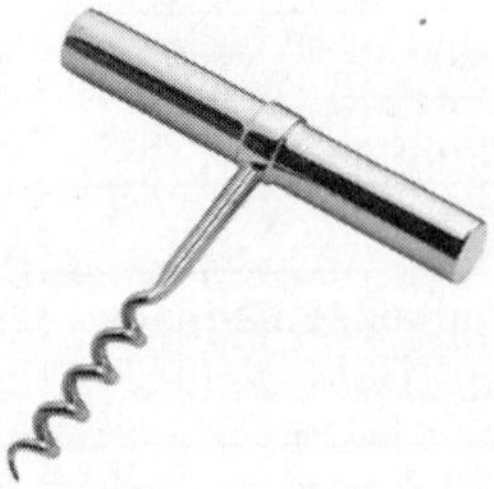

T shape wine opener

Types of wine openers

14.12 WINE CORK

Types of wine corks

To seal a wine bottle, cork is used. The cork is made up of bark of Oak tree (*Quercus suber*) which grows only in the western Mediterranean and Portugal. Cork has unique physical properties as its cells form microscopic 'suckers' that grip the bottle neck. It is inert and impervious to the liquids and neither reacts with wine nor rots. Only weevils and fungi are likely to affect it, but these can be avoided. Occasionally, some bottles will have a ' corked ' or tainted aroma and flavour. Nowadays, synthetic corks made from plastic foams and screw caps are also being used by many wine producers.

Advantages of screw cap

- Maintains the freshness of the wine.
- Easy to open as compared to the cork.
- Wines can be stored vertically as well.
- No cases of withered cork.

Screw cap

- Most of the people do not have a wine opener at home.
- Screw cap is made of aluminium which is totally recyclable.
- The liner known as Saran film is totally non reactive to the wine.

Tannin

Tannin is a mouth drying chemical that comes from the grape skins and from the oak barrel in which wine is aged or externally added tannin powder. Tannin is only found in red grape varieties, extracted from the skins during maceration or they may develop during storage in barrels. Their quality and quantity is defined by various factors such as grape variety, maturity of the grapes and duration of maceration. Tannins are responsible for the structure of the wine and play an essential role in ageing. Tannins are noticeable as a sensation of astringency (or dryness) which gives a chewiness to the wine.

REVISION QUESTIONS

1. Differentiate between old world wine countries and new world wine countries along with examples.
2. Write down step-by-step procedure of making red wine, white wine and rose wine.
3. Write down various common aromas found in wines. Also write a short note on tannin.
4. Name various wine openers.
5. Name any one preservative used in making wine.
6. What are the various faults in wine?

RESEARCH ACTIVITIES

- List down different red grape and white grape varieties used in winemaking and also paste their pictures in a scrapbook.
- Prepare a PowerPoint presentation on classification of wine.
- Visit a nearby public bar and wine shop and list down the name of various red wines, white wines, rose wines and sparkling wines available.
- Collect various wine corks and wine labels and paste in a scrapbook.
- Practice the pronunciation of various red grape varieties and white grape varieties.

15

World Wines

15.1 INTRODUCTION TO FRENCH WINES

France is not just home to most of the world's greatest classic wines but remains the foremost country in the world, in its diversity and experience of wines. Wine production in France has become a major industry to an extent which no other country of Europe can match. French wines are exceptional in their quality and variety.

After reading this chapter, you will be able to understand:

- The various wine producing countries, regions, grapes and their wine laws.

15.1.1 Wine Regions of France

There are 35 districts in France, but the major wine producing regions are as follows:

- Bordeaux
- Burgundy
- The Loire Valley/Val de Loire
- The Rhone Valley (Cote du Rhone)
- Champagne
- Alsace (bordering Germany)
- Jura
- Provence
- South West France

Did you know?

The red wines of Bordeaux district are known in England as clarets.

1. Bordeaux

Bordeaux region is one of the three most famous French wine producing regions. Bordeaux produces wines of remarkable quality. It produces one - twentieth of wine of France. Main grape varieties of Bordeaux region are:

Red wines	White wines
Cabemet Sauvignon, Cabernet Franc, Merlot, Petit Verdot and Malbec (*Used as a part of mixture)*	Sauvignon Blanc, Semillion

Greatest wines from Bordeaux
• Chateau Haut Brion
• Chateau Latour
• Chateau Mouton Rothschild
• Chateau Margaux
• Chateau Lafite Rothschild
• Chateau Petrus

The classic flavour of Red Bordeaux is of black currant laced with vanilla and spices, young red wines are tannic and astringent. Red wines are aged for two years in new oak barrels whereas white wines are luscious, fruity, full-bodied. There are five classic regions in Bordeaux producing mainly red wine, but also a small top quality dry, sweet white wine. These five regions are:

- **The Medoc:** Produces best red wines of France and is part of the larger Bordeaux area. When young, they are full, heavy and tannic. After maturing it becomes delicious, complex, often rich, peppery fruit, spicy/cigar box (cedar wood) overtones.
- **Graves:** The Graves district named after the gravel soil produces wines having beautiful colour, full body and bouquet with a faint perfume of pine. Produces both red and white wine.
- **St. Emilion:** St. Emilion, adjoining Pomerol, is in chalk hill county and the wines are grown on chalk and clay, there are some three hundred chateaux (french term for village). It produces soft, velvety, heavy, full bodied and rich wines with less bouquet and finesse than those of the Medoc.
- **Pomerol:** This region came to be known after the Second World War and has no official classification.
- **Sauternes:** Sauternes is known for producing very sweet white wines made from Sauvignon blanc, Semillon and a small percentage of muscadelle grapes. Wines from this region have 13-15% alcohol content. Sauternes wines with age become golden yellow in colour.

2. *Burgundy*

Burgundy lies in the heart of France. The vineyards of the Burgundy region cover a narrow strip of land on the eastern slopes of the hills running south-east from the Burgundian capital, Dijon. The heart of the Burgundy wine growing region is also the historic city of Beaune. The best Burgundy wines are the reds, the best of which can be kept for a good 20 to 30 years. However, Burgundy also produces some top quality, though not too distinctive, white wines. The main grape varieties of Burgundy are:

Red wines	White wines
Pinot Noir and Gamay	Chardonnay and Aligote

Burgundy is the land of small estates and wine farmers. Burgundy wines are therefore not known by chateau names. The wines are sold to various shippers who may blend them before sale. The red wines of Burgundy differ from those of Bordeaux in that, on an average, they are more full-bodied, have a pronounced flavour but contain less tannin. The wine regions of Burgundy are as follows:

The Chablis Region: Chablis is famous for producing best white wine in France. Chablis can be matured in oak barrels and stainless vats. Oak barrels are used for later maturing wine; and steel vats for bottling the wine for early drinking.

- **The Cote D'Or:** The Cote D'Or produces red and dry white wine from fairly basic to some of the most fabulous wines in the world like *Gevery Chambetin* - Red wine, *Corton* - Red wine, *Cote De Beaune* - Red wine, *Pommard* - Red wine, *Montrachet* - White wine, *Meursault* - White wine and many more. The Cote D' Or is split in two areas *Cote De Nuits* (produces red wine) and *Cote De Beaunne* (produces both red and white wine).

Greatest wines from Burgundy

- Chablis (white)
- Pouilly Fuisse (white)
- Beaujolais
- Pommard

- **Cote Chalonnaise (or region de Mercurey):** The Cote Chalonnaise is often said to produce wines like mini Cote D'Or wine. It produces red as well as white wines.
- **The Maconnais:** This region produces predominantly white wine but some red wines also. The famous white wines from this region are *Pouilly Fuisse* and *Pouilly Loche*
- **Beaujolais:** In the south of the Burgundy region, bordering the Rhone valley vineyards, a large area around Beaujeu produces a light red wine known as Beaujolais, one of the most famous French wines. This is a wine that does not usually survive for many years, and over the last fifty years it has been successfully marketed as a "*vin primeur*", or young wine, to be drunk after just a few weeks of maturing.

3. The Loire Valley (Val De Loire)

The Loire Valley is referred as "the garden of France". The region is named after the river, Loire which is the longest river in France. It is one of the most attractive and versatile wine producing areas. For almost whole of its length is bordered by vineyards. The varieties of wines which are produced in Loire are white, red, rose, dry, semi-dry or sweet sparkling like *Anjou Rose, Muscadet* and *Pouilly Fume.* The major grape varieties of Loire are:

Greatest wines from the Loire

- Vouvray
- Pouilly Fume (White)
- Anjou (Rose)
- Muscadet (White)

Red wines	White wines
Cabernet Franc and Gamay	Chenin Blanc, Muscadet and Sauvignon Blanc

The Loire valley, however, is also France's second largest producer of sparkling wines, after Champagne. The region also produces vin gris, "grey wine", which is actually a very pale rosé, being a white wine made from black grapes. Two of the more prestigious varieties are *Vouvray* and *Saumur*. The wine regions of Loire Valley are:

- The Pays Nantais
- Anjou - Samur
- Touraine
- The Central Vineyards

4. The Rhone Valley (Côtes du Rhône)

Côtes du Rhône is one of those French wines that has become famous on account more as a result of the extent of the vineyard than of the quality of the wine. The Côtes du Rhône vineyard runs for over 200 kilometres down the Rhone valley from the south of Lyons to the Camargue. Within the region, there are a number of prestigious smaller areas such as Côte Rotie (in the northern part of the region), Hermitage or Chateau Neuf du Pape. The principal grape varieties of the Rhone Valley are:

Greatest wines from the Rhone

- Chateau Neuf du Pape
- Côte du Rotie
- Hermitage
- Tavel Rose

Red wines	White wines
Syrah, Grenache	Viognier

5. Champagne

Centred on the towns of Reims (Rheims) and Epernay, is the most northern of France's major vineyards. Unlike most of the best French wines, Champagnes are blended in order to produce either non-vintage Champagnes (blended from different years) or vintage Champagne, blended from wines of the same harvest. Consequently, since the quality of the Champagne ultimately depends on a balance between the quality of the grapes and the skill of the blenders, Champagnes are also ranked and promoted by producer, not by any more finely delimited appellation. Possibly the most highly rated of blends is Krug, other well appreciated brands include Mumm, Bollinger and Heidsieck, Moët & Chandon and Taittinger. The distinct taste and purity of real Champagne is certainly due to the chalky soil and the continental growing conditions that abound the Champagne region.

6. Alsace

Situated on the lower eastern slopes of the Vosges mountains, in the Rhine valley is rather different from any other French wine growing area. Most Alsatian wines are white and usually named after their grape variety like Alsace Riesling. Alsace was a part of Germany during 1817-1917 therefore has a influence of German wines as compared to French wines, hence produces mostly dry or fruity white wines. The wines of Alsace have Germanic touch tall, fluted bottles with Gothic print. Major grape varieties found in Alsace region are Riesling, Gewürztraminer, Muscat, Tokay, Pinot Blanc and Sylvaner.

7. Jura

The Jura vineyards lie eastwards, near the Jura Mountains which separate France from Switzerland. The region is famous for outstanding and peculiar type of golden wines and straw wines. The best and most distinctive of Jura whites are made from the Savagnin grape variety, which is found only in this region, and gives the wine a delicious sherry-like taste. However, most Jura wines are blended from different varieties, and as in Alsace, the grape variety tends to be indicated on the label. The Jura vineyard also produces dark rosé wines, sometimes called reds, as well as the famous "yellow wine", Vin Jaune, an expensive apéritif wine. Other famous Jura wines are Vin De Paille (straw wine) and Vin Gris (coloured rose wine).

8. Provence

Provence is a large wine producing area, best known for its rosé wines, the most famous of which are Côtes de Provence and Côteaux d'Aix, however it also produces red wines. Provence is sun and sand, fabulous hilltop villages with wonderful smell of wild herbs, thyme, basil and rosemary. Note that the Provence vineyard also includes the southern end of the Côtes du Rhone AOC area.

9. Midi

Consists of Languedoc and Roussillon wine regions which makes an enormous quantity of inexpensive wines and is the largest vineyard in France. Midi is also known as "The Belly of France" as the Midi region produces 40% of the French harvest.

10. South-West France

There are a number of smaller less well known wine growing areas, producing some quite good wines at very reasonable prices which includes-

- Bergerac
- Cahors
- Gaillac
- Jurancon
- Madiran
- Irouleguy
- Cotes de Buzet
- Cotes de Duras

Table 15.1: Wine regions in France

Wine region	Grape varieties	Wine style
Bordeaux	Cabernet Sauvignon, Cabernet Franc, Merlot, Petit Verdot, Malbec, Sauvignon Blanc, Semillon	Prestigious tannic reds, dry medium, and luscious whites.
Burgundy	Pinot Noir, Gamay, Aligote, Chardonnay	Powerful, silk-smooth reds, crisp reds, dry to soft, full, flavoured whites.
The Loire Valley	Cabernet Franc, Pinot Noir, Cabernet Sauvignon, Chennin Blanc, Muscadet	Light fruity reds, semi-sweet roses, dry, medium, sweet whites and fine sparkling wines.
The Rhone Valley	Syrah, Grenache, Marsanne, Viognier	Big, dark full flavoured red. Some excellent whites and sparkling wines.
Champagne	Pinot Noir, Pinot Meunier, Chardonnay	Finest sparkling wine. May be white or pink. Ranges from extremely dry to sweet.
Alsace	Riesling, Gewürztraminer, Muscat, Tokay, Pinot Noir	Dry crisp to full-bodied and spicy whites.
Jura	Pinot Noir, Chardonnay, Savagnin, Poulsard	Red, white, yellow wine (Vin Jaune), straw wine (Vin De Paille), coloured wine (Vin Gris).
Provence	Grenache, Ugni blanc, Syrah, Marsanne, Sauvignon Blanc	Reds, whites and rose wines of reasonable quality.
Midi	Grenache, Syrah, Cabernet Sauvignon, Chennin blanc, Cahrdonnay, Mouzac	Light to distinctive reds, tart to medium dry whites, excellent sparkling wines.
South West France	Merlot, Malbec, Cabernet Franc, Gamay, Syrah, Semillon, Mauzac, Sauvignon Blanc.	Fruity, light sometimes tannic reds, orange pink roses, crisp dry to flowery whites.

15.1.2 French Wine Controlling Terms/Wine Quality Control

The French government has established the governing body to control the quality wine production in France, this body is known as *Institut National des Appellations d' origine* (INAO). It has framed certain rules and regulations to have a strict control on French wines. It has designed certain grades which indicate the quality of French wines. These grades are as follows:

Grade 1- Appellation d' Origin Controlee (AOC)

It represents around 52% of all French wines. It is a guarantee of origin of wine and are of highest quality that adhere strictly to production requisites, i.e.,

- An exactly defined growing area
- The type and blend of grape varieties used

- Care of vineyard and grafting
- Maximum harvest per acre
- Minimum alcohol content
- Wine production and storage methods
- Official tasting, final grading of wine.

Within each region there is a laid down hierarchy of appellations also which, in general are geographical. The more specific the geographic description, the higher the appellation, and the stricter the regulations. In some areas, an individual vineyard may be eligible for several ACs of different quality levels. Some regional and district appellations have the right to the additional qualification superieur, e.g., *Bordeaux Superieur, Macon Superieur*. These wines simply have an extra half or full degree of alcohol compared with the equivalent basic appellation.

Grade 2- Vins Delimites De Qualite Superieure (VDQS)

It is a grade down from AOC. This is an official category of French wine, and was introduced in 1949. VDQS wines are of a high quality from a limited growing area. This accounts for less than 5% of French wine. VDQS wines are subject to regulations like:

- Growing area
- Grape variety
- Minimum alcohol content
- Cultivation and wine production

Grade 3- Vin De Pays/VDP (Country Wines)

It was created in 1970 and formalized in 1979. It is related to country wines and gives some guarantee of authenticity and quality, e.g., Vin de pays Chablis. It contributes to 33% of the total production (unblended).

Grade 4- Vin De Table/VDT (Wine of the table)

The table wines are meant to be almost consumed in the country. It is meant for everyday use and does not improve with age. It is for the ordinary wines or table wines. It was earlier known as Vin De Consommation Courante (VCC) or Vin Ordinaire. These wines can be blended with wines from the EU(European Union).

15.2 WINES FROM GERMANY

Germany takes sixth place among the wine producing nations of the world. Much of the production is intended for export, while Germany itself imports huge volumes of wines. Compared with the other major wine producing countries, the consumption in Germany is very low as the Germans tend to prefer beer and other imported wines. While looking at the history of German wine, it shows that it was the Romans who introduced viticulture in Germany. During middle ages, vineyards were situated all around Germany but due to new techniques in making beer (as brewing industry created considerably greater income than winemaking) and increase in the imports of wine, the vineyards decreased and later on many grape varieties disappeared due to the attack of vine louse phylloxera in all the vineyards of Germany, resulting in the introduction of phylloxera-resistant American rootstocks. Although a few winemakers succeed in making excellent red wines, Germany is known as a white wine country because of its climate. More than 85% of the area cultivated by vine in Germany is planted with white grape varieties. Yet Germany produces an abundance of light, fruit flavoured, low alcohol and low priced table wine which are greatly popular in America and Britain. The country is also renowned for exquisite, expensive, sweet, honeyed, golden wines as result of sophisticated harvesting procedures.

15.2.1 Wine Laws

German wines are produced and sold under the German wine laws, which came into existence in 1971 and till date has a number of amendments made it to since. Wines here are categorized by the degree of ripeness measured in natural grape sugar upon harvest. The term used to measure the level of sugar present in the must is *'Oechsle'*. In 1971, the German wine laws divided the wine into two major categories: **Tafelwein** (table wine) and **Qualitätswein** (quality wine).

1. Tafelwein (Table Wine)

This is the lowest category of German wine. While this is made entirely from grapes which have been grown in Germany it is sold under one of five wine regions or *Weinbaugebiete*; these wines are German table wines. *Deutscher Tafelwein* may state the vintage. When the wines are blended with wine from other European countries it is sold as EU *Tafelwein*. *Landwein* is a higher grade Tafelwein, which must be sold as either trocken (dry) or halbtrocken (medium dry). There are seventeen regions for Landwein and these are different from both Tafelwein and Qualitätswein bestimmster Anbaugebiet regions. For further understanding, you can say *Tafelwein* can be divided into two subcategories :

- Deutscher Tafelwein (German Table wine)
- Deutscher Landwein (German Country wine)

1 A Deutscher Tafelwein

This is the basic table wine made from grapes grown in Germany. There is a simple *Tafelwein* made when wines are blended with European wines or grapes.

1. B Deutscher Landwein

Similar to the French *Vin De Pays,* it is superior to the *Deutscher Tafelwein* and will have a slightly greater alcoholic content. The wine is dry or semi-dry and can be produced in any of the seventeen designated *Landwein* areas.

2. Qualitätswein (Quality Wine)

This category can be subdivided into:

- Qualitätswein mit Prädikat (Qmp)
- Qualitätswein bestimmter Anbaugebiete (QbA)

2 A Qualitätswein mit Prädikat (Qmp)

These wines are of superior quality. They are completely natural wines with no sugaring of the must allowed. There are six ***Prädikat* (distinctions or degrees of ripeness)** which indicates detail of the harvesting of the grapes. The harvesting of these grapes must be authorized by the local wine authorities and minimum must weights (sugar content of the juice) are laid down for each district. The label for these wines show the same details as QbA wine in addition to the *Prädikat,* and must shows the *Anbaugebiete.* The six *Prädikat* are as follows:

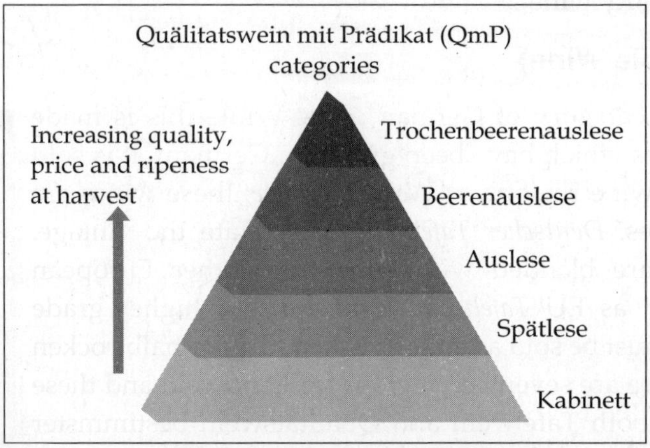

- **Kabinett:** Produced from the first harvest. Minimum must weight - 73° Oechsle.
- **Spatlese:** The term literally means 'late harvest' usually three weeks after the general harvest. Minimum must weight - 85° Oechsle.
- **Auslese:** This is a late selective harvest, which means that each individual bunch of grapes is inspected to determine its ripeness. These wines are richer and sweeter than Spatlese. Minimum must weight 95° Oechsle.
- **Beerenauslese:** Overripe top quality grapes, high concentration of sugar due to botrytis. In Germany, they are termed 'edelfaule'. They are picked individually after ripeness has been determined. Minimum must weight - 125° Oechsle.

- **Trockenbeerenauslese:** Very high concentration of sugar, and top quality wines made from top years. The grapes are almost shrivelled in this case. Minimum must weight 150° Oechsle.
- **Eiswein:** Ice wines are made only when conditions are favourable. Made from overripe grapes which have been left on the vine until caught by the frost, then picked at –8°C or colder and pressed to separate the frozen water from sweet juice. These frozen grapes produce a wine that is both sweeter and more concentrated than the average *Pradikat* wine.

Features of Qualitätswein mit Prädikat (QmP) are:

- 9.5% natural alcohol as no chaptalization is allowed.
- Origin should be in one of the 11 regions.
- Made from an approved grape variety of an approved vineyard.
- Wine must go through a testing panel and carry a test serial number.
- If 85% of grapes used is from one vineyard, they can carry the name of the vineyard.

2 B Qualitätswein Bestimmter Anbaugebiete (QbA)

These are second highest quality wines. The wines have to be made from authorized vine stocks. The must weight expressed in *Oechsle* degrees, has to reach a certain minimum level. This is gauged by using a hydrometer which has a graduated scale of measurement. This will reveal the potential alcohol content of a wine by comparing the specific gravity of the must to the specific gravity of water. Qba wines will also undergo a chemical and sensory evaluation and they must not be blended with wines from outside their regions. These wines are normally made from fully ripened grapes but like Tafelwein and Landwein, these wines can be improvised by chaptalisation. Features of QbA wines are:

- Made with addition of sugar.
- 7.5% natural alcohol.
- Origin should be in one of the 11 regions.
- Made from an approved grape variety of an approved vineyard.
- Wine must go through a testing panel.
- If 85% of grapes used is from one vineyard then can carry the name of the vineyard.

3. Sekt

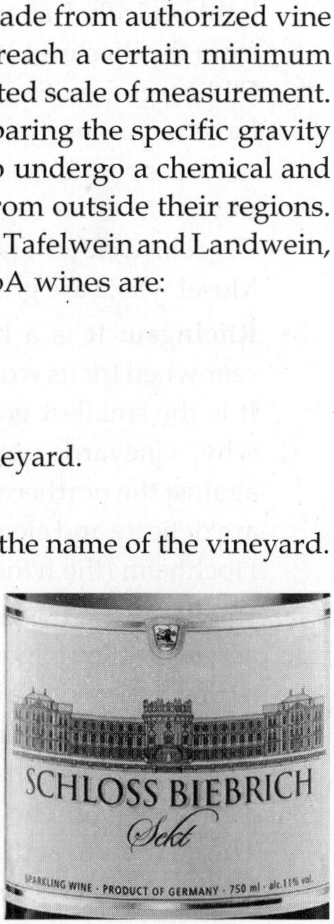

Sekt is a sparkling wine from Germany made in all regions. The term Sekt is a short term for *Qualitatsschaumwein,* meaning quality sparkling wine. Schaumwein itself is basic, cheap, bubbly and cheerful. *Deutscher Sekt* must now be made from grapes grown in Germany. Sekt BA is quality sparkling wine made from grapes grown in the region declared on the label. Most Sekt is produced by the charmat method, that means the second fermentation takes place in a sealed tank and the wine is then filtered and bottled under pressure. However, real star quality Sekt is made after the fashion of Champagne.

15.2.2 Wine Producing Region

The main wine producing region of Germany is situated in the south-west quarter of Germany. It is the most northerly wine region of Europe and crosses latitude 50ºN; it is not normal elsewhere for grapes to fully ripen. It is in these borderline districts that some of the finest white wines are produced. Germany has 13 designated wine regions for quality wines, most surrounding the Rhine River and its tributaries. Thirteen designated wine areas of Germany are described below.

- **Mosel:** The valley is watered by Mosel river and its tributaries, Saar and Ruwer. The vineyards are sited on steep slopes above the Mosel river. Primary grape used here is Riesling. Wines produced in Mosel are usually light in alcohol about 9% and are made from the Riesling, Muller-Thurgau and Elbling grapes. Some of the wines also have a property called 'Spritzig' – natural sparkle. Some of the important towns in the region are, Piesport, Graach, Ockfen and Kasel. Bottles of Mosel wines are green in colour.

Wine producing regions of Germany

- **Rheingau:** It is a historic centre, also renowned for its wonderful landscapes. It is the smallest grape growing region that produces greatest of all wines. This is why, vineyards are located on large hillsides facing the south and are protected against the northern climate by the Taunus mountain chain. The wines of this region are delicate and elegant. The important villages are Johannesberg, Steinberg, Erbach, Hochheim (the wine from this region was termed as Hock wine by the British).
- **Rheinhessen:** It is the largest of Germany's thirteen winemaking regions, sprawling across a valley of gently rolling hills along the Rhine River. This tremendously fertile region is home to all kinds of agriculture, and just a portion of it is devoted to fine wines, but the quality of these wines is high, and getting higher each year. Most of Germany's wine that is exported is made here. It has a warmer climate than Mosel and Rheingau. The primary grape varieties used are Sylvaner and Muller Thurgao. The wines are soft, sweet with delicate bouquet. Some well known vineyards are Oppenheim, Worms and Bodenheim.

- **Rheinpfalz:** Located near the French border is the second largest wine producing region in terms of area. This is the warmest and driest part of Germany. The principal grapes used in the region are Muller-Thurgau, Morio-Muskat, Kerner and Sylvaner. The white wines of the regions are soft, spicy, aromatic yet clean and fresh whereas the red wines are mild and mellow.
- **Nahe:** Located to the west of Rheinhessen on either side of the river of that name. The main grapes used in this region are Reisling, Sylvaner and Muller-Thurgao and it produces wines of varying tastes and quality. Some well-known villages are Schloss Bockelheim and Rudesheim.
- **Franconia (Franken):** The grapes used are Muller-Thurgao and Sylvaner and the wines are pleasant, dry and mellow. The distinctive feature of the region is the special flagon-shaped bottle known as 'bocksbeutel' or 'boxbeutel' in which wines are exported.
- **Ahr:** One of the smallest wine producing regions in Germany known for red wines. However, the volcanic origin of the soil along with lots of slate make the region suitable for producing white wines too.
- **Baden:** South east region of Germany offers great diversity, producing aromatic and powerful wines.
- **Wurtemberg:** Separated from Baden by Black Forest, it produces pleasant red and white wines.
- **Mittelrhein:** Situated on the Rhine slopes, it produces hearty and stylish wines.
- **Hessische Bergstrasse:** Very small region; production takes place for local consumption only.
- **Saxony:** New wine region of Germany that produces dry white wines with fruity acidity.
- **Saale/Unstrut:** Most northern wine areas of Germany produce light, soft, flowery dry wines.

Also note that the bottles from Rhine region are brown in colour and from Mosel are green in colour.

15.2.3 Grape Variety

There are nearly 40 grape varieties permitted to be used in Germany. The most important of these are Riesling, Müller-Thurgau and Silvaner followed by Kerner. The most notable black grape for the red wines is Spätburgunder, the net most planted is Portugieser and Dornfelder. To name a single grape variety on the label, the wine must contain a minimum of 85% of that grape.

Müller-Thurgau

Table 15.2: Principal grape varieties of Germany

Red Grape	White Grape
Spätburgunder (Pinot Noir)	Riesling
Dornfelder	Müller-Thurgau
Portugieser	Silvaner
Trollinger	Rulander (Pinot Gris)
Mullerrebe (Pinot Meunier)	Elbling
Domina	Kerner
	Morio - Muscat
	Weißer Burgunder (Pinot blanc)

15.2.4 Reading A Wine Label

German wine labels are very informative and easy to understand once you know the terminology. Wine regions are called *Anbaugebiete*. Each region is divided into districts known as *Bereiche* or into village or communities (*gemeinde*). Every Bereiche will have a collection of vineyards (*grosslagen*) and each grosslage will have single vineyards (einzellagen). For example:

- Mosel -Saar-Ruwer is a region- *Anbaugebiete* or *Gebiete*
- Bernkastel is a district - *Bereich*
- Bernkasteler Badstube is a collective site - *Grosslage*
- Bernkasteler Doktor is a single vineyard - *Einzellage*

The following information is also labelled in the wine:

- The wine category.
- *Erzeugerabfullung:* Estate bottled. Sometimes the bottler's name (abfuller) is also given.
- The vineyard name preceded by the district name carrying the suffix 'er', so *Bernkastel* becomes *Bernkasteler.*
- The vintage year, also in the possessive form such as 2016 er.
- Taste or style of the wine.
- QbA: Quality wine from a designated region.
- QmP: Quality level and distinction of the wine and manner of harvesting, such as *Spatlese.*

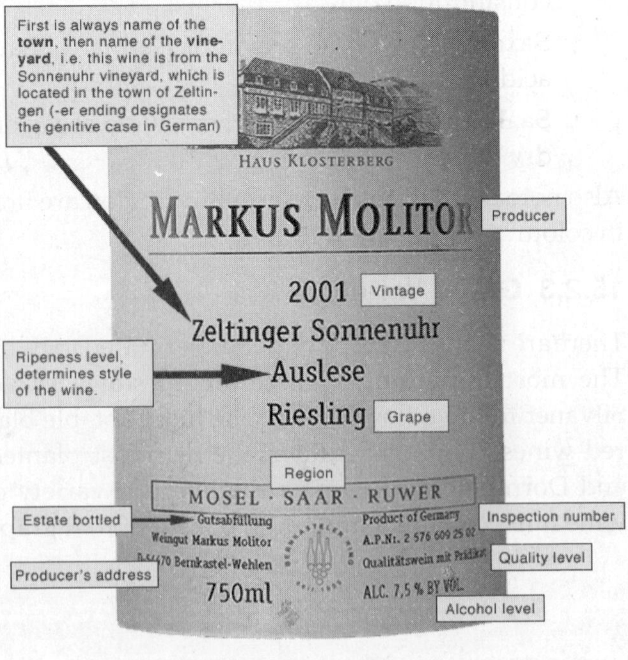

- Ripeness level: Determines the level of wine
- Inspection number: The term A.P. no. denotes the inspection number which proves that the wine has passed official chemical and sensory tests. The last two digits indicate the year the wine was sent to be tested.
- Alcohol percentage: It will be stated in alcohol by volume.

15.2.5 German Wine Terms

- **Sekt:** Used for German Sparkling wine
- **Hock:** Wines from the Rhine valley
- **Trocken:** Dry
- **Halbtrocken:** Medium dry
- **Perlwein:** Also known as Spritzig, this is a lightly sparkling white or red wine which may be artificially injected with the help of carbon dioxide.
- **Rotling:** Pink wine made from a combination of black and white grapes.
- **Schaumwein:** Sparkling wine.
- **Erzenger Abfulung:** Bottled by producer.
- **Gebiet:** Refers to the region; there are eleven wine growing regions.
- **Bereich:** This refers to the districts within the region.
- **Grosslage:** These are the sub-districts that are made up of a collection of vineyards.
- **Einzellage:** Single vineyard

15.3 ITALIAN WINES

The ancient Greeks called Italy's Oenotria (its southern part), the land of wines. Italy has remained steeped in viticulture for over 3000 years and today is second only to France in production of wine. The majority is drunk in Italy itself and is considered the world's largest wine consumer as an average Italian family consumes wine during both mid-day and evening meal and is also a vital ingredient in Italian cuisine. Early viticulture in Italy is credited to the Etruscans, who lived in central Italy before the founding of Rome. A separate wine tradition was introduced farther south by Greeks who colonized Sicily and the southern Italian peninsula. Rome, which was founded as a small city within the Etruscan realm, began its rise to greatness after asserting its independence from Etruscan rule around 500 BC. Thereafter, Rome expanded and learned from their former enemies and absorbed their best technologies and ideas, including winemaking. Everywhere they went, the Romans planted grapevines, thereby establishing the basis for today's wine industry. After fifth century, economic conditions in Europe declined and the former empire broke up into myriad of constantly changing political entities. As a luxury, viticulture might have almost disappeared throughout Europe for two things. First, water quality in much of medieval Europe, especially in the cities, was poor and unhealthy, whereas alcoholic beverages like wine were inherently more hygienic. Second, the Church required wine for sacramental purposes, so monks continued to pursue viticulture and improve on winemaking techniques. As the home of the Popes, Italy was naturally one of the centres of winemaking in medieval Europe. Italy was so fragmented by political boundaries, cultural rivalries, and mountainous terrain, hundreds of unique grape varieties developed in relative isolation throughout the country. The foundation was set for the vast array of wine appellations, styles, and varieties that exist today in Italy. In addition, in more recent times, a few grape varieties that were renowned in other countries were introduced into Italy, especially in the areas that had cultural or political ties with France, Spain, or the Germanic countries. In this chapter, students will understand the major wine producing regions along with the grape varieties and wine laws that exist. We will also try to examine the method of reading wine labels of Italian wines along with the various wine terms used.

15.3.1 Wine Producing Regions of Italy

Italy has twenty administrative regions, each having its vineyards and own range of microclimates and soils. Mountains which form the backbone of the country account for 40% of the area cultivated for wine. Vineyards can be found in every sheltered valley. Although there are countless microclimates throughout Italian vineyards, in general terms the north has a continental climate while the south enjoys a Mediterranean climate. The vineyards are never far from the sea so that extremes of temperature are moderated. Italy has twenty wine regions which are further subdivided into many provinces. Every wine region is known for its diverse culture helping in creating unique style of wine. Some important wine producing regions in Italy are as follows:

- **Piedmont:** The northwestern region of Piedmont is located in the foothills of Alps mountains and is famous for producing medium and high quality red wines. The capital is Turin (Torino), famous for its heavy industry although the rest of the area remains traditionally agricultural. Piedmont is best known for its sweet effervescent wine Asti Spumante (Asti is the town where the foaming, sparkling wine is made) made from Muscat grapes by Charmat (bulk) method. Using Nebbiolo grape also known as Spanna, fabulous red wines Barolo, Barbaresco, Barbera d' Asti is also produced here which have even more prestige. Another red grape Dolcetto is used to make Dolcetto d' Acqui and other good red wines. Of the whites, Muscat or Moscato and Gavi are the best. Today Piedmont, together with Tuscany is temple to the art of winemaking.
- **Veneto:** It is the major wine producing region of northeast Italy. The best known wines of Veneto whose capital is Venice are the dry, white Soave, the dry light red Bardolino and the immensely popular, red Valpolicella. Renowned sparkling Prosecco wines are made in this region.

- **Tuscany:** Along with Piedmont, Tuscany is the most significant part of Italy in quality wines and occupies a special place at the cultural heart of the country. This region is renowned for its truly great red wine Chianti. Sangiovese or a local clone, Brunello is used as the prime grape. Chianti used to be marketed in a globular-shaped, wicker covered bottle called a fiasco (flask). Modern technology has made it impractical to continue with such presentation; nowadays more emphasis is on the quality of the wine. Chianti has seven sub-districts including Classico, Colli, Fiorentini and Rufina. Classico is the historic centre of the zone. Along with Chinati ,Tuscany is also very famous for its dessert wines Vin Santo which refers to Holy Wine that uses the grape Trebbiano.

- **Valle D' Aosta:** This is the northwestern corner of Italy occupied by a small river bordering both France and Switzerland and is smallest of the twenty regions. It has one DOC which accounts for 85% of the production comprising red, white and rose which are consumed locally. Wines produced here are made from a number of native grapes, backed up by a smattering of Burgundy and Alsace varieties.
- **Lazio:** This region is famous for Frascati, a white wine that can be dry or sweet and sometimes sparkling and the equally well known white wine called Est ! Est !! Est !!! di Montefiascone made from Trebbiano.
- **Liguria:** An arc-shaped mountainous region that runs along the Mediterranean coast of northwest Italy. It is not a significant winemaking district and many of its traditional wines are made from raisined grapes such as syrupy dessert wines. Famous grape varieties grown here are Bosco (white) and Rossesse (red).
- **Lombardy:** It is geographically the largest of Italy's wine region and has been leader in producing quality wines.
- **Campania:** The cultivation of vineyards in Campania is a proof that ancient Greeks and Romans were very skilled in growing grapes. Despite all the modern technology, the best wines of Campania are still produced from the same place as 2000-4000 years ago. The grapes introduced by the Greeks way back have survived till date. The Aglianico (red) and Greco (white) vines of today both originate from the original vines planted by the ancient Greeks.
- **Apulia:** Apulia or Puglia region produces more wine than any other. Negroamaro grape is a prestigious grape of this region. Most of the wines are sent to Turin to make Vermouth.

- **Sicily:** The largest Mediterranean island, Sicily produces good table wines and exceptionally fortified wines. Marsala is made mainly from white grapes but some red grapes are also permitted. These fortified wines can be sweet or dry.
- **Sardinia:** This island produces some good quality wines, most of which comes from the co-operatives. Cannonau and Monica are the famous red grapes whereas Nuragus is the significant white grape here.
- **The Marches:** This is an eastern region on the Adriatic coast which produces wines by pairing red DOCs, Rosso Conero and Rosso Piceno made from blends from the eastern Italian variety, Montepulciano with Tuscany's Sangiovese.
- **Calabria:** Also known as the foot of Italy, it is not much renowned for its wines as the old and famous wines have more or less disappeared, although the classic version of Ciro white from the Greco Bianco is of good quality. White and red wines are also made here, but the area is much famous for red wines.
- **Fruili-Venezia-Giulia:** The region bordering Austria, Slovenia and Croatia is another region that has achieved some notable success with international varieties. Collio or Colli Orientalli is a varietally named wine. The reds Cabernet Sauvignon, Cabernet Franc, Merlot and Pinot Noir and the whites Traminer Aromatico, Ribolla Gialla, Pinot Grigio are all fine wines. The sweet whites, Picolit is a lovely golden dessert wine of this region.

- **Emilia-Romagna:** The most popular wine of this region is Lambrusco which comes in all colour but is usually sparkling, high in acidity and often of little discernible quality. Another famous wine of this region is Albana di Romagna which is the first wine in Italy to be graded a DOCG status.
- **Trentino-Alto Adige:** French varietals are grown here producing light wines. The most important red grape is the local Schiava, which is used to produce Santa Maddalena, the most famous wine from the area.
- **Umbria:** The region was once synonymous with Orvieto, the semi-sweet (*amabile*) white wine. The popular modern version Orvieto Secco, *amabile* (meaning soft in the mouth) is also available. The best wine however is, Torgiano Rosso Riserva closely followed by Sagrantino di Montefalco. Both are quality red wines.

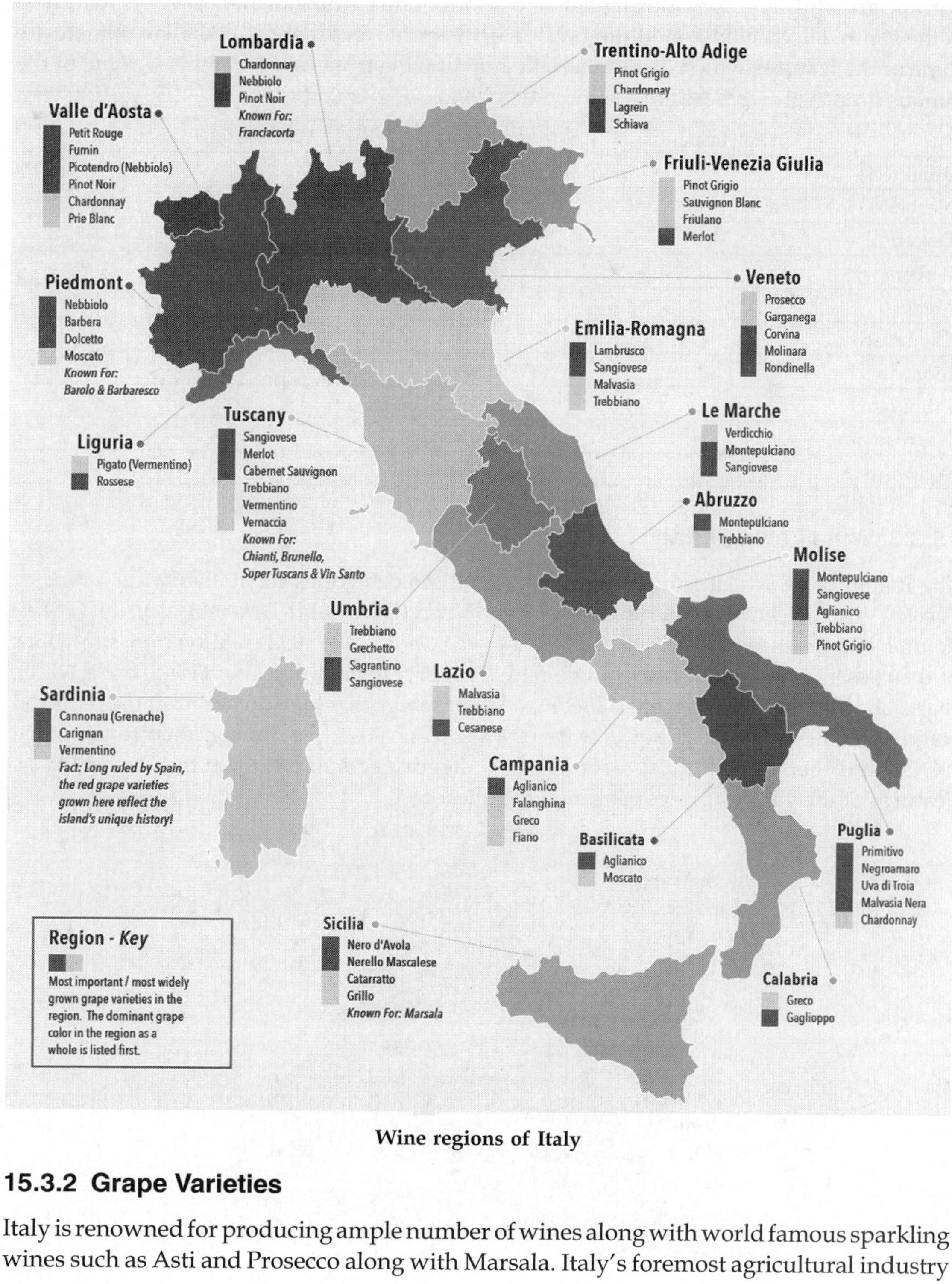

Wine regions of Italy

15.3.2 Grape Varieties

Italy is renowned for producing ample number of wines along with world famous sparkling wines such as Asti and Prosecco along with Marsala. Italy's foremost agricultural industry is grape growing as grapes are planted across the country from northern borders to its heel in the south. High acidity, medium body, earthy aroma and distinctive Italian climate are some of the features which distinguish the Italian wine from other countries. Some of the famous grapes grown here are mentioned below:

Red Grape	White Grape
Sangiovese	Pinot Grigio
Nebbiolo	Trebbiano
Dolcetto	Traminer
Barbera	Moscato
Merlot	Malvasia
Lambrusco	Gavi
Montepulciano	Soave
Primitivo	Vermentino
Negroamaro	Fiano
Aglianico	Verdicchio

15.3.3 Wine Laws of Italy

The Italian wine law of July 1963 introduced three categories for Italian wine - *Vino da Tavola* (VDT), *Denominazione di Origine Controllata* (DOC) and *Denominazione di Origine Controllate e Garantita* (DOCG). The 1963 law was updated in 1992 creating new sub-zones of the present DOC and introducing a new category, *Indicazioni Geografiche Tipiche* (IGT). It also allowed wines to be declassified to a lower category if they do not meet the required standards. For example, a DOCG wine of a sub-zone could be downgraded to the zonal DOCG and then down to a sub-zonal DOC category and so on down *to Vino da Tavola.* Features of the various categories are given ahead:

- **Vino da Tavola (VDT):** This is simply a table wine and is the lowest category of Italian wine.
- **Indicazioni Geografiche Tipiche (IGT):** This is similar to the *Vin de pays* of France and *Landwein* of Germany. These wines are generally superior to the VDT wines and reference to colour, grape, place or typology will appear on the label.
- **Denominazione di Origine Controllata (DOC):** This is equivalent to the French AOC. These wines have controlled origin, grape varieties, methods of production, yields and characteristics of the district of origin. When DOC appears on the label, it indicates that the wine is made from specified grape grown in a demarcated area and that the wine was vinified and aged according to prescribed standards. Since 1992, DOC wines must pass a laboratory and tasting examination.
- **Denominazione di Origine Controllata e Garantita (DOCG):** This category guarantees authenticity of origin, controls the grape variety used and has more stringent restrictions on yield, alcohol content, vinification and ageing. Generally these wines have a lower yield per hectare and are of high quality. These wines have to be tasted and officially approved by panel of experts. This top tier ranking only includes a few wines. Some of the famous wines within this group are Chinati, Barolo, Barbaresco, Asti Spumante and many others. All DOCG wines must be passed by a laboratory and tasting examination.

15.3.4 Reading A Wine Label Of Italian Wines

Italian wine label is very informative and easy to understand as it provides all the necessary information. Information stated in Italian wine label is shown here.

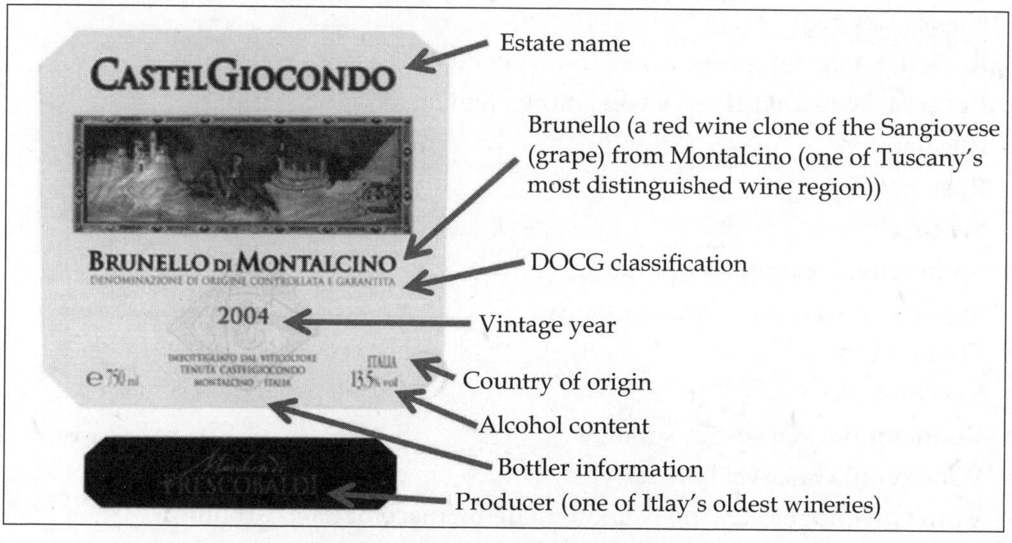

Italian wine label

1. Estate Name: It denotes the name of the producer.
2. Grape and Region: It identifies the name of the grape and region where the grape has been grown.
3. Classification: It tells wine belongs to which classification/law.
4. Vintage: It tells the harvest year.
5. Alcohol Content: It tells the alcoholic strength of the wine in alcohol by volume.
6. Bottler information and the name of the producer.

15.3.5 Terms Related to Italian Wine

- **Abboccato or amabile:** Slightly sweet
- **Annata:** Vintage
- **Azienda:** Estate
- **Bianco:** White
- **Cantina:** Cellar, winery
- **Casa vinicola:** Wine company
- **Chiaretto:** Deep rose
- **Classico:** Classical or best zone of a wine area
- **Consorzio:** Voluntary association of producers who ensure high standards above the minimum requirements.
- **Dolce:** Sweet
- **Imbottigliato:** Bottled by
- **Metodo Classico or Tradizionale:** Champagne method for making sparkling wine.
- **Nero:** Dark red
- **Recioti:** Some dry sweet wines from Veneto
- **Reserva:** Wine that received additional ageing.
- **Rosata:** Pink
- **Rosso:** Red
- **Secco:** Dry
- **Spumante:** Foaming or Sparkling
- **Superiore:** Wine of superior quality
- **Tenuta:** Estate
- **Vecchio:** Old
- **Vendemmia:** Harvest or Vintage
- **Vendemmia tardiva:** Late harvest
- **Vino Novello:** New wine usually made by macerazione carbonica

15.4 PORTUGUESE WINES

Portugal is the seventh largest wine producer in the world, exporting over half of its production. Apart from classic fortified wines Port and Madeira, Portugal also produces good quality full flavoured table wines. The wine growing vineyards are spread all over the country in the following areas:

Famous Portuguese wine terms

- **Vinho Tinto** Red Wine
- **Vinho Branco** White Wine
- **Quinta** Wine farm. It is mentioned as part of a winery's name on the label of wines from Portugal.

- **Alentejo:** The white wines produced here are distinguished for being slightly acidic and for its aroma of tropical fruit. The red Alentejo wines are full-bodied, rich in tannins having aromas of wild and red fruit.
- **Algarve:** The wines aren't designed to age but some particular red wines are aged. These drought-climate varieties result in juicy acids, creating, more smoky sweet, dusty notes in the wine.
- **Bairrada:** Known for good quality red wines which are rich in tannin when young but become mellow and soft with ageing. White wines of average quality along with some sparkling wines are also produced here.
- **Beiras:** Produces some rose wines along with some excellent red wines and a well known sparkling wine called *Raposeira*. The white wines produced here are slightly acetic.
- **Bucelas:** Produces white wines from the classic *Arinto* grapes.
- **Carcavelos:** This region is renowned for its flavoured fortified wines.
- **Colares:** Famous for producing red wines from *Ramisco* grapes.
- **Dao:** Famous for its full-bodied, earthly red wines. They are mostly blended and have an agreeable smoothness because of their unusual rich glycerine content.
- **Douro:** Also declared by UNESCO a world heritage site is famous for producing *Port* wines.
- **Estremadura:** This region is famous for both red and white table wines.
- **Minho:** Produces one of the most distinctive wines in Portugal called *Vinho Verde* (green wine). The green refers to the youth and the personality of the wine which is made from underripe grapes. These wines can either be red or white. These wines undergo Malolactic fermentation in order to breakdown the strong malic acid present.
- **Setubal:** This is famous for the fortified, intensely sweet amber coloured Moscatel De Setubal.
- **Tras-os-Montes:** Famous for producing internationally renowned *Mateus* Rose. This wine is beautifully labelled and presented in a Flagon-shape bottle.

Grape varieties of Portuguese wines

Red wines	White wines
Agua Santa, Alfrocheiro Preto, Azal Tinto, Bastardo, Borracal, Ramisco, Temapranillo, Tinta Pinheira, Touriga	Arinto, Bical, Boal, Moscatel, Ovelha, Trebbiano, Verdelho, Malvasia

15.5 WINES FROM SPAIN

Spanish sparkling wine

CAVA is the most important and well known sparkling wine from Spain which comes from the *Catalonia* region in the district of *Penedes.*

Spain has more vineyard acreage than any other country, but comes third behind Italy and France in terms of volume of wine produced. The vineyard is extremely arid in many regions and therefore, cannot be densely planted because the vines do not get enough moisture. The pre-eminence of Sherry has overshadowed the considerable merits of table wines. Use of modern equipment, cool fermentation techniques and stringent control on standards of production ensure that Spanish wine is well made. Spain is divided into six main regions as described below:

1. **Rioja:** Produces mainly red wines by using Tempranillo and Garnacha grapes.
2. **La Mancha:** Produces both red and white wines, but is known for its strong red wines.
3. **Catalonia:** Its main city is Barcelona which is divided into three districts:
   - **Allela:** Produces white wines.
   - **Penedes:** Known for its sparkling wines which is divided in two categories Cavas and Granvas.
   - **Tarragona:** Known for its fortified and sweet wines.
4. **Valencia:** Produces sweet red table wines.
5. **Galacia:** Produces a green white wine similar to the Portugese Vinho Verde.
6. **Andalucia:** This region produces lovely fortified dessert wine, Malaga.

Grape varieties of Spanish wines

Red wines	White wines
Azal Tinto, Baga, Borracal, Espadeiro, Ferron, , Tempranillo, Pinot Noir, Cabernet Sauvignon, Merlot	Airen, Albarino, Verdelho, Palomino, Pedro Ximenez, Planta Nova, Torrontes, Trajadura, Verdil, Xarel-Lo, Cabernet Franc, Chardonnay, Sauvignon Blanc

Wine laws that regulate the wine industry in Spain are:

- **Vinos de la Tierra (VT):** Country wines
- **Vinos de Calidad con Indicación Geográfica:** Quality wines with a geographical indication

- **Vinos de Denominación de Origen (DO):** Denomination of origin wines.
- **Vinos de Denominación de Origen Calificada (DOCa):** Qualified denomination of origin wines.
- **Vinos de Pago:** Estate wines
- **Consejos Reguladores:** Governing bodies

> **Did you know?**
> **Vino de Mesa (VdM):** A Spanish wine law states that these are wines that are the equivalent of most country's table wines and are made from unclassified vineyards or grapes.

15.6 HUNGARIAN WINE

The Romans likely planted the first vines in this region, then called Pannonia. Hungarians, originally nomadic who came here from Asia during the 9th and 10th century developed the vineyards across the following centuries. It was during the 18th century that Hungary, by then allied with Austria, started marketing its most famous wines, Tokaj throughout Europe. The greatest wine produced in Hungary is Tokaji, also spelt as Tokaji made around the town of Tokay. The wines come in various styles, but they are all made from the white grapes. Furmint, Harslevelu and Muskotaly. There are three styles of Tokay – Tokay Szamorodni, Tokay Aszu and Tokay Aszu Essencia. All Hungarian wines marketed for export are controlled by the state monopoly called Monimepex. The wines are usually named after their production zones: Eger, Balaton, Pecs, Mor, Sopron, Badacsony and Somlo.

REVISION QUESTIONS

1. Differentiate between new world wine and old world wine.
2. List down the information mentioned in the label of Italian wine bottle.
3. Write down the various wine producing regions of France with their characteristics.
4. Mention the various wine laws of France, Italy and Germany.
5. Write in brief about Portugal, Spain and Hungarian wines.

RESEARCH ACTIVITIES

- Collect wine lists from various five-star hotels situated in and around your city and study them.
- Search five red wines and five white wines of the following countries :
  - ◊ France
  - ◊ Portugal
  - ◊ Italy
  - ◊ Spain

16

New World Wines

16.1 INTRODUCTION

After reading this chapter, you will be able to understand:

- Differences between the old world wine producing countries and new world wine countries.
- Features of various new world wine producing countries like United States, Australia, New Zealand, South Africa, Japan, India Chile, Argentina and Canada.

Many wine producing areas have emerged in the New World countries since 1980. The New World in the context of wine, is a term used to describe wines that are either grown outside of Europe and the Mediterranean growing regions or it can also be known as the wines produced outside the traditional wine growing region of Europe. The New World countries are new to wine production. Most New World wines come from the United States, Australia, New Zealand, South Africa, Chile and Argentina however some other countries like Japan, China and India are also coming up with some fine wines. New World wines based much of their early production on European standards, but have since expanded and, in some cases, improved upon those ideals. In this chapter we will examine wines from the New World countries, grape varieties used along with the major wine growing regions and also differentiate between the Old World wine with the New World wines.

Table 16.1: Differences between old and new world wines

Old World wine countries	New World wine countries
Wines from European countries	Non-European wine producing countries
Winemaking techniques are customarily based on tradition rather than science	Winemaking techniques are modern and science based
Labelled by region	Labelled by grape variety
Wines with subtle character and charm	Intense fruit flavours
Wine laws are more rigid	Wine laws are more flexible
Wines are aged for long time	Generally wines are young

Generally comes with cork	Mostly comes with cap screws
Countries: France, Spain, Germany, Italy, Portugal, Austria, England, Greece, Croatia, Hungary.	**Countries:** Argentina, Australia, Chile, South Africa, United States, New Zealand, Brazil, Japan, China, India and many more.

Old World Merlot and New World Merlot

16.2 WINES FROM USA

USA is the fourth largest producer of the wine in the world and is now the leading wine consumer market. There are almost 1500 wineries in the United States but the production is concentrated in four states: California (accounting for about 90% of its national total), Washington State, Oregon and New York State. Washington State is the second largest wine producer in the country whereas in Oregon, wine industry has recently realized its potential for fine wines and has earned a reputation in producing quality wine from Pinot Noir. The state of New York is the third largest wine producer in the country including both *vinifera* or hybrid varieties. California is the home of north American wines and have cooler areas where the temperature is often regulated by sea mists coming in from the Pacific which produces the best wines. Site, situation, soil and climate in California is well suited for wine production. Napa and Sonoma are the best known regions and produce the finest wines in America.

16.2.1 Wine Regions of California

- **Sonoma county:** It is the diverse wine producing region due to the rolling hills, coastal mountains and rugged Pacific coastline. This county includes the very cool

Sonoma coastline, the Russian River Valley and the slightly more temperate, Alexander Valley. This region produces world-class Chardonnay, Pinot Noir, Merlot and Cabernet Sauvignon.

- **Napa county:** One of the California's top wine region. It is only 30 miles long and a few miles wide. This valley is revered for its grape, Cabernet Sauvignon.
- **Mendocino county:** Situated in the northern-most area and the rugged mountains near the coast.
- **Santa barbara county:** Because of its consistently mild climate, the Santa Barbara region is affectionately called the "Riviera" of California's central coastline. Here, a narrow coastal corridor forms the Santa Maria Valley which is one of California's few east-west valley's opening to the Pacific Ocean. The morning and afternoon fog that rushes through this corridor cools the Santa Maria Valley which helps in nurturing Chardonnay and Pinot Noir grapes.

Basically, two qualities of wine are made in United States; table wine and premium wine. Blush wines is an American invention, is a pale pinky-blue wine made from black grapes. The skins are only in contact with the must for an hour or two during fermentation.

Table 16.2: Major grape varieties of United States

Red grape	White grape
Zinfandel	Chardonnay
Cabernet Sauvignon	Sauvignon Blanc (Fume Blanc)
Pinot Noir	Riesling
Merlot	Pinot Gris
Syrah	Müller Thurgau
	Semillion

16.2.2 United States Wine Laws

In 1980 an appellation American Viticulture Area/Approved Viticultural Areas (AVAs) is formed however in contrast to the European system, any such geographic designation is not linked to constraints on grape variety, yield or production techniques, nor is there any system of grading wines by tasting. Features of AVAs are as follows:

- Varietal wines must use a minimum of 75% of grape named on the label.
- Within a geographical source indicated, atleast 75% of the wine must come from there.
- Wines from a specific vintage or from a nominated particular estate must have atleast 95% of that wine in the bottle.

16.3 WINES FROM AUSTRALIA

The vines were introduced to Australia by an English naval captian, Arthur Phillip, in 1788. Between 1820 and 1850, viticulture became a significant agricultural activity in southeastern Australia, the region surrounding the developing townships of Sydney, Melbourne and Adelaide. Throughout the 19th century, there were many private initiatives to import grape varieties from the Old World as immigrants, explorers and farmers who arrived from Europe with a few cuttings of *vitis vinifera*. From producing high alcoholic, heavily fortified and syrupy wines, Australia has developed production of good varietal wines. These wines are still reasonably high in alcohol, with strong characteristic grape flavours and intense fruit. Like many Californian wines, they are ready for drinking earlier than some of the better known European wines made from the same grape varieties. The red wines have less astringent tannins than their European counterparts, and the modern cool fermentation techniques couples with enlightened blending have produced high quality table wines at competitive prices.

Port wine is also very popular in many Australian households along with the table wines. European migration after the World War II began the habit of consumption of table wines in Australia.

Today wine is successfully made in:

- **Victoria (VIC):** Great Western, Yarra Valley, Geelong, Milawa, Rutherglen, Goulbern Valley.
- **South Australia (SA):** Clare Valley, Murray river Valley, Barossa Valley, Coonawarra, McLaren Vale, Longhorne's Creek, Southern Vales, Padthaway, and around Adelaide.
- **Western Australia (WA):** Mount Barker, Margaret river, Coastal Plain and the Swan river Valley.
- **Queensland (QLD):** Granite belt and Roma.
- **New South Wales (NSW):** Upper and Lower Hunter Valley, Mudgee, the Murrumbidgee Irrigation area and Cowra.
- **Tasmania (TAS):** Pipers Brook and Launceston.

16.3.1 Understanding an Australian Wine Label

In 1990 a Label Integrity Programme, aimed at controlling claims on label information, came into legislation. Most Australian wines indicate the name of the grape variety although many producers also state the brand names or estate names to the most prestigious wines such as Penfolds Grange. Blended wines, a large and very successful part of the industry, must list the grape varieties used in descending order of importance, for example, Aldridge's Estate Semillon Chardonnay will have a higher proportion of Semillon than Chardonnay. Eighty per cent of the wine bottled must be of the grape and region indicated.

If the label shows a vintage year, the bottle must contain at least 95% of that year's wine. Austalian wine labels are very informative, detailing product description which might include, when appropriate, terms such as oak matured and late harvest. Bin numbers and Vat numbers are often used to distinguish different styles or class of wine. Many wines are marketed under their grape name but they do not match the same quality as comparison to European counterparts, however some grapes have a good resemblance.

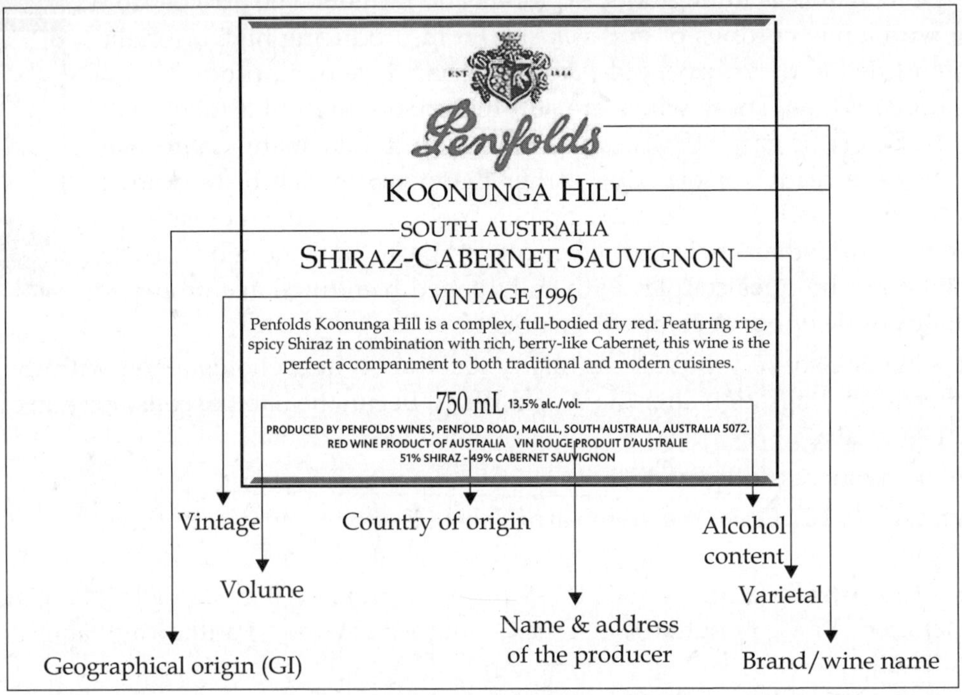

Australian wine label

16.3.2 Australian Grape Varieties

Over 60 grape varieties are cultivated, some for experimental purposes, but all originate from the classic European family *Vitis Vinifera.* Chardonnay (white), Shiraz (red) and Cabernet Sauvignon (red) remains the main grape.

Table 16.3: Principal grape varieties of Australia

White grape	Red grape
Chardonnay	Cabernet Sauvignon
Rhine Riesling	Shiraz (Hermitage)
Semillon	Pinot Noir
Sauvignon Blanc	Merlot
Gewurztraminer	Malbec

Colombard	Cabernet Franc
Marsanne	Petit Verdot
Muscat	

16.3.3 Wine Laws of Australia

Although nowhere near as strict as the French AOC, Australian wine regulations are enforced by the Australian Wine and Brandy Corporation, and include the following:

- When using a state, zone, region, or sub-region on a label, 85% of the wine must be from the stated place.
- If a grape variety is stated on the label, 85% of the wine must consist of that grape.
- If a vintage is stated on the label, 85% of the wine must come from that vintage.
- When blending grapes, if two or three grapes make up at least 85% of the wine, each of the grapes that make up 20% or more of the wine must be stated. If four or five grape varieties are used, and each makes up at least 5% of the wine, each of these grapes must be stated. Additionally, the grapes must be stated in the order of importance, such as Cabernet-Merlot when the wine contains more Cabernet Sauvignon than Merlot.

16.4 WINES FROM SOUTH AFRICA

South Africa, a country of about 44 million people, produces about 3.5% of the world's wines and is the world's seventh largest producer. Most of the vineyards in South Africa are located with in 100 miles of Cape Town, the major port city and located at the southernmost tip of the nation. The Cape has some of the best vineyard land and soil; climate and seasons suited to maturing grapes. Fifty per cent of the must was distilled in South Africa to make Brandy. However, nations, export strategy has been to move out of the market for bulk, brandy and fortified wines into that of high quality vinifera wines. South African wine history has witnessed a series of problems and obstacles since its very inception till date. Problems faced by the South African wine industry in the recent past has been the long wait for 15 years, imposed by the government that delayed availability of new vines to the farmers, a local population whose consumption of wines is only 9 litres per year and a climate that alternates between too warm and too cool, thereby producing either overripe grapes or under ripe fruit. The most critical problem, which will take a few more years to be rectified, is that South Africa's social and political policies had resulted in sanctions and resistance to almost all products of the country including wine industry. After the failure of the apartheid policy, South Africa was isolated from the international community, and its wine industry was kept out of touch with the latest wine production methods and contemporary viticultural trends. The current issues faced by the industry is huge quantities of grapes being produced thereby giving the quality of the yield a second-class status. Second, is the failure of the proprietary grape of the country, *Pinotage,* in the international market. The wines made of these grapes are muddy, cooked, too earthy and a bit flat.

16.4.1 South African Grape Varieties

Most of the wines are sold as varietals. Red wine production is in full-bodied style.

Table 16.4: Grape varieties grown in South Africa

White grape	Red grape
Cape Riesling	Cabernet Franc
Chardonnay	Cabernet Sauvignon
Chenin Blanc or Steen	Cinsault (Hermitage)
Muscat d' Alexandrie	Merlot
Sauvignon Blanc	Pinotage
Palomino	Pinot Noir

16.4.2 South African Wine Laws

Wine law system was established in 1973 called South African wines-of-origin (WO) with appellations applied to regions, districts and wards to increase specificity. It is a highly organized control system.

The law specifies the following:

- The label must specify the area of wine's origin.
- Must have name of the producer.
- Can have vintage date if 75% of the wine is from that year.
- A varietal wine must have 75% of the grape variety after which it is named.

The wines are produced by small cooperatives and are sold to the main producing company of which the biggest and most important is KWV *(Kooperatiewe Wijnbouwers Vereniging)*. All growers must belong to this association.

16.4.3 Wine Producing Regions of South Africa

Coastal regions

- **Stellenbosch:** Known as "Napa Valley of Cape", it is one of the most important regions in the Cape. The main producers of this region are **Stellenbosch farmer's winery, Berkgelder** and **Gilbeys**.
- **Constantia:** This is home to the oldest vineyards of the Cape. It is also the home of the first and most famous vineyard lands in South Africa, **Groot Constantia**. This region makes light reds and whites but is famous for dessert wines made from Muscat.
- **Durbanville:** A very small region, however, some of the vineyard locations are believed to be the best. Some of the main producers are **Parker family,** famous for nations' only Barbera and Gewürztraminer.

- **Paarl:** It is famous as the home of KWV. It is also famous for sherry made by the Solera system. This region also manufactures sweet fortified wines in style of port.
- **Swartland:** Viticulture is confined to southern section of Swartland. Famous varietals arc Chenin Blanc and Sauvignon Blanc.
- **Tulbaugh:** Famous for Cap Classique Brut from Pinot Noir.
- **Overberg:** Famous producers are Walker Bay and Elgin.

Inland regions

- **Klien Karoo:** Known for Porto style fortified wines.

16.5 WINES FROM CHILE

Chile has an ideal geography, geology and climate to produce wines that are both distinctive and outstanding. As its natural borders are protected by the Andes in the west and the Pacific Ocean in the east with a coastal range of hills running north to south between the plain and ocean the vine eating louse phylloxera has not found its way to Chile, meaning that the older vines remain healthy and ungrafted. Grape growing arrived with the Spanish conquistadors in the 1500s. The early grapes were very likely to be the País or Mission grapes from Spain or the Canary Islands. Today Chile is one of the highly export-focused markets. A further winemaking advance occurred in the early 1980s, with the introduction of stainless steel fermentation tanks and the use of oak barrels for ageing. Chile has many unique wine regions with distinct terroir. From the Atacama desert in the north, to Bío Bío in the south, each region has its own unique personality and grapes that thrive. The Casablanca Valley by the coast is cool and foggy—perfect for Pinot Noir and Sauvignon Blanc; Maipo and Colchuago in central Chile have hotter days so also suited to big hearty reds such as Cabernet and Carménère. Maule, to the south of Maipo also grows Cabernet and Carignan. The DO (Denominacion de origin) designation has existed here only since 2002. Five regions have been recognized, divided into subregions that correspond to particular valleys. The notion of named places of origin as an index of wine style is still emerging as most of the Chilean wines are produced as blends of different subregions.

16.6 ARGENTINIAN WINES

Argentina is the world's fifth largest producer of wine and it exports its delicious wines to countries all over the world, keeping enough in the country itself to satisfy its local wine lovers. Argentina has cleverly conserved the rains and snow of the Andes mountains which later can be distributed through a system of irrigation to keep the vines and other crops healthy. Mendoza is the best and largest producing region accounting for up to 70%

of the national output. The other centres of wine production are San Juan, Rio Negra, La Rioja, Catamara and Salta. Malbec is the country's most recognized grape variety; the country also offers a mixture of reds in the way of Bernado, Syrah, Cabernet Sauvignon and Pinot Noir, amongst others. When it comes to whites, Argentina is renowned for its aromatic Torrontés but has also gained recognition for its Chardonnays and Sauvignon Blancs. As per the Argentina's wine regulation, wines displaying a varietal on the label must contain 80% of that varietal.

16.7 CANADIAN WINES

The wine production in Canada dates back to the middle of the nineteenth century and has now developed a serious industry after the introduction of vinifera vines varietals. The other great influence was the success of the ice wines which were originally and still are produced from hybrid Vidal and later also from the Riesling, whereas Chardonnay and Merlot are also quality wines produced here. The four provinces which produce wines in Canada are Ontario, British Columbia, Nova Scotia and Quebec with Ontario and British Columbia being the far most important. A federal appellation control system has been introduced called the Vintners Quality Alliance (VQA) which both Ontario and British Columbia have joined. There are controlled appellations (VAs) and all wines bearing the VQA seal must have been passed by analysis and a tasting panel. Wines displaying a designated VA must contain 85% grape from that area. Wines displaying a varietal on the label must contain 85% of that varietal with the other 15% coming from their respective province.

16.8 NEW ZEALAND WINES

Vines were introduced in New Zealand in 1819. Europeans who migrated to New Zealand pioneered the wine industry. Purity, vibrancy and intensity makes New Zealand wines different from other wines. The long ripening period due to cooler climate develops flavour whilst retaining fresh acidity, a balance for which New Zealand wines are known. Chardonnay is the most widely planted varietal in New Zealand, followed by Sauvignon Blanc and Muller Thurgau along with Riesling, Chenin Blanc, Semillon and Gewurztraminer. Among the reds, Cabernet Sauvignon produces the best wines often blended with some Merlot. Major wine producing regions of New Zealand are Hawke's Bay, Marlborough, Canterbury/Waipara, Central Otago and Coudy Bay. New Zealand producers have used French and German names to identify their style of wines for many years, the most popular modern approach is to list the name of the grape variety. A registration system established in 1994 delimits growing areas by setting out the borders of recognized regions, subregions and even of individual estates but wines detailing their region of origin tend to be exported. A regional name may be featured on the label if 100% of the wine originates from there with the grapes both grown and processed locally.

16.9 WINES FROM BRAZIL

Brazil a native to North America has got a hot, damp climate which tends to suit the Isabella (*Vitis labrusca*) better than the European classic *Vitis vinifera*. Modern technological development and expertise has resulted in the cultivation of the classic grapes like Merlot, Cabernet Sauvignon, Pinot Noir for reds and the Riesling, Sauvignon Blanc, Semillon, and Trebbiano for whites. Most styles of wine are made but the sparkling is best of all made either traditionally or by the sealed tank method. The two main centres of production are Rio Grande do Sul and Sao Paulo.

16.10 WINES FROM JAPAN AND CHINA

Japan which is prone to monsoons and typhoons, does not have a climate conducive to vine cultivation. Yet the country produces some good red and white wines, for instance those sold under the Chateau Lumiere label and good sweet wine from Chateau Lion. The main grapes used are Labrusca, Delaware, Campbell's Early and the indigenous Koshu. Some European vines like Cabernet Sauvignon, Merlot, Chardonnay and Semillon are also cultivated. The principal wine districts are Honshu, Kyushu and Hokkaido, which has favourable microclimate for vine cultivation whereas in China there are six wine producing regions; Kiangsu to the north of Shanghai, Hebei northwest of Peking, Liaoning in Manchuria, Sheris near Sian on the Yellow River, Sinkiang and the Shantung peninsula. Some indigenous grapes used in China are Dragon's eye, Cow's Nipple, Cock's Heart and Beichun as well as Cabernet Sauvignon, Cabernet Franc, Pinot Noir, Gamay, Gewurztraminer, Riesling and Muscat.

16.11 WINES FROM INDIA

India has been making wine for many centuries but most Indians prefer hard drinks (whisky and rum) to wines, but due to the recent westernization of urban middle and upper classes the perception of wine in India has changed. A new market has grown dramatically here for wine. Within more than 40 estates, the state of Maharashtra is country's leading wine region followed by Karnataka and others. Many of the leading wines producers of the country including Sula vineyards located in Nashik, Maharashtra where the grapes are grown at high altitude on the slopes of the Sahyadri mountains. Sauvignon Blanc, Cabernet Sauvignon and Syrah are the most popular grape varieties including Isabella, also known as Bangalore Blue and Muscat Hamburg also known as Gulabi. Other known Indian grapes are Anab-e-Shahi, Bhokri, Thomson, Dilkhush, Sharad seedless and many more.

REVISION QUESTIONS

1. List down the various differences between new world wines and old world wines.
2. Name famous wine regions of the following:
   U.S.A., South Africa, Australia.

RESEARCH ACTIVITY

Paste the wine label of Australian wines in your notebook and write down the information mentioned on it.

17

Champagne

17.1 INTRODUCTION

> **After reading this chapter, you will be able to understand:**
> - Difference between Champagne and sparkling wine.
> - Various methods of making Champagne.
> - Grape varieties used in making Champagne.
> - Reading Champagne label.
> - Champagne glassware.

Champagne is a light sparkling wine which is made only in the Champagne region of northeastern France that is 90 km north-east of Paris and 300 km from the coast. It is part of the northern-most wine growing belt of France having very cold winters whereas summers are long and cool with a topography of low hills. Soil here is chalky which lends to the acidity in wines. These chalky slopes of Champagne provide effective drainage and also provide enough moisture to nourish the plants. The soil is rich in minerals. Champagne is a blended wine. It is different from all other sparkling wines in the world for three major reasons. First, a wine can only be labelled as "Champagne" if it is made in the Champagne region of France. Second, to be called "Champagne," it must be made only from the Pinot Noir, Pinot Meunier, or Chardonnay grapes which grow in that region. Third, true Champagne, as opposed to other sparkling wines has to have gotten its bubbles by undergoing the fermentation process twice: once in barrels and again in bottles. Champagne can be produced elsewhere, as long as credit is given to the "*methode champenoise*" on the label.

17.2 GRAPE VARIETIES

The grapes of Champagne are primarily black; about two-thirds of the vineyards grow black grapes. Although the skin is black, the juice is white. The chief grape is Chardonnay. The three main grape varieties are:

- **Chardonnay:** White grape produces a lighter, fresher juice. Provides freshness, elegance and finesse.

Chardonnay
Adds freshness, elegance and finesse.

Pinot noir
Adds body, structure and a complexity of flavours.

Pinot meunier
Adds fruitiness and floral aromas.

- **Pinot Noir:** A black grape that does not have much depth and alcoholic strength. It provides body structure and complexity of flavours.
- **Pinot Meunier:** This is also a black grape that provides fruitiness and floral aroma.
- The ratio of the grapes used are :

The Champagne region is divided into the areas of production:

- Montagne de Reims
- Vallee de la Marne
- Cote des Blancs
- Aube

17.3 MANUFACTURING OF CHAMPAGNE

17.3.1 "Methode Champenoise"

1. **Picking:** It is critical that the grapes are picked at the correct ripeness. Immense care must be taken in handling the grapes to avoid damaging them.
2. **Pressing:** It should be done rapidly so that the skin of black grapes does not colour the juice. The wooden press called the *marc* holds about 4000 kg of grapes. The law allows only 2666 litres of juice to be extracted in the first press known as the *vin de cuvee* and all the best Champagnes are made from this. The next 666 litres is *premier taille* and is used for blending. The last press results in *rebeche* and is used to make *Marc de Champagne.*

3. **Liqueur de triage:** A small amount of cane sugar and old wine is added along with a special type of yeast. This ensures that every bottle undergoes a secondary fermentation. The bottles are sealed by hand with corks or mechanically by crown caps. The bottles are then stacked on their sides in underground chalk caves.
4. **Secondary fermentation:** Best carried out at 10-12°C and takes 6-8 months. The yeast turns the sugar into alcohol and carbon dioxide, which dissolves into the wine thus creating a desired stream of bubbles called the mousse. A long slow fermentation produces a very fine and lasting mousse.
5. **Ageing:** The best wines are aged for 3-5 years, but the legal requirement is one year. During this time the alcohol reacts with acids to produce sweet smelling esters, which give Champagne its exquisite bouquet.

Champagne riddling rack known as pupitre

6. **Remuage/riddling:** The bottles are placed in racks with oval holes called *pupitre,* their necks being tilted slightly downwards. The *remuer* grasps the bottom of the bottle and gives it a slight shake, turns and tilts. This happens to each bottle every three days for about six weeks and at the end of this time, the bottles will be standing vertically with their necks down and the sediment settles down at the cork.

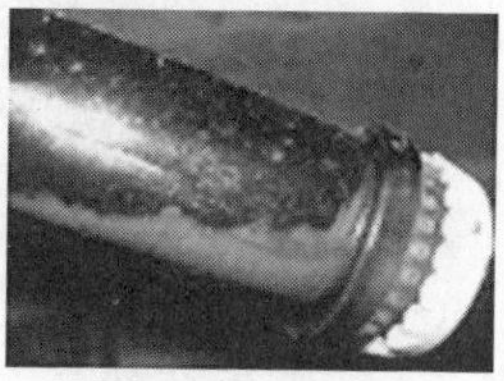

Disgorgement

7. **Disgorgement:** The neck of the bottle is dipped in a freezing brine solution, forming a small block of ice at the neck. The pressure built up in the bottle expels the ice when the cap is removed.
8. **Dosage:** A dosage is added to top up each bottle and give the Champagne the desired sweetness. The dosage is also called *liqueur d' expedition,* and it is a mixture of wine and cane sugar. The younger the wine, the greater the dosage needed to balance its acidity.
9. **Recorking:** A compound cork of three sections is wired down to resist the pressure of CO_2.
10. **Shaking:** This is done to distribute the dosage evenly.
11. **Resting:** A wine is rested again for 4-6 months.
12. **Packaging:** Bottles are cleaned, labelled and dispatched.

Did you know?

The pressure in a Champagne bottle is typically between 70 and 90 pounds per square inch. That's two to three times the pressure in a car tyre, about the same as in a double-decker bus tyre.

17.3.2 The Tank Method/Bulk or Charmat Method

It is named after its inventor Eugene Charmat, a French wine scientist, who wanted to reduce the time and money involved in the process. In this, after primary fermentation the various base wines are blended together. The blended base wines are put into another fermentation tank for 1-5 years. For secondary fermentation to take place the yeast and sugar is added. After 1-5 years the tank is cooled to filter the dead yeast. Afterwards dosage is done then bottled, corked and labelled. This method is also known as *cuvee close*.

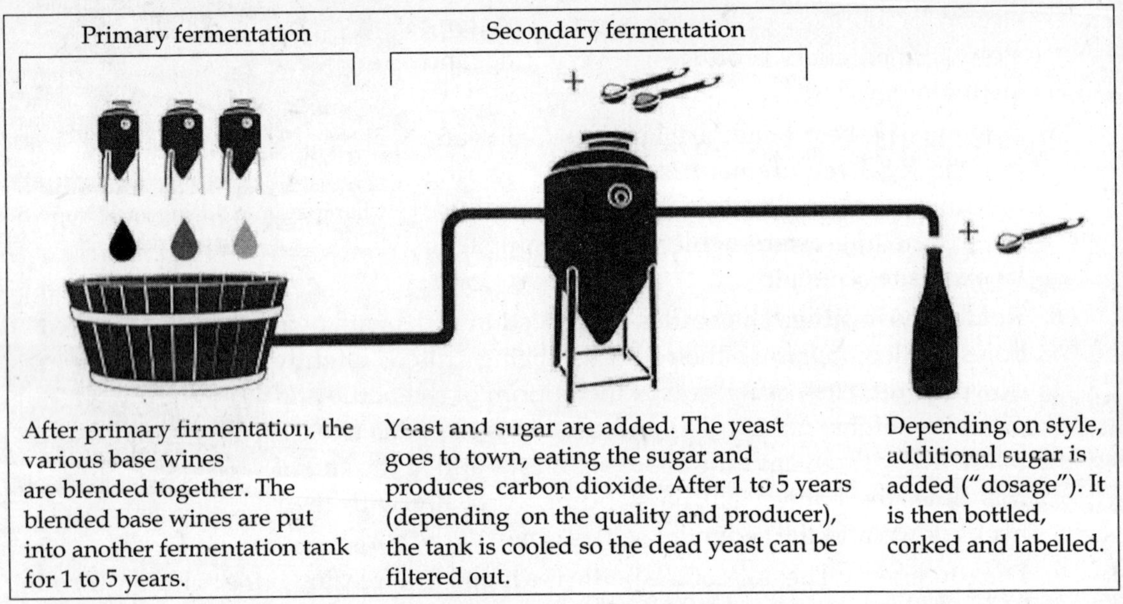

Tank method (Charmat method)

17.3.3 The Transfer Method

Also known as *méthode transfert* in French. This method was developed in Germany in 1930s and is a modification of the *methode champenoise*. In this process the riddling technique is not used, instead after ageing all the wine in the bottles are transferred to a large tank and the temperature brought down to 32ºF. After filtration, the wines are bottled with addition of dosage.

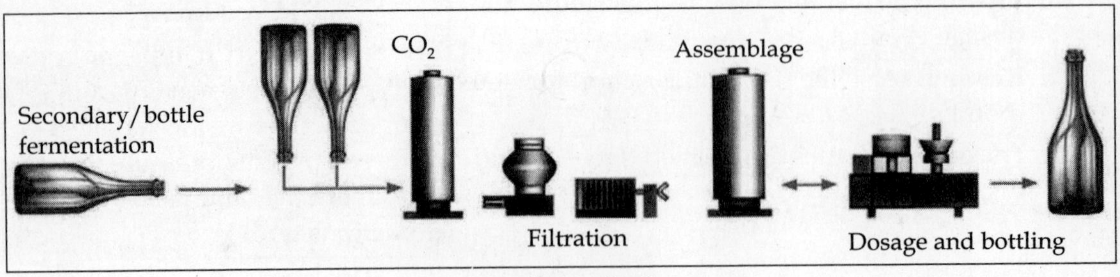

Transfer method

17.3.4 Artificial Carbonation

The quickest and cheapest method of making sparkling wine – similar to the way soft drinks are made to fizz, by injecting carbon dioxide. In this, the bubbles are not an integral part of the wine nor does it last for long.

Did you know?

Why Champagne bottles have Punt?

For Champagne and sparkling wine, the punt helps to give structural integrity to the bottle, which has to be pretty strong to hold during pressure of the bubbly wine. Also, it helps the bottles stack if putting them one on top of the other during the second fermentation stage.

Did you know?

Bruno Dutertre headed a three year, $7 million joint project between Moet & Chandon and Heineken to understand and study the influence of chemical and physical parameters on the formation of bubbles and the stability of the mousse between 1986 and 1989. At the heart of this research was a camera-based, computer-linked "artificial vision" system built by ITMI (Industrie et Technolgie de la Machine), which actually recorded the release of bubbles and counted them. As per its result, there are on average 250 million bubbles in a bottle of Champagne and the stream of bubbles is known as Mousse.

17.4 BOTTLE SIZES

- Split - 187.5 mL (About 1.5 Glass)
- Half - 375 mL (About 2.5 Glasses)
- Bottle - 750 mL (About 5 Glasses)
- Magnum - 2 Bottles (About 10 Glasses)
- Jeroboam - 4 Bottles (About 20 Glasses)
- Rehoboam - 6 Bottles
- Methuselah - 8 Bottles (About 40 Glasses)
- Salmanazar - 12 Bottles (About 40 Glasses)
- Balthazar - 16 Bottles (About 60 Glasses)
- Nebuchadnezzar - 20 Bottles (About 100 Glasses)

17.5 STYLES OF CHAMPAGNE

Various styles of Champagne are as follows:

- **Blancs de blancs:** An increasing common style from Chardonnay grapes. The style is usually fresh and bright, and many deluxe types of Champagne are now labelled Blanc de Blancs.
- **Blanc de noirs:** This rare style is made from 100 per cent black grapes.
- **Rose:** It is an increasingly popular style. Traditionally, the pink colour is gained by a careful and short maceration of the Pinot Noir and Pinot Meunier grapes skins with the juice.

- **Cremant:** A Champagne with only half the normal amount of fizz. If the base wine is good, that is still good enough.
- **Deluxe:** Premium Champagne, beautifully packaged, highly priced and grapes from Grand Cru region.
- **Vintage:** Wine of a single, usually good quality year; deeper and better than a non-vintage.

17.6 LEVEL OF SWEETNESS

The amount of dosage determines the degree of sweetness or dryness in the wine. Following are the guidelines for designating Champagne.

Extra brut	Less than 6 grams of sugar per litre
Brut	Less than 15 grams of sugar per litre
Extra dry	12-20 grams per litre
Sec	17-35 grams per litre
Demi sec	35-50 grams per litre
Doux	More than 50 grams per litre

17.7 READING A LABEL OF CHAMPAGNE

Apart from various terms on the back of the label, there are certain numbers that indicate the type of producer and the numbers following will indicate each different winemaker. Main letters are as follows:

(i) **RM—Recoltant manipulant:** Harvester handler. This indicates that the wine is from a single grower.

(ii) **CM—Cooperative manipulant:** Cooperative handler. This means that the wine comes from a Cooperative.

(iii) **NM—Negociant manipulant:** Merchant handler. Also called Merchant's wines. They are traditionally the most powerful and famous of the Champagne trade. Their wines are likely to be of the highest standard.

The following items also appear on the label:

- The word 'Champagne'.
- Brand name.
- Nominal value - The amount of the wine in the container.
- Alcohol content - As a percentage of volume.
- Professional registration code
- Producer
- Location of producer
- Country of origin

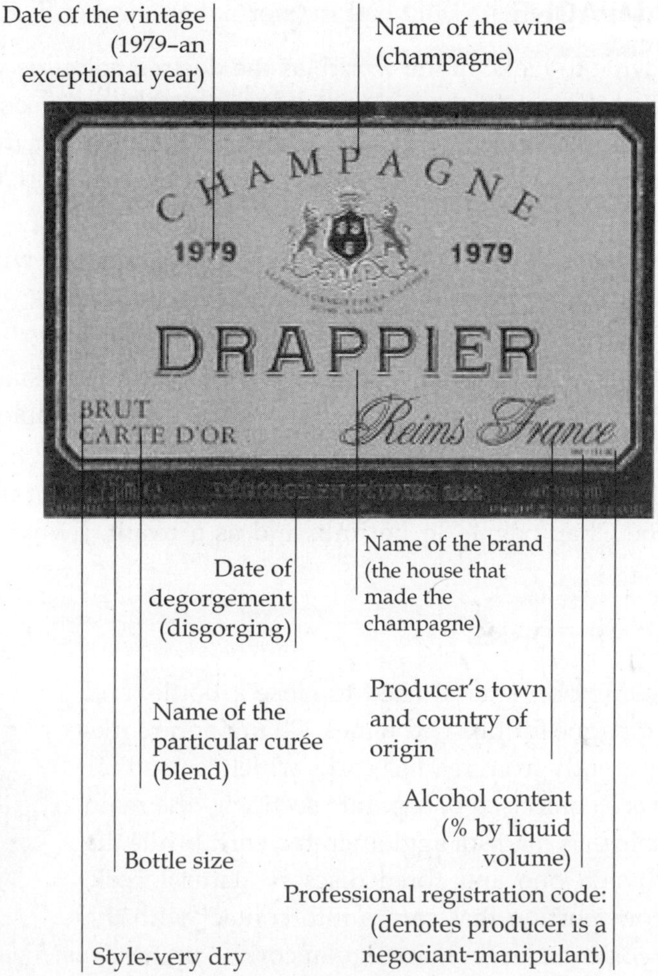

Parts of a Champagne label

17.8 THE LAW

Only sparkling wines made in the Champagne district of France can be called Champagne. The *Comite Interprofessional du vin de Champagne* is the authority responsible for coordinating the interests of the many thousands of vineyard owners and their workers with those of their outlets for the finished product, Champagne.

> **Other sparkling wines**
>
> - **Spanish:** Cava wines; largest producers are Cordoniu & Frexinet Cava.
> - **Italian:** Asti spumante
> - **German:** Sekt
> - **French sparkling wines:** Burgundy and Alsace make Cremants, also in the Loire valley.

17.9 ROSE CHAMPAGNE

The most difficult wine to make in the world, as the desired colour is very unpredictable and there are always chances of the pigment to precipitate out as sediment. As a result people also indulge into illegal practices by adding artificial colour in the form of some berry juice, cochineal or red vegetable dye. The ways of making Rose Champagne are as follows:

1. Traditional method, wherein the grape juice is left in contact with the skin leading to transfer of colour. The colour is again unstable and there are always chances of the pigment separating out.
2. Addition of red wine to White Champagne. This addition usually happens in the secondary fermentation stage. Again the colour is very unstable and may separate out.
3. Addition of red wine can also occur at the dosage stage. But in this case, the red wine and the Champagne do not mix and as a result, the wine develops an off flavour.

17.10 CHAMPAGNE CORKS

Cork is the most common material used to close a bottle, and mandatory in Champagne for finished wines. Champagne corks are constructed differently from regular corks which is used for still wines, as they are composed of separate sections - the main body, called the *manche,* is made of agglomerated cork, while the *miroir* consists between one and three discs of natural cork, affixed to the bottom portion that comes into contact with the wine. Champagne corks are larger than regular corks—up to *48 mm high* and *31 mm in diameter*—and are highly compressed when they are inserted into the bottle, reduced in diameter to only 17 mm. This provides for a tight seal, allowing them to retain the carbon dioxide in the bottle. Cork in a bottle of Champagne is secured by a large metal clip or the wire cage that keeps the cork in a bottle which is known as *Agraffe.*

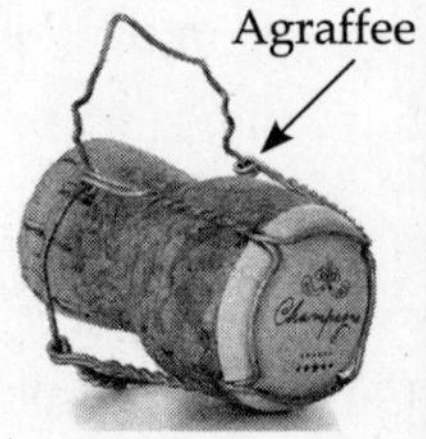

17.11 CHAMPAGNE GLASSES

Champagne should be served in long-stemmed flutes or tulip-shaped glasses. These are designed to enhance the flow of bubbles to the crown and to concentrate the aromas of the wine. Champagne or sparkling wines should not be served in Champagne saucer glass or coupe glass as in this glass, the bubbles dissipate quickly due to the large area exposed to air, and spillage is a constant problem. The perfect glass to serve Champagne or sparkling wine is Champagne tulip glass. Never chill or ice the glass as it would take away from the enjoyment of the wine. Incidentally, since the surface texture of crystal is rougher than ordinary glass, more bubbles form on these glasses.

	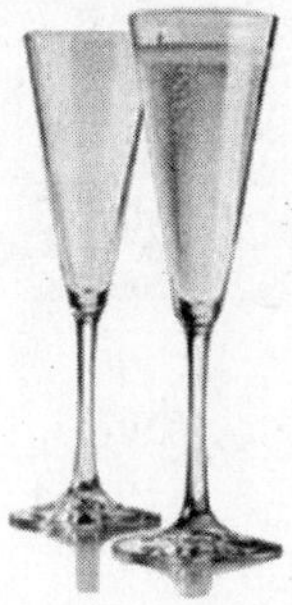	
Champagne tulip	**Champagne flute**	**Champagne saucer**

17.12 SERVING TEMPERATURE

Serving Champagne at the proper temperature is essential. Champagne should be served at a temperature between 39 and 48 degrees Fahrenheit (4 to 9°C). Non-vintage and sweeter Champagnes can take the lower side of that scale, but a fine Champagne should be served between 43 and 46°F (6 to 7°C). Remember to always leave the bottle corked until it's time to serve.

Champagne in wine chiller

17.13 MAJOR CHAMPAGNE PRODUCERS

- Krug
- Lanson
- Dom perignon
- Bollingers
- Tattingers
- Charles hiedsieck
- Veuve clicquot pont sardin
- G.H. Mumms
- Laurent periere
- Piper hiedsieck
- Moet et chandon

Some interesting facts about Champagne

- Legend has that Marilyn Monroe once took a bath in 350 bottles of Champagne.
- All Champagnes are blend of thirty to sixty separate still wines.
- Dom Perignon, who was a monk is referred to as father of Champagne.
- The name Champagne is derived from **Campagnia**, a Latin term for the countryside north of France.

Some interesting facts about Indian sparkling wine

- Sula Brut is a sparkling wine produced by Sula Vineyards.
- The first and only sparkling wine made by **Methode Champagnoise** is Marquise De Pompadour.
- The first sparkling wine exported from India is **Omar Khayyam**, which comes from the abode of Champagne Indage.
- The first Indian sparkling wine to win an international award was Marquise De Pompadour which won a Bronze medal at **International Wine & Spirit Competition** in 1986.

Brand Names of Other Sparkling Wines

- **Carta Nevada:** Spain
- **Cordon Nigro:** Spain
- **Processo-di-valdob:** Italy
- **Henkell Trocken:** Germany
- **Sula Brut:** Indian
- **Henkel Kardinal:** Germany

Sparkling wine glossary

- **Vin Mousseux:** French term for sparkling wine.
- **Phil/ant:** French term for sparkling wine.
- **Perlant:** French term for lightly sparkling.
- **Spritzig:** German term for slightly sparkling.
- **Schaumwein:** German term for sparkling.
- **Perlwein:** German term for slightly sparkling.
- **Sekt:** German term for sparkling.
- **Spumante:** Italian term for sparkling.
- **Espumante:** Portuguese term for sparkling.
- **Espumosos:** Spanish term for sparkling.
- **Trocken:** German dry sparkling wine.

- **Lagenbach:** Germany
- **Dienhard Cabinet:** Germany
- **Asti Spumante:** Italian
- **Cobetchoe White:** Russian

REVISION QUESTIONS

1. Differentiate between Champagne and sparkling wine.
2. Write five brand names of sparkling wine.
3. What is the ratio of the grapes used in making Champagne? Also write down the name of the grape varieties used in making Champagne.
4. What does the brut and extra brut signify in a Champagne.

RESEARCH ACTIVITIES

- Prepare a PowerPoint presentation on the different Champagne making methods.
- Search the different brand names of Champagne served in major hotels of India.
- Search the different brand names of sparkling wines served in major hotels of India.
- Paste a Champagne label in your notebook and write down all the available information from it.

18

Fortified Wines

18.1 INTRODUCTION

After reading this chapter, you will be able to understand:

- Meaning of fortified wines
- Types of fortified wines
- The solera system
- Types of sherry and port.
- Madeira and Marsala

In general, the term fortified means *strengthened* or *in addition to*. Fortified wines or liqueur wines are those wines in which alcoholic percentage has been increased to 16%-22% ABV by the addition of neutral spirit brandy, however any neutral spirit distilled from grapes, grains or sugar can also be added. But in general, brandy is used as an addition. The reason behind fortification is to stop fermentation by adding spirit because sometimes inactive yeasts activate and start fermentation process, passing through different climatic conditions. Fortification halts the fermentation process by killing yeasts and the unfermented sugar makes the wine sweeter than other wines. Fortified wines are generally served after meals with dessert or between meals except sherry (fino). The reason for this addition goes back hundreds of years, when in some wines brandy was added before they were shipped so that the wines reach their destination in a reasonable condition. Transportation of wine in those early years was unreliable and dirty. The wines were shipped in containers that were unhygienic, sometimes in animal skins. It was a side product of the fortifying that the wines arrived at their destination, sometimes after months at sea, having travelled through a variety of climate zones, very different in character from how they started their journey, very often much improved. One of the examples of this type of wines are the wines of the island of Madeira. The process of manufacture of these wines imitates the heat variations that the wines experienced on their long ocean journeys. Fortified wines are stronger than usual, so they are poured in smaller quantities while serving.

There are many factors which affect fortified wine:

- The point at which the spirit is added to grapes/must during the fermentation process (this affects how sweet or dry the wine will be); sometimes sweetness is added after the fermentation process.

- The type of spirit being used.
- The type of wine the spirit is added to.
- Any additional botanicals, aromatics or flavours.

Fortified wines can be either dry or sweet. Dry varieties are ideal for an aperitif, either on their own or mixed into a cocktail, and sweet varieties, which often feature on dessert menus, are ideal after dinner with some pudding.

18.2 TYPES OF FORTIFIED WINES

18.2.1 Sherry

> **Did you know?**
> **Mistelle**
> It is a grape juice or slightly fermented white wine to which brandy has been added that is used in the production of other wines (as some vermouths and Malaga).

Sherry is a fortified and blended wine, made through the solera system containing 17 to 22 per cent alcohol. Sherry originated in southwest Andalusia in the region of Jerez. The town Jerez was founded by the Phoenicians in 1100 B.C. who brought their sailing ships to an inland city near the Bay of Cadiz off the Atlantic coast, and named it Xera. After the Roman conquest, Xera was latinized to Ceret, which the Moors pronounced as Scheris. This was subsequently hispanicized to Jerez, and anglicized, in reference to the beverage, into sherry. The official sherry-producing zone, known as the zona de jerez superior, or "zone of superior sherry," is bounded by three major towns: Puerto de Santa Maria, Sanlucar de barrameda, and Jerez de la Frontera. The Jerez area is triangular in shape and lies between the Guadalquivir and Guadalete rivers in southwest Spain, with the Atlantic Ocean on the west. The entire Jerez area consists of some 55,000 acres of vineyards.

18.2.1.1 Law

The Spanish regulatory agency established in 1933 to guarantee the authenticity of sherry is the Consejo Regulador do la Denominacion de Origin Jerez-Xeres-Sherry. The tribunal High Court of England ruled in 1967 that only wine from Jerez may be identified simply as sherry, and that imitations must be labelled by their country of origin.

18.2.1.2 Grape Varieties

Grapes used in making sherry are white. *Palomino, Pedro Ximenez* and *Muscatel* are the grapes used for making sherry wine. Palomino Blanco grapes are pale in colour, fairly large, and grow predominantly in albariza soil. This grape is used in the production of 85 per cent of all sherry wine whereas Pedro Ximenez and Muscatel grapes are used to sweeten sherry wine.

18.2.1.3 Production Process

Grapes are harvested, crushed and destemmed, and immediately sent to a press, where the first 85 to 90 per cent of the liquid obtained is used to produce sherry. The remaining

10 to 15 per cent, which is usually of a lower quality, is distilled into brandy, to be used later to fortify the sherry wine. The must is allowed to ferment in large 130-gallon barrels made of American white oak. After all of the sugar has been metabolized by the yeast, resulting in a wine with 11 to 13 per cent alcohol, the wine is racked off the lees (which separates the wine from its sediment, such as dead yeast, pits, and grape solids). It is then put into other barrels, which are only partially (about 80 per cent) filled and loosely "bunged" (referring to the tightness of the coopering on the barrels), which will help develop a sherry style. The wine is then fortified with brandy made from the sherry wine, raising its alcoholic content to 15.5 per cent. The high alcohol content favours the flor action and is sufficiently high to prevent acetification (vinegar production). Flor is a yeast-like substance (*Saccharomyeces cerevisiae*) that forms a whitish film on the surface of certain sherries when the temperature in the cellar is between 60°F and 70°F. After a year or so the wine under the flor develops a distinctive yeasty taste, which is technically due to a large increase in the aldehyde content of wine. The longer the sherry "sits on" the flor, the more flavour it extracts, and the finer it becomes. All types of sherry start out the same, for some relatively unknown reason flor forms on the surface of some barrels of sherry and not on others. When the flor forms a very thick white blanket, the sherry becomes a fino. If a thinner film forms, the sherry becomes an amontillado. If no film forms, the sherry becomes an oloroso. After a period of 18 to 24 months of ageing undisturbed under the blanket of flor (if it forms), the wine is transferred to the winery's solera system. A fino will be sent to the fino solera, an amontillado to the amontillado solera, and so on.

> **Did you know?**
>
> **Flor**
>
> **Flor** is a yeast-like substance (*Saccharomyeces cerevisiae*) that forms a whitish film on the surface of certain sherries when the temperature in the cellar is between 60°F to 70°F. After a year or so the wine under the flor develops a distinctive yeasty taste, which is technically due to a large increase in the aldehyde content of wine. The longer the sherry "sits on" the flor, the more flavour it extracts, and the finer it becomes

18.2.2 The Solera System

Sherry has a unique and rather complex system of maturation using a large number of casks and fractional blending. This system is called **solera**. Barrels in a solera are arranged in different groups or tiers, called criaderas or nurseries. Each scale contains wine of the same age. The oldest criadera, confusingly called *solera* as well, holds the wine ready to be bottled. When a fraction of the wine is extracted from the *solera* (this process is called the saca), it is replaced with the same amount of wine from the *first criadera*, i.e., the one that is slightly younger and typically less complex. This, in turn, is filled up with wine from the *second criadera* and so on. The last criadera, which holds the youngest wine, is topped up with a new wine named *sobretabla*. Taking away part of the wine and replacing it with the contents of other scales, is called *rociar* or *to wash down*. A *saca* (taking out part of the old wine) and *rocío* (replenishing the casks) will usually take place several times a year, but the actual number may vary and specific figures are rarely disclosed. In Jerez, a Fino solera is resfreshed two to four times a year. A Manzanilla solera can easily have six to ten sacas a year. By law there is a maximum of 35% that can be taken out, but normally between 10 and 15% of the 500-550 litres capacity of the butts will be taken out and refreshed. It is a bit less in Manzanilla soleras. Note that it is not common for wine to be drawn off from all the casks of a solera at the same time – this is usually spread out over time.

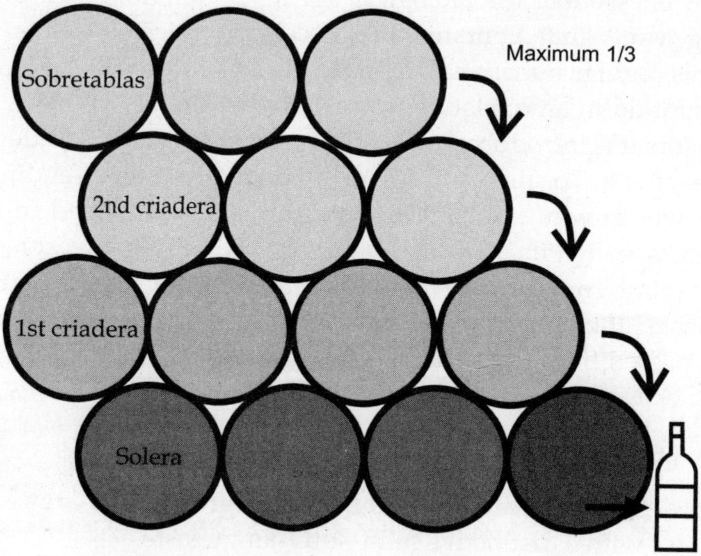

Maturation of sherry through solera system

18.2.2.1 Organisation of a Solera

Solera comes from the word suelo, meaning ground or land and it refers to the butts (casks) nearest to the ground. The solera system involves a series of American oak barrels arranged in rows or tiers, often eight to ten barrels high. Although a solera is usually represented as layers of casks stacked upon each other, with the solera level at the bottom of the pile. In practice, barrels are stacked in blocks of casks rather than actual rows. We are talking about hundreds of casks here, so sometimes a whole room is filled with just one criadera. Some of the largest soleras are even distributed over different buildings. Also, there are two technical reasons behind this placement: first, stability can be problematic when more than three or four casks are placed on top of each other, and secondly, it is better to place Fino and Manzanilla casks near the floor, where it is cooler. The number of tiers between the solera and the last criadera, varies largely and depends on the style of the wine and the preferences of the bodega. In general, Manzanilla and Fino soleras have more criaderas than those of Oloroso and other oxidatively aged sherry. A typical Fino solera ranges between three and seven criaderas. A Manzanilla solera has at least nine criaderas, up to fifteen. By law, the maximum amount that can be drawn out of a barrel of a fully mature sherry is 33 per cent.

18.2.2.2 Purpose of a Solera

The most significant result of the solera system is ensuring continuity and consistency. By blending multiple vintages, the possible variability of each year will be lowered and – after a certain amount of years - the bottled wine will maintain a constant average age. New wines are only gradually introduced to the system, and the influence of the new wine will disappear as it takes on the characteristics of the older sherry quite rapidly. Furthermore, the solera system is essential for biological ageing under flor since every refreshment brings in young wine that contains the necessary micronutrients to support the yeast. Without this regular nutritional input, the layer of flor will die and the sherry will continue its maturation in an oxidative way. Note that the new wine is never poured in directly from the top, it is introduced in the cask gently and always underneath the film of flor without damaging it. To sum up, a solera is essentially a never-ending ageing system, gradually but slowly growing older. Once mature and maintained in a proper way, it shows a unique personality, the identity of the solera. One of the reasons for the blending is to "tame" the young, rough wine. The key to the solera system is that aged sherries in the bottom "educate" the younger ones by giving them character and taste. The wine is also aerated as it passed from tier to tier, and in addition picks up subtle nuances from the oak barrels.

18.2.3 Styles of Sherry

- **Fino** sherries are made entirely from Palomino grapes, and are very dry, light, and pale in colour, with a distinctive mild nutty-tangy taste.
- **Amontillado** sherries have more colour and body than finos, with a medium dry taste and nutty flavour. True amontillado sherries are the best to use for cooking, for they impart a nutty-tangy flavour to food. Fino sherry is too dry for cooking and seems to lack the amontillado sherries' charm and depth, while oloroso and cream sherries are simply too sweet.
- **Oloroso** sherries are even fuller-bodies than either fino or amontillado sherries, and have an even deeper colour. Olorosos are semi-sweet and display a more well-rounded flavour than the other.
- **Cream** sherries are rich, deep amber to golden brown in colour, and usually display an exquisite bouquet. They are very sweet and "creamy" to the taste. (An even sweeter cream sherry, made entirely from Pedro Ximenez grapes is called a "brown" sherry.)
- **Manzanilla** is the palest, lightest, and driest fino-type sherry and is produced in the town of Sanlucar de Barrameda. Manzanillas are also more astringent or "tonic" in taste than fino sherries, which is probably due to both the ocean breezes and the unique soil content of the vineyards where the grapes are grown.
- **Palo cortado** has a very fresh and clean bouquet, somewhat resembling a well-made amontillado, yet its taste is reminiscent of a full-bodied oloroso. They do not develop

any type of flor, and are quite rare. A sherry producer cannot make this style of sherry every year, and its production amounts to less than one per cent of the total.

- **Pedro Ximenez** is the sweetest and most viscous of the sherries. It is rich, dark brown and liqueur-like in its concentration. It is traditionally served after meals in place of a brandy or cordial.

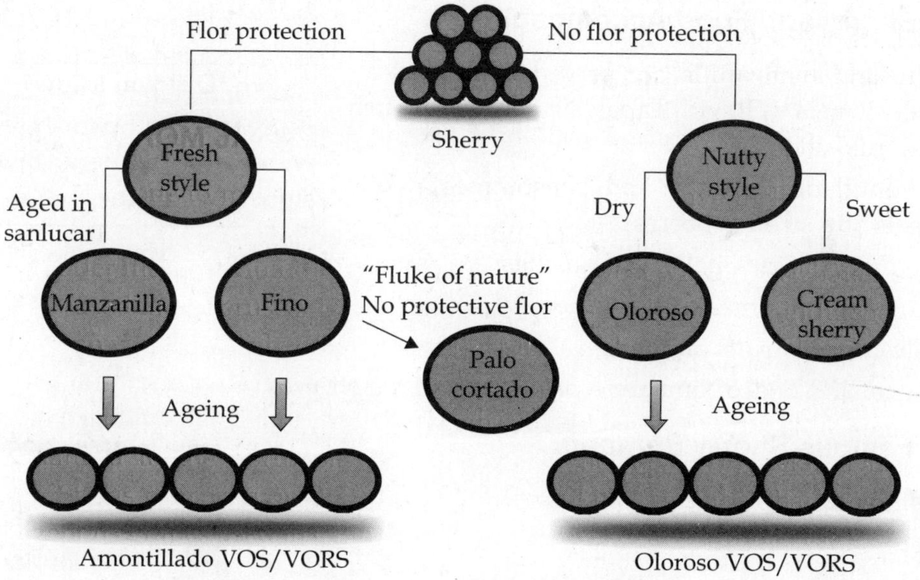

Production of Amontillado and Oloroso

18.2.4 Storing Sherry

Like other fine wines, sherry should be stored in a cool, dark place free from humidity or variations in temperature, and preferably free of strong light, vibrations or smells. Because sherry is meant to be consumed soon after bottling, it is not necessary to lay the bottles on their sides.

18.2.5 Serving Temperatures

Different sherry styles can be enjoyed at different temperatures. The guidelines are given below:

Sherry type	Serving temperature
Finos	Well chilled: 1-2 hours in the refrigerator before serving
Amontillados	Lightly chilled: 1 hour in the refrigerator before serving
Olorosos/cream sherries	Room temperature or lightly chilled or 'on the rocks' with a wedge of lime or a slice of orange

18.2.6 Glasses

Sherry copita

Although there are special sherry glasses, called *copitas* it is smaller than port glass but similar in shape. Any small, tulip-shaped white wine glass will also work. Because of sherry's higher alcohol content, serving sizes are generally 2-3 ounces.

18.2.7 Sherry and Food Accompaniment

- Fino and manzanilla are served chilled as an aperitif; gels well with Tapas, seafood, white fish and mild cheeses.
- Amontillado – soups and consommés, white meats and strong cheeses.
- Medium sherry – pates and quiches.
- Olorosso – red meats and game.
- Pale cream – fruits and foie gras.
- Cream and Pedro Ximenez – pastries and blue cheeses.

Did you know?
Bodegas is the Spanish term for wine cellar, winery, tavern or store selling wine.

18.2.8 Famous Sherry Shippers

- Callejuela
- Bodegas Yuste
- Bobadilla
- Cruz Conde
- Juan Piñero
- Alvear
- Díez Mérito
- Bodegas Luis Pérez
- Gutiérrez Colosía

18.3 PORT

Port has been the official drink used for toasts by the English royal family for two centuries. In Portugal, its history goes back to before the birth of Christ. In fact, the Douro is the world's second legally demarcated wine region (Italy's Chianti Classico region was demarcated in 1716 by the grand duke of Tuscany). In 1756, during the era of the marquis of Pombal (almost two-hundred years France's appellation controlee regulations became law), the Douro region was defined to protect the quality and good name of port (known as Porto, in Portugal). In that same year, Pombal reestablished the Oporto Wine Company. The production of port is limited to a strictly defined area of approximately 1500 square miles along the river Douro in northern Portugal. The slopes of the Douro, which has a very slate-like soil known as schist, are cut out and terraced for planting with vineyards. These walled terraces prevent erosion of the previous soil. Port is made in three regions, i.e., Cima Cago, Baixo Cargo and Douro Valley.

18.3.1 Law

The production and marketing of port are strictly controlled by the **Instituto do Vinho do Porto** (Port Wine Institute). Stringent laws govern the production of all port from the vine to the final product. An official certificate of origin is issued by the Port Wine Institute after careful tasting and examination of each lot. The official seal of guarantee over the neck of the bottle indicates approval by the Port Wine Institute.

18.3.2 Grape Varieties

More than forty grape varieties are planted in the region and used to produce port. The varieties listed below are those most commonly used:

Red:

- **Touriga Nacional** (tor-EE-ga NASH-ee-oh-nal)- gives intense aroma.
- **Touriga Francesa** (tor-EE-ga fran-shay-huh)- gives fruit and aroma to blend.
- **Tinta Roriz** (TEEN-ta ror-EEsh)- provides great colour.
- **Tinta Barroca** (TEEN-ta Bar-ok-ah),
- **Tintã Cão** (TEEN-ta cow) adds fineness and complexity to a blend.
- **Tinta Amarela** gives a dark red colour.

White: Francisca, Malvasia Fina, Moscatel Galego, Rabigato.

18.3.3 Production

> **Did you know?**
> Vineyards in Portugal are known as Quinta.

The grapes are picked by hand and the harvest generally begins in the second half of September, although it may start earlier in the hotter eastern areas. When the grapes have been picked, they are carried to the winery where they are crushed to allow the fermentation to start. Once fermentation is under way, care is taken to ensure that the grape skins are kept in constant contact with the fermenting juice so that their colour, tannin and flavour are released into the wine. Traditionally, this is achieved by treading the wine by foot in wide granite tanks called 'lagares'. In most wineries, foot treading has now been replaced by mechanical methods. When about half of the natural sugar in the grape juice has been turned into alcohol, the treading stops and the skins are allowed to float to the surface of the 'lagar'. The fermenting wine is then drawn from under the skins into a vat where a carefully selected neutral grape spirit is added to it. This raises the strength of the wine and stops the fermentation. As a result, much of the natural grape sugar is preserved in the finished port. Fermentation and fortification are only the beginning of the process of making port wine. They must always be followed by a period of ageing, which allows the wine to mellow and its flavours to develop and mature. One of the unique properties of port is its ability to enhance richness and flavour over very long periods of ageing in wood. This is partly because it is fortified and partly because it is a wine of extraordinary concentration and aromatic potential. The way port is aged determines how much contact it has with the wood and with the air and will shape its character and style.

18.3.4 Styles of Port

Ports fall into two categories: *Wood aged ports* – those that age in barrels and *bottle aged ports*. The vast majority of ports are wood aged, remaining in cask, or vat, until they are deemed to be fully mature. These wines are bottled when ready to drink and require no further ageing.

Within wood aged ports, it is possible to distinguish three broad styles.

- Firstly, there are the **fruity and full bodied** ports which include Ruby, Reserve Rubies, Vintage Character and Late Bottled Vintage. These wines generally age for no more than five or six years in large oak vats, where contact with the wood is relatively limited. As a result they retain their deep red colour and their fruitiness, vigour and intensity. They are the perfect choice for the classic combination of port and cheese or for drinking at the end of a meal.
- Next there are the **mellow, complex** ports which have had the benefit of greater contact with the wood, being aged in small oak casks and for longer periods. These include **Tawny ports**, including the sublime aged Tawnies. They also include a small category called **'Colheita'**, which is a Tawny bearing a harvest date. The characteristic of Tawny port is its seductive amber hue and its opulent nutty, spicy, plum-pudding flavour. Tawny ports make superb dessert wines, particularly delicious with a crème brûlée or a plate of figs. Tawnies are an excellent choice for summer drinking as they can be served slightly cool.
- Lastly, there are the **white** ports. These are usually aged in cask or vat for a relatively short time so that they develop mellowness and complexity but keep their fruity freshness. There are sweeter and drier styles, the dry white ports making a perfec aperitif served cool with a plate of olives or roasted almonds.

The main type of bottle aged port is vintage port. It is the finest and rarest of all ports the most sought after by wine lovers, collectors and investors. It is a selection of the very best wine from a single exceptional year and represents only a very small proportion of the crop. A bottle of vintage port must always be stored lying down so that the cork is in contact with the wine and does not dry out. Vintage port remains for only two years in wood, usually in a large vat. It is then bottled, long before it is ready to drink, and continue to age for many years or decades in bottle, gradually developing the sublime comple aromas which are the hallmark of a great mature vintage port. During the ageing process, a sediment, or crust, will form in the bottle. Before serving a vintage port, it is often necessary to decant it to separate the wine from the crust. Decanting also brings the wine in contact with the air, allowing the aromas, or 'bouquet', of the wine to open out after the long period during which the wine has been enclosed in the bottle.

18.3.5 Types of Port

1. **Ruby port:** Young, fresh, full-bodied wine, sold and drunk young. These are blended wines containing 3 to 7 years old wines. Ruby port tends to deteriorate rather than improve in the bottle.
2. **Tawny port:** Cheap blend of young red and white ports.
3. **White port:** These are often taken as aperitif and are made of red grapes. They are not very popular.

18.3.5.1 Types of Ruby Port

1. **Basic ruby port**
    - It is cheapest.
    - Is kept for less than one year for maturing.
2. **Vintage character port**
    - Blended for various years.
    - Matured in casks for four years.
3. **Crusted port**
    - Blend of very high quality wines from two or more years.
    - Matured for four years in casks and three years in bottle.
    - It has a characteristic crust formation that requires decanting.
4. **Late bottled vintage**
    - Wines for one year, matured for 5-6 years and then bottled so that wines improve in bottles.

18.3.5.2 Types of Tawny Port

1. **Basic tawny port**
    - Blend of red and white port.
    - Matured in casks for eight years.
2. **Aged tawny port**
    - Aged for 10, 20, 30 and 40 years. Also known as fine old tawnies.

Did you know?

The major difference between a Ruby Port and a Tawny Port is that Ruby Port keeps maturing in a bottle whereas Tawny Port ages only in the cask and will stop maturing once it is bottled.

18.3.6 Serving Port

Port, because of its high alcohol and sugar levels, is usually best consumed during cool or cold weather. When it is time to open a bottle of vintage port, the bottle should be stood upright for three to five days, which allows the crusted sediment to settle to the bottom. The bottle should be opened at least one to two hours prior to drinking; this will dissipate any "off" odours or gasses that might have developed under the cork. Port need not be chilled, and is best when drunk at cellar temperature. Contrary to popular belief, port has limited shelf-life once opened, and should be consumed within several weeks - vintage port deteriorates eight to twenty-four hours after opening and should be consumed at one sitting. The English believe that the best accompaniment to port is Stilton cheese (from the blue cheese family) or a well-aged cheddar served with freshly shelled walnuts.

18.3.7 Port Wine Shippers

- Quinta Do Noval
- Warre's
- Taylor's
- Graham's
- Fonseca's Guimaraens
- Niepoort
- Dow
- Smith Woodhouse
- Sandeman

Port wine brands

18.4 MADEIRA

The island of Madeira, in the Atlantic Ocean is some 360 miles from the coast of Morocco. The island showed no sign of earlier occupation, and because of its dense covering of forest was given the Portuguese name Madeira (island of wood). Before the island could be occupied, huge coast-to-coast forests had to be burnt. It was reported that the fire actually lasted for seven years. When the ashes finally blended with the fertile volcanic earth, a unique soil was formed which is composed of deep deposits of wood ash and humus, ideal for the making of Madeira wines.

18.4.1 Production

The grapes are grown on steep terraces all over the island. Most wine growers also grow vegetables for themselves or for the local market between the vines. This slows the growing of the grapes which become more aromatic and more concentrated. The grapes are mostly grown in the pergola-style, low in height and covered with a roof of their own leaves. This protects the grapes from the strong winds and sometimes the dramatic changes in temperature. The distance between the vines is two to three yards. The different varieties are grown in different heights above sea level. Boal and Malvasia are best grown in lower altitudes, whereas Verdelho and Sercial like the higher altitudes. The versatile and robust Tinta Negra Mole imitates the other varieties depending on the altitude it is grown at and depending on the processing, the harvest is mostly done manually. Malvasia is the first, the dry varieties Verdelho and Sercial go last. This sounds like a paradox, but since the aromas are not backed up by sweetness, these grapes simply have to get as much sun as possible for the development of their aromas. The grapes are then carried up to the next street, sometimes hundreds of yards, and are collected on small trucks. Then they go to the winepress, where the grapes are crushed and pressed. Until into the late 1970s this used to be done with feet and wooden presses. The fermented juice is carried by the Borracheiros in goatskins containing up to 70 litres or 15 gallons to the wine cellar downhill. The fermenting of the must is stopped with brandy; the time of adding the brandy depending on the grape variety. The must from the Malvasia grape gets the brandy right at the beginning of fermentation, Boal and Verdelho around the fourth day, and Sercial about a month after the fermentation started. In this way the resulting wine will be sweet or dry, depending on when the fermentation of the grape's sugar was stopped, but all the wines have high alcohol content. The adding of brandy is known as fortification. The fortified young wine is then transferred to the estufa. In the simplest version, this is a large container, usually stainless steel, with a pipe system in it. The pipes circulate hot water in them and so heat the wine over several days to a temperature of about 50 degrees celsius or 120°F. This final temperature is then kept for some weeks or months. Since the heating in this way is rather fast, some of the wine's sugar turns to caramel. The wine will then feature the typical burnt taste of the lower qualities of Madeira wine. The better qualities of madeira are put into large wooden casks, standing in a heated room. The best wines and all the vintages are treated with the canteiro method. The casks with the young fortified wine are transferred to the roof, where they will be exposed to the sun's heat. The beam carrying the casks is called canteiro, giving this method it's name. Wines treated with the canteiro method do not display so much caramel, but rather have a fresh fruity taste. Once the wine is in the estufa or cask, the Madeira Wine Institute will impose a seal on the container and register it's contents. When heating is finished, the wine in the estufa is allowed to cool and will then be transferred into wooden casks to be stored for years to come. Depending on the intended use, this can be three to fifteen years. There is always some air in the casks and so the wine completely oxidizes, i.e., the organic contents of the wine react with the air's oxygen and thereby change the colour, the smell and the taste of the wine. Finally, the wine goes into the blend. The cellar master tries to keep the characteristic taste of the shipper's wine by blending different wines together. The normal everyday Madeira wine is such a blend, the age given on the label indicating the youngest wine in the blend. Blended wine with the name of a grape variety on the label must contain at least 85% of this grape. The other 15% can be filled up with other varieties, usually tinta negra mole. Good wines are treated in a different way, they can become vintage Madeira; this means that they will stay in cask for a minimum of twenty years, most of them much longer, up to hundred years and more. In this time, the sun's heat leads to further concentration and oxidation. Before overconcentration makes the wine undrinkable it will be transferred to glass Demi-Johns containing 22 liters or 5 gallons of wine. Those Demi-Johns are then sealed airtight which stops further development of the wine and enables long-time storing. In earlier times, this was the way for the madeira lover to store its wine in large quantities. Finally, the wine is bottled and will then rest another two years before it goes to the market. Madeira wine, because of the complete oxidation, is very robust and will keep for years to come, even centuries. Once a bottle is opened, the contents will also keep at least for weeks or months. So you can take your time and slowly sip on history without having to worry about the wine getting bad.

18.4.2 Types of Madeira

There are five types of Madeira, four of which are named after the grape variety used.

- **Sercial:** The sercial grape variety is viticulturally similar to the German Riesling, and was in fact brought to Madeira from Germany. In reality, however, it bears absolutely no resemblance to the Riesling in taste. Sercial is the driest Madeira; it is similar to a fino sherry, although slightly sweeter.
- **Verdelho:** The Verdelho grape is a cross between the Spanish Pedro Ximenez and the Italian Verdea grape varieties. The wine is semi-dry and has a clean taste and a gentle, smooth flavour.
- **Rainwater:** This wine was believed to have been created by Mr Habisham, a local Madeira shipper from Savannah, Georgia. He made special blends of Sercial and Verdelho that were lighter and quite a bit paler (almost like rainwater)than most of the Madeiras that were consumed during that era (the early nineteenth century).
- **Bual or Boal:** The grape variety descended from the Pinot Noir of Burgundy, France. The wine is darker in colour than either Sercial or Verdelho, with a sort of buttery aroma and a definite sweet taste.
- **Malmsey:** Prince Henry, the navigator, transplanted the Malvasia (Malvoisie) vines from Crete to Madeira. Malmsey is a luscious, sweet, rich wine, quite dark in colour, similar to a cream sherry but with more character.

18.4.3 Serving and Storing Madeiras

Madeiras are fortified wines and therefore last a great deal longer than table wines. It is best to keep bottles of Madeira lying on their sides until several days before serving. The bottles should then be carefully stood up to allow any sediment to settle to the bottom, and then decanted. Madeiras, once opened, have an unusually long shelf-life provided they are not exposed to high temperatures or excessive sunlight and air. In serving Madeira, never use ice, but rather chill the wine in the refrigerator. Sercial, Verdelho, and Rainwater Madeiras should be chilled and served as aperitifs. Bual and Malmsey should be served at room temperature after dinner in long tulip-shaped glasses that hold five to seven ounces. Verdelho is the perfect Madeira to use when cooking, because it lends just enough flavour to the food. It is excellent in sauces, gravies, and in soups, especially turtle soup. Madeiras are among the longest-lived wines in the world, some lasting as long as two-hundred or more years.

18.4.4 The Estufa System

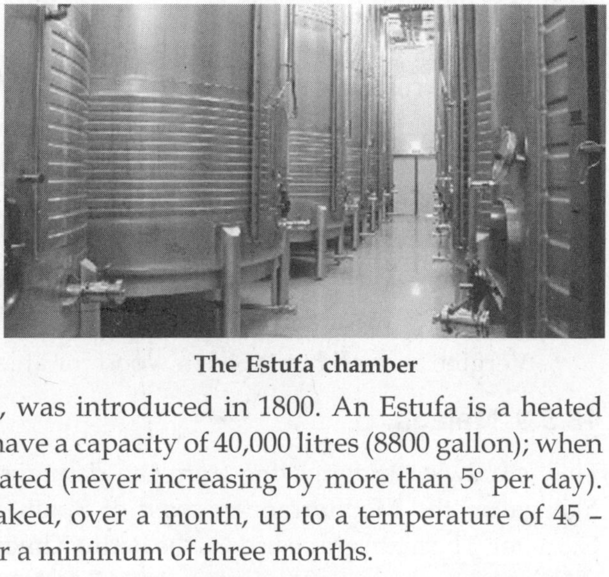

The Estufa chamber

It was noticed in sixteenth century that casks of Madeira when used as Ballast (heavy substances carried by ship) on ships going to and from the East Indies had improved considerably in flavour on their return. It seemed that crossing the equator twice, on the long sea journey going in and out of the tropics, imparted an attractive "cooked" flavour to the wine. When this practice was no longer commercially viable, a simulated version, known as **Estufagen**, was introduced in 1800. An Estufa is a heated chamber/room. It contains tanks which have a capacity of 40,000 litres (8800 gallon); when filled with wine, the tanks are slowly heated (never increasing by more than 5° per day). As temperature increases, the wine is baked, over a month, up to a temperature of 45 – 50°C (113–122°F). It is held at this heat for a minimum of three months.

Some shipper's gauge their maximum temperature lower and keep the wine longer – up to sixteen months – as they feel lower and slower gives better results. Another month is then taken to turn the heat down in the same slow, gradual manner. A thermometer, with a government's seal, is attached to each Estufa. If Estufa is heated beyond a certain temperature, the seal will break and the wine cannot be sold as Madeira. The wine is given a light fortification before going into the Estufa and more substantial one when it comes out. Madeira is eventually bottled as an alcoholic strength of 21%; before that it is matured and blended through solera system and rested before sale.

18.5 MARSALA

Marsala is the best-known fortified wine of Italy. Like Málaga, it takes its name from the town that produces it, the name comes from the Arabic name of the town 'Marsah el Allah'. John Woodhouse, an English merchant and connoisseur of fortified wines, created Marsala. It was produced with the intention of competing with already existing Sherry and Madeira. The vine growing region occupies the western end of the Island of Sicily. The soil is volcanic mixed with iron oxides. The climate is hot, dry and sunny, ideal condition for tough, sugar-laden grapes.

18.5.1 Grape Varieties

- Catarratto
- Inzolia
- Grillo

Marsala comes in three different colours:

- Oro (golden)
- Ambra (amber)
- Rubino (ruby)

18.5.2 Styles of Marsala

- Fine (aged for a minimum of one year)
- Superiore (aged in wood for two years)
- Superiore riserva (aged in wood for four years)
- Vergine (always dry and aged in wood for five years)
- Vergine stravecchio (aged in wood for at least 10 years)

18.5.3 Malaga

This is a sweet brown wine from the demarcated region of Malaga on the Mediterranean coast of Spain, 160 km from Gibralter. The main grape used is the Pedro Ximenez. Although extremely popular in the past, only a small amount is now produced. Many of these are blended in solera system.

REVISION QUESTIONS

1. What is fortified wine?
2. Differentiate between solera system and Estufa system.
3. List various grapes used to make sherry.
4. Write various styles of port and also differentiate between ruby port and tawny port.
5. Give short notes on port, sherry, Madeira and Malaga.

RESEARCH ACTIVITIES

- Paste the pictures of grapes used in making sherry and port.
- Search the various shippers of port wine and sherry.

19

Aperitifs and Bitter

19.1 INTRODUCTION TO APERITIFS

> **After reading this chapter, you will be able to understand:**
> - Meaning of aperitif.
> - Types of aperitif.
> - Meaning of vermouth.
> - Ingredients of vermouth.
> - Types of vermouth.
> - Other aromatized wines.
> - Bitters and their types.

The word aperitif derives from the Latin word ***aperire***, meaning "to open," in the sense of opening up the appetite. It should be something to prepare the palate for the meal and should be offered within the first thirty seconds after the guests have been seated. An aperitif can be categorized as hors d'oeuvre (beverage appetizer) and treated as welcoming drink. It should be low in alcohol, so as not to numb the taste buds. It should be dry, so as to stimulate the appetite, as sweet drinks can cause the guest to feel full before the meal has even begun. All true aperitifs carry a bittersweet character that stimulates the production of gastric juices and promotes appetite. Aperitif in one line can be said as '*before meal drink*'.

19.2 KINDS OF APERITIFS—WINE BASED AND SPIRIT BASED

> **Aperitif wines**
>
> An aperitif is a drink served before meals to stimulate the appetite by engaging the gastric juices and preparing the taste buds for food. Aperitif wines are usually served in short glasses and contain alcohol between 15 - 22 per cent ABV. Examples are Vermouth, Dubonnet and Dry Sherry (Fino).

No single type of alcohol can be taken as aperitifs. Generally, aperitifs can be divided as wine based aperitifs and spirit based aperitifs. Wine based aperitifs include dry crisp white wines, sparkling wine or Champagne, dry fortified wines like sherries (*Manjanilla and Fino*), Byrrh (*made of red wine, mistelle, and quinine*), slightly chilled light-bodied white wine like Chablis, Sauvignon Blanc and White Burgundies. Wine based cocktails like Kir and Kir Royale aromatized wines (*Wines which are fortified and infused with botanicals that add flavour and colour)* include Vermouth, Dubonnet and Lillet. Relatively low in alcohol from 16 - 24% and with distinctive bittersweet flavours as they promote conviviality without diluting the palate for the food to come. Some of the famous spirit based aperitifs include mixed drinks like gin and tonic water, Cynar, Pastis, Ouzo, Campari, Amer Picon bitters and before dinner cocktails.

Popular classic aperitifs

Breakfast aperitifs:	Lunch aperitifs:	Dinner aperitifs:
• Bloody Mary	• Gin and tonic	• Vodka martinis
• Champagne and orange juice	• Beer shandy	• Campari and soda
• Earl Grey tea	• Pimm's No. 1 cup	• Kir Royale
• Virgin Mary	• Sparkling wines	

19.3 DIGESTIFS

Digestifs are elegant, luxurious spirits and liqueurs served at the end of a meal. Their high alcoholic content helps guests to comfortably digest the meal they have enjoyed. The purpose of digestifs are:

- Aids digestive process.
- Relaxes guests after a meal.
- Enhances mood.

19.3.1 Popular Digestifs

Several regions of the world enjoy digestifs specific to the preferences and traditions of the people there. Another factor influencing these preferences is gender. Men usually prefer robust and potent digestifs, while women tend to prefer more subtle flavours. Some popular digestifs are:

- Limoncello
- Grappa
- Brandy and Cognac
- Cordials and liqueurs
- Bitter digestifs like Amari
- Ouzo
- Schnapps

19.4 VERMOUTH

Vermouth is classified as an aromatized wine, containing between 16 to 20 per cent alcohol. It is derived from a German word *wermut-* meaning wormwood. Wormwood infusions were used to cure intestinal worms. The specialists in making modern vermouth are Italians and French. Marseille in France and Turin in Italy are very well known for vermouth production. Italian vermouth refers to sweet and red vermouth whereas French vermouth refers to classical dry and white vermouth, though both the countries make all types of vermouth.

19.4.1 Ingredients for Making Vermouth

(a) **Flavouring agents:** Vermouth is flavoured with about 50 different ingredients which include:

- Wormwood
- Quinine
- Citrus
- Peels
- Roots
- Flowers
- Herbs

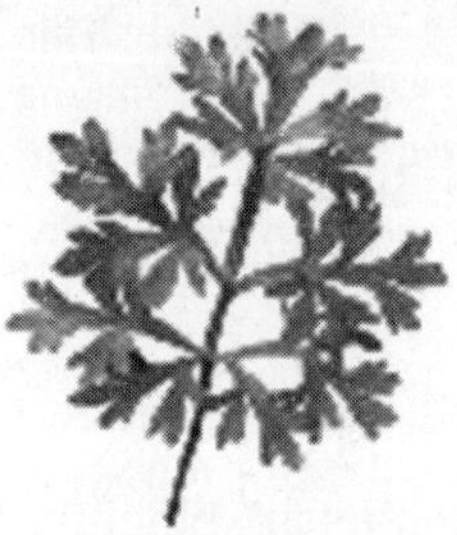

Wormwood leaf

These ingredients are chosen for their aroma and medicinal values and called flavouring agents. The recipe is secret and closely guarded.

(b) **Wine:** A placid, two or three years old, high strength wine is used. For Italian vermouth, the wine can come from any part of the country, but the French rely on the wines from Midi region.

(c) **Sweetener:** Sugar syrup is used as sweetener.

(d) **Spirit:** The spirit is usually neutral brandy.

19.4.2 Production

- The flavouring agents are steeped or infused in the spirit.
- The flavoured spirit is added to the sweetened wine.
- The liquid is fined to free it from any haze forming substances.
- After maturing, it is bottled and distributed.

19.4.3 Types of Vermouth

- **Sweet Vermouth or Bianco**
  - ◊ Usually 15-16 per cent alcohol with up to 15 per cent sugar.
  - ◊ Clove and licorice flavoured
  - ◊ Made with dry white wine which is flavoured. Fortified and sweetened with *mistelle* (grape juice or slightly fermented white wine to which brandy has been added that is used in the production of other wines).
  - ◊ Used as an aperitif as well as in slightly sweet cocktails such as the Manhattan.

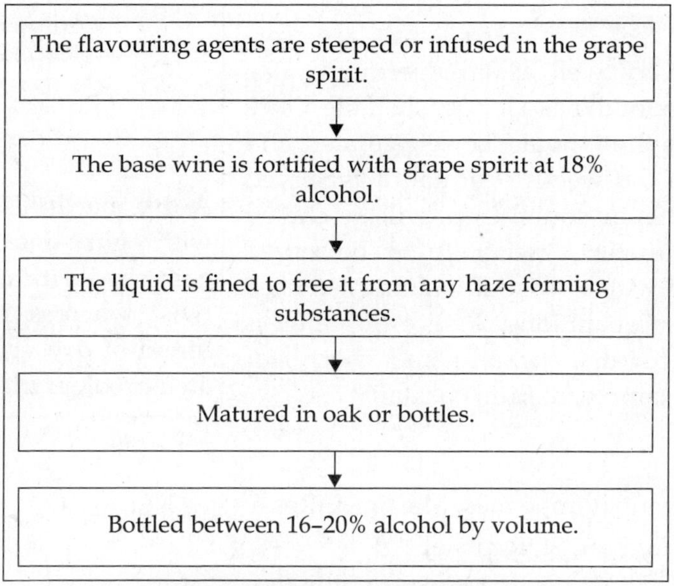

Vermouth production process

- **Dry Vermouth**
  - ◊ Often called French vermouth or simply French.
  - ◊ Lightly floral and herbal.
  - ◊ 18 per cent alcohol and contains at most 5 per cent residual sugar.
  - ◊ Has a base of dry white wine and is yellow with green tinges in colour.
  - ◊ Served with ice and lemon and sometimes with a splash of soda.
  - ◊ Prime ingredient for the Dry Martini cocktail.
- **Rose Vermouth**
  - ◊ Has a white wine base.
  - ◊ A little of the sweetener is added to the wine and it is flavoured and fortified and then coloured pink with the addition of caramel.
- **Red Vermouth**
  - ◊ Often called Italian Vermouth.
  - ◊ Made from a white wine base which is well sweetened, flavoured and fortified.
  - ◊ The reddish brown colour comes from a generous addition of caramel.
- **Chambery**
  - ◊ A light and very delicate vermouth made in the foothills of the Alps mountains at Savoie.
  - ◊ Flavoured with the alpine herbs and is the only vermouth produced in France with an A.O.C.
- **Chumberyzette**
  - ◊ A vermouth flavoured with wild Alpine strawberries.

19.4.4 Service

Vermouth goes very well as an aperitif. Unlike sherry or port, vermouth has a longer shelf life. Once the bottle is opened, it should be refrigerated and consumed within 6-8 weeks. Vermouth is served mostly on the rocks or straight up, will be chilled and garnished with citrus twist. It can be served chilled or over ice with a twist of lemon. Also used in many cocktail preparations. A slice of lemon is used as garnish for dry cocktails and cherry for sweet cocktails. Example, martini cocktail.

> **Did you know?**
>
> ?
>
> A dry martini is a cocktail made with gin and dry vermouth garnished with an olive or a lemon twist whereas martini dry is a brand of dry vermouth, which is an ingredient in a dry martini.

19.4.5 Brands

- **Italian:** Cinzano, Punt e mes, Martini & Rossi
- **French:** Noilly Prat, St. Raphael
- **Dry:** Chambery, Cinzano, Martini, Noilly Prat, Torella
- **Bitter:** Punt e Mes
- **Sweet:** Cinzano, Bianco, Cinzano Red, Martini Bianco, Martini Rose, Martini Rosso, Noilly Prat Red

19.5 OTHER AROMATIZED WINES

- **Dubonnet:** Flavoured with quinine and herbs and available in two varieties: blonde (white) and rouge (red). It is from France.
- **St. Raphel:** Bitter-sweet drink, flavoured with quinine and herbs; it is available in red and white. It is from France.
- **Lillet:** Made from white Bordeaux wine and flavoured with citrus fruit peels and herbs and fortified with Armagnac, it is aged in casks. It is also from France.
- **Byrrh:** Has a base of red wine and brandy and flavoured with quinine and herbs.

19.6 BITTERS

Bitters refer to spirits that are flavoured with roots, herbs and spices which generally have medicinal properties. In other words bitters are an aromatic flavouring agent made from infusing roots, barks, fruit peels, seeds, spices, herbs, flowers, and botanicals in a spirit. The origins of bitter lie in the flavouring elements that were commonly added to the earliest spirits. Bitters were called 'elixir of life' meaning magical cure, taken as restoratives and

> **History**
>
> First made in 1824 in Venezuela by a German physician as a cure for seasickness and stomach pains. He then proceeded to form the 'House of Angostura' to sell his invention to sailors. It is now served as a *digestif*, as its high alcoholic content is believed to help digest food.

remedies for any number of conditions, ranging from headache, indigestion, stomachache to constipation. Three to five drops of bitters are used while making cocktails.

Table 19.1: Types of bitters

Name of the bitter	Description	Colour	Aroma	Taste
Fernet Branca	• Aromatic Italian spirit made with a base of grape spirit. • More than 40 herbs and spices such as wort, myrrh, rhubarb, chamomile, cardamom and saffron are used. • Used as a hangover cure.	Dark brown  	Complex, fresh,. grassy mint	Menthol and a dry herb finish.
Angostura	• Produced in Trinidad • Best known bitters in the world. • Recipe is a closely guarded secret. • Flavour is produced from extracts of Seville orange peel, angelica roots, cardamom, cinnamon, cloves, gentian roots, and quinine. • It is one of the essential ingredients in classic old fashioned bourbon cocktail.	Dark and deep amber  	Herbs, roots, molasses and a balance of rum	Bitter but finely balanced with herbs and rum.
Aperol	• A bitter from Italy made from a blend of spirits, along with rhubarb, gentian roots and herbs. • Alcohol content is 11% ABV.	Dark orange  	Complex and well balanced with herbs, orange and spices	Sweet with a blend of orange, rhubarb and spices.

Boonekamp	• Traditional bitter from Germany. • Made from a mixture of herbs. • Strong alcoholic content, i.e., 43-48% ABV.	Dark orange - amber from the herbs and spices 	Pungent flavour	Sweet liquorice, spicy and a warm, bitter finish.
Suze	• Complex of wild gentian roots and herbs that have been thoroughly macerated and distilled. • Quite oily and has a bitter-sweet character similar to Campari. • Often drunk straight with ice, or diluted with tonic water or even black currant cordial.	Medium yellow 	Unusual, distinctive; gentian with apricot, vanilla, citrus and caramel	Oily, round and full; bitter-sweet with gentian, citrus, vanilla; long finish.
Aveze	• Made from must of fresh gentian roots that have been macerated for nine months. • This prolonged maceration results in unusual, dry flavour with a mildly bitter, herbal character.	Light golden yellow 	Aromatic and pungent with herbs and spices	Herbal, dry and slightly bitter.
Campari	• Best known bitter in the world. • More often drunk with soda water or lemonade. • Contains quinine, rhubarb, ginseng, bitter orange peel and many aromatic herbs. • Sweetened with sugar and tinted red with cochineal dye. • Alcohol % is 24 ABV.	Deep, red pink due to the addition of cochineal 	Elegant distinctive, orange fruit and spice	Refreshing dry, bitter-sweet taste of orange and herbs; fresh finish.

REVISION QUESTIONS

1. What is an aperitif? Name any two wine based aperitifs and any two spirit based aperitifs.
2. What do you mean by vermouth? Name various ingredients used in making vermouth.
3. Name any three aromatized wines.

RESEARCH ACTIVITY

- Paste the pictures of any ten types of bitters in a scrapbook describing about their colour, taste and aroma.

20

Food and Wine Pairing

20.1 INTRODUCTION

> **After reading this chapter, you will be able to understand:**
> - The rules and elements of food and wine pairing
> - Cheese and wine pairing

Most of the wines are an accompaniment to the food and there are many established guidelines for pairing wines with food. Originally, wines evolved to complement the cuisine of a region, so this is often a good starting point for finding a good wine and food combination. There is no single choice of wine that must be drunk with a certain dish, but some are definitely a better match than others. It is important for a wine sommelier and bartender to have the knowledge of food and wine parings. Some of the general rules for food and wine combination are as follows:

- Dry wine before sweet wine
- White wine before red wine
- White wine with white meat
- Red wine with red meat
- Light bodied wines before full-bodied wines
- Sweet food with sweet wines
- Acidic food with highly acidic wines
- Serve good wine before great wine
- Commence with a grape aperitif rather than spirit based aperitif
- Champagne or sparkling wines compliment with most foods
- Avoid combining savoury foods with high tannin wines
- Avoid chewy or high protein content food with tannic wines
- Avoid salty food with sweet wines
- Avoid fatty food with highly acidic wines

When selecting the food for wines, do keep in mind:

1. The food item being paired
2. The cooking method of that item
3. The additional flavours or sauces

The fundamental rule is to begin by pairing delicate wines with delicate flavours, medium-bodied wines with medium-weight or intensity flavours, and strongly flavoured foods with wines that will stand up to their pungency. To achieve the best match it is necessary to analyze the basic components in both the wine and the food. The principle is to try to balance them so that neither the food nor the wine overpowers the other. The main elements of food and wine matching to consider are:

- Weight/body
- Flavour, intensity and characteristics
- Acidity
- Salt
- Tannin
- Sweetness

20.2 ELEMENTS FOR MATCHING FOOD AND WINE

20.2.1 Weight/Body

Try to match the weight of the food with the weight of the wine. Rich, heavyweight foods, like game, roast meats and red meat casseroles need full-bodied wines. Normally, it is powerful red wines that are the favoured choice but it is the weight of the wine, not the colour or flavour, which is the most important consideration.

- Hence a full-bodied white wine is usually a better match with meat than a light-styled red wine.
- Lightweight food like poultry and fish are complemented by more delicate wines.
- Whilst a white wine is the instinctive choice; light, low-tannin reds also work.

Also remember the contribution of sauces. A rich creamy sauce will need a wine of sufficient body to match the food and flavours that will complement the smooth creamy, buttery taste.

Classic pairings: Full-bodied Chardonnay with thick cream- or butter-based sauces, medium-bodied Pinot Noir with salmon, light-bodied Sauvignon Blanc with delicate fish.

20.2.2 Flavour, Intensity and Character

It is the most important element to consider. Flavour intensity is not same as weight. For example, plain boiled potatoes or plain boiled rice, both are heavy in weight but light in flavour whereas thinly sliced red or green peppers are low in weight but high in flavour. Match full flavours together, like Sauvignon Blanc and asparagus, mild flavours like

Muscadet and oysters. The flavour characteristics of some foods and wines are very similar and consequently they make good combinations:

- Light fruit-based desserts can be matched with the "grapey" flavour of the Muscat variety.
- Spicy dishes can be matched with Gewurztraminer, a variety often described as spicy or Gruner Veltiner. (Spicy wines may have white or black pepper, cloves, ginger, allspice aromas and flavours for example.)
- Steam dishes or food cooked by gentle method of cooking requires light flavoured wines.
- Smoked food pairs well with enough flavour intensity wines to cope up with the strength of smoking.
- Cream or butter sauces go well with wines that have been fermented or aged in new oak barrels. Oak imparts vanilla-scented, buttery, creamy flavours to the wine.
- Delicately flavoured wines like Italian whites (Vementino, Pinot Grigio, Gavi, Soave, Verdicchio, Orvieto) and Loire Muscadet complement shellfish and seafood.

20.2.3 Acidity

Sour flavours in food makes wine taste sweeter and frutier but less acidic, and therefore less vibrant and refreshing. For this reason, any acidity found in the food should be matched with acidity in the accompanying wines. Food and wine can both have acidity. Citrus fruits, tomatoes, lemons, pineapples, vinegar and green apples are all high-acid foods. A classic example is Champagne served with smoked salmon and a squeeze of lemon. High-acid wines are also used to cleanse the palate when eating oily food. In Italy, many dishes are made with lots of olive oil, tomato and lemon. The majority of Italian red wines have noticeable acidity and so complement the regional dishes perfectly. The acid in the wine serves the same purpose as the acid in fresh lemon, so often squeezed on these dishes. Acidic wines also often pair well with salty foods, helping to cut the salty taste on the palate. However, low-acid wines often clash with acidic foods therefore the pairing of the two should be avoided. As a general rule, acidic wines are very food-friendly.

Classic pairings: Sauvignon Blanc with fish, Chianti with fresh tomato sauce.

20.2.4 Salt

Salty foods are enhanced and balanced by a touch of sweetness. Blue cheese and port is a classic combination. For a dry wine to work with salty food, it should have low tannins and noticeable acidity. It is easier to find white wines with these characteristics than reds, but there are some red wines like Beaujolais.

20.2.5 Tannin

Food with high protein content or oily foods such as lamb, pate, rare red meat pairs with wines with high level of tannin. The more textured the food like duck, chewy - like steak, the more acidity needed in the wine. Typically detected in red wines, tannin comes from the grape skins and stalks used in red winemaking. Food cooked by frying method also requires wines with high acidic content as frying increases the fat content. Tannic wines pair well with low-salt and high-fat foods as fat lessens the astringency of tannins, and conversely tannins prevent fat from seeming too rich. *Cabernct sauvignon, Sirah, Malbec* all pair very well with roast red meats and steak.

Classic pairings: Cabernet Sauvignon with steak.

20.2.6 Sweetness

The wine should always be sweeter than the food. Sweetness in wine also acts as a foil to rich foods. Sweet foods make wines seem more bitter and acidic. The general rule of thumb is to serve a wine at least as sweet or sweeter than the food being served. Sweet food goes well with wine that has a similar or higher degree of sweetness. The sweeter the food, the sweeter the wine. Sweetness also balances salt and so sweet wines are classic companions of blue cheeses, e.g., port with Stilton. Sweet wines are also often served alongside desserts. The general rule with sweet and semi-sweet wines is to pair them with foods that are less sweet than the wine itself.

Classic pairings: Sauternes with foie gras, Riesling with spicy Asian dishes, Sauternes with créme brûlée.

Also note that if a dish is prepared with wine, such as Coq au Vin or pasta with white wine garlic sauce, consider matching the serving of wine to the wine used in making the dish.

Table 20.1: Examples of food pairing

White wine	Cheese	Seafood	Poultry	Meats	Herbs/spices
Chardonnay	Brie, Gauda	Crab, Shrimp, Scallops, Lobster, Snapper, Salmon, Trout	Chicken, Turkey, Goose, Duck	Veal, Pork	Basil, Thyme, Ginger, Nutmeg, Saffron
Sauvignon Blanc	Feta, Mozzarella, Parmesan, Brie	Shrimp, Oysters, Sole, Snapper	Chicken, Turkey	Veal, Pork	Basil, Cilantro, Dill, Tarragon, Thyme, Lemon Grass
Pinot Grigio	Ricotta, Mozzarella	Mussels, Sole, Shrimp, Oysters, Salmon, Trout, Snapper, Smoked Salmon	Chicken, Turkey	Ham, Salami	Tarragon, Thyme, Oregano, Basil
Riesling	Blue cheese, Feta	Crab, Mussels, Smoked Salmon, Shrimp	Chicken, Duck	Baked Ham, Pork, Smoked Pork	Mint, Tarragon, Xilantro, Ginger
Gewurztraminer	Smoked Gauda, Smoked Mozzarella	Scallops, Mussels, Shrimp, Crab, Salmon, Smoked Salmon	Turkey	Pork, Ham, Sausages	Cilantro, Gineger, Cinnmon, Clove

Red wine	Cheese	Seafood	Poultry	Meats	Herbs/spices
Pinot Noir	Chevre, Feta, Bries, Camembert	Salmon, Tuna	Chicken, Duck	Beef, Lamb, Pork, Veal	Mint, Basil, Tarragon, Rosemary, Anise, Fennel seed, Cinnamon
Merlot	Camembert, Smoked Gauda, Cheddar, Parmesan	Salmon, Tuna	Duck	Beef, Lamb, Pork, Veal	Mint, Rosemary, Tarragon, Thyme
Shiraz/Shyrah	Parmesan, Pecorino, Smoked Gauda	Salmon, Tuna	Duck	Beef, Lamb, Pork, Veal	Bayleaf, Lavender, Mint, Rosemary, Thyme
Zinfandel	Feta, Smoked Gauda, Parmesan	None	Duck	Sausage,Beef, Lamb, Pork	Bayleaf, Mint, Oregano, Rosemary, Black pepper, Fennel Seed, Clove, Cinnamon
Cabernet Sauvignon	Gorgonzola, Brie, Camembert	None	Chicken, Duck	Beef, Lamb, Pork, Veal, Venison	Basil, Mint, Oregano, Rosemary, Thyme

20.3 WINE AND CHEESE PAIRING

In the case of wine and cheese pairing, most of us think of red wine with cheese but in fact white wine is actually a much better match for many types of cheese because red wines, especially full-bodied red wines mask the flavours of cheese. Fortified wines and lighter red wines are often a much better match. Wine, cheese and bread together is known as *trinity of the table.*

Table 20.2: Major wine and cheese pairing

Style of wine	Cheese
Port, Sweet wines	Stilton (English blue veined cheese)
Chardonnay	Camembert, Brie or any other creamy cheese
Sauvignon Blanc, Chenin Blanc, Semillon	Goat cheese
Red wine (Sauvignon, Merlot, Syrah, Zinfandel)	Gauda, Cheddar or other semi-firm, firm and aged hard cheese
Madeira	Sheep's cheese

Note: Cheese are served with a selection of dried fruit, nuts, sour cream, bread or crackers that helps in bridging any imperfections in the wine and cheese pairing.

20.4 WINES AND COURSES

- The starter courses are best accompanied by a dry white or a dry rose wine.
- National dishes should be complimented by the national wines of that country, example, Italian red wines can be served with pastas.
- Fish and shellfish are most suited to a well chilled dry white wine.
- Red meats such as beef and lamb harmonize well with red wines.
- White meats such as poultry are acceptable to medium white wines.
- Heavier red wines should be served with game dishes to compliment the full flavour of the dish.
- Well chilled sweet wines should be offered at the end of the meal.

Wine and cheese

REVISION QUESTIONS

1. Write down the various rules of wine and food pairing.
2. Suggest the type of wine for the following food dishes:
   (a) Seafood
   (b) Roast lamb
   (c) Penne Arabiatta
   (d) Stilton cheese
3. List down the various points to be considered while suggesting wine with food dishes.

RESEARCH ACTIVITY

Visit a nearby bar situated in any five-star hotel and check for their offerings of various foods with wine.

21

Cocktails

21.1 INTRODUCTION

After reading this chapter, you will be able to understand:
- Types of mixing methods while making a cocktail.
- Bar measurement and types of garnishes
- Decide on the method, equipment and garnishes to be used each time when drink is being prepared.
- Cocktail families
- Various cocktail recipes.

A cocktail is a mixed drink containing two or more ingredients. Originally, a mixture of distilled spirits, sugar, water, and bitters, the word has gradually come to mean almost any mixed drink containing alcohol. Cocktail is made by mixing spirits or wines with fruit juices, bitters, liqueurs or other ingredients either by stirring, shaking and blending all of them. The ideal cocktail combines two or more ingredients having a base of alcoholic beverages in a harmonious manner so that no element should dominate the other. The term cocktail was first introduced by American bartenders in 1920.

21.1.1 Ingredients of Cocktail

Cocktails usually consist of three different 'classes' of ingredients.

- **Base:** It is most often some sort of spirit, like vodka, whisky, gin, tequila and occasionally wine.
- **Flavouring:** The main flavouring is added to bring out the aroma of the base and to modify its taste such as vermouth, fruit juices or even eggs or cream.
- **Special flavouring:** It is added to enhance the taste of the base, and often also adds the colour to the cocktail. Common special flavourings include Grenadine, Blue Curacao, and others.

21.1.2 Equipment

There are many types of equipment used for making a good cocktail. First out of the essentials is the cocktail shaker. There are two basic types of shakers available. A European cocktail shaker is usually made of metal, or glass with a metal top. It is, basically, a container which holds about half a litre, fitted with a top which closes tightly around the upper edges of the container. This top also has a smaller top, usually fitted with a built-in strainer, through which the shaken cocktail is poured. American shakers, however, consist of two cones about the same size. One is often made of glass, and the other is metallic. These cones are held together to form a closed container, and the shaken cocktail is poured from either one. Most American shakers do not have built-in strainers. Peg measures, also known as jiggers, are also essential. Jiggers are most often made of metal, but glass jiggers are common, as well. The standard measurements of a jigger can vary widely, depending on where you are. In India, jiggers are available at 60 mL/30 mL and 50 mL/25 mL. In addition to the equipment mentioned above, there are other equipment as well like ice bucket, water jugs, ice crusher machine, muddler, bar caddy, bar pad, salt and sugar rimmer, electric blender, ordinary kitchenware such as fruit knife, pairing knife, corkscrews, chopping board, lime squeezer, speed pourer, bar guns, lemon squeezer, store and pour, zester, scooper, straws, toothpicks, stirrers (small stirrers known as swizzle sticks) and hand towel and cocktail napkin. To serve cocktail in an appropriate glass is also very important. Glassware like cocktail glass, martini glass, margarita, rolly polly, rock , high ball, tom collins, slim gin, hurricane are most common glassware used to serve cocktails.

21.1.3 Mixing a Cocktail

Not all cocktails are made in the same manner. Just as the ingredients may vary, there are several ways in which to mix a cocktail. The most frequently used methods are as follows:

- **Shaking:** The cocktail is mixed by hand in a cocktail shaker. The shaker is first filled three quarters with ice, preferably cubes, as crushed ice will tend to melt and dilute the cocktail. The ingredients are then poured on top of the ice, in order of alcohol content (highest first). When shaking a cocktail, hold the shaker in both hands, one hand on the top and the other supporting the base of the shaker, and shake vigorously. When water has begun condensing on the outside of the shaker, the cocktail is sufficiently chilled, and the cocktail should immediately be strained into the glass. In general, shaking creates a colder cocktail than stirring does, but also a cloudier one.

Steps of shaking

- Add ice, spirits, liqueurs and mixers into a cocktail shaker.
- Place the lid and cap on the shaker facing over shoulder.
- Shake vigorously for ten seconds ensuring that ice hits the top and bottom of shaker a number of times. Condensation on shaker base indicates that drink is ready.
- Remove the cap and pour drink gently in the glass.
- Remove cap and place hawthorn strainer over shaker if using American shaker.

- **Stirring:** The cocktail is stirred with a glass or metal rod in a mixing glass, before the cocktail is strained into a glass. As with shaking, crushed ice should not be used, and water condensing on the outside shows that the cocktail is finished.
- **Blending:** An electric blender is used to mix fruit juices, alcohol, fruit, etc. Blending is an excellent way of mixing ingredients which do not blend easily in any other way. Blend the cocktail till it has reached a smooth consistency. If the recipe requires ice, add crushed ice last, but be careful not to add too much, as the cocktail may be watered down. Blending is a much disputed method of mixing a cocktail, and in general, blending should be avoided unless the recipe demands it.
- **Building:** When building a cocktail, the ingredients are poured into the glass in which the cocktail will be served. Usually, the ingredients are float on top of each other, but occasionally, a swizzle stick is put in the glass, allowing the ingredients to be mixed.
- **Muddling:** When one or more of the ingredients needs to be crushed into the drink. It is commonly used to mix granulated brown sugar or white sugar with fruits and herbs like mint leaves which helps to extract the flavours from them.
- **Layering:** In this mixing method, a mixed drink is layered to create a contrasting colour effect. Usually a 30 mL or 60 mL short glass is used for this drink and alcohol used for making layered drinks. The contents should vary in their densities so that layers are formed.

Steps of stirring

- Chill the glass.
- Add ice in mixing glass.
- Pour ingredients like spirits, liqueurs and mixers into mixing glass.
- Stir the ingredients in mixing glass by rotating bar spoon around edge of glass without melting the ice.
- Place strainer on top of mixing glass and pour gently into the chilled ice.
- Garnish.

Steps of muddling

- Add ingredients to an appropriate glass.
- Crush sugar and herbs/fruits by pressing muddler firmly downwards and twisting clockwise until ingredients are thoroughly mixed.
- Most of the bartenders used to shake the cocktail after muddling to ensure consistent flavour throughout the cocktail.

Steps of building

- Take glass and add ice.
- Pour spirits and liqueurs over ice.
- Add mixers and garnish.

Note: Glassware for built cocktails is usually larger.

Steps of layering

- Take a shot glass and place mixing spoon upside down into glass and pour ingredients one by one over back of spoon, gently raising spoon as glass fills.

- **Combination:** This mixing method applies combining any two mixing methods to create an interesting effect. Examples:
  - ◊ Layer blended over shaken mixture.
  - ◊ Layer blended over built mixture.
  - ◊ Layer a shaken mixture of ingredients over built mixture.

Muddling technique

Blending

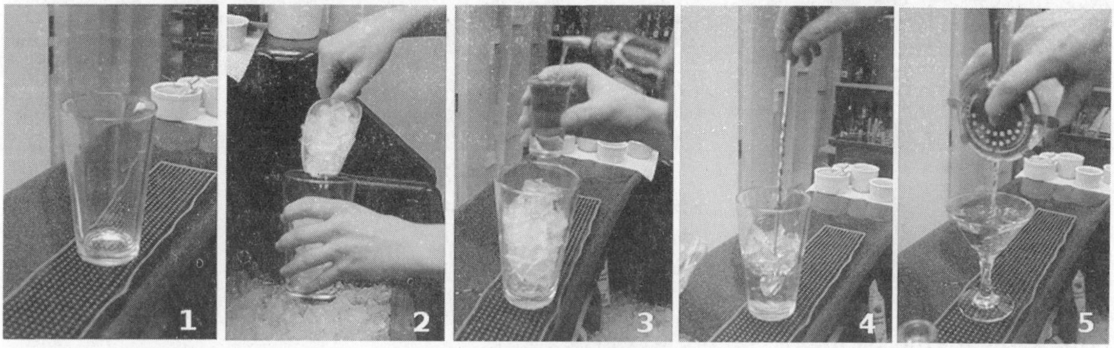

Stir method

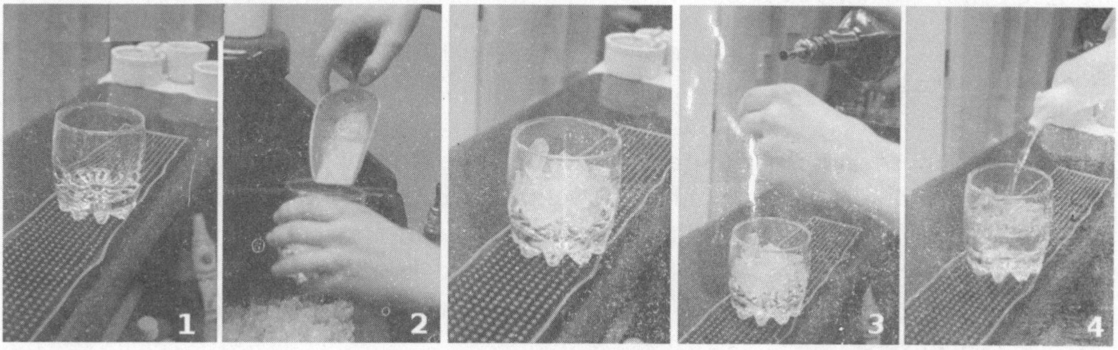

Building method

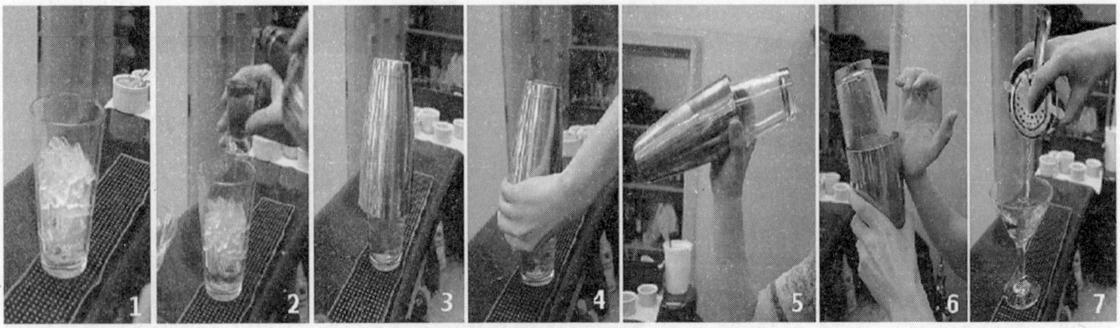

Shaking method

Layering method
Steps in mixing a cocktail

21.2 TYPES OF COCKTAILS

Following are the six major categories of cocktails:

1. Pre-dinner cocktails
2. Creamy cocktails
3. Long cocktails
4. Sour cocktails
5. Shot cocktails

1. **Pre-dinner cocktails:** These are usually intended for consumption before drinking. The intention is to stimulate the appetite and increase the enjoyment of the meal. The base spirit for the pre-dinner cocktail is usually clear but rye whisky or brandy can be used.
2. **Creamy cocktails:** These are usually served after a meal. They contain cream and heavy mixers.
3. **Long cocktails:** These are served in long glass and can be served any time during lunch or dinner. They consists mainly of fruit juices and soda and are generally lower in alcohol content by volume than the [illegible] categories. The base spirit for a

long cocktail is nearly always a white spirit as they are more suitable to mix with soda and juices.

4. **Sour cocktails:** These are balanced combination of spirits and liqueurs, lime/lemon juice and sugar syrup. Suitable for drinking on any occasion but are best consumed in the late afternoon or early evening.
5. **Shot cocktails:** These are often served as accompaniments to other beverages. They are usually layered and served in 30 mL shot glass and can be sipped or shot. Shot cocktails are often served to celebrate a special occasion and are mainly served later in the evening. In order to mix shot cocktails properly, one must be acquainted with the density of spirits and liqueurs. Density is determined by sugar content. Higher the sugar content, higher will be the density. Example: Kahlua is heavier than a spirit vodka as Kahlua has a higher sugar content. Spirits and liquers higher in density sink to the bottom.

21.2.1 Mocktails/Non-Alcoholic Cocktails

Also known as virgin cocktails that contain no alcohol. The base for these drinks are normally juices. As with cocktail, mocktails look and taste better than any of their individual components. Mocktails or non-alcoholic drinks are typically a blend of different fruits and juices with sugar syrup used to provide sweetness.

21.3 RULES FOR MAKING COCKTAILS

1. Use the appropriate glass.
2. Make your tools ready. For example: Cocktail shaker, peg measure, etc.
3. Get equipped with cocktail recipes.
4. Use only the finest ingredients.
5. The chilling process: As soon as you are equipped and ready, start by chilling the cocktail glasses. It can be as simple as putting the glass in the freezer for some hours or pouring in water with ice. Take them out only when you are ready to pour the mixed drink. This way the drink is kept smooth and cool for a longer time after it has been served.
6. Adding the ice. If ice is desired then it should be placed last into the cocktail shaker and in case of build cocktails, it will be vice versa.
7. Adding the ingredients in the order: **Base spirit → 1st Mixer → 2nd Mixer → Garnish**
8. If the cocktail needs shaking then shake it well near the shoulder hitting ice top and bottom inside the cocktail shaker, till the moisture can be seen outside the shaker.
9. Dress up or garnishing the cocktail: Cocktail drinks look empty without proper garnishing. Garnishes generally used are sweet lime, lemon, orange, pineapple, strawberry, cherry, olives, etc. Right garnishes for right cocktail make it more appealing. A general rule for selecting garnish is:

- No garnish with dark spirits.
- White spirit should be garnished with that fruit which is used in the cocktail either as a juice or chunks, etc.

21.4 COCKTAIL GARNISHES

Almost all cocktails are garnished in one way or another, most often with some kind of fruit. Garnishing is a part of the ritual of making cocktails. It adds to any drink a special feature than the others giving colour, flavour and style. The purpose of the garnishes is either to enhance the appearance of the drink or both. Garnishes should not hinder the cocktail while drinking. Most of the classic drinks have their own garnish, but it is in your imagination and creativity where you can find lots of models. A garnish should be attractive for its main function is to please the eye, which invariably pleases the palate. While garnishing any cocktail, it is always important to use fresh ingredients. The most common garnishes include fruits such as lemons, oranges, apples, cherries, pineapples. Some drinks require more elaborated garnishes like olives, celery sticks, berries, cherries, mint and cucumber. Sometimes coffee beans, nutmeg, cinnamon sticks can also be used as cocktail garnishes depending on the creativity of bartender and nature of cocktail. Although the garnishes for some classic cocktails never changes but nowadays, there is a trend towards less garnishing and more cocktail hence giving better value for money to the customers. When garnishes are used, drinking straws should be offered to prevent the guest having to fight with the garnish to get to the drink. When the garnish is placed on the rim of the glass, it is primarily for ornamental purpose and drinks can be made without it. Following are the factors to consider while preparing a garnish for any cocktail:

- **Colour:** Colour of the garnish should be compatible or a contrast to the colour of the drink, e.g., a pink coloured drink benefits from a red cherry and a blue drink with a pineapple slice which is yellow in colour.
- **Taste:** If an edible garnish is used, it should be compatible with one or more of the ingredients in the cocktail. Edible garnishes also impart flavour to the drink, e.g., a cocktail containing pineapple juice would be benefitted by a garnish of pineapple slice and a cocktail containing lime/lemon juice by a lime/lemon slice/wedge.
- **Shape and size:** The shape of the glass helps in determining the best garnish to use, e.g., lime/lemon wheels complements a Martini glass whereas adding pineapple slice in a Martini glass will look odd with the shape of the glass. Size of the garnish should also be appropriate for the size of the glass, e.g., a mixed drink rather than in a small glass may benefit from a small cherry, a large orange slice.

Garnish can be placed in different ways in a glass		
Mounted	Place on the side of a glass.	E.g., lime wheel in Margarita
Floated	Floated in the mixture	E.g., lime/lemon slice in vodka and lemonade
Sunk	Dropped into the bottom of the glass	E.g., cherry in Manhattan

Garnishes are normally floated for mixed spirits and mounted or sunk for cocktails.

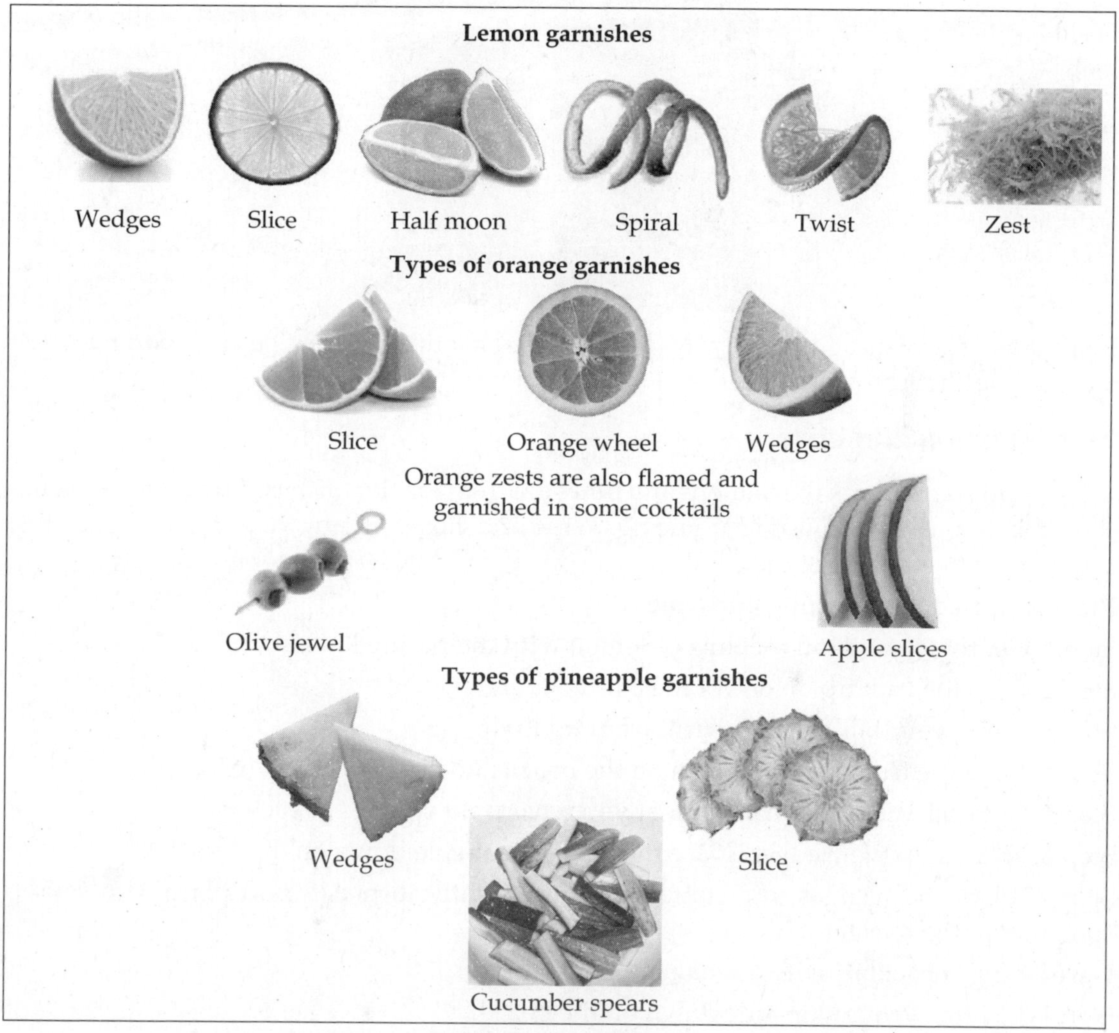

Types of garnishes

Cherries: Cherries are speared onto orange slices, pineapples, limes and lemons. This type of decoration is called "flag" in the cocktail world. The most common are: Maraschino Cherries, Red Cherries, Yellow Cherries and Green Cherries.

Flags: Fruit flags and boats are the flashiest of the standard cocktail garnishes. Flags are garnishes that skewer a Maraschino cherry on top of another garnish, such as an orange slice or pineapple wedge whereas boats are the garnishes made from citrus fruit wheels that have been folded in half with a Maraschino cherry pinned into the fold.

Remember: Garnishes should always be presented in odd numbers, because odd numbers are more aesthetically pleasing.

21.4.1 Lemon and Lime

Before shift starts, check that lemons and limes are free from blemishes. Any with blemishes should be set aside and used for juicing. Wipe and rinse off any wax on the skin as this could affect the flavour of the drink.

Preparing wedges of lemon and lime:

Step 1: Gently top and tail the lime or lemon with the paring knife.

Step 2: Prop the fruit up on one of the cut tips.

Step 3: Using your knife, cut the fruit from tip to tip.

Step 4: Place the fruit cut-side down on the board and cut the fruit in half again.

Step 5: Cut each quarter in half, so that you have eight wedges of each.

Step 6: Neaten up the wedges. Place the wedges cut-side down on the board.

Step 7: Place the wedges in a container, cover tightly in plastic and place it in a prep container in the refrigerator.

Garnishing a cocktail with a wedge during service:

Step 1: Lay the wedge skin-side down on the board.

Step 2: Run your knife three-quarters of the way between the skin and the flesh.

Step 3: Cut a third of the skin flap off so that it looks neat.

Step 4: Prop the wedge on the rim of the glass so that the flesh of the wedge is touching the liquid.

Muddling with lemon and lime:

Step 1: Top and tail the lemon or lime.

Step 2: Cut down the centre of the fruit, from tip to tip.

Step 3: Lay the halves cut-side down and cut in half from tip to tip.

Step 4: Cut the quarters the other way now, giving you eight pieces.

Slices of lemon and lime:

Step 1: Top and tail the lemon or lime, in a way that exposes the flesh.

Step 2: Cut the fruit horizontally in five mm thick slices.

Step 3: Make an incision to the centre of the slice so that it can then be placed onto the rim of the glass.

Working with lime and lemon

21.4.2 Oranges and Grapefruit

- Check that the produce is fresh.
- Remove any wax that may be present on the skin of the fruit.
- Prepare all garnishes before service starts.

Preparing wedges of orange and grapefruit:

Step 1: Halve the fruit, from tip to tip.

Step 2: Top and tail the fruit.

Step 3: Halve the fruit again to make quarters.

Step 4: Halve again to make eighths.

Step 5: Trim pith.

Step 6: Wrap and pack away for service.

How to finish the wedge during service:

Step 1: Place the wedge skin-side down.

Step 2: Run a knife three quarters of the way between the skin and flesh.

Step 3: Trim one-third of the skin.

Step 4: Arrange the wedge on the glass.

Muddling with oranges and grapefruit:

Step 1: Top and tail.

Step 2: Halve.

Step 3: Halve into quarters.

Step 4: Divide, turn and halve into eighths.

Step 5: Halve again to make eighths.

Step 6: Check that the pieces are small enough for muddling.

Preparing slices of orange and grapefruit:

Step 1: Top and tail the fruit.

Step 2: Cut the fruit horizontally into five mm thick slices.

Step 3: Cut the rounds to the centre.

Working with oranges

21.4.3 Zest

Zest is the skin of a citrus fruit that is used to add flavour and aroma to drinks. The zest contains oils that burst from the skin when it is squeezed or twisted. Ensure that your zest is firm, shiny and blemish-free.

Remove the pith from the zest before adding to the drink.

Zest must be prepared before service, but begins to shrivel over time and must be wrapped in an air-tight container and refrigerated.

Preparing zest:

Step 1: Using a potato peeler or a paring knife, peel the zest in long strips from tip to tip without removing any flesh.

Step 2: Lay the zest pith side up on a board and, using a sharp knife, gently shave off any pith that is attached to the zest.

Step 3: Trim the zest so that it is even, neat and to the establishment's standards.

Extract the oils from the zest:

Step 1: Once the drink has been prepared, squeeze and twist the prepared zest over the surface of the drink.

Step 2: Rub the zest on the lip, stem and base of the glass.

Flaming with zest:

Step 1: Place the prepared zest between your fingers, facing the cocktail.

Step 2: Use a lighter to warm the zest.

Step 3: Squeeze the zest firmly so that the oils ignite over the drink.

How to make the Horse's Neck:

Step 1: Using a potato peeler, peel an entire lemon, beginning from the top and spiralling down to the tail.

Step 2: Coil the zest in the glass, with the top end hanging out of the glass.

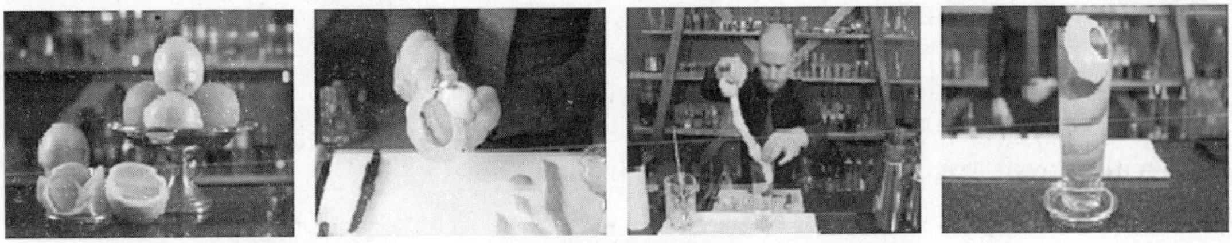

Working with zest

21.4.4 Mint

Always have a station that is stocked with mint.

Adding a sprig of mint makes the drink look fresher and more exciting, while adding extra aromas to the surface of the drink.

Before adding the sprig of mint, gently tap it a few times in your hand to release the minty aroma.

Muddling with mint

You will need:

- A bar spoon or muddler
- Mint
- The glass that you'll make the drink in

Step 1: Place the spirit or ingredient into your glass.

Step 2: Add eight or nine mint leaves into the glass with the ingredient.

Step 3: Gently tap the mint with either your bar spoon or muddler

Place the straw right next to the sprig of mint so that each and every time a guest takes a sip, there is a fresh smell of the mint.

Using mint as garnish

21.4.5 Sugar and Salt

Salt and sugar are used in drinks for two reasons:

- To add a strong burst of flavour.
- To add great texture and interest to a drink.

Crusting with salt

Because salt has such a powerful flavour and is rarely used in drinks, it must be approached carefully. It's usually a flavour coupled with citrus-based drinks, such as a Margarita.

Step 1: Fetch the appropriate glass.

Step 2: Take a wedge of citrus that suits the drink.

Step 3: Rub the flesh of the wedge on the outside of the glass, starting at the rim and working approximately three centimetres down.

Step 4: Angle the glass downwards over a sink or bin and, from a high angle, sprinkle the salt over the damp half of the glass where the salt will stick.

Crusting with sugar

A sugar crust will add sweetness to the drink, so the drink should be quite refreshing or sour, such as the Crusta.

Crusting with sugar is simple and looks best when made using castor sugar. Follow the same steps as when you crusted with salt, however, because sugar is more palatable than salt, dampen the entire rim of the glass for an even coating.

Crusting with powdered sugar

Crusting with powdered sugar provides lot of sweetness and no crunch, whereas cocktails crusted with salt and castor sugar have a crunchier texture.

21.4.6 Apple

Apples are delicate fruits that need to be refrigerated. They can be easily damaged and they oxidise quickly. The only way to prevent this is by squeezing lemon juice, or an acid, over the top of the cut apple. They must only be prepared to order.

Making slices of apple

Step 1: Cut the cheek off the apple, avoiding the seeds and core.

Step 2: Cut the cheek into two mm thick slices.

Step 3: Squeeze fresh lemon or lime juice over the cut apple.

Making a caramelised apple fan

- To be made before service
- Does not oxidise

To caramelise the apple:

Step 1: Coat the apple slices in castor sugar.

Step 2: Lay the slices out on a heat-proof surface.

Step 3: Using a blow torch, caramelise the castor sugar until the apples are golden brown.

Using the caramelised apples:

Step 1: Prepare caramelised and fresh apple slices.

Step 2: Arrange a caramelised apple slice, then a fresh apple and then another caramelised apple and splay them like a deck of cards.

Step 3: Using a skewer, secure the apple fan.

Step 4: Position the fan on top of a cocktail.

Fruity, floral, non-alcoholic cocktails work very well with apple.

Using apple as a garnish

21.4.7 Pineapple

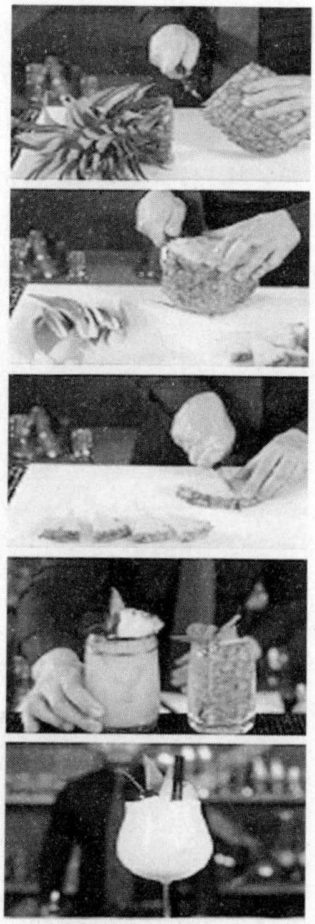

Pineapple garnishes

Refrigerate pineapples to extend their shelf-life. Pineapple does not oxidise and can be prepared before service.

Preparing wedges of pineapple

To prepare wedges perfectly:

Step 1: Cut off the head of the pineapple, but don't throw it away.

Step 2: Cut the pineapple into one centimetre thick slices.

Step 3: Cut the slices into quarters.

Step 4: Halve the quarters to create triangles.

The skin can be left on for texture and presentation.

Working with pineapple skin and leaves

Some cocktails, such as the Piña Colada, are beautiful when garnished with pineapple leaves and skin.

To garnish a drink with the pineapple skin:

Step 1: Remove the head of the pineapple.

Step 2: Using your knife, remove the skin without wasting any fruit.

Step 3: Set the fruit aside and neaten the pineapple skin into even strips.

Step 4: To garnish the drink, place the skin against the inside of the glass and pour in the drink.

21.4.8 Spices

Spices are aromatic and fragrant natural substances that add flavour and interest to drinks and foods. They can be made from seeds, pods, bark, stamens and leaves.

Vanilla pods should be stored frozen and, as far as possible, spices should be purchased whole to preserve the maximum amount of flavour.

Garnishing with grated spices

Cocktails, such as the Egg Nog and the White Russian, benefit from the warming, spicy flavour of nutmeg. To achieve the perfect coating of nutmeg, follow these steps:

Step 1: Place the microplane, or fine grater, over the top of the cocktail.

Step 2: Grate the nutmeg over the top of the drink to produce a fine, even dusting.

Step 3: Serve.

Note: Try to grate the nutmeg directly over the drink instead of grating it before service to get a fine, even layer of spice!

21.4.9 Floating Garnishes

A floating garnish can be shaved chocolate, shaved coconut, edible flowers and berries. In order for a garnish to float, it has to be lighter than the liquid on which it sits. This means that the garnish needs to be stored in a cool, dry place, except for fresh garnishes, such as edible flowers and berries.

When to use a floating garnish

The floating garnish must only be used when it complements the drink, or is part of the flavour base. For example, coffee beans are the perfect floating garnish for a White Russian, and Angostura Bitters compliment the Whisky Sour with its bitter, herbal flavours.

Floating garnishes

21.4.10 Skewers

Skewers are very useful items behind the bar. Skewers are used to make the guest's experience comfortable and easy.

They are best used with small berries, olives and cut fruit. They can be made from wood, bamboo, plastic and metal. Wood, bamboo and plastic skewers should only be used once and then discarded, but metal skewers can be washed and sterilised for reuse. Always keep skewers covered in a clean, dry place, and only touch the end that the Guest will touch, so as not to contaminate the garnish.

Remember: Garnishes should always be presented in odd numbers, because odd numbers are more aesthetically pleasing.

Using skewer as a garnish

21.5 MIXERS

Mixers are non-alcoholic liquid ingredients, often added to drinks and cocktails and usually kept in bottles, cans and boxes. A mixer should highlight its flavour but never overpower it. Even though mixers are the least expensive ingredients in a recipe, they play an important part in the final result when making a cocktail. Mixers are often kept in plastic casing for storage to prevent contamination, but they can become dirty and dusty. To ensure that the mixers are always clean, wipe any dust off with a clean cloth after removing them from the storeroom. Pack them into the fridge, in the correct place, with labels facing you. Following are the uses of mixers:

Types of mixers

- They change or enhance the flavours of a drink.
- They dilute a drink and lower the ratio of alcohol in a drink.
- Some change the texture or consistency of a drink, making it either thicker or more watery.
- Some change the colour or appearance of a drink.
- Can be served on their own for guests who do not drink alcohol.

Table 21.1: Popular mixers

Name	Mixed with
Cola	Spirits such as brandy, whisky, vodka and rum.
Ginger ale	Whisky, brandy, vodka and rum
Lemonade	Vodka, brandy, whisky and rum
Soda water	Vodka (and lime cordial), brandy, whisky and rum as well as aged spirits
Tonic water	Gin and vodka
Red bull	A variety of mix options based on guest preferences

21.5.1 Tips and Tricks

- 1/2 oz. of liquor is equal to 1 count, assuming you are using a pourer on your bottles. To measure 1 1/2 oz. of liquor, count "1001...1002...1003" as you are pouring. After a while, you should be able to do it by eye.
- To make highballs, fill glass two-thirds of ice before adding liquor. Always pour liquor in before the mixer. Do not stir drinks containing carbonated mixers.
- To make cocktails, low balls, and other shaken or stirred drinks, fill shaker half full of ice. For low balls, fill the glass about half-full of ice before pouring drink.
- Most shaken drinks which contain light cream can also be made as blended drinks, substituting vanilla ice cream for the light cream.
- To make blended drinks, first fill blender half-full of ice. If necessary, add more ice as you are blending.
- Always keep fruit juices and other mixers refrigerated.
- In fruit drinks, e.g., strawberry margaritas always use fresh fruit, not frozen.

21.6 TERMS RELATED TO THE BAR

- **Mixing:** When using a cocktail shaker, there is one golden rule to remember. Always put the ice in the shaker first, and the liquor last. This is to ensure that all ingredients are properly chilled by the ice when they are poured over the ice, and by adding the liquor last you reduce the chance of dilution.

A well-stocked bar should have: cola, ginger ale, tonic and soda water, sprite, seven up and sour mix. A sour mix is made from equal parts of lemon and/or lime juice and simple syrup.

- **Stirring:** A drink that is stirred instead of shaken retains its clarity and is free of ice chips. Drinks based on clear liquors, like a Martini, should always be stirred and not shaken (heard James Bond when he orders his Martini "shaken, not stirred"?). When stirring a cocktail you should stir it enough to mix the ingredients, but not stir it too much. If you stir too much, the ice will begin to dilute the liquor. A general rule is that 10-15 stirs are sufficient for proper mixing. A drink containing carbonated beverage(s) should be stirred gently and briefly to retain the sparkle.
- **Shaking:** Instead of stirring, you can shake the drink. This will mix the ingredients more than stirring, but will also result in a less clear drink. Drinks which contain ingredients that are hard to mix, such as cream, fruit juices and eggs, should be shaken vigorously to ensure that the ingredients have been well mixed.
- **Blending:** Use an electric blender to mix fresh fruit, liquor, juices and ice instead of a shaker. Not too popular everywhere, but perfect for making frozen cocktails or to blend ingredients that are otherwise impossible to mix.
- **Floating:** The purpose of floating is to keep each ingredient in the drink in separate layers that do not mix with the others. This will create a drink with separate layers, and this is why floating often is referred to as layering. The easiest way to float one liquor on top of another is to use a demitasse spoon, holding it over or in the glass and slowly trickle the ingredient over the back of the spoon.
- **Muddling:** Muddling is a simple mashing technique for grinding herbs, such as mint, smooth in the bottom of a glass. You can use a wooden muddler that you buy in a bar supply store or buy a bar spoon with a muddler on the end. It crushes the herbs, much as the back of a soup spoon might, without scaring the glass.
- **Frosting:** To frost a glass, first dip it in water and then put it in the freezer for half an hour or so. Also note that metal and silver mugs and cups will frost better than glasses.

21.6.1 Standard Bar Measurements

- Oz = 1 ounce = 30 mL approx. / 29.573 mL
- Tbsp = tablespoon = 1/2 oz = 15mL
- Tsp. = teaspoon = 1/6 oz = 5 mL
- Dash = 1/6 teaspoon = 1 mL
- 1 part = any equal part
- 1 splash = 1/4 ounce
- pinch = whatever that gets between fingers and thumb
- 1 pony = 1 ounce
- peg measure = 30 mL and 60 mL
- 1 quart (qt) = 9.4635 decilitres
- 1 gallon (gal) = 3.7854 litres

- 1 millilitre (mL) = 1/30 ounce
- 1 centilitre (cl) = 1/3 ounce
- 1 decilitre (dl) = $3\frac{1}{2}$ ounces
- 1 litre (l) = 34 ounces

21.7 FAMILIES OF DRINKS

- **Bucks:** A buck is a long drink made from a single liquor with the addition of citrus juices and ginger ale. Example, Gin Buck.
- **Collins:** A long, refreshing drink containing just one spirit (gin, whisky), lemon juice, sugar and soda water. The Collins is a close relation to the *Fizz* and the *Sling* but is always built and never shaken. The Collins is always served in a Collins glass. Example, Tom Collins.
- **Daises:** These are short drinks containing any number of spirits and are often served with cracked ice. A Daisy must be shaken very hard and served freezing cold. Example, Rum Daisy.
- **Fixes:** A close relation of the Daisy but is built and not shaken and poured over crushed not cracked ice. Example, Gin Fix.

Use of ice

Ice can only be made using still water or clean water which has been boiled first and then purified.

- Ice is used to keep drinks and cocktails cool. It can be blended into smoothies and cocktails to create texture.
- Ice does not just cool drinks down but can also be used to 'temper' or balance alcohol in drinks. Ice melts when it's added to aged spirits and releases water which 'invigorates' them. This is called '*awakening the dragon*'.

- **Fizzes:** These are a shaken version of the Collins but have highly pressurized soda water to give them a strong sparkle. The Fizz must be consumed very quickly to avoid losing the sparkle. Example, Silver Fizz
- **Flips:** A drink made from any base (spirit, wine, liqueur) that contains a whole egg. It is advisable to only use fresh eggs and no milk (unlike egg noggs). Shake the drink very hard to mix the ingredients thoroughly. Example, Brandy Flip.
- **Frappes:** This is a single spirit or liqueur drink served on crushed ice. These are also known as Mists. Example, Wards Frappe.
- **Highballs:** A highball is basically a drink that contains a single spirit and a mixer (soda, ginger ale) served over ice. The name comes from a signal that used to inform train drivers that they were behind schedule in the early days of the American railroads and is used to indicate a drink that is prepared quickly. Example, Horses Neck.
- **Hot Drinks:** Any drink that contains boiling water or any other hot ingredient; they are very popular in colder countries. They can be made with hot chocolate, milk, coffee and certain juices. Example, Keoke Coffee.

- **Juleps:** The word Julep means tonic and is credited as the first cocktail to be created. The drink can contain any spirit, liqueur or wine but must contain sugar and mint. The most famous Julep is the Mint Julep made with Bourbon. Example, Mint Julep.
- **Pousse Café:** A mixture of spirits and liqueurs, but the different ingredients are separated by means of careful floating, this creates a rainbow effect. The reason the ingredients float is due to the amount of sugar present in the different ingredients, the higher the sugar content, the less the alcohol and therefore the heavier the spirit or liqueur. Lighter ingredients float on heavier ingredients thus creating the rainbow effect. Examples include B52, Slippery Nipple and Cucaracha.
- **Punches:** A mixture of spirits (usually rum or brandy), juices (lime, orange, etc.), spices and sugar, punches were originally served in large bowls but can be served as single drinks. The punch can be served hot with extra juices and spices (Hot Rum Punch) or cold with less juice and spice (Planters Punch). Example, Rum Punch.
- **Rickeys:** An unsweetened version of the Collins or Fizz, it was created by a bartender at the Shoemakers Bar in Washington DC at the end of the 19th century. The drink was named the Rickey after Colonel Jim Rickey, a political lobbyist from Kentucky. The base of the drink is gin, with the addition of fresh limes and soda water, it is always served long. Example, Gin Rickey
- **Sangrees:** The word sangree comes from the word "Singari" which is Indian for "blood drink". The drink can be made from liquor, wine or beer which is sweetened and served in a short glass over crushed ice. Example, Brandy Sangree.
- **Slings:** The sling is a close relation of the Collins, fix or fizz but are usually connected with hot weather countries especially the Far East. It is a sweetened spirit with lemon and soda, the most famous example is the Singapore Gin Sling. Example, Raffles Gin Sling.
- **Smashes:** A smaller version of the Julep, made without the addition of soda water and served over crushed ice. The most famous example being the Mojito.
- **Sours:** A short and sharp drink that always contains lemon or lime juice, liquor and sugar. The most famous type is the whisky sour. Some bartenders always put an egg white in to their sours; this is not necessary but it does make the drink smoother and look more appealing. Example, Whisky Sour.
- **Toddies:** Originally a hot drink made since the early Victorian era, today they can be served both hot or cold. The toddy is basically a sweetened liquor with water and various spices such as cinnamon, nutmeg or cloves. Hot toddies contain a slice or twist of lemon, whereas cold toddies also contain lemon juice. Example, Hot Whisky Toddy.

21.8 BAR TERMINOLOGY

For being a good bartender, it is important to have a good knowledge of beverage apart from food dishes and he should try to memorize and understand bar terminology as well.

- **After-dinner cocktail:** Sweet cocktails, which are served after dinner.
- **Pre-dinner cocktail:** Dry cocktails, which are served before dinner (sometimes standing cocktail) and should be stimulating.
- **Blend:** To mix drinks, but as well to mix whiskys during production (blend of malt and grain whisky).
- **Blending:** Mixture of 2-3 components.
- **Build-in glass:** The preparation of a cocktail or mixed drink is done in the glass served.
- **Chasers:** Long drinks which are filled up with tonic waters, bitter lemon, ginger ale, coke, fruit juice, beer, etc.
- **Chilled:** Cooled down, chilled glass from the freezer.
- **Dash:** Drop, "spritzer", is a pouring unit used with strong aromas like angostura, grenadine, syrups, etc.
- **Fill:** "To fill-up", to fill a drink up with fruit juice, lemonade, soda water or sparkling wine.
- **Filler:** Other word for chaser.
- **Float:** Kind of preparation technique; aromas which are put on top of the drink for garnish.
- **Frosted:** Frozen, a glass or bottle is covered with a film of thin ice.
- **Gill:** Original whisky pouring unit of $1\frac{1}{2}$ oz.
- **Gom, Ghomme:** Another name for sugar syrup.
- **Grind:** To grate or grind an ingredient finely to powder.
- **Iced:** Like frosted
- **Jigger:** Measuring unit of 20 or 40 g.
- **Sugar syrup:** 1 kg sugar and 1l water boiled; and then cooled down, used for cocktails.
- **Long drink:** Name for every drink which has more than 8 cl content of beverage.
- **Marge:** Spirits with high alcohol tend to lose slight volume especially when heated.
- **Mixer:** Other name for chaser or filler.
- **Muddler:** A pestle or the other end of the bar spoon, to grind or smoothen ingredients like rock sugar, herbs or fruits (Caipirinha).
- **Mug:** Old description for big beer glass with handle made out of clay or tin.
- **Nip:** To drink a fairly small amount or taste.
- **Nutmeg:** Freshly grated, used in some cocktails.
- **On-the-rocks:** Type of order for drinks served with ice (whisky on the rocks).
- **Peel:** A piece of skin of citrus fruits, lemon, lime, orange to flavour drinks and for decoration.
- **Pitcher:** Water pitcher, wine pitcher to be put on the table for self-service.

- **Plain:** Not diluted, not mixed, type of order for drinks (no ice !).
- **Poures:** Pouring unit for bottles, with 20 or mostly 40 g. To be installed on the bottle neck.
- **Pouring drink:** A basic drink like cognac, whisky; if the guest does not specify what kind without giving a brand or name.
- **Sediment:** A deposit especially found with aged red wine, sherry or port.
- **Shake:** Called the preparation technique using a cocktail shaker.
- **Short drink:** Name for drink which contains less than 8 cl liquid.
- **Soothe:** Conserved egg white in aerosol/spray bottles, used for creaming
- **Sparkling:** Foam, sparkling wine.
- **Squeeze:** To press, especially for citrus fruit.
- **Stir:** To mix or stir a drink as preparation technique whereby ingredients are carefully mixed in the glass served with a bar spoon.
- **Straight up:** Other name for plain or up.
- **Strain:** To strain or hold back ice or ice pieces in the shaker, when pouring the drink into the glass.
- **Straw:** Formerly the natural straw used for drinks, now of course made of plastic in various colours and shapes.
- **Sugar edge:** Sugar on the rim of the glass, dipped in lemon or lime juice and then into a sugar bed on a saucer.
- **Sugar lip:** Like sugar edge, part of the garnish.
- **Sugar rim:** Other word for sugar edge.
- **Swizzle stick:** Used for mixing drinks, twirling stick (small).
- **Topped:** Covering drinks with cream or whipped cream.
- **Twist:** To twist citrus fruit on the rim of the glass to release the aroma.
- **Under liner:** Underliner for the glass, usually out of small, round white linen, or paper with property logo.

21.9 RIMING A COCKTAIL GLASS

Cocktails like Margarita require to rim a glass with sugar and salt to provide an extra-special touch along with a visual addition to the cocktail. Cocoa powder, brown sugar, chilli powder, dried or fresh herbs are being used nowadays in various innovative cocktails. To rim a glass, take a saucer and arrange the sugar or salt as needed in a circle corresponding roughly to the size of the rim of your glass. Hold the Margarita or a cocktail glass by its stem at about a 45 degree angle and moisten the rim and outer edge of the rim of the glass with a lime or lemon wedge. Dip the moistened glass in the saucer containing circle of salt/sugar. If more salt or sugar is needed, hold the glass perpendicular to the saucer and gently roll the outside of the rim in the salt/sugar. Then shake off the excess salt or sugar. Be sure to get any flakes that might have fallen into the glass.

Table 21.2: Important cocktail recipes

Screwdriver	Ingredients	Qty (mL)	Method
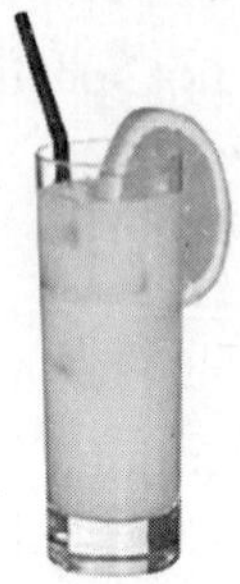	Vodka Orange juice	60 150	Build the ingredients over ice into a Collin glass, stir and serve with an orange slice. Garnish: Orange slice Glass: Collin glass
Harvey Wallbanger	**Ingredients**	**Qty (mL)**	**Method**
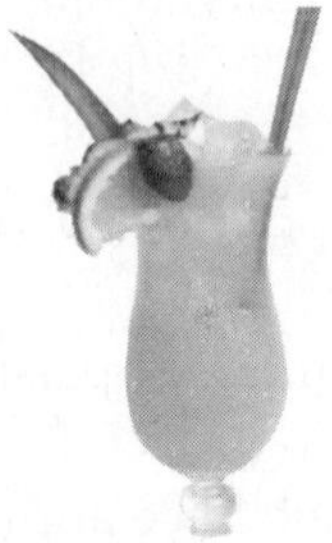	Vodka Galliano Orange juice	45 15 120	Build the ingredients over ice into a hurricane glass, stir and serve with an orange slice. (You can float Galliano on top as well) Garnish: Orange slice Glass: Hurricane glass
Black Russian	**Ingredients**	**Qty (mL)**	**Method**
	Vodka Kahlua	30 30	Shake the vodka and Kahlua over ice and strain into an old fashioned glass filled with ice. *For White Russian, float cream over the same cocktail. Garnish: Cherry with stem Glass: Old fashioned
Kamikaze	**Ingredients**	**Qty (mL)**	**Method**
	Vodka Triple sec Lime juice	30 30 15	Shake all the ingredients over ice and strain into the glass. Garnish and serve. Garnish: Lemon wedge Glass: Old fashioned

Caprioshka	Ingredients	Qty (mL)	Method
	Vodka	60	Muddle lemon chunks with white and brown sugar in an old fashioned glass, add crushed ice and vodka, cover with mixing glass and shake well. Pour into another old fashioned glass.
	Lemon (chunks)	1	Garnish: Lemon
	Brown sugar	10	Glass: Old fashioned
	White sugar	5	

Bloody Mary	Ingredients	Qty (mL)	Method
	Vodka	60	Stir all ingredients in the mixing glass and strain into an old fashioned glass.
	Tomato juice	120	Garnish: Celery and lemon slice
	Worcestershire	Dash	Glass: Rolly Polly / Rock
	Tabasco	Dash	
	Lemon juice	15	
	Salt & pepper		

Cosmopolitan	Ingredients	Qty (mL)	Method
	Vodka	45	Add all ingredients to a cocktail shaker with ice cubes. Shake and strain into a martini glass.
	Cointreau	15	Garnish: Orange slice/zest
	Cranberry juice	60	Glass: Martini
	Lemon juice	10	

Long Island iced tea	Ingredients	Qty (mL)	Method
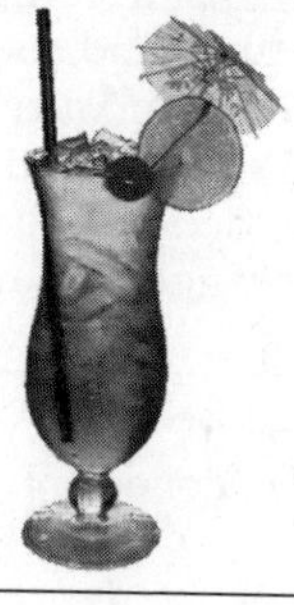	Vodka	15	Add all the ingredients in a hurricane glass, put ice and top up with coke.
	Gin	15	Garnish: Lemon wedge, cherry
	Rum	15	Glass: Hurricane
	Tequila	15	
	Cointreau	15	
	Coke	1	
	Lemon juice	10	

Perfect Manhattan	**Ingredients**	**Qty (mL)**	**Method**
	Rye whisky Sweet vermouth Dry vermouth Angostura	45 7.5 7.5 Dash	Add the ingredients to a mixing glass filled with ice and stir the mixture until chilled. Strain into a cocktail glass, add the garnish and serve. (Can be made shaken as well) *There can be variants like Dry or Sweet Manhattan, based on Vermouth. Garnish Cherry Glass Cocktail/Martini

Rob Roy	**Ingredients**	**Qty (mL)**	**Method**
	Whisky Sweet vermouth Angostura	45 15 Dash	Add the ingredients to a mixing glass filled with ice and stir the mixture until chilled. Strain into a cocktail glass, add the garnish and serve. Garnish Cherry Glass Cocktail/Martini

Rusty Nail	**Ingredients**	**Qty (mL)**	**Method**
	Scotch whisky Drambuie	45 15	Add the ingredients to a mixing glass filled with ice and stir the mixture until chilled. Strain into an old fashioned glass, add the garnish and serve. Garnish Orange zest Glass Old fashioned

Old fashioned	**Ingredients**	**Qty (mL)**	**Method**
	Rye whisky White sugar Angostura	60 15 Dash	Place sugar in the glass and soak with the bitters. Muddle the mixture and pour whisky slowly on ice until all the whisky has been added and the sugar is dissolved. Run orange zest around the rim of the glass. Garnish Orange zest Glass Old fashioned

Mint Julep	Ingredients	Qty (mL)	Method
	Rye whisky	60	Crush the mint and sugar in the glass. Fill the glass with crushed ice and add the whisky. Stir the mixture and serve.
	White sugar	10	Garnish: Mint leaves
	Lemon juice	10	Glass: Old fashioned
	Mint sprigs	5	

Whisky Sour	Ingredients	Qty (mL)	Method
	Whisky	60	Add all the ingredients to a shaker filled with ice and shake sharply. Strain the contents to a cocktail glass filled with ice, garnish and serve.
	Lemon juice	15	Garnish: Cherry
	Sugar syrup	10	Glass: Cocktail
	Angostura	Dash	

Daiquiri	Ingredients	Qty (mL)	Method
	White rum	45	Pour all the ingredients into an ice filled shaker. Shake and strain into a cocktail glass. Garnish and serve.
	Cointreau	15	Garnish: Lemon slice
	Lemon juice	15	Glass: Cocktail/Martini
	Sugar syrup	10	

Mojito	Ingredients	Qty (mL)	Method
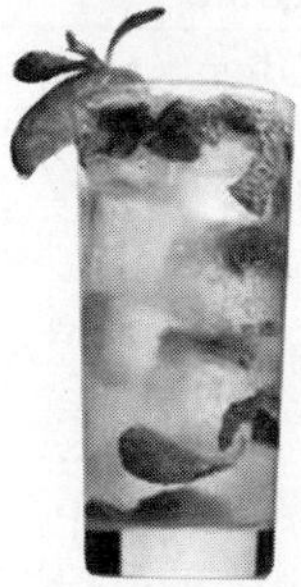	Bacardi	45	Crush the mint and sugar in the glass. Fill the glass with crushed ice and add the rum. Stir the mixture, top it with sprite and serve.
	Dark rum	15	Garnish: Mint sprigs
	Sprite	120	Glass: Collins/Old fashioned
	Brown sugar	10	
	Mint sprigs	5	
	Lemon juice	10	

Planter's Punch	Ingredients	Qty (mL)	Method
	Dark rum	60	Build the ingredients into a Collins glass filled with ice. Gently pour the grenadine on the side of the glass, float the dark rum. Garnish and serve.
	Orange juice	60	Garnish: Orange slice
	Pineapple juice	60	Glass: Collin
	Lemon juice	10	
	Grenadine	5	

Mai Tai	Ingredients	Qty (mL)	Method
	White rum	45	Add all the ingredients to a shaker filled with ice, shake and strain into an ice filled old fashioned glass. Garnish and serve.
	Triple sec	10	Garnish: Orange slice
	Cherry brandy	10	Glass: Old fashioned
	Pineapple juice	60	
	Angostura	Dash	
	Sour mix	10	

Pinacolada	Ingredients	Qty (mL)	Method
	White rum	60	Put all the ingredients in a blender, add a scoop of crushed ice and blend. Pour into a hurricane glass, garnish and serve.
	Pineapple juice	100	Garnish: Pineapple slice
	Coconut cream	25	Glass: Hurricane glass
	Sugar syrup	10	

Negroni	Ingredients	Qty (mL)	Method
	Gin	20	Shake all the ingredients together over ice and strain into a cocktail glass. Garnish and serve.
	Sweet vermouth	20	Garnish: Orange twist
	Campari	20	Glass: Cocktail/Martini

Gimlet	Ingredients	Qty (mL)	Method
	Gin	60	Add the gin and cordial to a shaker filled with ice. Shake very sharply and strain into a cocktail glass.
	Lime cordial	30	Garnish: Lemon slice
			Glass: Cocktail/Martini

Martini	Ingredients	Qty (mL)	Method
	Gin	60	Add the ingredients to a mixing glass filled with ice and stir. Strain into a Martini glass, garnish and serve.
	Vermouth	Dash	Garnish: Olive
			Glass: Martini

Singapore Sling	Ingredients	Qty (mL)	Method
	Gin	30	Add all the ingredients to the cocktail shaker, shake and pour into an old fashioned glass.
	Cherry brandy	15	Garnish: Pineapple & cherry
	Triple sec	7.5	Glass: Old fashioned/Collins
	Benedictine	7.5	
	Pineapple juice	120	
	Grenadine	10	
	Angostura	Dash	
	Lemon juice	10	

Tom Collins	Ingredients	Qty (mL)	Method
	Gin	60	Build the ingredients into a Collins glass filled with ice. Stir gently, garnish and serve.
	Soda	120	Garnish: Lemon slice
	Angostura	Dash	Glass: Collins
	Lemon juice	20	
	Sugar syrup	15	

Margarita	Ingredients	Qty (mL)	Method
	Tequila Cointreau Lemon juice Sugar syrup	45 15 15 10	Add all the ingredients into a blender. Add a scoop of crushed ice and blend. Pour into a margarita glass, garnish and serve. Garnish: Lemon slice Glass: Margarita/Cocktail

Tequila Sunrise	Ingredients	Qty (mL)	Method
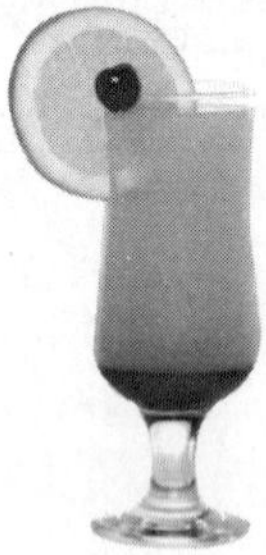	Tequila Orange juice Grenadine Lemon juice	60 120 15 10	Build the tequila and orange juice into the glass with ice. Gently pour the grenadine down the inside of the glass so the syrup fills the bottom. Garnish and serve. Garnish: Orange slice Glass: Hurricane/Highball

Kir Royale	Ingredients	Qty (mL)	Method
	Sparkling wine Crème de cassis	120 5	Add a small dash of crème de cassis to a Champagne flute and gently top with sparkling wine. Stir gently and serve. Garnish: Not required Glass: Champagne flute

Bellini	Ingredients	Qty (mL)	Method
	Sparkling wine Peach Schnapps	120 15	Add the peach schnapps and gently top with sparkling wine. Stir gently, garnish and serve. Garnish: Peach slice Glass: Champagne flute

Sidecar	Ingredients	Qty (mL)	Method
	Brandy	45	Shake all the ingredients together over ice and strain into a Martini glass. Garnish and serve.
	Cointreau	15	Garnish — Lemon slice
	Lemon juice	15	Glass — Cocktail/Martini

Brandy Alexander	Ingredients	Qty (mL)	Method
	Brandy	45	Shake all the ingredients over ice and strain into the glass. Garnish and serve.
	Crème de cacao	15	Garnish — Grated nutmeg
	Cream	15	Glass — Brandy balloon/Martini

Grasshopper	Ingredients	Qty (mL)	Method
	Crème de menthe	30	Shake all the ingredients over ice, strain into a glass and serve.
	Crème de cacao	30	Garnish — Mint leaves and cherry
			Glass — Martini

B52	Ingredients	Qty (mL)	Method
	Kahlua	15	Make layers in the order of ingredients written.
	Bailey's Irish Cream	15	Garnish — No garnish
	Grand Marnier	15	Glass — Shot

Note: QTY is in mL.

21.10 SYRUPS AND MIXES

In the bar, following syrups and juices are prepared in advance for the smooth operation of the bar.

- **Sugar syrup:** Also known as gomme syrup used for make the drinks sweet.

To prepare sugar syrup

1. Fill a jug three quarters full with white sugar.
2. Add sufficient boiling water to be able to stir the mixture of sugar and water.
3. Stir the mixture till its consistency like honey.
4. Allow the mixture to cool.
5. Pour the mixture into a bottle and label it to identify.

Note: The basic proportion is 0.5 kg of sugar to 1 litre of water.

- **Sour mix:** It is a mixture of lemon/lime juice, water and sugar. Sour mix eliminates the need for the bartender to have to balance the ingredients while mixing and contributes to faster, better prepared cocktails.

To prepare sour mix

1. Add two cups of sugar in a bowl.
2. Now add one cup of hot water.
3. Add one cup of fresh lemon juice or to taste.
4. Egg white (optional) can also be added.

- **Lemon/lime juice:** Extract the lime/lemon juice with the help of lemon squeezer and pour the juice in a bottle and label it. Remember that seeds should not be in the lime/lemon juice.
- **Bloody Mary mix:** It can be prepared in busy bars where Bloody Mary is served in large numbers.

To prepare Bloody Mary mix

1. Tomato juice - 600 mL
2. Lemon juice - 60 mL
3. Tabasco sauce - 8 drops
4. Worcestershire sauce - 20-30 mL
5. Salt and pepper to taste

   Mix all these ingredients and fill it in a bottle and label it.

21.11 LIQUEUR SUBSTITUTE CHART

A good bartender must have the knowledge of the substitutes of the various liqueurs used in the cocktail as sometimes the specific liqueur is not available in the bar. At that point of time the substitute liqueurs can be used to prepare the cocktails.

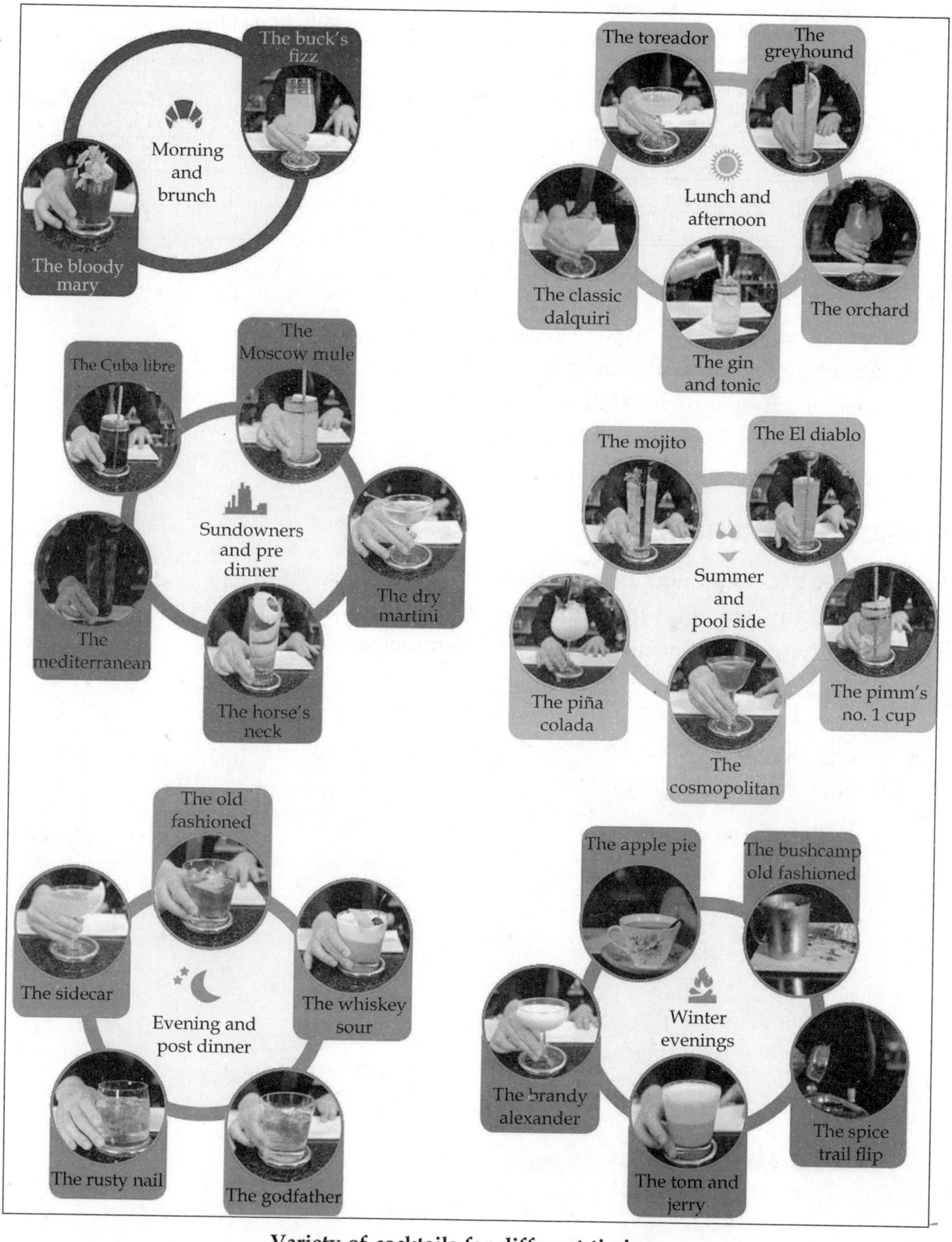

Variety of cocktails for different timings

Liqueur	Substitute Liqueur
Cointreau	Triple Sec
Midori	Melon Liqueur
Malibu	Coconut liqueur
Kahlua	Creme de cafe
Lena	Banana Liqueur
Tia Maria	Creme de cacao

REVISION QUESTIONS

1. List any ten garnishes used in cocktail making.
2. Write any five cocktail recipes and methods.
3. Explain different cocktail mixing methods.
4. List down any five cocktail families.
5. Write any two mocktail recipes.

RESEARCH ACTIVITIES

- Practise to cut various garnishes from lime, oranges and pineapple.
- Prepare any two innovative cocktails using your own creativity.
- Learn five cocktails of each along with their recipes and methods:
  - ◊ Vodka
  - ◊ Gin
  - ◊ Whisky
  - ◊ Rum
  - ◊ Tequila

22

Cellar Management

22.1 INTRODUCTION

> **After reading this chapter, you will be able to understand:**
> - The various functions performed by cellar.
> - Storing beverages in cellar
> - Cellar control procedures

Cellar is the area or a storeroom where all the alcoholic beverages used in the hotels or clubs are kept. Its primary function is to record, maintain and to protect all alcoholic beverages such as wines, beers and spirits from theft and helps in maintaining the quality of the beverages by storing them at appropriate temperature. Cellar also monitors and records all the movement of beverages inside and outside the cellar. Traditionally, the cellar is located underground with a cool and constant temperature so that the alcoholic beverages do not get disturbed by the change in temperature and vibration by the machines working at the upper level. Cellar might be of any sizes as it doesn't make any difference to the cellar's basic functions of storing alcoholic beverages. Nowadays in hotels and clubs, bulk beer is also being kept in the wine cellar where major concern is the operation and maintenance of the beer reticulation system along with the operation and maintenance of bulk wine and spirit dispensing systems. Cellar man is responsible for taking care of cellar; his main duties are as a follows:

- Store alcoholic beverages according to the temperature required to prevent them from spoilage.
- Issuing alcoholic beverages to various restaurants, bars and clubs whenever required against the requisition form duly signed by authorized signatory.
- Stock the cellar with adequate amount of wines, beer, spirits and other alcoholic beverages.
- Maintain and update the records of cellar room.
- Check for any discrepancy and report to senior authority.
- Ensuring the uninterrupted supply of alcoholic beverages to various outlets.
- Storing the beverages in proper racks.
- Maintaining various stock registers of cellar room.

22.2 STORING BEVERAGES IN CELLAR

As soon as alcoholic beverages are received from the supplier, they are immediately transferred to the cellar for proper storing and control so that they can be issued to various departments against the requisition. Beverages such as wines and beers should be handled with utmost care and stored carefully at appropriate temperatures in assigned racks to prevent them from spoilage in comparison to spirits which are not as sensitive to wines and beers. Ideal location for the cellar is basement which is dark, cool and free from any vibration which may affect the wines and the temperature should be constant. Cellar should also be well ventilated and clean with dim lighting. Some cellars also have bottle cooling shelves for efficient control on the temperature to store beer and wines. A cellar is divided into five subsections to store the various beverages as follows:

- Front part of the cellar having a temperature of 13-16°C to store spirits, red wines and also keg beers if the movement of keg beers is high in the premises.
- Refrigerated area having temperature of 50°F for storing white wines, rose wines, sparkling wines and Champagnes.
- Depending on the low movement of keg beers, a refrigerated area maintaining the temperature of 6-8 degrees centigrade is also maintained in the cellars.
- Bottled, canned beers, mineral waters and soft drinks are stored in the refrigerated area maintaining the temperature of 13-15°C.
- A separate area for empty bottles received from various outlets and bars are also maintained to avoid their misuse and to sell them off.

Wines stored horizontally in cellar

Wine bottles with cork should always be stored horizontally in the designated racks so that cork remains in touch with the wine or else the cork will get withered and the cork particles will mix with wine resulting in corky wine. It is almost important to check that cork remains airtight so that it doesn't allow air to enter, whereas other spirits, liqueurs, syrups and cordials should always be kept on the shelves. Fortified wines are stored upright except vintage port which are to be stored on their sides. Unopened bottle cases are stored in the lower racks whereas opened cases should be emptied and bottles from it be stored properly in their place at upper rack by placing new arrivals at the back and the old stock in the front, allowing the cellar man to issue the old stock first. All bottles are to be assigned bin numbers to implement better control and to be stored as per the bin number.

22.3 CELLAR TOOLS AND EQUIPMENT

Cellar should possess all the essential tools and equipment and be stored in one part of the cellar in a rack. Equipment and tools required in the cellar and beer storage areas are as follows:

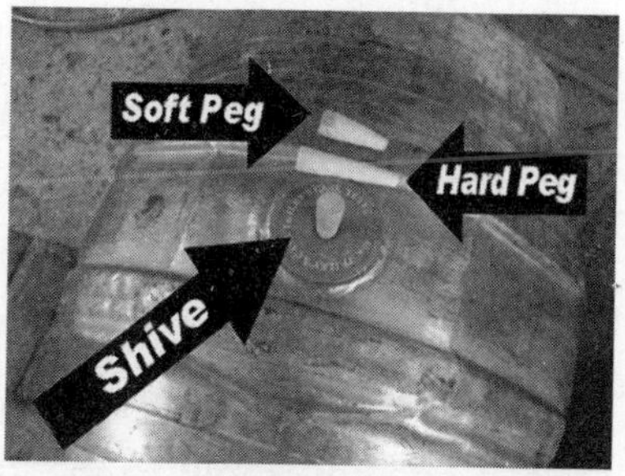

- **Stillions/thrawls:** Casks are supported on stillions or thrawls which are made up of wooden rack or brick platforms on which the casks are placed for service. In many cellars, casks of keg beers are situated together in one area of the cellar with the carbon dioxide gas cylinders bracketed into the wall.
- **Shives:** These are round pieces of hard wood placed in the bung hole of the cask just before it is sent out from the brewery. The shive has a small hole in the centre which does not go completely throughout the wood. When the case is vented, the hole is completed by punching out the thin centre with the help of wooden mallet. This allows the gas to escape from the casks.
- **Spiles:** These are used to bung the hole to prevent the carbon dioxide from escaping which helps in building the pressure in the cask as a result, beer regains its condition (frothy head). Spiles can be hard or soft. Hard spile is made of hardwood whereas soft spile is made of bamboo which allows the gas to escape and so prevents the beer from being too gassy and difficult to serve.
- **Filters:** These are used in the cellar to return good quality beer to the cask which was drawn out of the pipe before cleaning the pipe line. Filters should always be kept clean and use clean filter papers.
- **Beer taps:** These are the taps made from brass used for dispensing cask-conditioned beers from the cask. These taps must be cleaned and sterilized after use for hygiene purposes.
- **Dip sticks:** This is used as an indicator to check the quantity of beer left in the cask. Dip stick is immersed in the cask through shives and then taken out showing / indicating the quantity of beer left.
- **Inline coolers:** Provided for cooling the keg beer which are adjusted to the correct temperature for each beer.
- **Scotches:** These are wooden triangular blocks used to stop the cask from rolling.
- **Electrical impelled pump:** These dispense accurate amount of beer into the glass when the beer man presses the button.

22.4 PRACTICES FOR A GOOD CELLAR MANAGEMENT

Following points are to be practised for managing cellar operations:

- The cellar should be clean and well ventilated.
- Cask after receiving should be placed on stillions.
- Temperature in the cellar to be maintained so that changes in temperature do not spoil the delicate beverages like wine and beer.
- Spilling to be done to reduce the excessive pressure held inside the cask.

- Before a cask is required in the bar, tapping must be done at least 24 hours before.
- During regular intervals, pipes and engines should be cleaned for hygiene purpose.
- After closing time, excessive beer left in pipes should be taken out.
- If a beer is returned, it should be filtered back into the cask.
- Cellar should not be overstocked as it can make the cellar look dirty.
- Beverages should be supplied regularly to the various outlets situated in the hotels.
- Issue beverages to the various outlets against the requisition received only.
- Spiles removed during service should be replaced after the service is closed.
- Equipment available in the cellar should be cleaned on a regular basis.
- Ullages should be returned to the cellar so that proper entries can be marked in the Ullages book.
- Cellar area should be cleaned on a regular basis with the help of mild solution.

22.5 CLEANING THE CELLAR AREA

Cellar area should be cleaned regularly so that beverages should be stacked properly in the area to avoid any breakage of bottles and bad odour.

22.5.1 Equipment

Kegs, casks and other gas equipment are expensive and may carry a deposit, so they should be placed in a secure place and must be returned to the supplier whenever next supplies are received from the supplier and recorded on a return slip. Empty cask- conditioned beer containers should have a hard spile knocked into the shive and the tap hole should be sealed with a cork. Gas cylinders are given a five-year check up, so it is most important to use them in strict rotation and to return empty ones as soon as possible after use to allow the supplier to have them maintained correctly. Empty bottles should be stored out and packed into their respective crates, either at the end of a service or during the preparation time on the morning of next day. Afterwards, crates should be stacked in a secure area.

22.5.2 Walls, Floors and Ceilings

As the cellar remains damp, it encourages moulds to grow on the walls and ceilings which may increase the chance of infecting cask-conditioned beer therefore, walls and ceiling of a cellar should be whitewashed or painted in a light colour at regular intervals. Besides, the cellar will also acquire an unpleasant smell. Unnecessary wetting should be avoided and ventilation be provided as far as possible. The cellar cooling air vents and intakes must be free from dust and dirt and any filters cleaned or replaced whenever necessary. If the cooling is on contract, then the contractor should be informed about the non-working or cleaning of cooling vent for necessary action. The floor should be scrubbed and washed down at least once a week and dried afterwards to make the cellar area neat. Little mild diluted bleach or chloride of lime may be sprinkled over the floor as this will inhibit the growing of mould. Avoid using strong disinfectants as they may spoil the wine and beers.

22.5.3 Drainage

The drains, gulley and sump (if any) must be kept clean and fresh. If there is a sump, it must be scrubbed at least once a week using bleach and chloride of lime. Also ensure that the sump pump filter and grating are kept clean and in position.

22.5.4 Rubbish

Rubbish may not be allowed to deposit or accumulate or left lying around as it can act as an obstacle to free passage or a possible fire risk. Rubbish must be properly binned outside the building in an area especially constructed for this purpose.

22.5.5 Other Equipment

Corks and spiles used for cask-conditioned beers should be kept tidy in plastic bags in the cellar. All items of equipment such as beer taps, dip sticks, beer filters, jugs and buckets must be washed out after use and dried. They should be put away when not in use.

22.6 CELLAR CONTROL PROCEDURES

Strict monitoring and controlling process is required for proper cellar control as it is a major area where all the alcoholic beverages are kept. To ensure the proper flow of beverages inside and outside the cellar, many types of records are maintained. All the F&B outlets where alcoholic beverages are served get the beverage issued from the cellar after providing duly filled requisition form to the cellar, this may be on daily or a weekly basis depending on the organization policy. Requisition forms should be duly signed by the authorized signatory for a control purpose. All the outlets situated in the hotels or bars are required to maintain the par stock of the alcoholic beverages sufficient for a day or a week. Entries in the bin card are maintained while receiving and issuing beverages to check the amount of stock left at any given point of time, it also helps the cellar man to know when the beverages are to be ordered for the cellar. In the bar as all drinks are checked before issue, a daily consumption sheet is completed each day after the end of the service by copying down the sales shown on the top copy of the wine sheets. The consumption sheet will also list the complete stock held in the dispense bar, later on at the end of the week the consumption sheets are totalled, thereby showing the total sales for that period. These totals may then be transferred to a bar stock book for costing purposes.

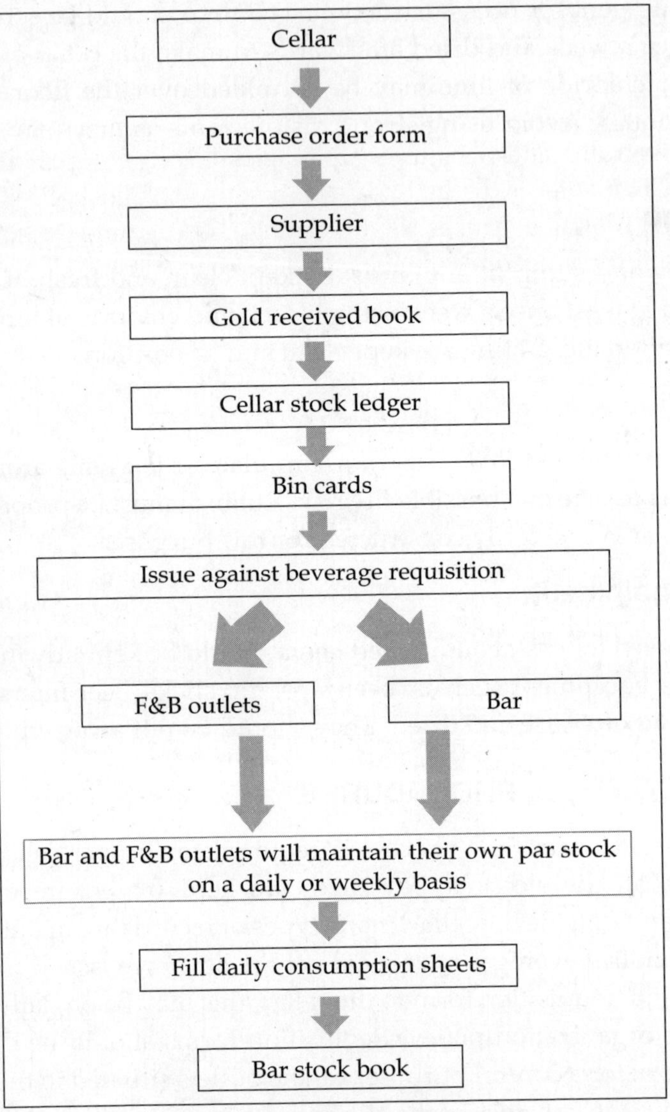

Flowchart of cellar management

Drink Name	Bin card No.	Day 1	Day 2	Day 3	Day 4	Day 5	Day 6	Day 7	Total

Daily consumption sheet

22.7 CELLAR CONTROL AND RECORDS

Cellar control is of utmost importance to any establishment as it stores more valuable stock and fetches more percentage of profit by the sale of beverages. It also tempts dishonest staff to indulge in fraud and various malpractices which compels the cellar to have a foolproof system. The cellar is the main source of supply of alcoholic beverages to various outlets in the hotel for sales. It uses the following records to maintain strict control and ensure that every bottle is accounted for.

Date No. 1185

The Harborside Restaurant and Lounge

PURCHASE ORDER

Please furnish the following – All carriers charges prepaid

Qty.	Unit	Description	Unit price	Amount

Received by .... Purchasing agent......................

Invoice must accompany merchandise

Invoice of the cellar stock

(a) Purchase order: A purchase order is a form or a format used to list down the beverages to be purchased containing the essential information such as

- Price of the beverage
- Expected delivery date
- Other important information.

The purchase order is a primary cellar control tool helping the supplier to know about the beverages to be supplied along with their quantity and type to be supplied as per the requirement of the cellar.

(b) Cellar inwards book: Also known as Goods Received Book, details of the goods received are recorded in this book. All deliveries should be recorded in detail. While receiving all the items/beverages are to be checked properly for any damages, expiry, broken bottles and so on. Each delivery should show the following information:

- Name and address of the supplier
- Delivery date
- Delivery note
- Invoice number
- Order number
- Lists of items delivered
- Price of the item
- Quantity and unit
- Total price
- Discounts if applicable

WAZOBIA HOTELS LTD

Cellar Inwards Book

Date:

Date	Beverage	Delivery/ Invoice No.	Bin card No.	Bottle	Halves	Other sizes

(c) **Bin card:** Bin card is used in the cellar to check the stock level of each item at any given point of time. These bin cards are attached to shelves or racks for each type of beverage. Each beverage will have an individual bin card and all the entries pertaining to receiving and issuing of that beverage is recorded in that individual bin card. It also shows the maximum and minimum level of stock of individual item helping in determining the reorder level. When the stock gets minimum in bin card, cellar man gives further order of that beverage after obtaining proper permission from the concerned authority. Information like brand name, size, quantity, storage information, date of receiving, date of issuing are mentioned in the bin card. Modern cellars for security reasons also stamp the expensive beverages like wines and spirits with their own stamp.

WAZOBIA HOTELS LTD
Bin card

Bin No.
Type:
Size:

Date	Received	Issued to bar				Balance
		A	B	C	Total	
05/02/10	12	2	–	1	3	9
07/02/10	–	1	1	2	4	5

(d) **Beverage requisition:** Every outlet selling beverages should fill a beverage requisition form to get the items from the cellar. These requisitions may be controlled by either serial number or by colour and are normally prepared in duplicate or triplicate, details of which are given below:

Beverage Requisition Slip

Serial No.

Outlet____________

Date ____________

S. No.	Item	Unit	Par stock	Stock in hand	Quantity		Unit Cost	Total cost
					Required	Issues		

Prepared by	Authorised by		Issued by	Received by

- First or top copy of the requisition form is forwarded to the cellar.
- Second or duplicate copy is forwarded to the accounts department or F&B Controls.

- Third or triplicate copy remains with the bar or the outlet for their reference to check the items received from cellar.
- Outlet or bar name
- Date of filling the requisition form
- List of beverages required from the cellar
- Quantity, size and number/unit of beverages required
- All beverages should be duly signed by the authorized personnel deputed by the management.

Beverage requisition form also helps in controlling the movement of items from the cellar to the bar/outlet and to avoid too much stock being taken at one time, thus overstocking the bar. The level of the stock held in the bar is known as par stock.

(e) **Cellar control book/ cellar stock ledger:** This format is used to record all daily receiving and daily issuing of each beverage to and from cellar. All the movement of beverages are recorded in the cost price. Goods are accepted with invoice or delivery note and verified against the bin card and the perpetual inventory record.

Cellar Control Book									
Item	**Unit**	**Op. stock**	**Issues**	**Total issues**	**Returns**	**Book stock value**	**Balance by stock taken**	**Variances**	**Values issued at cost**
Signature of cellar man: ____________									

(f) **Ullages, breakages and spoilage record:** The term *ullages* refers to all inferior quality or damaged bottles, wines with faulty cork, weeping wines, damaged beer casks and so on which require immediate action and to be returned to the supplier for replacement. To record all ullages, a book known as Ullages Book is maintained in the cellar. The value of returns and the items returned are recorded in Returns book and Credit memo is issued. Breakage of bottles due to mishandling should be recorded in the breakage column of the book to know the value of beverages lost. All these records should be entered with a proper explanation and countersigned by the authorized signatory as frequent ullages and breakages needs investigation.

SPOILAGE REPORT

Section : Date: Time:

S. No.	Item	Quantity	Unit	Unit cost	Total cost	

Recorded by________________ Checked by ________________

(g) Credit memo: It is requested from the supplier for the value of the goods returned due to damages or for any discrepancies between the purchase order and the invoice. It includes the items invoiced but not delivered, it is prepared in duplicate; one copy goes to the supplier and another to the accounts department for information. Credit memo is prepared for the following:

- Wrong goods shipped
- Wrong quantity shipped
- Wrong quality shipped
- Broken or damaged merchandise
- Not in stock (back order)
- Items invoiced but not delivered
- Short on delivery
- Old or expired good
- Empties
- Computational errors

(h) Empties return book: Suppliers charge for the containers sent along with the goods such as crates, kegs and so on. Therefore, it becomes necessary to maintain the record of all those empties and must be returned in good condition to the suppliers to claim the credit. For the same, Empties Return Book is maintained to keep the record of empties in hand and returned to the supplier.

(i) Transfer book: This book is used in the various F&B outlets/bar to record the movement of stock between F&B outlets or bars.

INTER BAR TRANSFER				
From: ________________		To : ________________		
Date:				
Item	**Size**	**Quantity**	**Unit cost (Rs.)**	**Total cost (Rs.)**
Ordered by________________		Bar Manager/Bar In charge:________________		

(j) **Barcode system:** Barcodes are now a vital part of many modern stock control systems. It identifies items precisely for stock control and ordering purposes. When used in cellar the barcodes on all stocks being received or issued can be swiped in the same way as seen in supermarket, quickly recording its movement and adjusting the stock records immediately.

22.8 BAR FRAUDS

While having controls in the bar, we come across the various frauds undertaken by the customers and staff. It is very important to know such frauds for beverage controls so that beverage cost may be minimized and profit can be increased. Following are the bar frauds usually seen in the bar:

(a) **Customer walking without paying:** The primary kind of customer fraud is customers walking out without paying their checks. However, customers may also cheat an establishment by a number of other methods. They may claim that the food was unsatisfactory and thus indicate (usually the manager or host will make the suggestion) that they will not pay for it.

(b) **Bringing foreign article:** Another possibility, which has occurred frequently, is for customers to indicate that their food contained some foreign matter, such as glass or china, or even an insect (perhaps even brought in by the complaining customers).

(c) **Customer making unnecessary complaints:** Complaints are generally made to the waiter or waitress, who should, in turn, call the manager or host to solve the problem. Since there is always the possibility that the events did occur in reality, the normal policy is to grant free drinks or dinners to the guests to avoid embarrassment, to prevent possible lawsuits, and, of course, to encourage the customers to return. In most cases of fraud, the guests will not return to perform the same type of fraud nor will they return merely to buy a dinner. In the case of falsified complaints, the establishment has no recourse except to treat the affair as a normal business expense.

In cases of walkouts, the house may have legal recourse, and, of course, it can set up a control system that minimizes the chances of this type of theft. Customers normally cannot perpetrate any other type of theft, since they do not have access to food or beverages. Disputes may arise, however, as to the exact number of drinks that were served. In cases of parties where the payment is based on head counts, lower figures may be presented by the guests. However, verification can readily be made by staff members. Only one or two systems of cash collection can eliminate the walkout fraud. Cash prepaid (for fast food) or collected either by a cashier stationed at the beginning of food service (single-priced dinners or buffets) or a cashier at the end of the line in cafeteria eliminate customer frauds of this nature. A COD system comparable to those used for beverages is occasionally used in food service. In every other system, there remains a possibility that the customer will walk out despite precautions by management and by employees. It is impossible for a waiter or waitress to watch a table continually. Even with team systems in which two servers work together—one remaining in the dining room and the other placing orders and relaying food from the kitchen—the team cannot watch every customer continually. A team system, however, certainly is an improvement over the individual server system. Likewise, a cashier cannot be expected to stop every customer to determine if the check was paid, particularly during busy meal hours.

(d) **Using false credit card:** Customers may also use credit cards that are worthless or attempt to pay with checks that are not honoured by banks. Unless customers are known, it is best to avoid cashing checks if possible. If a check must be cashed, adequate identification should be provided, and no check should be honoured for more than the value of the dinner.

(e) **Counterfeit currency:** Occasionally customers will attempt, either intentionally or unintentionally, to give to cahier counterfeit currency. In most cases, this currency will be easy to detect if proper cash handling procedures are followed. All bills should be quickly examined on both sides and placed on the ledge of the register. It is hoped that this cursory examination will detect most of the counterfeit money, although in some cases help of the expert can be taken.

(f) **Thefts by waiter and waitress:** Intentional omission of items from the bill in order to establish a rapport with customers, to increase tips, or perhaps to give free merchandise to friends or fellow employees. This type of fraud occurs when inadequate dupe system or validating systems are utilized. A full control system in organizations having full services is impractical, since accounting for items with a retail sales value of less than $1 is too costly. Bookkeeping costs would be excessive in relation to income.

In some cases, the items to be sold are already under the control of the service staff, as in the case of milk in individual containers or a 6-gallon refrigerated carton in the service area. No records are maintained when a waitress or waiter pours a glass of milk. Should this charge be omitted from the check, it would be impossible to track down the guilty party, since a number of personnel may have access to the milk supply.

(g) **Reusing of checks:** This type of theft may occur in any kind of establishment. For high volume operations, it is possible that a large number of sales may be of a small amount. Thus, customers presented with a particular check would have no way of verifying whether it was their own or not, since the amount was correct and the items were the same. With the abbreviation normally used on checks, it is impossible for the guest to read a check without an interpreter. So long as the amount is correct, they are satisfied unless the amount is higher, most customers do not care if they receive their own check.

(h) **Pocketing checks or using unauthorized checks:** It is often possible to reproduce the checks that are used by an establishment. Certainly if stock checks (not specially imprinted ones) are being used, they may be readily purchased by anyone from dealers. It is also possible when checks are not numbered or recorded (and in those cases where the numbers are recorded but not audited) for a waiter or waitress simply to pocket the check and the cash received, if other control systems are not utilized.

Checks can be counted automatically by the utilization of a check numbering system similar to UPC (universal product code) or those systems being used by banks. Each check is imprinted with a number that can be read by a machine. If a number is omitted or the check not closed out, the machine will report this omission. Such systems are readily available through electronic technology.

(i) **Overcharging:** This practice may occur when staff members are allowed to make corrections on the checks without supervision. The customers may be charged for merchandise not received. Or higher prices may be entered on the check. After the customer has paid the staff member, the correct prices and amounts are entered, the check is retotalled, and the difference is pocketed by the server. Incorrect addition, intentionally adding money to each check and pocketing the money when check is properly totalled can readily be performed, particularly if amounts are handwritten on the checks. Should the error be discovered by the customer it is normally excused, since an error of overadding can be quickly explained as poor arithmetic.

(j) **Substitution:** In some establishments with fairly tight system of control, it is impossible for a waitress or waiter to supply friends with free merchandise. However, substitution can be made by ordering higher priced items from the kitchen and charging for lower priced ones. The server orders a higer priced item but records a lower priced item on the check. The friend is presented with a check for the smaller amount. Falsification of tips or other charges, in some areas of the country, where many food and beverage sales are complimentary, other incidents occur where a dinner is being paid for by someone other than the guest. Extra amount of beverages or food may be placed on the checks to increase the value of the sale. This extra food can be sold to other guests and the cash received pocketed by the waiter or waitress. This padding of the bill may also be done whenever the tip may be a fixed proportion of the total bill. If the sales are increased by 1000 rupees, the tip may go up to 100 rupees or more. When given a free dinner, the guest does not closely inspect the items on the bill. Instead, he or she merely gives a brief inspection, signs for the full amount, and leaves a tip based on the total value listed on the check.

(k) **Split rings:** When waiter or waitress also handles the cash registers, split rings may occur. This situation arises when for example, a check for 1000 rupees is rung up 500 rupees and 400 rupees. The owner has lost 100 rupees which the waiter or waitress pockets. By ringing the second time, the waiter or waitress prevents the customer from seeing the actual amount of the first ring-up. The customer usually presumes there was a simple error. Should anyone question the two rings for one check, the waiter or waitress merely states that he or she made an error on the first ring and rang 900 rupees by mistake. Using a cash register with a tape and giving guests receipts, will help to alleviate this type of fraud.

(l) **Bartenders' fraud or errors:** A bartender who handles cash (using a register) has the same opportunity of theft as a waiter or a waitress, and the same chance of error.

(m) **Cashier theft or error:** The possibility of theft for cashier is more restricted than with either bartender, waiters, or waitress, since they normally do not handle the products sold. If the cashier is responsible solely for cash collection, errors or theft may occur under any of the following categories:

1. Cashier keeps the money and pockets or destroys a check.
2. Cashier changes the total of check after collection.
3. Cashier bunches sales, split-rings, or underrings.
4. Cashier gives incorrect change.
5. Cashier performs incorrect addition.
6. Cashier falsifies payout or adds items to complimentary checks and removes them from other checks.

REVISION QUESTIONS

1. Which of the following wines are stored on the sides?
   (a) Vintage port
   (b) Sherry
   (c) Madeira
   (d) Marsala
2. The person responsible to take care of cellar is:
   (a) Bar man
   (b) F&B controller

(c) Cellar man
(d) Receiving clerk

3. List down the various equipment found in cellar area.
4. In which of the following situations is a credit memo not made?
   (a) Overcharging
   (b) Wrong delivery
   (c) Bottle broken by accident
   (d) Rate wrongly charged
5. Weeping wine bottle is an example of ____________.
6. To draw the beverages from the cellar area, one needs to fill:
   (a) Transfer from
   (b) Requisition form
   (c) Purchase order form
   (d) Wine demand form
7. List down the information recorded in the Cellar Inwards Book.
8. Wooden triangular blocks which are used to prevent a beer cask rolling from side to side is known as ______________.
9. Write down the various points to be considered for good cellar management.
10. Explain various bar frauds.

RESEARCH ACTIVITY

Draw the specimen of any five forms/formats used in cellar along with the information provided in them.

23

Tobacco

23.1 INTRODUCTION

After reading this chapter, you will be able to understand:
- Meaning of tobacco
- Types of tobacco
- Uses of tobacco
- Meaning of cigar
- Parts/structure of a cigar
- Classification of cigar
- Brand names of cigar
- Judging a cigar
- Anatomy of a cigarette
- Service of cigar

Tobacco is an agricultural product processed from the fresh leaves of plants in genus Nicotina. Only two species are preferred namely ***Nicotina rustica*** which grows in Eastern Europe, Russia, Turkey, India and North America. The other species is the ***Nicotina tobaccum,*** which is cultivated in South America, West Indies and Cuba. Tobacco has never been found growing in the wild, yet it is the most widely grown non-food crop plant on the earth.

23.1.1 Types of Tobacco

- **Virginia:** Most popular type of tobacco used in pipe tobacco. It is the mildest of all blending tobacco and has the highest level of natural dextrose sugar, which basically gives it a light sweet taste.
- **Burley:** This is the next most popular tobacco for pipe tobacco blending. It contains almost no sugar, which gives a much dryer and fuller aroma than Virginia. Burley is used in many aromatic blends because it absorbs the flavourings.
- **Spice tobacco:** It is not actually one type of tobacco but rather a broad variety of more special types, used in small amount to create interesting blends. These would include Latakia, Perique and Kentucky among others.
- **Oriental:** It is a variety of tobacco, grown in Turkey, Balkans and Russia. A common characteristic is dusty, dry and sometimes slightly sour aroma. Some of them are also used in "erotic" cigarettes from Egypt and other Arab countries.

Tobacco leaf

- **Latakia:** It is the result of a curing process involving fire curing the leaves over controlled fires of aromatic woods and fragrant herbs. It is probably the most well known spice tobacco, and mainly grown in Cyprus and northern Syria.
- **Perique:** It is a red burley type of tobacco, grown and processed in St. James, Louisiana near New Orleans. Perique is a rare, slow burning, strong-tasting tobacco. Production is small so its value is quite high.
- **Kentucky:** This is actually a specially treated burley tobacco. Unlike Burley, Kentucky is fire cured. Its aroma is not heavy as with Latakia but very aromatic and antique. The nicotine content tends to be rather high and therefore it is used in limited amounts.
- **Havana:** Cuban and other cigar tobacco are used in a limited range of Virginia blends and mixtures.
- **Cavendish:** It is more a method to treat tobacco than a type of tobacco. English Cavendish uses a dark flue or fire cured Virginia, which is steamed and then stored under pressure to permit it to cure and ferment for several days to several weeks. When done well, this tobacco is excellent. Cavendish can be produced out of any tobacco type.

23.1.2 Tobacco Plant, Leaf and Processing

- The tobacco plant grows to a height of 6 feet in 8-10 months.
- Leaves at the tip of the plant are succulent and those towards the base are tougher. The different leaves have uses specific to their character. Each leaf varies in size.

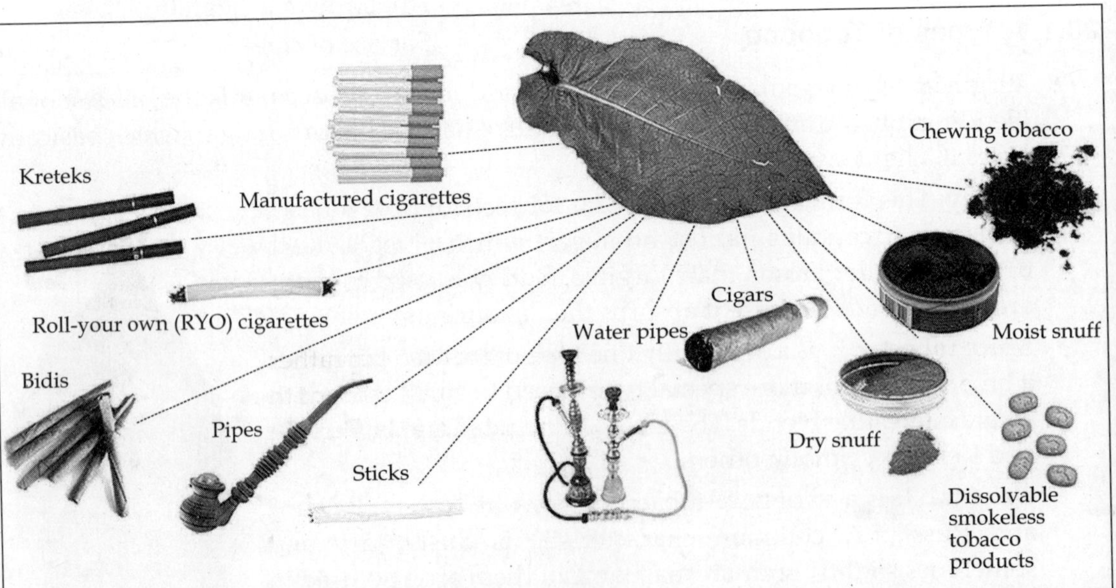

Uses of tobacco

- The harvest of tobacco leaves begin in mid to late February and carries onto March. Each leaf is plucked and segregated as per size and type.
- The harvested and sorted leaves are then taken to warehouses where they are allowed to hang from poles and dry out in the warm air that is circulated.
- This process takes 4-5 days. After this, the leaves are allowed to dry in heaps.
- Due to uneven drying, the leaves rot and eventually fermentation takes place and the leaves change colour to a silky brown.
- The leaves are collected in bundles of 5 and these are matured in dark warehouses for about 5 months.

Tobacco is used in many different ways around the world such as:

- **Smoking tobacco:** Cigar, cigarette, pipe, roll-your-own (RYO), bidis, kreteks (clove flavoured cigarettes), water pipe (hukkah).
- **Smokeless tobacco:** Dry snuff, moist snuff, dissolvable smokeless tobacco products, chewing tobacco.

23.1.3 Curing

Curing is a process of controlled drying of tobacco in which physical and chemical changes take place in the leaf to give it smoking and other desired properties. Tobacco can be cured through either of the methods:

- Flue curing
- Air curing
- Fire curing
- Sun curing

Flue curing (for virginia/cigarette tobacco): Flue curing is done in air-tight barns or kilns with adjustable top and bottom ventilation or forced draft system. Air in the barn is heated either indirectly by floor level flues from a furnace or directly by space heaters. The tobacco cures in 4-9 days. This process produces cigarette tobacco which is high in sugar and has medium to high level of nicotine.

Sun curing (for oriental and native tobacco): Sundried tobacco dries uncovered in the sun. Tobacco leaves are strung on open air sacks for 10-20 days. This method is used in Turkey, Greece and other Mediterranean counties to produce oriental tobacco. This tobacco is low in sugar and nicotine and is used in cigarettes.

Air curing (for Burley, Cigar, Maryland and dark tobacco): Air curing is done on sheds with limited ventilation control and provision of supplementary heating if natural conditions are too cold or moist. Drying is carried out on the whole plant or individual leaves. This process is sometimes preceded by sun curing and may take up to three months. Air cured tobacco is low in sugar and gives a light, sweet flavour and is high in nicotine.

Fire cured tobacco (for non-cigarette tobaccos needing high aroma): Fire cured tobacco is hung in large barns where fire of hardwood are kept on continuous or intermittent low smoulder. The wood smoke circulates among the leaves giving it a characteristic creosote aroma. This process is carried out for 3-10 weeks depending on the tobacco. Fire cured tobacco is low in sugar and high nicotine. Pipe tobacco, chewing tobacco and sniff are fire cured.

23.2 CIGAR

Cigar is a tightly rolled bundle of dried and fermented tobacco. Cigar may be defined as a cylindrical roll of tobacco meant for smoking. This is formed in a binder leaf around which spirally wrapped is a wrapper leaf. The wrapper leaf, which is the most expensive, must be strong, elastic, silky both in colour and texture, possessing pleasant flavour and good burning qualities. Best cigars come from Cuba.

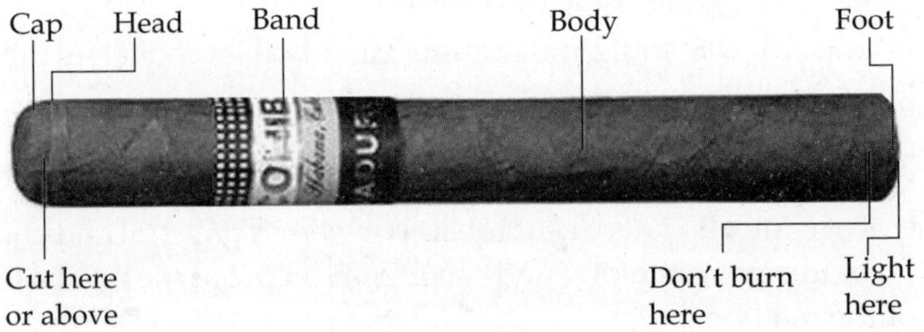

Anatomy of cigar

23.2.1 History of Cigar

Christopher Columbus and his contemporaries introduced cigars to the society. The expedition that set out from Spain and reached the American continent found native Indians smoking bundles of tobacco wrapped in dried palm leaves or corn leaves. The word cigar originated from the Mayan word Sik'ar believed to have meant smoke, which led to the Spanish word Cigarro and later translated into the English word, cigar. An excavation carried out in Mexico discovered pots with figures of people smoking bundles of rolled leaves presumed to be cigars. They found their way into the Spanish society. Initially, affordable only by the rich and the royalty, by 1660 they were introduced to the rest of European society.

Corojo plant **Criollo plant**

23.2.2 Structure/Parts of a Cigar

There are three parts to a cigar as described below:

Parts of a cigar

(i) Filler

Filler is the tobacco that makes up the heart of the cigar and gives it its bulk. It is the source of rich flavours and aromas. The leaves used to make the filler comes from the Criollo plant taken at different levels of the plant.

- **Ligero:** The topmost part of the plant, provides strength.
- **Seco:** The middle part of the plant, provides aroma.
- **Volado:** The bottom part of the plant, provides combustibility.

Good quality leaves are used. 2-3 leaves with their veins removed are rolled tightly to form the centre core of the cigar called filler. The leaves used must be well matured.

(ii) Binder

It is the tobacco leaf that holds the filler in place. It defines the shape of the cigar and the smoking quality. Binder comes from the Criollo plant, grown in direct sunlight. Leaves are much coarser and darker, matured for 12 months before use.

(iii) Wrapper

It is the exquisitely thin leaf that forms the outer surface of the cigar. Wrapper is wound around the cigar and binds the whole cigar. It stands as the ultimate symbol of the cigar's perfection. The wrapper comes from the Corojo plant grown under tents of cheesecloth. It is matured and used within 18 months. Only the very best leaves are used for this purpose. The end of the leaf forms the tip of the cigar and only this tip is stuck by means of a vegetable gum, which is odourless and tasteless. The vegetable gum is the only other substance used apart from tobacco leaves in the production of a cigar. The wrapper determines the flavour and character of the cigar; because of this cigars are often characterised by the colour of the wrapper.

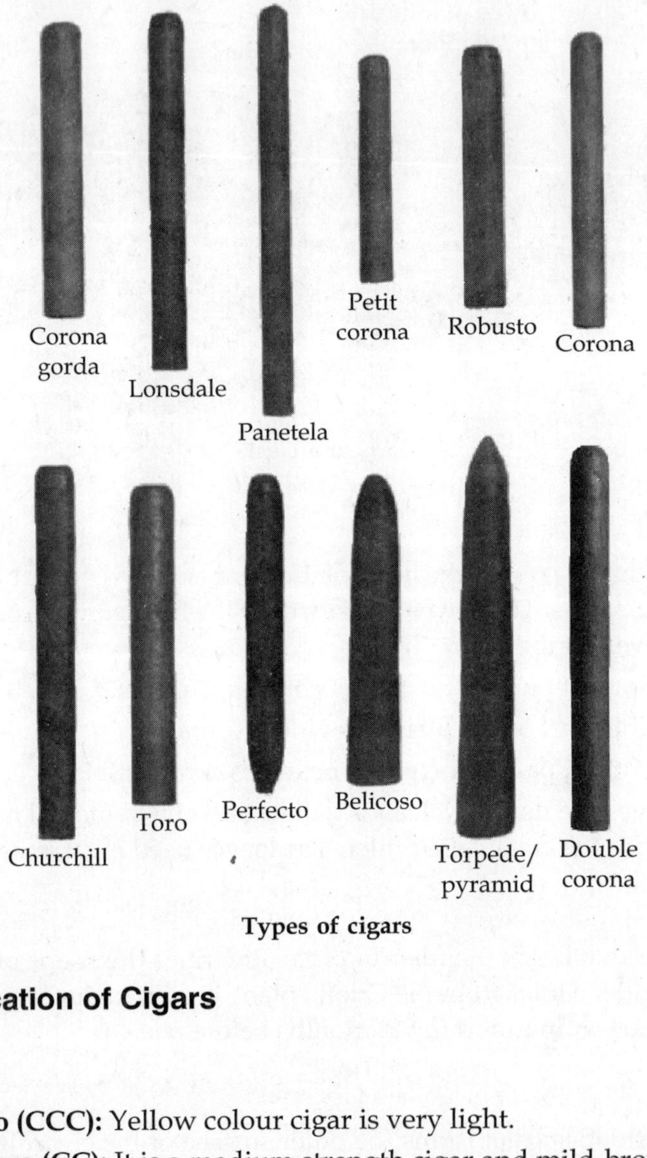

Types of cigars

23.2.3 Classification of Cigars

By Colour

- **Blonde/claro (CCC):** Yellow colour cigar is very light.
- **Colorado claro (CC):** It is a medium strength cigar and mild-brown.
- **Colorado (C):** Strong cigar, reddish brown.
- **Colorado maduro:** Very strong, dark brown.
- **Maduro:** Stronger than other cigars, very dark brown.
- **Oscuro:** Black.
- **Candella:** Greenish yellow.

Table 23.1: Types and characteristics of cigars

Type	Colour	Taste	Characteristics
Double claro	Light, slightly green	Slightly sweet	Quick-dired premature leaves
Claro	Very light tan, or yellowish	Mild	Grown under canopies
Colorado claro	Medium brown	Smooth, medium	Mostly sun-grown
Colorado	Reddish-brown	Strong, with a hint or spice	Usually shade-grown
Colorado maduro	Dark brown	Rich, aromatic	Grown from Cuban seeds
Maduro	Very dark brown or black	Smooth, rich	Fermented longer
Oscuro	Black	Very strong	Topmost leaf of the tobacco plant

By Size

Size of a cigar is measured by two dimensions, i.e., ring gauge (diameter) and length. The ring gauge is measured in units of 1/64th of an inch. A 64-ring cigar would be one inch in diameter. Most cigars are between 32 and 52-ring sizes. For example, a cigar that is called "8 × 48" is 8 inches long and 48/64ths of an inch in diameter. The girth determines how much of the cigar's burning tip is exposed to air. The fatter the cigar, the slower and cooler a cigar smokes because more of the filler is exposed to air. The shape is the length balanced with a particular ring gauge. Cigars come in 42 shapes and sizes varying from **length** of 4" to 9" and a **ring gauge** of 26 to 52 (which is the diameter measured in 1/64th of an inch).

By Shape

All cigars can be divided into two categories: parejos, or the straight-sided cigars, and figurados, or irregular shapes (torpedoes or perfectos and the like).

23.2.4 Storage of Cigars

- Cigars should be stored at optimum temperature of 16° to 18°C and relative humidity of 75% to 80%.
- They should be always stored away from food aromas since smells are absorbed quickly and the cigars get spoilt.

- In restaurants, cigars are stored in special intricately carved boxes known as humidors which are generally made up of cedar wood as it is porous in nature which allows the relative humidity and temperature that retain freshness in cigars. The humidor should be taken care of and the condition of the cigars within the humidor should be checked regularly.
- The **humidor** contains mainly a moisture pad, which keeps the cigars dry though during the dry season the pad may be moistened to prevent excess drying of cigars. The pad absorbs moisture during the humid season.
- The moisture source is the oasis located inside the cigar tray. When necessary this should be removed and damped with distilled water for about 10 seconds, then kept facing upwards until the surface water is absorbed, wiped dry and replaced.
- Humidor should be inspected each day, not only to check condition but also to ensure that the humidor is filled with cigars.
- Cigars are arranged according to nuances of shade. The darkest cigar is placed on the left of the humidor box, and the lightest is on the right.

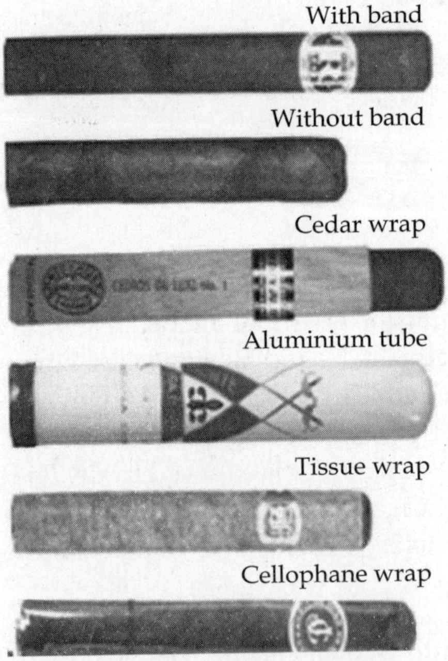

Wrapping styles of cigars

Brand Names

- Monte Cristo
- Romeo y Julieta
- Davidoff

- Cohiba
- H. Upmann
- Punch
- Partagas
- Hoyo De Monterrey
- Rafael Gonzalez
- Bolivar
- Cuaba
- Alcazar

Presenting cigar in humidor

23.2.5 Service of Cigars

- The cigar is presented to the guest in the **humidor** in its original wrapping.
- Guest selects and removes the cellophane paper.
- The edge may be clipped using a cigar cutter.

Cutting a cigar

- Cigar cutters are of two types, namely:
  - ◊ ***Guillotine*** which makes a vertical cut by removing a wedge.
  - ◊ ***Scissors*** which would cut off the tip.
- The guest himself may cut the edge or in rare cases, the steward may be asked for help.
- After the edge is cut, loose tobacco is tapped off by knocking against the fingers.
- This is lit either by a wooden matchstick, a butane lighter or a wooden spill.
- Petrol lighters, wax matches should never be used.
- Never remove the band from the cigar since it is tightly secured and its removal might damage the wrapper. If the guest wishes, suggest he smokes 3/4th of cigar for it to become soft ensuring no damage.

23.2.5.1 Smoking a Cigar

Cigar is always smoked according to one's personality and in leisure time. To enjoy a cigar, its smoke should not be inhaled. The true pleasure is found in appreciating the composition of tobacco flavours, and these are best detected on the palate by your sense of taste. Do not try smoking a cigar that has half gone out, as it will only offer a disappointing mixture of hot air and thin smoke. Half–lit cigars need to be coaxed back to full burn with a touch of re-lighting and a few vigorous puffs. Do not flick the ash as cigarette smokers do. Allow a long ash to form. Its evenness shows how well the cigar is being made. Cigar goes very well with cognac.

23.2.5.2 Judging a Cigar

- **Construction:** How well is the cigar made? How does it feel to touch? With a firm, but soft grip feel it from end to end. Does it feel consistent all the way through? Are there any hard or soft spots? A cigar that is too hard, too soft, or inconsistent will not draw properly.
- **Condition:** Cigars should be well conditioned before smoking. Cigars should be aged for several months to several years at the proper humidity (70% RH) and temperature (70° F). A dry cigar will burn hot, fast and can taste harsh. A damp cigar will be hard to light and can be hard to draw.
- **Causality (cause and effect):** How does the cigar taste? How does the cigar make you feel? Does the cigar build in taste, flavour and complexity as it burns? Or is it the same all the way through? Do you feel relaxed and calm after finishing it?

23.2.5.3 Cutting of a Cigar

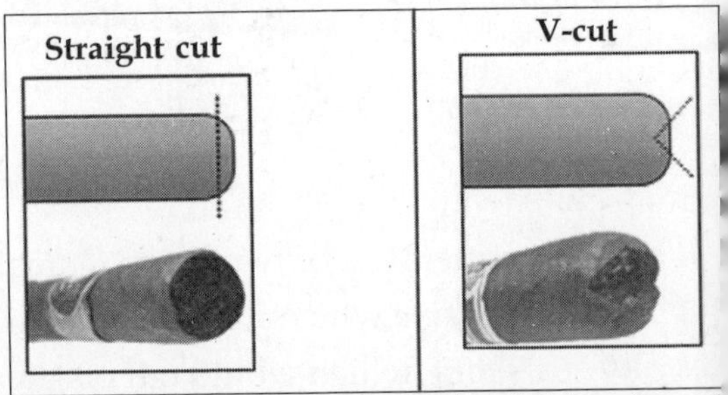

The first step involved in preparing a cigar for use is to open a passage way allowing air to circulate from one end to the other. Some smokers choose to bite the tip off the cigar; it is a quick and easy solution and there is no need to carry any tools along. Most cigar connoisseurs however use specialized clippers, that provide a clean, manicured cut. If a cutter is used, the incision should be made quickly and decisively. The cutter should be placed just above the cigar's cap line (the curved area that covers the head of the cigar) and clipped in one swift motion. This produces a clean cut which is desirable for smoking a cigar. Once the cigar has been clipped using the smokers preferred method, it is ready to be lit.

23.2.5.4 Lighting a Cigar

Lighting a cigar

Tobacco will absorb any aroma or fragrance that it comes in contact with. Paper and sulphur based matches or the use of a fluid based lighter can leave the cigar with an unpleasant taste. The preferred method to light a cigar is the use of a butane based lighter. A lit wooden match can be used once it has burnt off the chemicals used in the ignition process. Once the cigar is cut, hold the open end of the cigar over your flame and slowly rotate it. This will "Toast" the cigar and prime it for lighting. While it is still warm, place the cigar in your mouth and hold it at a 45° angle over the flame. Slowly puff and rotate the cigar while maintaining slight contact with the flame. A good cigar will light easy and burn evenly.

23.3 CIGARETTE

A cigarette (French "small cigar", from cigar + ette) is a small roll of finely-cut tobacco leaves wrapped in a cylinder of thin paper for smoking. Cigarette can also be called a finely shredded tobacco which is wrapped in paper, smoked, and inhaled for consumption. Commercially manufactured cigarettes are seemingly simple objects consisting mainly of a:

- Tobacco blend
- Rolling paper
- Glue to bond the outer layer of paper together, and filter often also a cellulose acetate-based filter.

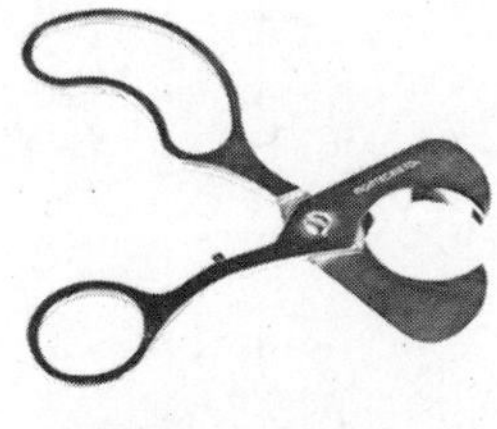

Cigar scissors

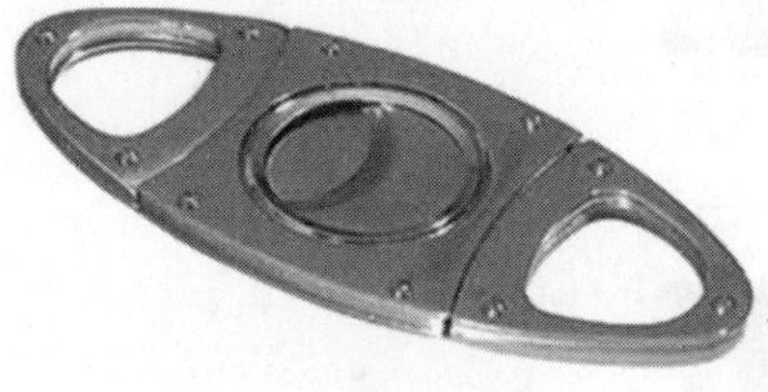

Guillotine cutter

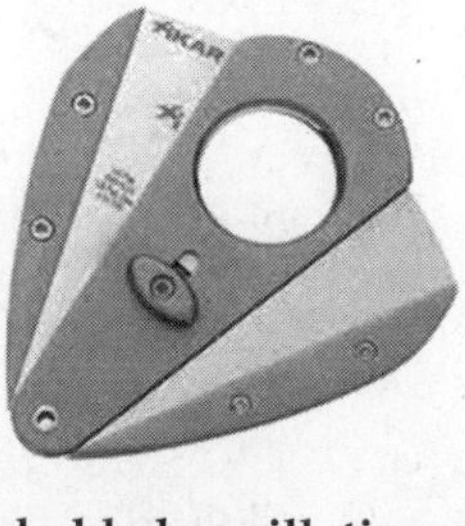

Double blade guillotine cutter

Guillotine cutter

1. Filter made of 95% cellulose acetate.
2. Tipping paper to cover the filter.
3. Rolling paper to cover the tobacco.
4. Tobacco blend

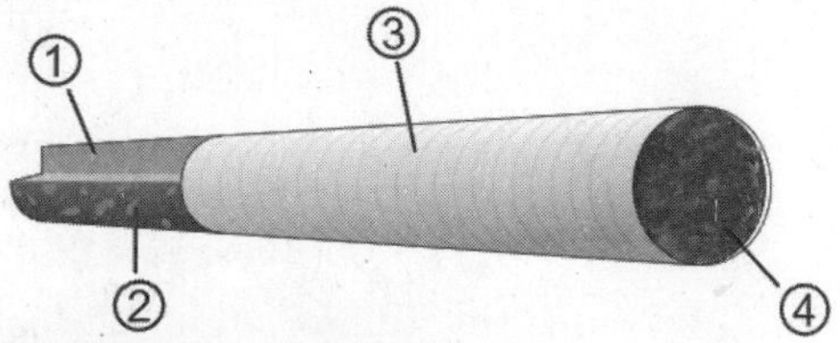

23.3.1 Service of Cigarettes: Standard Operating Procedure

- A packet of cigarettes must never be carried by hand to a customer.
- Always place a packet of cigarettes over a side plate on a beverage round.
- Outside wrapper is opened, the inside wrap pulled out and one or two cigarettes are tapped out, and not pulled out.

- Serve it along with a matchbox.
- The waiter or server should then stand by with a matchbox ready to light a cigarette.
- The waiter should strike the matchbox away from the guest and hold the flame only.
- Before extinguishing the match, the waiter must be sure that the cigarette is well lit.
- The used matchbox should not be disposed of in the guest ashtray.

Presenting a cigarette

- The waiter should clear the ashtray frequently.
- Cleaned ashtray should be placed on the table and it should be removed time to time.

Brands

(a) Vogue
(b) Benson and Hedges
(c) Camel
(d) Kent
(e) Columbus
(f) Davidoff
(g) Winston
(h) Dunhill
(i) Viceroy
(j) Marlboro

Brands available in cigarettes

REVISION QUESTIONS

1. Write down the various uses of tobacco.
2. Write down the classification of cigar.
3. Explain various parts of a cigar.
4. What do you understand by the humidor?
5. Explain how to judge a cigar.
6. Write down the serving procedure of cigar and cigarette.
7. Write five brand names of cigar.
8. Name any ten imported cigarette brands.

E-cigarette

E-cigarettes, also known as electronic cigarettes and vaporizer cigarettes are devices that emit doses of vaporized nicotine that are inhaled. The device is battery-operated and can also emit non-nicotine vaporized solutions. Generally, an e-cigarette consists of three parts:

1. A power source (usually a battery or wire that draws power from a USB port)
2. An atomizer (the part containing the heating element)
3. A cartridge (the part containing the liquid storage material).

Some E-cigarettes combine the atomizer and cartridge into one piece referred to as "cartomizers".

RESEARCH ACTIVITIES

- Purchase a cigar from the market and judge it. Also cut the cigar and understand its various parts like filler, binder and wrapper.
- List down any five imported cigars and cigarettes.

24

Bar Licence

24.1 INTRODUCTION

After reading this chapter, you will be able to understand:

- Need of bar licence
- Types of bar licence

To sell liquor in India whether in hotels, restaurants, pub, bars and in retail shops one is required to have liquor licence. It is illegal to sell liquor without such licence. Every state has its own rules to provide liquor licence through the excise department. Although the laws and regulations governing licensed premises vary, they are common in many respects. However, the permitted age for drinking alcohol varies from state to state and even the consumption and purchasing age of a alcohol varies state to state. In some states it is 18, in some states 21 and in some states it goes to 25 years and in some states, it is prohibited to sell liquor. Person working in bar should be familiar about this law to avoid any unwanted circumstances. Some of the types of liquor licences available in India are described below.

24.2 L-1 LICENCE

Every year government formulates the Excise Policy and in pursuance to this policy, the liquor licence (L-1) is granted for the wholesale vending to a company or a society or a partnership firm or proprietorship firm provided the applicant owns distillery / breweries/ manufacturing units/bottling plants. The applications for the grant of licence are invited through the public notice published in some of the leading newspapers of the country. An application for the grant of L-1 Licence is required to be made in response to the public notice in the prescribed format provided by the excise department. The prime job of L-1 Licence is to supply liquor to the holders of L-2, L-3, L-4, L-5, L-19 and L-19 A, L-52, L-53 licences.

24.3 L-2 LICENCE

L-2 Licence is for retail vend of foreign liquor/beer are granted only to selected undertakings of. Any proposal in respect of premises for opening of a vend would come from above corporations. As such an individual who wants to give his premises on rent for opening of vend has to approach any of these corporations, which after looking into suitability of the premises approach the office of the Commissioner of Excise for grant of L-2 licence in respect of the premises.

24.4 L-3/L-5 LICENCE IN HOTELS

On site consumption licences: Excise department grants licence to hotels which are holding star classification and approval of Department of Tourism, Govt. of India which are considered necessary for grant of licence in form L-3. This licence empowers the hotel to serve foreign liquor to the residents in their rooms. These hotels can also seek separate Licence in form L-5 for service of liquor in exclusive bar and in the restaurant / bar in the hotel premises. The service of liquor is restricted to specified premises of bar and restaurant only. The hotel is required to submit application on its letterhead accompanied by the documents required.

24.5 L-4 LICENCE FOR INDEPENDENT RESTAURANTS

L-4 Licence is granted to an independent restaurant approved by Department of Tourism, Govt. of India. Such restaurants can apply in the office of the Commissioner of Excise. The restaurant should be situated in commercial area with adequate parking space. Rest of the procedure for the grant of licence is the same as indicated in case of L-3/L-5 licence.

24.6 TEMPORARY LICENCE

At residence: No licence is required by an individual for serving liquor to his guests and family members at his residence provided the liquor served is within permissible possession limit.

L-20: This licence is granted to licenced hotels, restaurants and clubs for service of foreign liquor inside/outside their licenced premises on temporary basis for hosting a function on a specific day.

At any other premises (L-49A): L-49A licence can be obtained (after paying fees) for service of liquor in any party, function, marriage, etc., at a specific premise anywhere excluding public parks subject to the following conditions:

- The area is screened off from public view;
- Liquor is served to adults above 25 years of age.
- Liquor is procured from authorized source and the licence holder must be having the bill in original issued by retail liquor vend in Delhi from where the liquor has been procured.

Note: These licences vary from state to state. Above-mentioned licences are applicable in New Delhi, India.

REVISION QUESTIONS

1. Write down the purpose of the below-mentioned bar licences:
   (a) L2
   (b) L5
   (c) L20
2. Name the licence required to serve alcoholic beverages in a party at home.

RESEARCH ACTIVITY

- Visit the Excise Department office of your city and seek information on various licences applicable in your city.

25

Fruits, Nuts, Herbs and Spices

25.1 INTRODUCTION TO FRUITS

After reading this chapter, you will be able to understand:

- Types of fruits, nuts, herbs, spices and lettuces used in hotels and bars.

Fruits are the edible seed bearing portion of some cultivated or wild shrubs, trees and plants. They can be eaten raw, cooked and in many other forms. A fruit is used widely in the preparation of various food dishes. Fruits can be classified as follows:

- **Berries:** Blackberry, blueberry, raspberry, strawberry
- **Citrus:** Blood orange, grapefruit, sweet lime
- **Hard fruit:** Apple, pears
- **Tropical fruits:** Dates, figs, melons, pineapples
- **Stone fruits:** Apricots, plums, peaches, cherries

Table 25.1: List of fruits

Name	Picture	Uses
Apple (pomme)		• Eaten raw, stewed and poached. • Generally seen in fruit platter. • Used in salads, sauces (apple sauce). • Cooking apple is generally green, sweet and sour. • Cooking apple can be used as grilled and also goes with salads, and sauce.
Cooking apple		

Apricot (abricot)	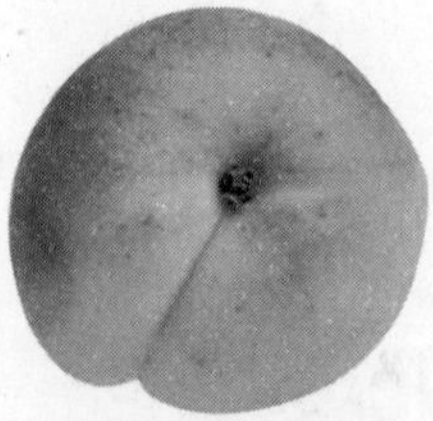	• Eaten raw, stewed and in salads. • Used as garnishes, filling for pies, pastries, puddings and in preparation of jams.
Avocado (avocat)		• Eaten raw. • Used in salads, soups and shakes.
Banana (banane)		• Eaten raw. • Used in shakes, desserts, ice creams. • Used in fruit platter. • Goes well with waffle, pancakes and desserts or as a banana fritter.
Blackberry (mure)		• Eaten raw, stewed. • Used as a filling for tarts, pies, puddings, jam.
Cherry (cerise)		• Eaten raw. • Filling for tarts, flans, pastries and pies. • Used as a garnish in different foods.
Currant (groseille)		• Eaten raw. • Filling for tarts, flans, pastries and pies. • Used as a garnish in various foods.
Date (datte)		• Eaten raw. • Used as a flavouring for cakes, pastries and puddings.

Fig (figue)		• Eaten raw. • Used in salads. • Goes with yoghurt, dry fruit. • Used in marinating as it gives tenderness to the meat.
Gooseberry (groseille verte)		• Eaten raw. • Used as a filling for pies, puddings and tarts.
Grapes (raisin)		• Eaten raw. • Used as a garnish for pastries, custard, puddings, fruit salad and in sorbet.
Grapefruit (pamplemousse)		• Eaten raw. • Used in breakfast. • Used in preparation of marmalade.
Kiwi		• Eaten raw. • Used in a fruit platter. • Served as a garnish in various pastries and desserts.
Lemon (citron)		• Used as a garnish. • Used as a flavouring agent. • Used in marination. • Used in various accompaniments such as grilled fish. • Lemon rind is also used in bakery. • Used in various alcoholic and non-alcoholic beverages.
Mango (mangue)		• Eaten raw. • Used in fruit platter. • Used in ice cream, shakes.

Melon (melon) Types of melon: • Casaba • Santa Claus • Charentais • Ogen • Cantaloupe • Honeydew • Crenshaw • Canary • Galia • Watermelon • Lavan • Honey ball		• Eaten raw in salads. • Used in cocktails, fruit salad and in sorbet and drinks.
Orange (orange)		• Eaten raw. • Used in fruit cocktails, salads, fruit salads. • Used as a juice, fresh and canned. • Used in various drinks, sorbets, mousse and souffle. • Widely used in the preparation of marmalades.
Papaya (papaye)	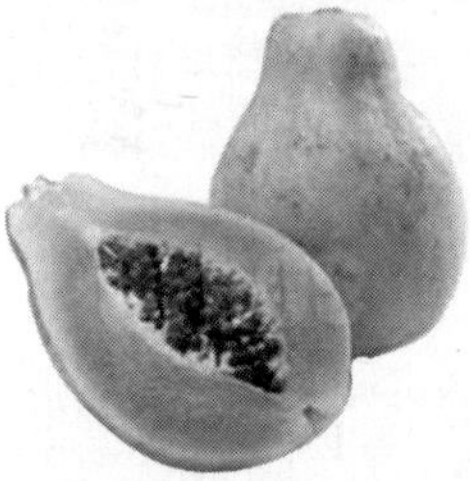	• Eaten raw. • Used in fruit salad. • Used in marination for tendering meat.
Peach (peche)		• Eaten raw. • Used in fruit salad. • Used as a filling for various pies and pastries. • Used in preparation of many dishes and garnishes.
Pear (poire)		• Eaten raw. • Used in fruit salad. • Used in tarts and also as a stewed fruit.

Pineapple (ananas)		• Eaten raw. • Used in fruit salad. • Used as a juice and garnish in many foods and drinks. • Used in many food preparations.
Plum (prune)		• Eaten raw. • Used in fruit salad. • Used in filling for tarts and pies as well as it is stewed.
Pomegranate (grenade)		• Eaten raw. • Used in fruit salad. • Used as a juice, syrup and in garnishes.
Raspberry (framboise)		• Eaten raw. • Used as a filling for pastries, tarts and pies. • Used in souffles, mousse, ice creams and jam.
Strawberry		• Eaten raw. • Used filling for tarts and pies. • Used in mousse and souffles. • Used as a garnish in many food and drinks.

Note: Fruits should not be stored in dry atmosphere. Hard, stone and citrus fruits are best stored in the boxes in which they are delivered. Berries are handled as little as possible and always be stored in the refrigerator.

25.2 NUTS

Nuts are single seeded, dry, hard-shelled fruits that have to be cracked to open or nuts can be described as any seed or fruit with an edible kernel in a hard or brittle shell. The seed inside the shell is called kernel. Nuts are used in many food preparations.

Table 25.2: List of nuts

Name	Picture	Uses
Almond (amande)		• Eaten raw. • Widely used in bakery and confectionery for preparation, decoration and garnishes. • Used as filling for various pies and tarts. • As an accompaniment for cheese.
Chestnut (marron)		• Braised, roasted and eaten hot. • Used as a garnish in many food products. • Used in bakery.
Coconut (noix de coco)		• Eaten raw. • Used in puddings, pastries, cakes. • Used as an oil and in curries. • Used widely in south Indian food. • Coconut milk is also used in many food preparations.
Hazelnut (noisette)		• Eaten raw. • Used in filling of pie, tarts and in cakes. • Used as an oil.
Groundnut (cacahouette)		• Eaten raw. • Used as an oil. • Used in filling of pies and tarts.
Pistachio (pistache)		• Widely used in bakery and confectionery to decorate cakes and other desserts. • Used in salads and dressings.
Walnut (noix)		• Widely used in bakery and confectionery to decorate cakes and other desserts. • Used as a stuffing and in pate. • Used as a garnish, in dressings and many salads.

25.3 HERBS AND SPICES

The name **"herb"** comes from the Latin word *"herba"*, meaning grass or herbage. Herbs have been the main source of medicine throughout human history. Culinary herbs are fresh or dried leaves used as food flavouring. There are literally hundreds of plants that can be grown for this purpose. Some of the more popular commercially grown herbs include basil, cilantro, chives, dill, mint, oregano, parsley, rosemary, sage and thyme. Both herbs and spices enhance the flavour of foods, and many have medicinal and nutritional properties. Herbs are the aromatic leaves of the fresh or dried plants whereas the spices are the aromatic parts of plants that thrive in the tropical regions. They are usually in the form of dried buds, fruits, berries, roots or barks.

25.3.1 Herbs

In former times, the term 'herbs', when used in cookery, included all plants and vegetables that grow aboveground, or in simple terms various aromatic plants that are used in cookery. **Pot herbs** traditionally include six vegetables: chard, lettuce, orache, purslane, sorrel and spinach. They are used not only to flavour soup but also as vegetables, salad ingredients and as a garnish. **Herbes a soupe**, which was traditionally used to flavour soups and stews, consisted of various green vegetables (carrot and celery tops, radish leaves, parsley stalks). **Herbes de provence** consists of a mixture of aromatic plants (thyme, rosemary, basil, bay leaf, savory). **Herbes venitiennes** are a mixture of aromatic herbs (tarragon, parsley, sorrel and chervil), which are finely chopped and incorporated into beurre manie. The herbs have been highly prized for centuries for their endless uses in cookery as well as in the field of medicinal and healing properties. In cooking, herbs can make a significant difference to a dish, making the simplest meal great with aroma and flavour. Fresh herbs can be easily grown at home in the garden, or in a pot or window box, and are also widely available from supermarkets, as sprigs, leaves and growing in pots. They are available in dried and frozen as well as fresh forms.

Though the range of herbs used in cookery is endless, this study will take into account the main herbs that are usually seen and used on a day-to-day basis in the hotel kitchens. The most common herbs are as follows:

- **Basil** has two types, common and sweet; both originated in India. Its name is derived from Greek word ***basilikos***, meaning royal. This delicate aromatic herb is widely used in Italian cooking. It is very important in Thai and Vietnam cooking; also used in salads and curries. The herb has a slightly pungent perfume, which can be noticed; just by brushing the leaves. Basil has a great affinity with tomatoes and other Mediterranean vegetables such as aubergines and fennel. There are numerous varieties of common basil. ***Purple basil*** has dark wine red leaves, while ***handkerchief basil*** has large leaves and ***Neapolitan basil*** has crinkly leaves. ***Sweet basil,*** also known as Asian basil or Thai basil, has a more aniseed flavour. There are a number of varieties and sweet basil comes closest to the basil with which we are familiar, that has glossy pointed leaves. ***Krapow,*** commonly known as holy basil, is another sweet basil but narrower leaves that tend to be dull rather than shine. It has a lemon scent and a peppery flavour.

- **Coriander/cilantro,** also known as ***Arab parsley*** or ***Chinese parsley*** in France and as cilantro in the United States can be used like parsley. The leaves feature especially in the cuisines of China, South-east Asia, South America and Mexico. It is an aromatic plant used both for its leaves and seeds. The origin goes back to the days of Romans who used this for preserving their meats. Its most classic use is for the preparation of ***vegetables a la grecque*** and of pickles in vinegar. Fresh coriander looks similar to flat leaf parsley, but the flavour is completely different with a piquant taste and intense aroma. Coriander is used extensively throughout the world, wherever a distinctive fresh pungency is required. In curries, dals and chutneys in India; in kebabs, meat balls and stir fries in the Middle East and Far East; and in salsas in South America. It is often sold with its root intact. The roots have a more intense flavour than the leaves and can be used in curry paste. The leaves also make a good garnish.

- **Parsley,** originated in southern Europe and cultivated mainly for its aromatic leaves, is used to garnish or flavour many dishes. There are mainly two types: ***flat leaf parsley*** which has large, flat, relative smooth leaves, has a strong flavour and ***curly leaf parsley,*** the most commonly available form which has bright green, crinky leaves and good flavour. There is another type, i.e., ***turnip rooted,*** which is cultivated for its swollen roots, is used in soups. It is one of the main ingredients of a bouquet garni. When mixed with garlic, it is often served with sautéed or fried fish dishes. Parsley is used to garnish many dishes and to add a touch of freshness. It is also used in the preparation of flavoured butters. It has a very good freezing quality also.

- **Thyme,** the basic herb used in cooking, is one of the main ingredients of the bouquet garni. It has a very good aroma and that is the reason it is used so extensively in various dishes. The other variety, i.e., wild thyme also called serpolet in France has clusters of pink flowers and has less pronounced flavour than garden thyme. It is used fresh or dried. It is very good for flavouring eggs, salads, tomato dishes and lentils. In Provencal cookery it is used to flavour ragout, mutton and rabbit. Otherwise it is considered to be a very mild herb and used most of the time as a great flavouring for chicken.

- **Dill,** also known as ***Russian*** or ***Swedish parsley,*** is an aromatic plant which originated in the east and introduced into Europe in ancient times. It is commonly called false anise or bastard fennel but it, in fact, has a very peculiar delicate flavour of its own. It grows wild in Spain, Portugal and Italy. It thrives in the warmer regions of the northern hemisphere and is widely used in Scandinavian cooking with salmon for making ***Gravadlax.*** Dill goes well in potato salads and with cucumber. It makes a good addition to creamy sauces and can be added to a wide variety of egg dishes. It is also used as a flavouring for dressings and dips, used in marinades and is a good partner to mustard. It should be added a few minutes before serving as the delicate flavours go away while cooking.

- **Fennel,** a plant of the Mediterranean origin, is now widely cultivated. The feathery leaves have a slightly aniseed flavour. The leaves are also used for garnish. The plant is a member of the same family as parsley and dill. It grows abundantly near the sea and in damp places, and has been used in cooking for thousands of years. The herb goes particularly well with fish and chicken. Chopped fresh fennel leaves may be added to mayonnaise and other yoghurt based dressings, creamy sauces, stuffings and soups. The fennel bulb can be used raw in salads or cooked in a wide variety of dishes.

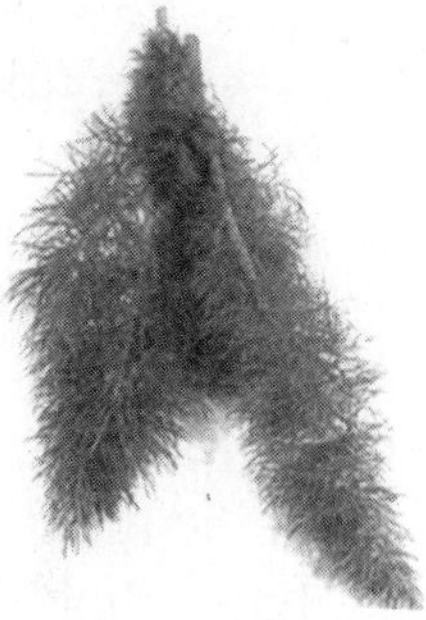

- **Tarragon** plant originated in Central Asia. Its name is derived from the Arabic ***tarkhun*** the herb was formerly reputed to cure snakebites. Fresh tarragon is deservedly one of the most popular herbs. The slender leafed ***French variety*** has a unique intense sweet vanilla flavour and is considered superior to the coarser tasting ***Russian tarragon***. This herb has an affinity with egg and cheese dishes, tastes good with poultry and can be added to green salads. It is used to enliven dressings and mayonnaise, and is finely chopped and stirred into cream and egg based sauces ***(Béarnaise)*** to serve with salmon and trout. Tarragon vinegar is a classic ingredient for many salad dressings and sauces. Its leaves are used fresh or they may be preserved by drying or freezing.

- **Chervil** originated in Central Asia but now common throughout Europe. It has a delicate flavour that goes well with soups, omelettes, sauces (béarnaise, gribiche, vinaigrette) and fish. It also looks very close to the flat leaf parsley. In addition to the ***common chervil,*** there is another variety which is ***curly*** and used for decoration. There is also ***bulbous chervil,*** its tuberous

roots, with high starch content, are eaten like Jerusalem artichokes. Chervil loses its flavour with prolonged cooking, so it is important to add it at the end of the cooking. It keeps very well when frozen.

- **Mint** is a fragrant aromatic plant used in infusion, to flavour liqueurs, sweets and syrups, and as a culinary herb. There are many varieties of this very famous and versatile herb. Some common ones include ***Spearmint***, the most popular mint. It has pointed serrated leaves with the fresh familiar flavour we mostly associate with mint. This is the preferred type mint jelly or mint sauce to accompany roast lamb. It is also used for tea in North Africa and Middle East, and for Kentucky mint julep. ***Pepper mint*** with its darker, longer leaves has a stronger flavour. It produces very pungent oil used mainly in confectionery. ***Japanese mint*** is a species from which menthol is extracted. The soft green leaves of ***apple mint*** have a more subtle fruitier flavour. Mint is widely used as a flavouring in a wide variety of dishes. It is an essential ingredient to the Mediterranean salad ***Tabbouleh***. In India, it is also mixed with yoghurt to make ***Raita and mint chutney*** accompaniments for Biryani and kebabs. ***Asian mint*** is more strongly flavoured than most European types, with a sweet cool aftertaste.

- **Marjoram** is closely related to oregano has three main known varieties: ***Sweet marjoram*** and more flavourful ***pot marjoram***. There is also another type known as ***wild marjoram*** which grows in abundance in Greece. Marjoram has a slightly sweeter flavour and a sweet, almost perfumed aroma. It goes particularly well Mediterranean style vegetable dishes such as ***ratatouille*** or in casserole and tomato sauces. It should be added at the last minute as it has a mild flavour which diminishes as it is cooked for long. It is also used in marinades and sometimes also in pizza toppings. In Greece, it is frequently used with lamb.

- **Oregano** is also known as ***wild marjoram*** and undoubtedly one of the most important herbs for pizza topping. As the use says, this herb is most commonly related to Italy where it grows in abundance. It has a very robust flavour. It has a warm aroma and a pleasant, slightly musty flavour that brings out the flavour of tomatoes and aubergines.

- **Rosemary** is a native of the Mediterranean countries. The name comes from the Latin word, ***Rosmarinus*** which means rose of the sea. The sprigs or spiky leaves are used either fresh or dried. They have a strong flavour and only a few are needed to flavour a marinade, a ragout or a grill. It goes particularly well with lamb, chicken and game. Its flavour can also enliven bean and vegetable dishes.

- **Sage** is widely cultivated in temperate climates for its leaves. The name comes from the Latin word ***salvus*** which means safe, in good health as traditionally it was considered to have curative properties. It also aids in digestion. It has a potent aroma and slightly peppery flavour and a little is required to flavour a dish. It goes excellent with pork dishes, especially grilled pork. It is used most frequently in Italian cuisine: ***Saltimbocca, osso bucco, paupiettes and rice minestrone*** that are flavoured with sage. In France, it is mainly used in Provence for flavouring white meats and certain vegetable soups. In Middle East, it is eaten with roast mutton and in China the tea is flavoured with sage.

- **Bay leaves:** This herb is from the Mediterranean region, which is obtained from an evergreen tree named *Bay laurel* or *true lorel*. It is widely cultivated in temperate regions for its glossy aromatic leaves known as bay leaf. It is one of the most commonly used culinary herbs. Its leaf is always incorporated into a bouquet garni to flavour any stock and soups, ragouts and various casseroles. This herb is hardly available fresh as most of the time it is sold dried. It can also be used fresh which will have a different flavour of its own.

- **Curry leaves** herb comes from a tropical tree of the citrus-rue family, which is native to southern India and Sri Lanka. The long leaves are shiny, dark green on top with paler undersides. It has a warm and spicy aroma when they are bruised or rubbed. It imparts a curry flavour that is unique to this particular herb. A classic way of using curry leaves is by adding them to the hot fat for a few seconds. This way the flavour is best extracted from the leaves. They can also be used chopped or whole in the curries, but in the latter case they should be carefully removed from the dishes as some people do not enjoy the leaves coming into their mouth while enjoying the meal.

- **Chives** members of the onion family, have a mild onion flavour. On the other hand, there is one more variety which is known as **Chinese Chives,** also called **Garlic chives** that have a delicate garlic aroma. They can be snipped with scissors and added to the egg dishes as garnish and for salads and soups also. They are an essential flavouring in **potato salad**. They are also a component of **fine herbs**. They make a good combination with soft cheese. When they are mixed to soften butter, they make a good alternative to garlic butter. Caution has to be taken if they are to be cooked along with some hot dish. They should be cooked briefly as they lose their flavour on prolonged cooking.

25.3.2 Spices

Any of the many aromatic substances derived from plants, which have a fragrant or sharp taste and flavour and used to season food are called spices. Most spices come from the east and the first spice to be introduced to Europe was the pepper from India. The use of spices in cooking was originally introduced by the Byzantines. Foodstuffs were preserved in spice sauces and sometimes to replace the flavour lost after lengthy cooking. Now the spices used in various cuisines are endless, everyone having their own style and way of using. The main purpose though remains the same that of providing flavour to the dish. Some of the main spices used in the kitchens are as follows:

- **Cardamom (Ilaichi)** is an aromatic plant from the Malabar region of south-western India. It has pods whose capsules contain seeds which are dried and used as a spice. It is an essential spice which is also the main ingredient of the whole as well as dried ground garam masala. The pungent and the warm bouquet of the cardamom seeds are unforgettable. It has a pleasing, slightly warm lemon like flavour. India is responsible for **80%** of the total cardamom growth world over. There are two types: the **green cardamom** and the **black cardamom**. Green cardamoms are the most common and useful. They are used extensively in curries, sweets and most commonly in flavouring tea. White cardamoms are the same pods which have been bleached. The black ones are used in long cooked, highly flavoured spicy Indian curries and chutneys. The spice is also used in German cooking, in pickles, with herrings and with cakes. It is also widely used as a mouth freshener.
- **Coriander seeds (Dhania)** is used in Indian cuisine as one of the main ingredients, finding its place in almost any curry prepared in India. The seeds look like tiny, pale, creamy-brown peppercorns. When they are dried and fried they have heady, slightly burnt orange aroma, which is very appealing. They are also used in the cuisines of Middle Eastern countries. In Germany, they are used in game marinades and also for flavouring and seasoning cabbage. Whole or coarsely ground coriander must be used in dishes cooked a **la grecque**.
- **Cinnamon (Dalchini)** is a bark which is obtained from several tropical plants. The bark is removed, dried and rolled up to make a tube, light fawn or dark grey in colour depending on the species. The most popular variety is from Sri Lanka. It imparts a sweet penetrating aroma and has a mild warm and spicy flavour. It is also commonly found in the form of a powder used as a topping and flavouring for coffee. In India, it is again used in garam masala and in France it is used in compotes and desserts. Apple and cinnamon are an all time combination (apple pie and cinnamon Danish).
- **Nutmeg (Jaiphal)** is the seed of the nutmeg tree widely cultivated in tropical Asia and America. It is a native to the Banda Island in the Moluccas. The best known variety is the nutmeg tree of the Sunda Island. The nutmeg is oval and rounded in shape, greyish brown in colour and wrinkled. It has a spicy flavour and aroma and

is always used freshly grated in little amount, as too much of it can cause the dish to taste bitter. It should always be stored in airtight containers as it tends to lose its flavour if left open. It goes excellent with béchamel base sauces, sautéed spinach, potato dishes, savory soufflés and cream based preparations. It is also used to spice cocktails and punches and is used in the manufacture of some fortified wines and spirits.

- **Mace (Javitri)** is also obtained from the same tree. It is nothing but the outer web-like covering of the nutmeg spice. It is pressed, dried and used as it is or reduced to powder. It has a slightly stronger flavour than nutmeg. It is used in garam masala in Indian cuisines. In Europe it is a popular seasoning for sausage meats and force meats, and it has an affinity with pork dishes. It can also replace nutmeg in potato puree and soufflés but the precaution has to be taken to add a little lesser.
- **Cloves (Long),** the name comes from the Latin word ***clavus*** which means a nail. It is a native to the moluccas in the southeast Asia, but they are now widely grown in Caribbean, Indonesia, Malaysia, Madagascar and Sri Lanka. They are picked when the buds are small and as they are dried in the sun, the colour changes to a dark brown. They are of great culinary significance. They are included in Indian garam masala and Chinese five spice powder. They are also used in the onion cloute for flavouring the béchamel sauce. They are arranged in a diamond pattern for flavouring and appearance on baked ham.
- **Cumin (Jeera)** seeds have a spindle shape that are used either whole or ground. They have a piquant and slightly bitter taste combined with warmth that is evident in their aroma. It is of great use in the Indian cuisines for tempering curries and dals and for making rice preparations such as pulao. It is also used in the Middle Eastern dishes in dolmas and rice preparations. It is a classic flavouring for breads in Europe and also used in the preparation of cold meats and cheeses, such as **Munster cheese**. It has two varieties: **the brown and black**. Black is also called as **Shahi Jeera** in India and is more powerful than brown cumin.
- **Turmeric:** This spice is hugely popular in India, and not only as a cheap alternative to saffron, it has a peppery aroma and adds a warm, musky flavour to food. It is used in its dried form and commonly available in the form of powder. It resembles a great deal to ginger but it is rare to see it fresh as most of the turmeric produced in India is sold dried. It has an amazing shelf-life provided it is stored in an airtight container to save its flavour. It is largely used in curries to provide colour and to lend a flavour which is unique to it. It is also used in various pickles and said to have great medicinal uses also.
- **Saffron** is one of the most expensive spice available on earth. It is the **stigma** of a flower named **Crocus sativus**. It has a distinctive and lasting aroma, and a pleasant pungency if used sparingly. Because of its striking colour, it is used in celebration dishes, e.g., **pulao in India, Paella from Spain and Risotto Milanese from Italy**.

Bouillabaisse, the classic French seafood soup is also flavoured with saffron. It is also commonly used in various sweets in India.

- **Mustard seeds (Rai or sarson)** are of different types: **white (alba), brown (juncea)** and **black (nigra).** The seeds have a mild smell or almost no smell. The real taste comes when they are crushed and mixed with a liquid. Mixing powdered mustard with a liquid activates the enzyme present in the seeds and it reacts with other constituents to develop the essential oil, which gives mustard its characteristic taste. Black seeds have the sharpest taste followed by white and then the brown. It has several culinary uses as a condiment. It is also one of the main ingredients in salad dressings. In India, its oil is used for cooking and in marinades. It is also used in a number of south Indian dishes as a tempering. It goes excellent with steaks giving them that extra tang as some people find the taste to be a little bland.
- **Carom (Ajwain)** is a famous Indian spice particularly used in *parathas*, an Indian bread done on a griddle. It is also used in pastries, snacks (*samosas*), and breads. It goes very well with bean and pulses all of which illustrate the affinity carom has with starchy food. It has a powerful thyme like aroma, which can be simply found by crushing the seeds in the hands.
- **Nigella (Kalonji):** These are the seeds of the onion, having little aroma. When they are rubbed in the fingers, they give off a peppery smell. They are sometimes used as a substitute for pepper also. It is widely used in Indian cuisines where it is known as kalonji. They are often sprinkled over naan, breads, etc. Nigella is one of the ingredients, in Bengali five-spice mix.
- **Chillies (Mirch)** are available in several different forms all around the world. The birthplace is Mexico where one can find the most varieties of chilly. They are available in all the supermarkets around the world in dried form as whole or powdered. They are largely used to provide pungency to the dishes. Chillies contain a pigment named capsaicin which is responsible for its flavour. It varies from species to species. The higher the capsaicin content in chillies, the higher the pungency. There are sweet chillies to fiery hot chillies (habanero). They are used in Indian cuisine in powdered as well as fresh form to provide colour and pungency. They are also used for tempering several south Indian dishes. Some of the other varieties of chilly are ancho, nyora, serrano, cascabel, bird's eye and pasado, all having a fiery hot taste. Serrano chillies are used to make the classic guacamole in Mexico.
- **Fenugreek (Methi)** is a highly aromatic spice. The seeds are used in a wide range of curry powders. They are also used dried and whole as a tempering. They have a good digestion property, which is the reason it is used in Indian cuisines. The seeds can also be used to make sprouts and can be used in sandwich fillings. The leaves after growing can be dried and used in gravies.

25.3.2.1 Some Combination Spices

These are some of the combination spices that have been accepted worldwide in a standard combination of different spices and each of these has a specific use in their respective cuisines. Following are some of the examples of the combination spices:

- **Jamaican jerk spice:** It is a combination of nutmeg, cinnamon, cloves, thyme (dried), black peppercorn, paprika in the ratio of 1:1:1:2:2:2. All spices are briefly broiled and ground to a fine powder.
- **All spice:** A spice also known as Jamaican pepper and in France as *poivre giroflee*, that is ground from the unripe berries of *Pimenta officinalis*, a tree which grows in the Caribbean, Honduras and Mexico. It has strong odours of nutmeg, cinnamon and cloves, which is why it is sometimes mistaken as a mixture of spices. It is used to season sausages, salt beef and pork, pickles, sauces, herrings, stuffing and even Christmas cakes.
- **Seven spice:** It is a combination of star anise, nutmeg, fennel, cinnamon, cloves, schezuan peppers and ginger.
- **Cajun spice:** Spice mix made with 1 tsp black peppercorn, 1 tsp cumin seeds, 1 tsp white mustard seeds, 2 tsps paprika, 1 tsp chilly powder, 1 tsp dried oregano, 2 tsps dried thyme, 1 tsp salt, 1 tsp garlic powder, 4 tsps onion powder.

25.4 TYPES OF LETTUCES

- **Aragula:** With its peppery and slightly bitter flavour, aragula is a terrific green to be used in a salad. It can be gently braised, too.
- **Belgian endive:** These crunchy, slightly bitter leaves are often used to make hors d'oeuvres, but they can also be chopped and added to salads, or braised to make an exquisite salad.
- **Cress:** This is a peppery green that is great in salads, sandwiches, and soups. It is attractive enough to make a good garnish as well. There are several varieties, including watercress, upland cress, curly cress, and land cress. Cress is highly perishable, so try to use it as soon as possible after you buy it.
- **Curly endive:** This crisp, bitter green leaf can be used in salads or cooked as a side dish. The outer leaves are green and somewhat bitter; the pale inner leaves are more tender and mild.
- **Iceberg:** This is prized for its crispness and longevity in the refrigerator, but it is a bit short on flavour and nutrients. It is one of the most readily available lettuces in India and is mostly used in salads.
- **Lollo Rosso:** This mild, tender lettuce has ruffled red edges.
- **Radicchio:** With its beautiful colouring and slightly bitter flavour, radicchio is wonderful when combined with other salad greens.

- **Romaine:** Romaine combines good flavour and crunch, plus it has a decent shelf-life in the refrigerator. It is the preferred green for Caesar salad. Green romaine is the most common variety, but you can also sometimes find red romaine, which is tender.
- **Red Sangria:** Thick rose blushed leaves over a blanched pale yellow heart make for an attractive lettuce.
- **Bibb:** This butter head lettuce has delicate, loose leaves and lot of flavour. The only downside is that it is expensive.
- **Mizuna or spider mustard:** Mizuna has tender leaves and a pleasant, peppery flavour.
- **Red mustard:** This has a pungent, peppery flavour that adds zip to salads.
- **Dandelions:** Dandelions have a somewhat bitter flavour, which Europeans appreciate more than Americans. Older dandelion greens should be cooked; younger ones can be cooked or served raw.

Types of lettuces

REVISION QUESTIONS

1. Name any ten spices used in Indian cuisine.
2. List down any ten herbs used in continental cuisine.
3. Write down the names of any five lettuces.
4. Write any three fruits used in bar for making drinks.
5. Name any three continental fruits.

RESEARCH ACTIVITY

- Visit a nearby vegetable market and list down the following along with their price:
  - ◊ Five continental fruits
  - ◊ Five continental vegetables
  - ◊ Five continental herbs used for cooking
  - ◊ Five lettuces
  - ◊ Ten Indian herbs and spices

26

New Trends in Bar

26.1 INTRODUCTION

> **After reading this chapter, you will be able to understand:**
> - Various upcoming trends in the bar.

Many new trends are being introduced in the bar in India and around the globe. Some of the trends are discussed in this chapter.

26.2 MIXOLOGY

It is another term for mixing drinks or bartending and a mixologist is another term for a bartender or bar chef. Mixology is generally accepted as a slang for a refined and in depth study of the art and craft of mixing. Mixology can be defined as "*the art or skill of preparing mixed drinks*". Mixology has become a more commonly used term in recent years and is generally accepted to be a refined, higher study of mixing cocktails and drinks.

26.2.1 Molecular Mixology

> **Mixologist**
>
> He is the bar equivalent of a culinary chef. A Mixologist not just pours the drink, he creates new ideas and signature cocktails by utilizing new culinary and savory concepts and knows how to use ingredients. A Mixologist's objective is to showcase the versatility of alcoholic beverages and enhance the guest experience by creating sophistication.

It is a special practice of mixing drinks using the analysis and techniques found in science to understand and experiment with cocktail ingredients on the molecular level. Inspired by the practice of molecular gastronomy (which works in similar ways with food dishes), this practice has become a popular study of many mixologists. The purpose is to manipulate states of matter to create new flavours, feel, textures and visuals that enhance the drink and make the drinker's experience more interesting. Popular techniques of molecular mixology include the use of foams, liquid nitrogen, gels, mists, heat, solidifying liquids, etc. There are many bartenders and establishments throughout the world that feature or specialize in molecular mixology, just as there are restaurants that specialize in molecular gastronomy.

However, the practice is sometimes touted as novel, gimmicky and, with the absence of discretion, can be overwhelming for some drinkers. Bartenders and chefs leading the molecular mixology have created incredible cocktails and drinking experiences. Cocktail spheres that explode in the mouth, cocktail caviar, edible cocktails, multi-colour layered cocktails, cocktails that resemble lava lamps, cocktails with foams and bubbles, cocktails infused with surprising leather and cigar are all new trends given by molecular mixology. Molecular mixology equipment ranges from simple blowtorches to vacuum chambers, cotton candy makers, liquid nitrogen, rotary evaporators and dehydrators.

26.2.2 Infusion : An Art & Science in a Jar

Herb infused spirits whether whiskies, vodkas or gins are gaining in popularity. Infusing alcohol is an ancient practice. It is the process of adding the flavours of herbs, spices, fruits and vegetables to alcohol to create a unique flavour combination. Infusing is simple process and has been used by distillers for centuries. Spirit infusions require a inventiveness, a sense of adventure, product knowledge and the ability to control the process. It is the simple practice of steeping or macerating a flavour into a spirit and letting it sit for a period of time. The time it takes for the spirit to absorb the flavours is determined by the product and the environmental factors. The basic concept is to combine a variety of choice flavours into a base liquor to create a custom flavoured spirit. Choosing an infused bottle of spirit can make drink a sweeter and smoother experience. It should also be noted that there is a difference between infused spirit and flavoured spirit. Makers of spirits have started adding flavours during production and now vanilla flavoured rums and raspberry flavoured vodkas sit side by-side with perennial standards on the shelves of a bar. Infusing spirits is a lengthy process, taking about two weeks but it is certainly not difficult if working as a bartender. Take hard alcohol and add in a source of flavour such as a fruit peel, herb or spice. Store the two ingredients together in a tightly-sealed mason jar and shake it vigorously three to five times a day. A good rule to go by when infusing is to start with oil based flavours such as citrus, chilies and similar fruits and vegetables. Using more succulent fruits such as strawberries could result in a mushy mess without careful supervision. The combinations of flavours are only limited by imagination but requires a great deal of patience. Vodka is the easiest spirit for infusing, as it is neutral as well as it pairs well with any flavour. But light spirits like gin, sake, light rum can also be used for almost any flavour. The flavoured vodka market appears to have exploded in the past few years. Brands like Absolut and Smirnoff are populating liquor store shelves with their fruity twists on classic vodka. From the flavours such as raspberry, citrus and vanilla to the unexpected treats like blueberry, mandarin and wild grape, there are options for every palate. Add just carbonated water and enjoy the enhanced taste of the guests. Tequila has also recently expanded into the infused drink market. Silver tequila from Sauza in both mango and açai flavours is one example. In many countries, tequilas and mezcal are also infused with rattle snakes and other insects. Though infusion need not be alcoholic water and sugar syrups can be infused too – the higher the alcoholic proof, the faster and more pronounced the extraction of flavours. When very high-proof alcohol is used, bartenders refer to the infusion as a tincture, which typically highlights a single flavour. Below are some tips for preparing infusion.

26.2.2.1 Preparation of an Infusion

I. Equipment required

- Clean glass containers or mason jars
- Empty wine bottles

Just make sure they are clean and free from any residue or odour of what was in them previously.

II. Gather all flavouring agents

Add fruit, spices, herbs and other flavouring ingredients of your choice. Use your judgment as to how strong the flavour of the ingredient is for how much you add. A good rule for fresh fruit is to fill the container half way up with the produce and then add liquor to fill the bottle. With herbs, a good handful or two is plenty. With something strong, like ginger, a three-inch piece should be enough for a 750 mL bottle. More ingredients can be added after a few days if more pronounced flavour is desired. Remember to cut the pieces small if using a small necked bottle. Use creativity to personalize the creations. For best results, use fresh ingredients only. Wash the ingredients and place them inside the mason jar or any other container.

III. Add alcohol

Fill the rest of the container with a decent spirit that is smooth and clean which will help in allowing the added flavours to shine. Remember to leave little space in the container so that the spirit can be shaken. Cover and close the container tightly.

IV. Infusion time

Store your infusion in a cool, dark place away from direct sunlight and shake it 3-5 times a day for the duration of the infusion. This can be done in the refrigerator as well. On an average, the ingredients should stay in the liquor for 3-5 days. Some of your more intense flavours will only need 3 days, less intense flavours should stay in the jar for a complete week or more. Taste the infused mixture after every few days to see if the flavours are sufficient. The longer you leave it, the more prominent the flavour, but it will level off eventually. Occasionally tip the bottle gently to redistribute the alcohol.

V. Strain, store and serve

When the infusion has reached its peak in flavour take the flavouring ingredients out of the jar. Use a fine strainer or paper coffee filter to strain the vodka into another clean jar or bowl and store in a cool place. Also note that containers and ingredients are thoroughly cleaned while infusing spirit. The high alcohol content should inhibit harmful bacteria from growing, but if at any point the concoction has an "off" smell, or starts to rapidly discolour or get cloudy, discard it. Remove rind and pith from citrus fruits as they make the infused liquor bitter. Common flavouring agents which can be used in a bar for infusing spirit are as follows:

- **Citrus:** Lemons, limes, grapefruit, oranges, blood oranges and tangerines.
- **Herbs:** Thai basil, lemon grass, mint, rosemary, dill, cilantro.
- **Fruit:** Mango, melon, berries, cranberries (fresh or dried), peaches, pineapple, apricot (fresh or dried), pomegranate, pear.
- **Spices:** Use whole spices like cinnamon sticks, dried chili peppers, peppercorns, star anise, cardamom and bay leaf.
- **Vegetables:** Fresh ginger, hot peppers, fennel, olives, horseradish, cucumber.
- Exotic flavour combinations can also be experimented like lemon with honey, lemon grass and ginger, fig and cardamom, apple and cinnamon stick and many more with fresh and interesting botanicals.

26.3 OTHER TRENDS IN BEVERAGES

- **Flavoured tonics:** Tonic water is the simplest mixer. A variety of new tonics are hitting the market, however, which can transform the most basic of mixers into something more sublime.
- **Cask-aged cocktails:** Drink mixes aged in wooden barrels for added nuance continue to gain popularity in major urban centres around the world.
- **Cocktails on tap:** For speed and consistency, many bars produce a selection of well-crafted cocktails in large.
- **Super-premium beverages:** Spirit enthusiasts and wine aficionados seem prepared to pay huge amount for a small taste of luxury potables. While they may not be willing to spend $300-$1,000 for a bottle of top-top-shelf cognac or Champagne, more and more enthusiasts are showing a willingness to pay a premium amount for an ounce or two.
- **Smoked spirits:** Flash smoking is making a move from the chef's kitchen to the bar top. Still a relatively new phenomenon, bar-top smokers used to infuse spirits with a mild smokiness are beginning to be found in a number of popular bars in most major cities.
- **Combination drinks:** More and more bar owners are discovering the benefits of combining two drinks and selling them together in order to boost sales. Whether it is the classic shot with a beer chaser, or a more inspired combination of two cocktails with complementing flavours, double-hitters promise to become a hit among bar patrons.
- **Return to the classics:** Cocktail menus have become chockful of creative concoctions and signature drinks. More and more drinkers, however, are starting to embrace some of the classics.
- **Skinny drinks:** Expect cocktail menus to offer more and more low-calorie beverages whether lighter versions of standard fare or entirely new concoctions. Popular

among the ladies and health-conscious patrons wanting to limit the number of "empty calories" they consume, skinny cocktails are a good way for drinking establishments to cater to this growing segment of their clientele.

- **Vintage beers, low-alcohol beers, microbrewery:** While higher-alcohol beers continue to be popular, rise in demand for flavourful, low-alcohol beers has also been increased. Microbrewery serving craft beers are also gaining much popularity among the youth.
- **Organic beverages:** Bars situated in the hotels around the world have already gone beyond organic food to start serving organic alcohol as well. In a short time organic liquor has expanded beyond beer, wine and vodka to tequila, gin, brandy, whisky and rum. Wine made from grapes that are grown, harvested, and processed according to the principles of organic agriculture is gaining traction with wine connoisseurs, and as a result many of the Asian hotel chains such as Ritz-Carlton, Marriott and Hyatt now carry organic beverages in their bars.
- **Craft beers:** Microbreweries serving craft beers have shown a tremendous rise. Many bars have planted a small microbrewery inside their bars to cater to their guests.

26.3.1 Cocktail and Food Pairing

It is the new concept in bars to pair cocktail with food. Cocktails and food pair beautifully and already many trendsetting restaurants and bars see cocktails as an inspired way to pair alcohol with foods and not just an aperitif. Following tips can be useful while pairing cocktail with food:

1. Consider cocktail pairing with food as same like wine pairing. Detect the flavour profiles and create a complementary drink accordingly.
2. Avoid cocktails that are overly sweet, especially when paired with a sweet dish.
3. Bring an ingredient forward in a dish by using it in a cocktail pairing.
4. Use fresh, quality ingredients in cocktails.
5. If compiling an entire cocktail pairing menu, keep the cocktail portions small.
6. Control the alcohol content as high alcohol content tends to numb the taste buds.

26.3.2 Designer Ice

One of the latest trends in the world of craft cocktails is using the designer ice. Different varieties, compositions, and shapes of ice is an essential ingredient in the new cocktail trend and with the help of such new innovations service of spirit has become more eye appealing. Serving whisky on the rocks with the help of ice ball is a latest trend in most of the high class establishments nowadays. Add just one big piece of ice that lasts longer in the drink, instead of a bunch of tiny pieces that melt quickly.

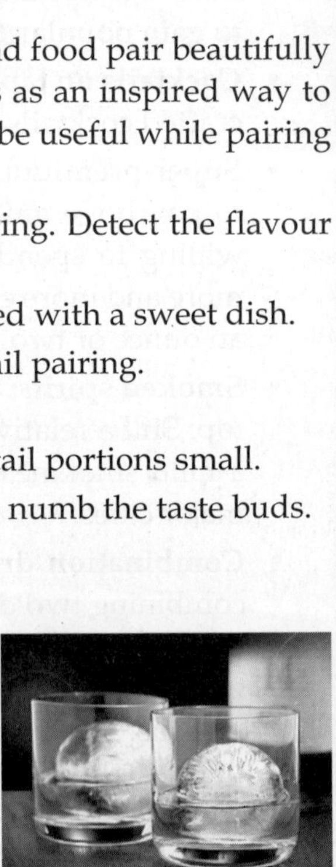

Ice ball

26.4 INFORMATION TECHNOLOGY

Use of online reservations is a rapidly growing trend, the use of the Internet to find where to go to eat and drink has become common nowadays. Smartphones, majorly tablets are being adopted more broadly in the hospitality industry not only as POS-integrated system but also as a replacement for the wait staff's order pads and as enhanced menus with photos, ingredients, the calorie count of foods, suggested wine pairings and many more. Many wine bars and restaurants are using tablets as a replacement to traditional wine menus. Tablets also provide an opportunity for cheap entertainment, in the form of interactive game play, to bar patrons. Use of social media has become a major marketing tool for the commercial bars as it combines the credibility of the word of mouth publicity with the reach of mass media. Many bar professionals are hiring social media managers to help promote their bars. LED's and new, cheaper and simpler-to-use DMX lighting software allows bars and nightclubs to modify the look and feel of their premises with greater ease, without having to overhaul the entire architecture. Whether as means of creating an entirely fresh look or as a way of changing mood lighting to match an event, a season, or a time of day DMX lighting is used more widely to create a fresh look and feel. Bars are using data and reviews from social media to update the menus and services.

26.5 OFFERING OFF-PREMISES SERVICES

With more options for consumers to eat and drink at home, it is becoming increasingly important for bars and restaurants to provide off-premise options for their customers to enjoy their experience from the comfort of their own home. With the rise of home delivery services it is more important than ever to ensure that bars offer some drinks as off-premises.

26.6 HIGH END NON-ALCOHOLIC DRINKS

There is also a rise in high end non-alcoholic drinks which includes house-made sodas and fresh juices, as well as premium coffee on nitro taps. This helps to offer those guests who want to stay healthier and may only want 1-2 drinks and for those who don't drink at all. It is also common for people to give up drinking for short periods during the year, and having great high end non-alcoholic drinks are a great way to keep customers coming to the bar even if they are not drinking at the moment.

REVISION QUESTIONS

1. Write in detail any five new trends prevailing in bars.
2. Write a note on the role of ICT in bar.
3. What is the process of infusing beverages with botanicals.

RESEARCH ACTIVITY

- Read various drinks magazine of last six months and note down the new trends followed by bars and restaurants in India and around the globe.

Service of Beverages

27

Bar Setup

27.1 OPENING A BAR

The following points should be considered before opening a bar everyday.

- Staff must report for duty on time.
- Uniform must be clean and the staff must be well-groomed.
- Use shift checklist to check the bar.
- Condition of chairs and tables must be examined.
- Condition of music player and speed pourer must be checked.
- Check the table set-up before shift starts. Keep clean ashtrays.
- Replace dirty linen.
- Check the bar counter set-up as per the stacking sequence.
- All bar station settings should be completed before the end of each shift.

27.2 ELEMENTS IN A BAR SETTING

- Carpet and tiles to be free from dust, stains and debris.
- Light fixtures to be fully illuminated.
- Air condition to be working properly.
- All walls to be clean and free from any chips or marks.
- All mirrors/glass to be polished and free from any smudges.
- All windows to be clean and free from any streaks.
- All plant and floral decorations to be fresh.
- Side stations to be stacked properly and must be neat and clean.
- Tables and chairs to be steady.
- Tables and chair legs to be free from any scuffs and scratches.
- Chair/couch upholstery to be clean, matching and in good condition.

- Appropriate music to be played at pleasant level.
- Hotel tissue box to be available at the bar on request.
- Hotel pad, pen and matchbox to be available at the bar on request.

27.3 MISE-EN-PLACE FOR BAR

- Bar and table setup should be completed before the opening time of the bar.
- All tables in the bar should be consistently laid and cleared within five minutes of guest's departure.
- Tables should be set as per the bar design specification.
- Beverage list should be placed on each table.
- Napkins and coasters should be free from any creases and stains.
- Correct cutlery as per bar design specification should be used for its intended purpose.
- Glassware as per bar design specifications should be clean and un-chipped.
- Crockery should be clean and un-chipped.
- Cutlery, crockery and glassware should be stored in designated areas.
- Ice bucket should be clean and well polished.
- Salt and pepper cruets should be made available on request.
- Sugar caddy selection should include white, brown and sugar substitutes.
- Salt rimmer should be ready.
- Bar caddy should be well arranged.
- Sugar crystals should be presented with sugar tongs and spoons.

27.4 BAR SETUP PROCEDURE

27.4.1 Equipment Required

- Functional bar
- Wiping cloth/sheet

24.4.2 Knowledge Required

- Standard recipes of cocktails/mocktails
- Types of glassware
- Handling glasses
- Par stock of beverage
- Beverage cost control

- Eye for detail
- Hygiene and sanitation

27.4.3 Procedure

- F&B associate should check if the floor has been cleaned the previous night.
- Bar area should be cleaned (inside and outside as applicable).
- Check the temperature of all the chillers and place the requisite items in the same. Call engineer if it is not working.
- Collect the fruits/lemon from the kitchen to make garnishes.
- Ensure that the straws, swizzle stick, cocktail sticks, coasters and napkins are placed in the bar caddy.
- Check the cordials, mixers and other cocktail ingredients and replace or replenish, if necessary.
- Prepare sour mix, squeeze lemon for lime juice, sugar syrup and fill them in thoroughly cleaned store and pour container.
- Wash the muddler, cocktail shaker and other bar equipment used for cocktail making.
- The bar steward should ensure that the bottles at the display are well laid and free from dust.
- Check if the required number of glassware is placed in the shelves inside the bar.

27.4.4 Standards

- All nooks and corners should be checked for cleanliness.
- All surfaces and areas should be free from stains, water marks and other sticky substances.
- The surfaces should be cleaned with soap solution and wiped dry with a clean red duster.
- The temperature of the chiller should be 4-7 degrees centigrade.
- Display all the bottles in the sequence of whisky, vodka from front, liqueur and tequila at last country-wise.
- Store and pour container should be labelled accordingly.
- The steward should ensure that the muddler, cocktail shaker, shaker glass, bar spoon, chopping board, paring knife, blender, ice crusher and peg measure are free from deposits and spotlessly clean.

Table 27.1: Procedure of effective working of a bar

STEP 1	Inspect the bar from inside and outside.	
STEP 2	Take out all bottles from the cupboard carefully. Clean and wipe the bottles with a duster.	
STEP 3	Clean and wipe the counter with a damp duster.	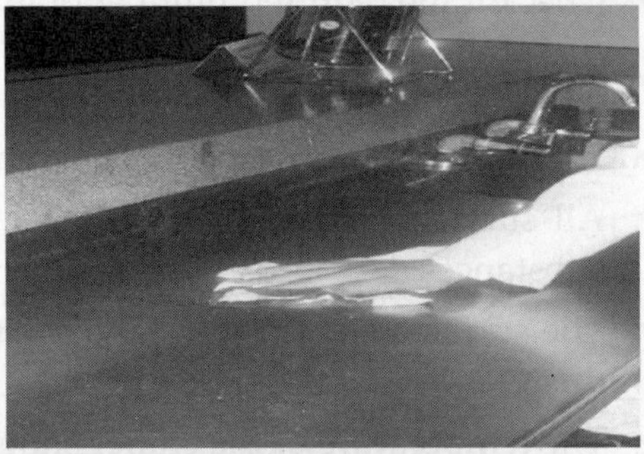
STEP 4	Stack the beverages and juices in the chiller situated under the bar.	

STEP 5	Cut and organize fresh garnishes in the garnish tray.	
STEP 6	Organize straws, swizzle stick, muddler, coasters, paper napkins for the meal period.	
STEP 7	Clean the cocktail shaker thoroughly with the help of a long brush.	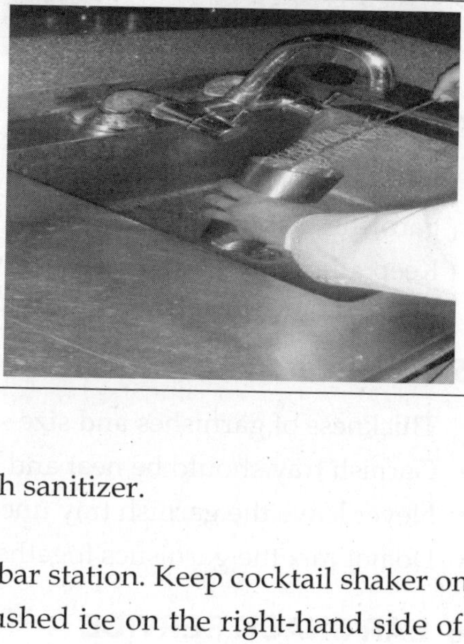

27.4.5 Setting Service Bar Counter

- Clean the bar counter using a clean cloth with sanitizer.
- Put ashtrays between every two chairs.
- Put four bar mats on the counter on the first bar station. Keep cocktail shaker on it.
- Keep ice cubes on the left-hand side and crushed ice on the right-hand side of the sink. Keep juices in the right sink.
- Two bar rails to be set on each counter; first rail to be set with white spirit and second with dark spirit. Lime cordial and sugar syrup to be kept in the second rail.
- All the ingredients of the cocktails like salt, pepper, angostura, honey, etc., to be kept on the side table.
- Prepare standard beverage garnishes like lemon wedges, lemon slices, lemon rings, lemon twists and mint sprigs.

27.5 PREPARATION OF GARNISHES

27.5.1 Equipment Required

- Chopping board
- Bar knife
- Fruits and vegetables
- Garnish tray
- Wiping cloth/sheet

27.5.2 Knowledge Required

- Types of garnishes used in bar
- Hygiene and sanitation
- Safety

27.5.3 Procedure

- Prepare yourself for cutting the garnishes to be used in bar.
- Put on a disposable glove to avoid cross contamination.
- With a clean bar knife cut according to the specific garnishes using the green coloured cutting board.
- Keep all garnishes separately in the garnish tray in a bed of ice or refrigerator to keep them fresh.

Placing garnishes

27.5.4 Standard

- Thickness of garnishes and size should be standard.
- Garnish tray should be neat and clean.
- Never leave the garnish tray uncovered.
- Do not mix the garnishes together.

27.6 BAR SNACK SERVICE

27.6.1 Equipment Required

- Menu card
- K.O.T. /B.O.T. pad
- Pen

27.6.2 Knowledge Required

- Types of snacks available

- Non-available items in menu
- Food pairing with various beverages
- Upselling and suggestive selling techniques

27.6.3 Procedure

- Observe the guest if he is ready for ordering.
- Approach the table to take order and stand in a position that allows you to have eye contact with the guest. Use standard phrases such as "Mr. Smith, May I take your order?"
- Guide the guest by suggesting the snacks according to the drink.
- Repeat the order to the guest after writing in the order pad – "Mr. Smith may I repeat your food order?"
- Speak to the guest slowly, clearly and politely.
- Punch the order in restaurant software and check that the order is received by kitchen department.
- Pick up the snack and present to the guest in an appealing manner.
- Snacks should be served at a right temperature.
- Appropriate condiments and accompaniments should be offered.

27.6.4 Standards

- The texture and colour of the snack should be acceptable.
- The portion should be as per the hotel/bar policy.
- Snacks should resemble their description on the menu.
- Snacks should be served within ten minutes of placing the order
- Guest should be informed of any unexpected delay.
- When the guest leaves temporarily, napkin should be folded neatly by F&B associate and placed appropriately.
- Order should be correct and complete.
- Condiments should be placed in an appropriate container.
- Tables should be visited to ascertain satisfaction on the level of service within five minutes of service of the snack.

28

Presenting Beverage Menu

28.1 PRESENTING A MENU

Equipment Required

- Beverage menu
- KOT/BOT

Knowlege Required

- Knowledge of the food and beverage items
- Upselling

Standards

Presenting beverage menu to the guest

- Menu should be presented within 1 minute of seating the guest.
- The menus should be clean and stain free.
- The number of food menus should be the same as the number of adult guests.
- There should be at least 1 beverage menu for every 2-3 guests at the table.
- The hostess should hold the menu firmly, from the right hand. The thumb should be on the upper side and four fingers should support the base.
- The menus should be offered from the right-hand side of the guests.
- The menu should not be presented to a group/guests with a pre-fixed menu.
- The menu should be handed over in the sequence:
  - ◊ Eldest lady
  - ◊ Other ladies

◊ Hostess
◊ Eldest gentleman
◊ Other gentleman
◊ Host

- In case the guest is occupied; the hostess should wait.
- Standard phrase for presenting the menu, "The menu card for you, Madam/Sir".
- The hostess/host/steward should know the "not available" beverages and the other "off menu" cocktails possible.

Procedure

- The hostess/host after seating the guests comes back to the hostess desk, picks up the menus and approaches the table.
- Present the beverage menu to the guest, ladies first. Then present the beverage menu to the gentlemen/host at the table. This menu should be presented irrespective if the guest chooses to have buffet or *a la carte*.
- The hostess/host should take the guest order if the guest is ready to order immediately.
- If the guest does not order at the same time, the hostess/host should inform the guest that the steward would be at the table shortly to take the order.
- If the guest orders the beverages, the hostess/host/associate should collect back the beverage menus.

28.2 UPSELLING

Equipment Required

- Beverage menu
- KOT/BOT

Knowledge Required

- Knowledge of the food and beverage items
- Complete knowledge of the menu
- Pricing of various items
- Description and brief history of all items on the menu
- Upselling techniques
- Knowledge of the hidden menu

Standards

- "Sir/Madam, I would recommend you to try our _____" (name of the drink and a brief description).

- "Sir/Madam, I would recommend you to try ______ (name of the wine). It will complement with your meal really well."
- "Sir/Madam, I would recommend you to try our specialty ________." The steward should give a brief description of the dish and its spice level.
- "May I recommend the Smirnoff vodka instead of the Magic Moment vodka in your Bloody Mary cocktail?"
- The guest should not feel like he/she is being forced.

Procedure

- The steward suggests some alcoholic and non-alcoholic cocktails to the guest and other house specialties if the guest asks for simple aerated drinks or juice.
- The steward suggests wine to accompany the food and provokes impulse buying.
- The steward recommends the house specialities to the guest.

28.3 SAMPLE WINE MENU

28.3.1 Champagnes

Moët et Chandon, Brut Impérial, NV
Épernay, CHAMPAGNE
Moët et Chandon, Cuvée Dom Pérignon, 1995
Épernay, CHAMPAGNE
Château Indage, Marquise de Pompadour, Brut, N/V
Narayangaon, Maharashtra, INDIA

28.3.2 White Wines

- **Chardonnay:** Chardonnays make consistently excellent, rich and complex white wines. Typically, these wines offer bold, ripe, rich and intense fruit flavours of fig, melon, pear, peach, pineapple, lemon and grapefruit along with spice, honey, butter, butterscotch and hazelnut flavours. This is a very versatile grape and grows well in a variety of locations throughout the world, particularly in Burgundy, Australia and California.

  Albert Bichot, Puligny-Montrachet, 2000
  Côte de Beaune, BURGUNDY
  Louis Jadot, Pouilly-Fuissé, 2001
  Mâconnais, BURGUNDY
  Chinkara Wines, "Chinkara", 2003
  Melbourne, Victoria, AUSTRALIA
  Maison Louis Jadot, Bourgogne, 2000
  Bourgogne AOC, BURGUNDY

Maison Louis Jadot, Meursault, 1998
Côte de Beaune, BURGUNDY

Château de Montpatey, Bourgogne, 2002
Bourgogne AOC, BURGUNDY

- **Sauvignon blanc:** Another great white varietal, this one is with a notable grassy or musky aroma. The pure varietal is found mainly in the Loire, at Sancerre and Pouilly-Fumé. New Zealand has had striking success with Sauvignon Blanc, producing its own perfumed, fruity style that spreads across North America and then back to France.

Henri Bourgeois, Pouilly-Fumé, 2002
St. Andelain, LOIRE VALLEY

Montana Wines, Marlborough Reserve, 2003
Blenheim, NEW ZEALAND

- **Clairette:** Originally from France, the Clairette grape is one of the Châteauneuf and Côtes-du-Rhône villages varieties. In its new "home" is Bangalore, it produces an attractively fruity wine with low acid.

Grover Vineyards, Blanc de Blancs
Nandi Hills, Bangalore, INDIA

- **Pinot Gris:** Originating in Italy as Pinot Grigio, this varietal comes into its own in Alsace, also known as Tokay there. This varietal is soft, gently perfumed and gives out more colour than other white wines.

Domaines Schlumberger Grand Cru Kitterlé, 1998
Guebwiller, ALSACE

- **Gewürztraminer:** Best grown in Alsace, the Gewürztraminer can yield magnificent wines. The Gewürztraminer produces a floral and refreshingly spicy wine with crisp acidity that pairs well with spicy food. The grape thrives in cool climates that allows it to ripen fully.

Domaines Schlumberger, Grand Cru Kessler, 2000
Guebwiller, ALSACE

- **Riesling:** The Riesling vine's hardy wood makes it extremely resistant to frost, therefore this variety excels in cooler climates. Although best known for the wines of Germany's Moser-Saar Ruwer, Pfalz, Rheinhassen and Rheingau, it also achieves brilliance in Alsace and Austria. Due to their higher acidity and distinctive floral, citrus, peach and mineral accents the Rieslings of Alsace have won many fans around the world.

Domaines Schlumberger, Grand Cru Kitterlé, 1999
Guebwiller, ALSACE

- **Muscadet:** A small district, Sevre-et-Maine, in Loire Valley produces the best classic Muscadet in France. The wine is distinctive and musky in aroma and is very light, a bit tangy and a little bit sparkly. It goes very well with seafood and often has a light green apple flavour.

  Gadais Père et Fils, La Grande Réserve du Moulin, 2002
  Muscadet de Sèvre-et-Main, Pays Nantais, The Loire Valley

Rosé

E. Guigal, Tavel, 2002
Tavel AOC, SOUTHERN RHÔNE
Grenache, Cinsault, Clairette, Carignan, Mourvèdre, Syrah, Bourboulenc

28.3.3 Red Wines

- **Cabernet Sauvignon:** This grape is a remarkably steady and consistent performer all over the world. In Bordeaux it is blended with Cabernet Franc, Merlot, and Petit Verdot to create some of the world's most famous wines. In California, it produces wines of uncommon depth, richness and longevity. For our Cabernet Sauvignon collection, we have selected a few outstanding styles of this great red grape.

  Jordan Winery, "Jordan", 1998
  Healdsburg, Sonoma County, CALIFORNIA

  Dominus Estate, "Dominus", 1999
  Yountville, Napa Valley, CALIFORNIA

  Château Margaux, Premier Grand Cru Classé, 1997
  Margaux, Médoc, BORDEAUX
  70% Cabernet Sauvignon, 20% Merlot, 5% Cabernet franc, 5% Petit verdot

  Château Latour, Premier Grand Cru Classé, 1997
  Pauillac, Médoc, BORDEAUX
  80% Cabernet Sauvignon, 4% Merlot, 15% Cabernet franc, 1% Petit Verdot

  Château Cos d'Estournel, Grand Cru Classé, 1997
  St. Estèphe, Médoc, BORDEAUX
  60% Cabernet Sauvignon, 38% Merlot, 2% Cabernet franc

  Stag's Leap Wine Cellars, "Napa Valley", 2001
  Napa Valley AVA, Napa County, CALIFORNIA

- **Shiraz:** Also known as Syrah in France, the Shiraz is a majestic red that can age for half a century. The grape itself seems to grow well in a number of areas and is capable of rendering rich, complex and distinctive wines, with pronounced pepper, spice, black cherry, tar, leather and roasted nut flavours, a smooth supple texture and smooth tannins.

Penfolds Wines, Grange, 1997
Barossa Valley, SOUTH AUSTRALIA
Mount Pleasant, Philip, 1998
Hunter Valley, AUSTRALIA

- **Cabernet-Shiraz**
  Grover Vineyards, Cabernet-Shiraz
  Nandi Hills, Bangalore, INDIA
- **Zinfandel:** The most widely planted grape in California, it may have originally come from Southern Italy as a variant of the Primitivo grape. Although much of it is vinified into a blush wine, real Zinfandel, the red wine is quintessential California wine. The grape has a zesty, spicy pepper, raspberry, cherry wild berry and plum flavours.
  St. Francis Vineyard "Old Vines", 2000
  Kenwood, Sonoma Valley AVA, Sonoma County, CALIFORNIA
  Duckhorn Paraduxx, 2000
  St. Helena, Napa County, CALIFORNIA
- **Pinot Noir:** Pinot Noir, the great grape of Burgundy offers the classic black cherry, spice, raspberry and currant flavours and an aroma that can resemble wilted roses, along with earth, tar, herb and cola notes. A fickle grape to grow as it reacts to environmental changes is therefore different in different parts of the world. Anderson Valley in California and Oregon produce interesting flavour variants to the classic Burgundy Pinot Noir.
  Maison Louis Jadot, Bourgogne, 1999
  Bourgogne AOC, BURGUNDY
  Louis Jadot, "Damodes" Premier Cru, 1999
  Nuits-Saint-Georges AOC, Côte de Nuits, BURGUNDY
  Pinot noir, Pinot gris, Pinot liébault
  Louis Jadot, "Gevrey Chambertin" Premier Cru, 1998
  Nuits-Saint-Georges AOC, Côte de Nuits, BURGUNDY
  Château de Montpatey, Bourgogne, 2002
  Bourgogne AOC, BURGUNDY
- **Merlot:** Merlot is the red wine success story of the 1990s: its popularity has soared along with its acreage. Although it dominates most of Bordeaux, it also produces great variants in Washington State and California. Unblended, the Merlots produce simple, light, balanced red wines highlighting their drinkability.
  Duckhorn Vineyards, "Duckhorn", 2001
  St. Helena, Napa County, CALIFORNIA

Stag's Leap Wine Cellars, "Napa Valley", 2000
Napa Valley AVA, Napa County, CALIFORNIA
Chinkara Wines, "Chinkara", 2003
Melbourne, Victoria, AUSTRALIA

- **Corvina Veronese**
  Amarone della Valpolicella Allegrini, 1999
  Valpolicella Classico, Veneto
  75% Corvina Veronese, 20% Rodinella, 5% Molinara
- **Sangiovese:** Sangiovese is best known for providing the backbone for many superb Italian red wines from Chianti and Brunello di Montalcino, as well as the so-called super-Tuscan blends. It is distinctive for its supple texture and medium to full-bodied spice, raspberry, cherry and anise flavours.
  Marchesi de' Frescobaldi, Castel Giocondo, Brunello di Montalcino, 1999
  Montalcino, Chianti, TUSCANY
  Marchesi de' Frescobaldi, Nipozzano, 2000
  Chianti Rufina, TUSCANY
- **Grenache:** The world's second most widely planted grape! Drought- and heat-resistant, it yields a fruity, spicy, medium-bodied wine with supple tannins. Particularly widespread in the Southern Rhône, it is blended to produce the famous Châteauneuf-du-Pape.
  E. Guigal, Châteauneuf-du-Pape, 2001
  Châteauneuf-du-Pape AOC, Southern Rhône, THE RHÔNE VALLEY
  Grenache, Syrah, Mourvèdre, Picpoul, Terret noir, Counoise, Muscardin

28.3.4 Wines by the Glass

- **White wines**
  Louis Jadot, Pouilly-Fuissé, Chardonnay
  Chinkara Wines, "Chinkara", Chardonnay
  Maison Louis Jadot, Bourgogne, Chardonnay
  Château de Montpatey, Chardonnay
  Henri Bourgeois, Pouilly Fumé, Sauvignon Blanc
  Montana Wines, Marlborough Reserve, Sauvignon Blanc
  Grover Vineyards, Blanc de Blancs, Clairette
  Domaines Schlumberger Grand Cru Kitterlé, Pinot Gris
- **Rosé wine**
  E. Guigal, Tavel

- **Red wine**

  Stag's Leap Wine Cellars, Cabernet Sauvignon
  Grover Vineyards, Cabernet-Shiraz
  Mount Pleasant, Philip, Shiraz
  St. Francis Vineyard Old Vines, Zinfandel
  Château de Montpatey, Pinot Noir
  Duckhorn Vineyards, Duckhorn, Merlot
  Chinkara Wines, "Chinkara", Cabernet - Merlot,
  Marchesi de' Frescobaldi, Nipozzano, Sangiovese

29

Service of Non-Alcoholic Beverages

29.1 SERVICE OF FRESH LIME WATER/SODA/JUICE

Equipment Required

- Glassware
- Straw and stirrer
- Salver
- Cocktail napkin
- Coaster
- Creamer for sugar syrup and lime juice

Knowledge Required

- Types of fresh lime soda available in the hotel
- To prepare fresh lime soda, sweet and salted
- Other cold non-alcoholic beverages available in the hotel.

Service of Fresh Lime

- Whilst taking the order, the order taker will check with the guest: "How would you like your fresh lime Sir/Mr. Scott, sweet or salted?" (Get response) "Soda or Water Sir?'
- While asking if another drink is required: "May I repeat your drink/s Sir/Mr. Scott?"

Standards

- Beverage orders will be taken within two minutes of seating.
- Fresh lime will be served within five minutes of taking order.
- Fresh lime will be served from a beverage round, unless served at the bar counter.
- Fresh lime will be served onto a coaster with a cocktail napkin. In case it is being served on to a table cloth, the coaster and cocktail napkin may be omitted.

- An empty glass, swizzle stick holder or B&B plate will be placed for used stir sticks.
- The server shall ask for a repeat order when the glass is 1/4th full.
- All common courtesies such as "Ladies first and host last" shall be followed.
- Glass will be cleared when the guest has finished the drink and declined a repeat order.
- All beverage orders shall be served from the guest's right (wherever possible).

Procedure

- Fill Collins glass with ice cubes and place a swizzle stick inside.
- Add lemon juice (30 mL).
- Put a lemon wheel on the rim of the glass.
- Add sugar syrup and/or salt.
- Add water and/or soda.
- Stir the drink.
- Place the following on salver.

Prepared Fresh Lime

- Sugar syrup in a decanter (in case fresh lime soda is sweet)
- Straws in straw holder.

At the Table

- Place the straw holder in the centre of the table.
- Place the drink and additional sugar syrup on right-hand side of the guest.

29.2 SERVICE OF ICED TEA

Equipment Required

- Glassware
- Straw and stirrer
- Salver
- Cocktail napkin
- Coaster
- Creamer for sugar syrup and lime juice

Knowledge Required

- Types of iced tea available in the hotel
- To prepare iced tea
- Other cold non-alcoholic beverages available in the hotel

Standards

- Beverage orders will be taken within two minutes of seating.
- Iced tea will be served within five minutes of taking order.
- Iced tea will be served from a beverage round, unless served at the bar counter.
- Iced tea will be served onto a coaster with a cocktail napkin. In case it is being served on the table cloth, the coaster and cocktail napkin may be omitted.
- An empty glass, swizzle stick holder or B&B plate will be placed for used stir sticks.
- The server shall ask for a repeat order when the glass is 1/4th full.
- All common courtesies such as "Ladies first and host last" shall be followed.
- Glass will be cleared when the guest has finished the drink and declined a repeat order.
- All beverage orders shall be served from the guest's right (wherever possible).

Procedure

- Fill Collins glass with ice cubes; place a swizzle stick inside and put mint leaves.
- Add lemon juice.
- Add sugar syrup.
- Fill with tea till top of the glass.
- Put a lemon wheel on the rim of the glass.
- Place mint leaves on top as garnish.
- Place the following on the salver:
  - ◊ Prepared ice tea
  - ◊ Sugar syrup in a decanter
  - ◊ Straws in straw holder.

At the Table

1. Place the straw holder in the centre of the table.
2. Place the drink and additional sugar syrup on the right-hand side of the guest.

Note: The tea leaves or tea bag needs to be brewed adequately before it can be poured over the ice. Most stewards do not allow the decoction to be brewed adequately, resulting in iced tea with very weak flavour of the tea itself. Also, brewing the mint leaf in the teapot with the tea helps enormously apart from the sprig of mint as garnish.

For Sugar Syrup

Boil briskly, equal quantities of sugar and water, with lemon juice or egg white. When the scum rises, take a skimming spoon and skim off the top. When syrup is clear, it is done. Let it cool and bottle for future use.

29.3 SERVICE OF JUICE

Equipment Required

- Glassware
- Straw
- Salver

Standards

- Collect freshly squeezed juice or canned juice as ordered by the guest in a clean glassware as per the hotel policy on a salver.
- Juices should be well stirred and properly placed on the salver.
- Serve from the right hand side of the guest
- Always mention the name of the juice.
- Place on the right side of the water goblet.
- Place it carefully and slowly.
- Do not spill.

30

Service of Tea and Coffee

30.1 SERVICE OF TEA

Equipment Required

- Salver with cloth napkin
- Tea pot, creamer
- Tea cozy
- Tea cup and Saucer
- Sugar caddy
- Tea spoon
- Tea strainer for masala tea

The tray setup

Knowledge Required

- Service of tea
- Varieties of tea available in the hotel

Standards

- The F&B associate should use tea leaves as per guest's requirement for strength of tea and covers. Tea should be brewed for minimum of 3 minutes before being brought to the table.
- The milk should be processed from the coffee machine and filled in a creamer.
- In case of lemon tea, 3 deseeded lemon wedges should be carried in a bowl/saucer (lemon wedges should be wrapped in a muslin cloth).
- In case of masala tea, the milk should be pre-mixed in the teapot and a dash of tea masala should be added.
- The teapot, teacup and saucer should be scrupulously clean and should be free from chips and stains.

- The teaspoon should be placed either parallel to the handle of the teacup or should be placed at 4 o' clock position and teacup at 5 o' clock position on the saucer.
- The teaspoon should be sparkling clean and without water marks or stains on the surface.
- The teacup, teaspoon and saucer should be placed on the right side of the guest using the right hand to hold the saucer.
- "Sir/Madam, would you like your tea with or without milk?" This step should be followed only if the specifications have not been confirmed at the time of order taking.
- The tea should be poured from the right side of the guest.
- In case of tea with milk, the associate should pour the tea till $3/4^{th}$ of the cup is full and then put 4-5 drops of milk at one go and allow the cloud of milk to come up. Ask the guest and pour milk again.
- In case of tea without milk, the associate should pour the tea up to $4/5^{th}$ level.
- The F&B associate should pour with a steady flow so as to avoid any spillage in the saucer or on the table.
- During tea service, three cookies are offered along with the tea.
  - ◊ For 2 people = 5 cookies
  - ◊ For 3 people = 7 cookies
  - ◊ For 4 people = 9 cookies
- The associate should ask for replenishment when the teacup is $1/3^{rd}$ full.

Procedure

- F&B associate picks up the order.
- The teapot, sugar caddy, strainer with slop basin (in case of leaf tea), teacup, saucer and teaspoon are taken to the table on a salver.
- The F&B associate places the teacup, teaspoon and saucer in front of the guest.
- The F&B associate asks whether the guest would like the tea with or without milk.
- The F&B associate pours the tea from the teapot into the cup and takes the teapot back to the side station.
- The F&B associate asks for replenishment of the tea.

Step 1: Approach the table

Step 2: Place cookies on the table

Step 3: Place sugar basin, slop basin, teacup and saucer

Step 4: Pour tea in the cup

Step 5: Pour milk in the tea

Stepwise procedure for serving tea

30.2 SERVICE OF COFFEE

Equipment Required

- Salver with cloth napkin
- Coffee pot, creamer
- Cozy
- Coffee cup and saucer
- Sugar caddy
- Teaspoon

Knowledge Required

- Coffee machine operations
- Classical service of coffee
- Types of coffee preparations available.

Standards

- The coffee should be processed from the coffee machine.
- The milk should be processed from the coffee machine and filled in a creamer.
- The outer surface of the cup should be clean and free from any coffee marks.
- Cup should be warm.
- Care should be taken that the coffee does not spill from the cup.
- The cup and saucer should be scrupulously clean and should be free from chips and stains.
- The teaspoon should be placed either parallel to the handle of the teacup or should be placed at 4 o' clock position and teacup at 5 o' clock position on the saucer.
- The teaspoon should be sparkling clean and without water marks.
- The cup, teaspoon and saucer should be placed from the right side of the guest.
- The coffee should be poured from the right side of the guest.
- In case of coffee with milk, the associate should pour the coffee up to 3/4th level and fill the cup with milk.
- In case of coffee without milk, the associate should pour the coffee up to 4/5th level.
- The associate should ensure that there is no spillage on the saucer or anywhere on the table.
- During coffee service, three cookies are offered along with the coffee.
  - ◊ For 2 people = 5 cookies
  - ◊ For 3 people = 7 cookies
  - ◊ For 4 people = 9 cookies
- The associate should ask for replenishment when the cup is 1/3rd full.

Procedure

- Associate picks up the order.
- In case the guest orders any coffee that is dispensed directly from the machine, it is pre-portioned in the cup.
- The sugar basin, cup, saucer, coffee pot and teaspoon are taken to the table on a salver.

Coffee tray setup

Step 1: Approach the table

Step 2: Place cookies on the table

Step 3: Place sugar basin, slop basin, tea- cup and saucer

Step 4: Pour coffee in the cup

Step 5: Pour milk in the coffee

Stepwise procedure for serving coffee

- The station associate places the cup, teaspoon and saucer in front of the guest.
- The associate pours the coffee from the coffee pot/carafe into the cup and takes the pot/carafe back to the side station. (This step is not applicable in the case of coffee by the cup.)
- The associate may ask for replenishment of the coffee.

31

Service of Beer

31.1 BEER SERVICE

Equipment Required

- Salver with cloth napkin
- Chilled beer goblet.
- Bottle of beer
- Opener

Knowledge Required

- Product knowledge
- Classification of beer
- Brands available in the hotel
- Basic knowledge of the beer

Standards

- Beverage orders to be served within five minutes of the guest's order.
- The beer glass should be placed at the 4 o'clock position to the water glass.
- The glass should be free from chips, stains and water marks.
- Handle the glass from the base using the forefinger and thumb only, leaving no fingerprints on the glass.
- Present the glass with the phrase–"______ (brand name of the beer), Sir/Madam."
- The bottle opener should be clean, free from dust and rust.
- Stop pouring 1 inch below rim.
- The head should not exceed 1 cm.
- In case the beer is not being shared, place the bottle in front of the consumer's cover.
- Present the glass with the phrase–"Enjoy your drink, Sir/Madam."
- To replenish the glass, use this phrase–"Would you like to repeat your drink, Sir / Madam?"

Procedure

- The F&B associate after taking the order from the guest gives the BOT to the bar, picks up the order and carries it to the station sideboard.
- The F&B associate should place the chilled beer glass on the table and then present the beer bottle to the host for approval.
- On getting the approval from the host, open the bottle and pour along the rim so as to avoid excessive head formation. Lift and tilt the glass to approximately 45 degree angle.
- Keep the bottle with remaining beer in the centre of the table on a coaster. Wish the guest while leaving the table.
- The F&B associate should ask for a repeat order when the glass is $1/3^{rd}$ empty.

Table 31.1: Stepwise procedure of serving wine

Step 1: The Station associate after taking the order from the guest gives the BOT to the bar, picks up the order and carries it to the station sideboard.	
Step 2: The F&B associate should place the coaster on the table if table cloth is not laid.	

Step 3: The F&B associate should place the chilled beer glass on the table.	
Step 4: The F&B associate should present the beer bottle to the host for approval. Host may check for the temperature of the beer.	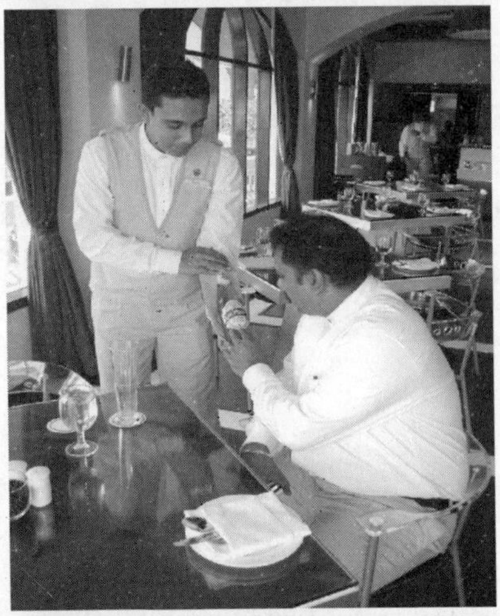
Step 5: Open the bottle and keep the crown cap in your pocket.	

Step 6: Pour the beer along the rim so as to avoid excessive head formation. Lift and tilt the glass to approximately 45 degree angle.	
Step 7: Serve the beer.	

32

Service of Straight Drinks/Spirits

32.1 WHISKY SERVICE

Equipment Required

- Whisky
- Salver with cloth napkin
- Appropriate glassware according to the drink
- Decanter
- Stirrer

Knowledge Required

- Product knowledge
- Principles of complementing mixers and spirits
- Types of glassware and hollowware

> **Did you know?**
>
> Single malt whisky should always be served at cellar temperature. It is not intended to be a thirst quenching drink, so avoid ice, which will only numb the subtle flavour of single malt. A splash of water can be added but choose spring water as it will not contaminate the flavour. Blended Canadian whisky has a rounded, fruity taste and benefits from being served on the rocks whereas Bourbon whisky is a highly versatile drink and mixes well with variety of mixers. Gin is mixed with tonic water and served with a slice of lemon.

Procedure

- The station associate should check with the guest which mixer she/he would like to have with her/his spirit.
- The associate after taking the order from the guest gives the KOT to the bar.
- The associate picks up the drink order from the bar and approaches the tables.
- Place the pre-filled glass on the table on a coaster.
- Offer ice to the guest. After two ice cubes have already been placed, check with the guest if he would prefer to have some more ice.
- The associate should then top up the glass with the mixer or as the guest desires.
- The remaining mixer, if any, should be placed next to the glass.
- Wish the guest while leaving the table.

Standards

- The F&B associate should always offer two relevant mixers. Example -"Madam/Sir, would you like to have tonic water or orange juice with the vodka?"
- Ice should be served with the help of the tongs.
- The decanter should be neat and clean and never touch the rim of the glass.
- Stirrer should also be provided along with the drinks in the glass.
- If spirit is being served in the Bar then cocktail napkin or paper napkin should be provided.
- Leave with this phrase—"Enjoy your drink, Sir/Madam".

Step 1: Pick up the drink order from the bar and approach the tables.

Step 2: Place the pre filled glass on the table on a coaster.

Step 3: Offer ice to the guest. After two ice cubes have already been placed, check with the guest if he would prefer to have some more ice.

Step 4: The associate should then top up the glass with the mixer or as the guest desires.

Stepwise procedure of serving spirits

Note: If table cloth is laid on the table then coasters are not provided, but if table cloth is not laid then t s necessary to provide coasters along with the drink.

32.2 COGNAC SERVICE

Equipment Required

- Cognac
- Salver with cloth napkin
- Brandy snifter
- Decanter
- Lukewarm water
- Wine opener

Knowledge Required

- Product knowledge

Procedure

- The F&B associate takes the order and raises BOT.
- Give the BOT in the bar and collect the bottle of cognac with all the accessories.
- Carefully cut the capsule below the level of the cork in front of the guest.
- Remove the capsule and cork.
- With the help of a neat napkin, clean the neck of the bottle to remove any dust and debris.
- Lay the brandy snifter on side of the bottle of cognac.
- Pour in the cognac until almost at level with the lip of the glass—this will help to deliver the right amount of cognac in the glass and serve from the right hand side of the guest.
- If brandy/cognac is desired only with lukewarm water, then pour lukewarm water from the decanter in the guest's glass.
- Repeat the order after consumption of drinks in the glass.
- At last present the bill to the guest, take the money, deposit it to the cashier and pass a thanks note to the guests for their visit. Tell the guests that they would be informed for any offers in the future.

32.3 TEQUILA SERVICE

Equipment Required

- Tequila
- Salver with cloth napkin
- Shot glass
- Lime wedge and salt

Knowledge Required

- Product knowledge

Procedure

- The F&B associate takes the order and raises BOT.
- Give the BOT in the bar and collect the drink with all the accessories.
- Bring the tequila in shot glass.
- Place the shot glass in front of the guest from the right-hand side.
- Place salt and lime wedge on the table.
- Repeat the order after consumption of drinks in the glass.
- At last present the bill to the guest, take the money, deposit it to the cashier and pass a thanks note to the guest for their visit. Tell the guests that they would be informed for any offers in the future.

32.4 GIN SERVICE

Equipment Required

- Gin
- Salver with cloth napkin
- High ball glass
- Decanter
- Tonic water
- Ice bucket with ice and ice tong
- Stirrer stick
- Lime slice (optional)

Knowledge Required

- Product knowledge

Procedure

- The F&B associate takes the order and raises BOT.
- Give the BOT in the bar and collect the drink with all the accessories.
- Bring the gin in high ball glass with a stirrer stick.
- Place the glass in front of the guest from the right-hand side.
- Asks for the preference:
  - ◊ If gin is preferred on the rocks, then ask for number of ice cubes to be placed.
  - ◊ If gin is desired only with tonic water, then pour tonic water from the decanter.

  - ◊ If gin is desired with ice and tonic water, then first place ice cubes and later add tonic water to it.
- Repeat the order after consumption of drinks in the glass.
- At last present the bill to the guest, take the money, deposit it to the cashier and pass a thanks note to the guests for their visit. Tell the guests that they would be informed for any offers in the future.

32.5 VODKA SERVICE

Equipment Required

- Vodka
- Salver with cloth napkin
- High ball glass
- Decanter
- Lemonade
- Ice bucket with ice and ice tong
- Stirrer stick
- Lime slice (optional)

Knowledge Required

- Product knowledge

Procedure

- The F&B associate takes the order and raises BOT.
- Give the BOT in the bar and collect the drink with all the accessories.
- Bring the glass with the vodka in it.
- Place the glass in front of the guest from the right-hand side.
- Ask for the preferences:
  - ◊ If vodka is preferred on the rocks, then ask for the number of ice cubes to be placed in the glass.
  - ◊ If vodka is desired only with lemonade, then pour lemonade from the decanter into the guest's glass.
  - ◊ If vodka is desired with ice and lemonade, then first place ice cubes and later add lemonade to it.
- Repeat the order after consumption of drinks in the glass.
- At last present the bill to the guest, take the money, deposit it to the cashier and pass a thanks note to the guests for their visit. Tell the guests that they would be informed for any offers in the future.

33

Service of Wine (Red and White)

33.1 WINE SERVICE

Equipment Required

- Salver with cloth napkin
- Wine glass
- Wine
- Wine chiller with stand for white wine
- Waiter's friend

Knowledge Required

- Winemaking and wine producing regions
- Wines available in the hotel
- Basic knowledge of wines
- Principles of wine and food pairing

Standards

- The wine glass should be placed at the 4 o'clock position to the water glass.
- The glass should be free from chips, stains and water marks.
- The glass should be handled from the stem using the forefinger and thumb only, leaving no fingerprints on the glass.
- The F & B associate collects the wine bottle from bar. The temperature of the wine is checked. In case of white wine, the wine should be chilled.
- The F & B associate should present the wine with a napkin under the bottle from the right of the host.
- The bottle should be held in the left hand and the thumb and index finger of the right hand should support the neck of the bottle.
- Label should be facing the host.

- Use the phrase—"Lindeman Bin 65 Chardonnay 2001, Sir / Madam."
- The F&B associate should be carrying a Waiter's friend, which should be in immaculate condition, scrupulously clean, shining and free from rust.
- Cut the seal with the knife of the Waiter's friend and discreetly place the seal in the pocket.
- Ensure there is little or no sound while removing the cork.
- The neck and mouth of the bottle should be free from fragments of the cork.

Wine chiller with stand

- The bottle should be wrapped with a clean napkin collar.
- The label should be facing the guest and not covered by the napkin.
- The service should be in the same sequence of etiquette.
- The wine should be poured gently without touching the rim of the glass.
- The glass should be twisted to one side with a jerk to avoid spillage.
- Use the phrase—"Enjoy your wine, Sir / Madam."
- Place the bottle on the side station if the table is too cluttered.

Standards for Service of Wine by Glass

The busboy should get the glass of ordered wine from the bar. The F&B associate should announce the name of the wine to the guest while serving the wine.

Wine collar

- Hold the glass by the stem while placing it on the table.
- Use the phrase—"Madam/Sir, the wine by glass is Grover's Sauvignon Blanc 2002."
- Place it at 4 o' clock position to the water goblet.

Procedure

- The F & B associate brings the wine glass on a salver and places at the table. (In case of white wine, chiller needs to be brought along with the wine.)
- Present to the host the wine bottle placed on a white napkin.

White wine in a wine chiller

- Announce the name of the wine with grape variety, and vintage year.
- Remove the seal after guest approval.
- Unscrew the cork to open the wine bottle.

- Wipe the mouth and the inner neck with a clean cloth. Smell the wine. Do not serve if you have a doubt.
- Hold the bottle in the right hand so that the label faces the host, and pour about 30 mL of the wine into the glass for approval.
- After the host has approved the wine, proceed to serve the guests.
- In case of white wines, place the wine chiller on the right hand side of the host or in a wine stand.
- In case of red wines, the bottle of wine should be placed on the table having wine collar.
- The F&B associate should always replenish the wine when the glass is 1/3rd empty. The bottle should be wiped dry when removed from the chiller for replenishment.

Step 1: The F&B associate brings the wine glass on a salver and places at the table.

Step 2: He presents to the host the wine bottle placed on a white napkin.

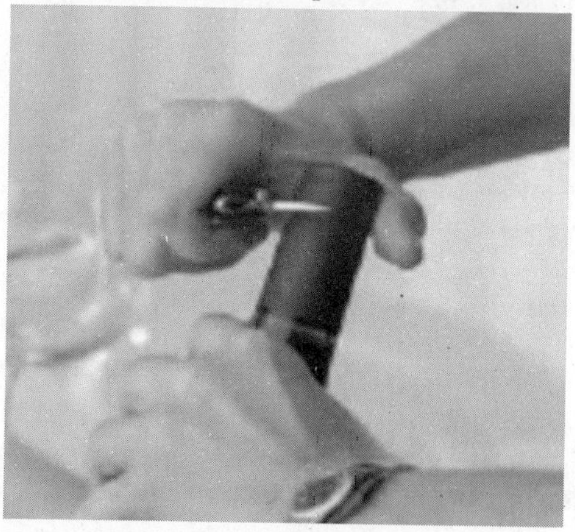

Step 3: With the help of waiter's friend, cut the capsule beneath the lip of the bottle. (Rotate the bottle as you cut.) Put the piece you have cut off in your pocket.

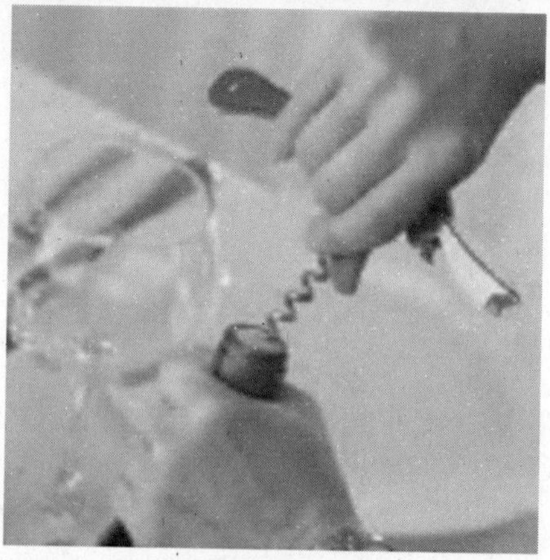

Step 4: Hold the bottle by the neck and insert the tip of the corkscrew at an angle and slightly off centre. (This helps to prevent cork breakage.) Turn the corkscrew until it is fully into the cork.

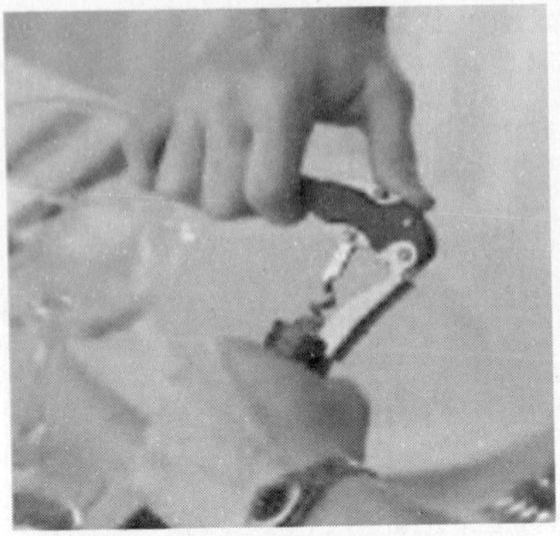

Step 5: After inserting the tip, turn the corkscrew just until the lever will sit on the rim of the bottle.

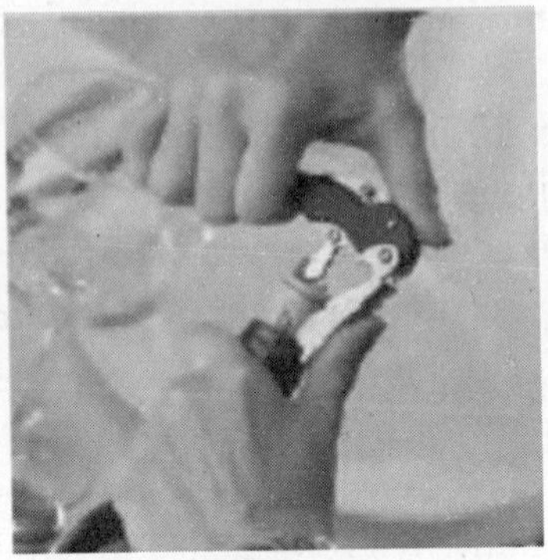

Step 6: Holding the lever in place, lift up the corkscrew until the cork is halfway or more out of the bottle. Turn the corkscrew the final turns it takes for it to be fully inserted, place the lever, and lift the cork out.

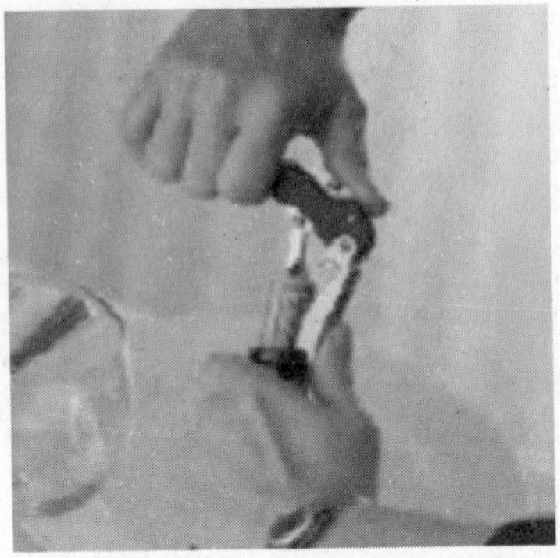

Step 7: Hook the lever of the corkscrew onto the rim of the bottle. Hold the lever in place with the thumb of the hand that is holding the bottle. Lift the corkscrew in one firm slow motion until the cork is fully extracted.

Step 8: Wipe the mouth and inner neck with a clean napkin.

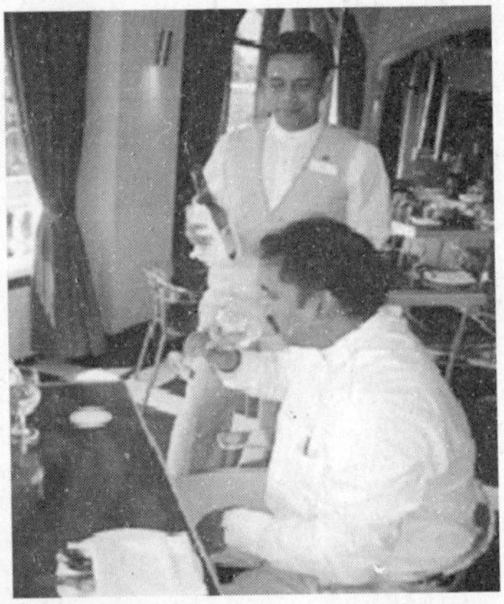

Step 9: Hold the wine bottle with the right hand and pour 30 mL into the host's glass for approval.

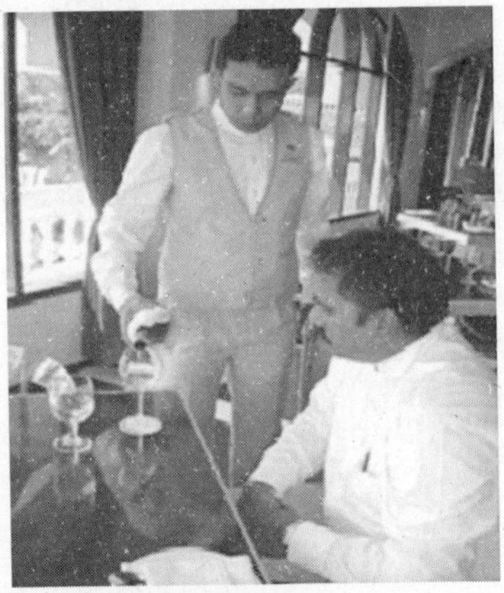

Step 10: After the host approves the wine, start serving wine to the guests and serve hot in the last.

Stepwise procedure for serving wine

33.2 WINE TASTING PROCEDURE

Wine tasting is not the same as drinking it. To experience the true flavour of a wine requires attention to the senses of sight, smell, touch, and taste.

See: Look at the wine colour against a white surface. Aside from the aesthetic value, colour tells a lot about the wine in the glass. As when white wine ages, it becomes darker, more golden in colour and when red wine ages, it loses colour. Oak ageing, grape varietal and climate also affect colour.	
Swirl: Swirling opens up the aromas and flavours and introduces oxygen which will help soften a young red wine's tannins.	
Sniff: Start smelling the wine a few inches above the rim of the glass. Do not plunge nose straight into the glass. Note the types of aromas, their intensity and harmony. If there are unpleasant smells, that may indicate that the wine is flawed.	
Sip: Take a sip and inhale the wine like a backward whistle. Move the wine around mouth. There are only four things which are being tasted, i.e., sweetness, saltiness, bitterness, and acidity.	
Savour: Think about the taste. Is it seamless, angular, full, light, crisp, buttery, well-balanced, overly acidic? Does it have a long finish or an abrupt end? Do you like it or hate it?	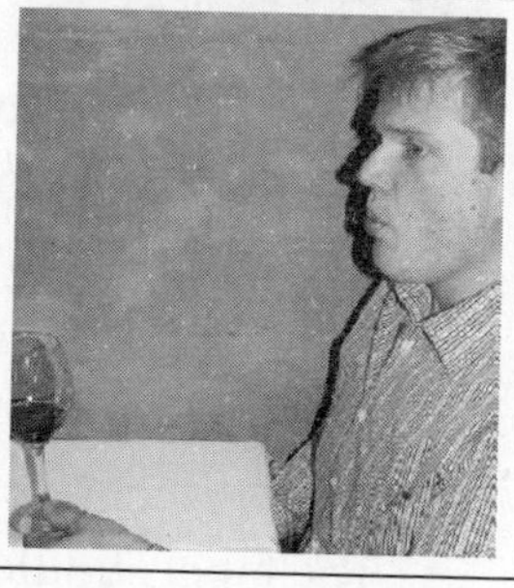

Stepwise procedure for wine tasting

34

Service of Champagne/Sparkling Wine

34.1 CHAMPAGNE/SPARKLING WINE SERVICE

Equipment Required

- Salver with cloth napkin
- Champagne tulip
- Champagne/ sparkling wine
- Wine chiller with stand
- Waiter's friend

Knowledge Required

- Difference between Champagne and sparkling wine and their making methods
- Champagne/ sparkling wine available in the hotel
- Basic knowledge of the Champagne/ sparkling wine
- Principles of wine and food pairing

Standards

- Place the Champagne tulip at the 4 o'clock position at the water glass.
- The tulip should be free from chips, stains and water marks.
- Handle the tulip from the stem using the forefinger and thumb only, leaving no fingerprints on the glass.
- The bottle should be twisted to one side with a jerk to avoid spillage.
- The Champagne should not be popped.
- It should not be given for tasting.
- The label should face the guest.

Champagne in wine chiller

- The wine should be poured gently without touching the rim of the glass.
- The glass should be only 3/4th full (180 mL).
- The wine chiller should be placed next to the host.
- The bottle should be wiped dry when removed from the chiller for replenishment.

Procedure

- Bring the Champagne tulip on a salver and place it on the table.
- The F&B associate should carry the bottle in the chiller to the host at the table.
- Collect the Champagne/sparkling wine from the bar. Check the temperature as Champagne / sparkling wine should be serve chilled.
- Present the Champagne from the right of the host.
- On getting the host's approval, hold the bottle with your left hand. Open the wire mesh using your right hand. Thumb should be placed on the bottle cork while unwinding the mesh. Index finger should be wrapped around the cork.
- Once the bottle has been opened, serve the host first and then the other guests.
- Place the bottle back into the chiller once every guest has been served.
- Top up the glasses regularly.
- When the Champagne gets over, place it inverted in the chiller and ask the guest whether he would like to order for another bottle.

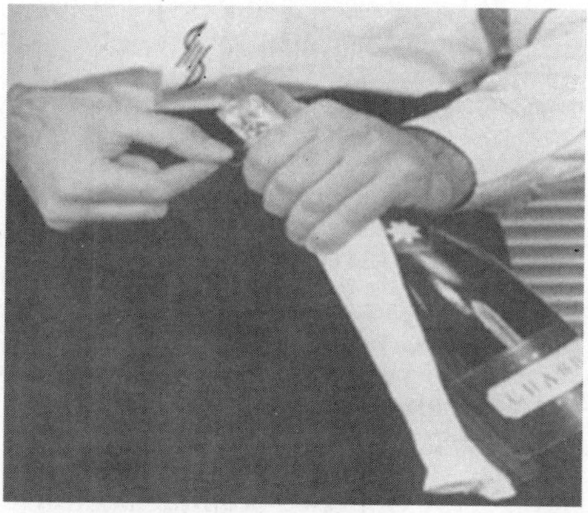

Step 1: Remove the foil wrap, untwist the wire mesh while keeping thumb over the top of the cork. Do not remove the wire cage.

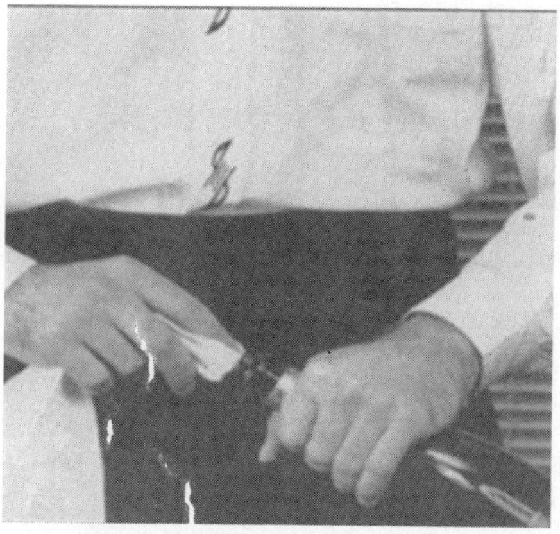

Step 2: Twist the cork off the bottle without shaking the Champagne/ sparkling wine.

Procedure to open a Champagne bottle

35

Service of Cocktails and Mocktails

35.1 COCKTAIL AND MOCKTAIL SERVICE

Equipment Required

- Salver with cloth napkin
- Appropriate glass as per standard of the drink
- Straw

Knowledge Required

- Menu Knowledge – beverage
- Standard phrases
- Types of glassware
- Point of sale

Standards

- The white copy of the KOT should be handed over to the bartender.
- The correct glass should be used according to the standard recipe for the cocktail/mocktail.
- The glass should be free from stains, chips and water marks.
- The beverage should be picked up from the bar complete with garnish. The garnish should be fresh and according to the standard recipe of the cocktail/mocktail.
- The juices should be picked up from the pantry kitchen.
- The associate should check with the KOT for the cover numbers – who is having what.
- Do not go to the table and ask who is having which drink.
- Use the phrase—"_____ (Name of the beverage), Madam / Sir."
- The glass is placed on the table to the right hand side of the cover at 4 o'clock position from the water glass.

- The glass should be held at the stem or at the base using the forefinger and thumb only, leaving no fingerprints on the glass.
- Use the phrase—"Enjoy your drink, Madam/Sir."

Procedure

- The F&B associate after taking the order from the guest gives the KOT to the bar, picks up the order and carries it to the station sideboard.
- The F&B associate should serve the beverage at the table. The F&B associate will announce the name of the beverage while doing so.

Setp 1: The F&B associate after taking the order from the guest gives the BOT to the bar and picks up the order from the bar.

Step 2: Serve the drinks according to the cover number. Always serve from the right hand side of the guest starting with the ladies first.

Serving procedure of cocktail/mocktail

Carrying drink tray guidelines:

- Salver/beverage round is carried on a slightly cupped hand on the pads of the fingers. This allows the waiter to adjust the balance of the tray as glasses are removed or added to the tray.
- When serving drinks to seated guests from a tray hold the tray behind the guest's head, and use your right hand to place the drink from the guest's right.

36

Service of Cigars/Cigarette

Equipment Required

- Cigars
- Humidor
- Ashtray
- Cigarette
- Matchbox
- Cigar cutter
- Side plate
- Beverage round

Knowledge Required

- Various types of cigars and cigarettes available in the bar/restaurant
- Handling cigars and cigarettes

36.1 SERVICE OF CIGARETTES

Procedure

- A packet of cigarettes must never be carried by hand to a customer.
- Always place a packet of cigarettes over a side plate on a beverage round.
- Outside wrapper is opened, the inside wrap pulled out and one or two cigarettes are tapped out, and not pulled out.
- Serve it along with a matchbox.
- The waiter or server should then stand by with a matchbox ready to light a cigarette.

Presenting a cigarette

- The waiter should strike the matchbox away from the guest and hold the flame only.
- Before extinguishing the match, the waiter must be sure that the cigarette is well lit.
- The used matchbox should not be disposed of in the guest ashtray.
- The waiter should clear the ashtray frequently.
- Cleaned ashtray should be placed on the table and it should be removed time to time.
- Some famous well known imported brands are:
  (a) Vogue
  (b) Benson and Hedges
  (c) Camel
  (d) Vin
  (e) Columbus
  (f) Gudangaram
  (g) Capri
  (h) Pine
  (i) Dunhill
  (j) Viceroy
  (k) Marlboro Lights

36.1.1 Changing Ashtray

Procedure

The following procedures are to be followed in the restaurant having smoking policy:

- Hold a clean ashtray in your right hand and place it over the dirty ashtray.
- The clean astray may be either way up.
- Remove the two trays together using one hand.
- Transfer the dirty ashtray to your left hand.
- Use your right hand to place a clean ashtray the right way up where the dirty one was.
- Dirty ashtrays should be held in the left hand or on a service tray, well away from the guests.

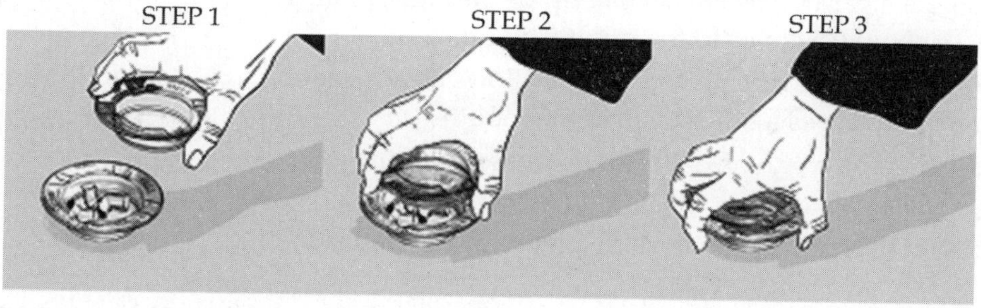

36.2 SERVICE OF CIGARS

Procedure

The best presentation and method of keeping cigars is in humidor. Humidor is a polished box with half a dozen sections each holding a different size and type of cigar. On the inside of the lid is a pad which is kept damp, but not wet, to maintain the humidity.

- Place a clean ashtray on the table.
- Present the glass case or humidor from the left side of the guest to select the cigars.
- Open the case and explain the different types, where they are from, sizes and how strong they are.
- Make recommendations as required.
- Carefully remove the selected cigar without any damage to the wrapper.
- A cigar should be smooth, firm and even to touch; it should be the same size and colour as its partners in the box.
- The wrapper should have a healthy glow to it and the open or cut end should be smooth and even.
- Collect the cigar from the guest for preparation. Ask the guest if the band of the cigar may be removed and what type of cut he/she prefers (straight or V-cut) before taking it to the sideboard.
- Within five minutes of order take the cigar to the sideboard to prepare according to be request of guest.
- If cigar is wrapped in cellophane, carefully remove the cellophane by applying gentle pressure at the end of the cellophane tube. Put the cellophane in your pocket and discard it later on.
- The band of the cigar should not be removed before lighting. It should be removed two minutes after the cigar has been lit with consent of the guest.
- Open the closed end of the cigar either by flat or V-cut as per guest's preference. If the cigar is not precut, then a clear V-shaped cut with a cigar cutter is recommended. This allows the cigar to draw easily.
- Using a cigar cutter, cut off the tip of the cigar mouth piece about 0.5 cm or to the guest's liking.
- Cigars should not be pierced as this allows an adequate draw and leaves a bitter taste in the mouth.
- Tap the cut cigar on side plate to remove any tiny particles.
- Present the cut cigar on the side plate from the left side.

Cigar brands

- Monte Cristo
- Romeo y Julieta
- Davidoff
- Cohiba
- H.Upmann
- Punch
- Partagas
- Hoyo De Monterrey
- Rafael Gonzalez
- Bolivar
- Cuaba
- Alcazar

- Strike a cigar match, hold the face of the cigar at 90° angle to the flames and rotate it between the thumb and the finger. From time to time remove it from the flame and wave it in the air. Within a minute, the cigar will be lit and ready to be offered.
- Once cigar is lit, place gently in cigar ashtray on the right side of the guest.
- Cigars must be lit with safety matches, cedar linings or a gas lighter and not a petrol lighter whose fumes would affect the taste of the cigar.

If the guest wishes to light their own cigar

- Place a box of cigar matches, which is especially made for lighting cigars onto a side plate with the cutter and the cigar.

Presenting cigar in humidor

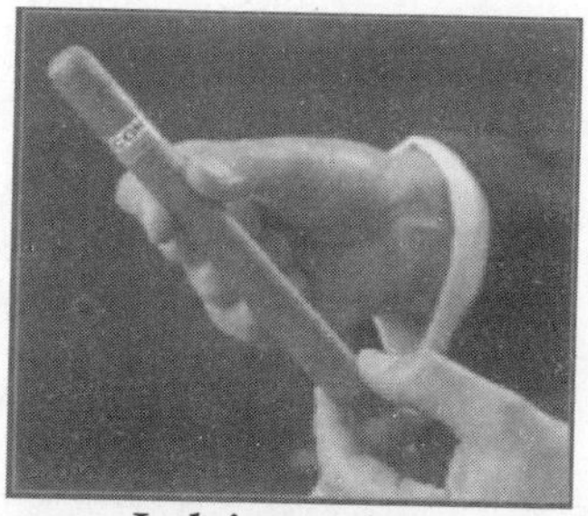

Judging a cigar

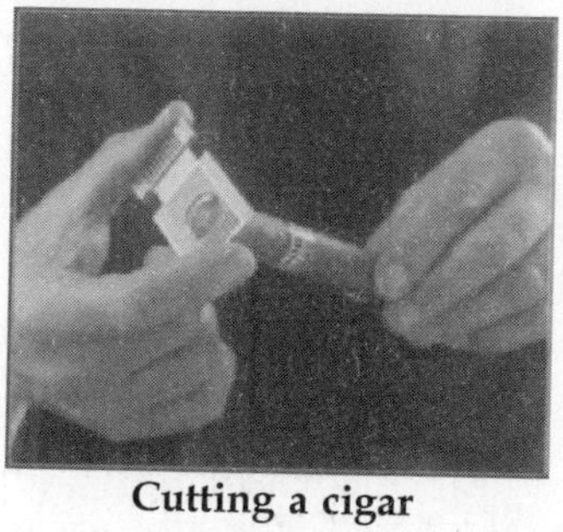

Cutting a cigar

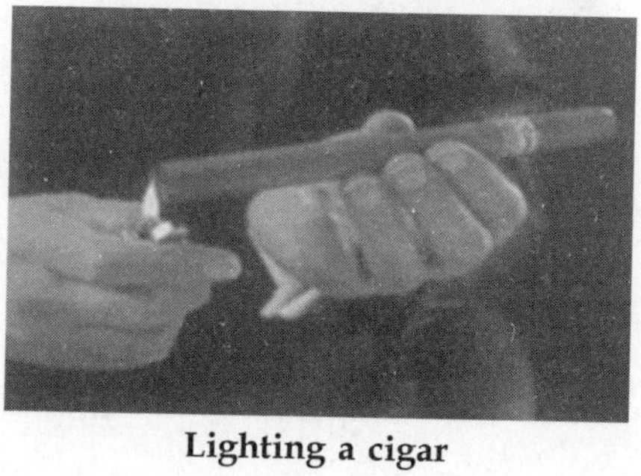

Lighting a cigar

36.2.1 Storage of Cigar

- Cigars are kept in the humidor, which keeps it at a constant level of humidity and temperature.
- Humidor needs to be checked on a daily basis, by asst. operations manager and cigar hostess.
- Ideal temperature should be between 68 to 72% humidity.

- The colleague checking the humidor should take appropriate action which may include adding distilled water, requesting advice from operations manager and chief engineer.
- Action taken should be noted in the outlet log book.
- Cigars are very delicate and are easily spoilt, if not looked after they will dry and lose their taste.

Points to remember:

- Offer cigar matches, ashtray, cutter and service detailed above to both customers who purchase cigars from outlet and those who bring their own.

Case Study

CASE STUDY 1: WEEPING BOTTLES

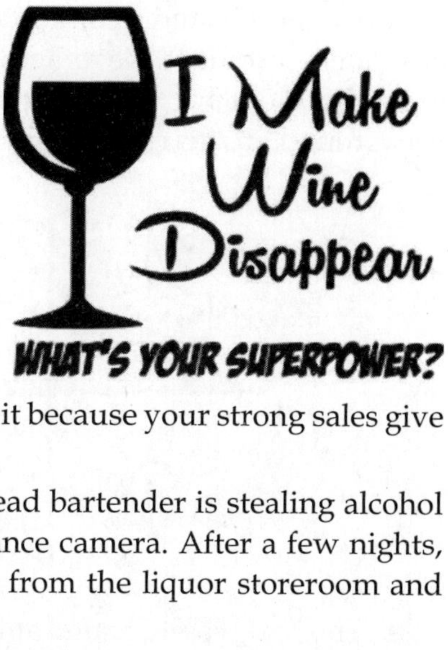

You are the general manager of a bar - The Brew Master located in New Delhi and have a clientele from the upper segments of the society. The bar has live performances regularly. You have a great staff that works in a team and enjoys working together. Strong customer volume includes regular locals and new guests. The customers enjoy their interaction with the staff and bartenders. When the staff gets off work before closing, they often become customers with the establishment. Sales are good and all costs are in line except the bar cost, which is one or two per cent high. You are not too worried about it because your strong sales give you a good profit and the owners are happy.

One day on a tip from an employee, you learn that a lead bartender is stealing alcohol from the storeroom. You set up a hidden video surveillance camera. After a few nights, you catch the bartender on surveillance taking products from the liquor storeroom and going out through the back door.

Lead bartenders are issued keys to the storeroom, as the bar often runs out of products during busy nights when management is busy with other operational issues. Inventory is taken weekly.

You do not know what to do. The lead bartender is very popular with your customers and the rest of the crew. Firing him would prove to be unpopular and could affect sales, customer volume and morale, but ignoring the problem would open the door to other employees taking products. Since you were tipped off, you know that at least some of the employees know what is going on.

- Should you dismiss the lead bartender? Why or why not?
- What are the ethics of setting up a hidden surveillance camera?
- Is the cycle for inventory a problem? Why or why not?

- Determine a method to solve the problem by tightening the policies and procedures of purchasing and storage of beverages.
- Identify several alternatives you have to solving the problem.
- Select the best solution.
- Determine how you would implement the solution.

CASE STUDY 2: SWOT ANALYSIS AT THE OAK BARREL BAR

The Oak Barrel Bar is located in South Goa near Warca Beach. It has been in business for just two years and has developed a solid local customer base made up mostly of local retired personnels. During the tourist season, the bar gets many referrals from various resorts in and around the area. The owner, Mr. John Lobbo wants to set some goals so that the Oak Barrel Bar can move closer to its vision and mission statements: 'To keep our customers coming back for locally sourced food, wide selection of alcoholic beverages, attentive service, and a comfortable welcome atmosphere' and 'Our mission is to provide customers exquisite beverages, healthy, organic cuisine with excellent service that exemplifies our heritage in South Goa.' The following information provides additional background on this establishment:

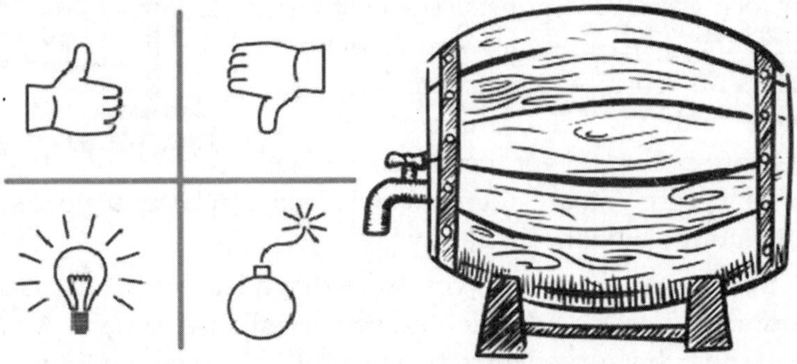

- The chef was educated at Le Cordon Bleu, Paris, and has been chef at several luxury resorts.
- The Lead Bartender has worked with many famous bartenders of India and United States.
- The State Government encourages local businesses to expand.
- Because of housing development in the area, more restaurants and bars are opening in the community.
- There is uncertainty regarding how an increasing housing market will affect things.
- A small influx of popular chain and fast food restaurants could wipe out the market.
- The Oak Barrel has a small staff.
- The Oak Barrel can create customized food and beverage menu selections upon request.

- The Oak Barrel does not have a lot of information about their competitors.
- The Oak Barrel has a small, select menu of healthy food, including fish and game.
- Cashflow can be unreliable at times.
- Several local residents have asked if the bar does outdoor catering.

Identify and list the strengths, weaknesses, opportunities and threats that the Oak Barrel may have. Upon identification of the factors, select three to focus on and develop further.

Strengths	
Weaknesses	
Opportunities	
Threats	
Top areas to develop further	

CASE STUDY 3: PLANNING A BAR

Mr. Hemant Negi won a lottery and dreamt about opening his own bar in the city but he had no idea about how to run one let alone where to begin. The city has about three lakh inhabitants and is only 30 minutes by car from a nearby tourist destination Nainital. The city has already three famous restaurants, two bars and several takeaways that are doing fine. All three restaurants are mid-ranged. A fine dining restaurant opened 3 years ago but it closed after 1 year.

Mr. Hemant Negi is unsure as to how to plan a bar and a selection of menu. Obtaining bar licence is not an issue as he has a reputation in the excise department. Money is also no object to him now that he has won the lottery but he also does not want to invest in an enterprise that is going to lose money for certain.

What are the various factors you would suggest to Mr. Hemant Negi to consider while planning a bar and bar menu?

If you were Mr. Hemant Negi how you would have planned the interior and decor of the bar along with the bar menu?

Index